Encyclopaedia of Architectural Technology

Jacqueline Glass

WILEY-ACADEMY

Acknowledgements

The author and publishers wish to thank the following individuals for their contributions and ideas. Their magnanimous efforts were greatly appreciated throughout the production of this book, which could not have been completed without their hard work and ingenuity. Individual entries in the Encyclopaedia are marked with the initials of their writers, as follows (those marked JG being by the author, Jacqueline Glass):

Efcharis Balodimou (EB)
Thomas Deckker (TD)
Zilah Deckker (ZD)
Eddie Heathcote (EH)
ir. William Holdsworth (WH)
Deborah Lazarus and colleagues at Ove Arup & Partners, London (OA)
Chris Simpson (CS)
Maggie Toy (MT)
Graham Webb (GW)

Thanks also to the following organisations:
British Cement Association
CIRIA
Ove Arup & Partners, London
Steel Construction Institute

The author wishes to personally thank the following people for their support during the production of this book:

Friends and colleagues at the Oxford Centre for Sustainable Development, School of Architecture, Oxford Brookes University
Dr Stephen Emmitt of Leeds Metropolitan University
Maggie Toy and colleagues at Wiley-Academy, John Wiley & Sons
Friends and colleagues at the British Cement Association
My parents, friends and everyone else who has inspired me along the way – thank you

First published in Great Britain in 2002 by
WILEY-ACADEMY

A division of
JOHN WILEY & SONS
Baffins Lane
Chichester
West Sussex PO19 1UD

ISBN 0-471-88559-2

Typeset in 10/12.5pt Bodoni by Laserwords Private Limited, Chennai, India.
Printed and bound in Great Britain by TJ International Ltd, Padstow, Cornwall.

Introduction

Dear Reader,

Welcome to the *Encyclopaedia of Architectural Technology*.

I hope you enjoy reading this book, whether you read it from cover to cover or find that you use it as a reference book, dipping in and out of it from time to time. In either case, I think you will find there is much to learn about and discuss. I recognised there was a need for this book a few years ago in my own teaching experience because there was no single sourcebook to recommend to my students that would give them a grasp of where 'architectural design meets technology'.

The content of the book will be useful for students on a range of undergraduate and postgraduate courses in the fields of Architecture, Architectural Technology, Building, Construction Management and Civil Engineering. Lecturers will find the text suitable to use in their own preparation in addition to being able to recommend it to their students as a core textbook. For students, the aim of this book is to equip you with a reasonable amount of technical knowledge, terminology and act as a sign-post to further information, which in combination should mean that you will be well prepared for that daunting first day in the office or on site.

Any designers and engineers already in practice will also find the book a useful tool in providing a source for quick and easy reference on an everyday basis. For readers new to the field of architectural technology, the book provides easy to read 'bite-size' insights into the world of construction, structures, building services, materials and detailed design. Entries on specific architects and their practices will be of particular interest – these demonstrate how technology and design intentions are brought together to best effect.

The technical content of the book is oriented towards UK practice, but there are frequent references to Europe and elsewhere. Where possible, technical terms have been used in combination with their colloquial equivalents to reflect 'real life'. Reference is made to both new build and refurbishment projects.

In summary, the book has been written from a 'technically-informed' architectural perspective that should appeal to a broad audience. My own view is that the best of all architecture is characterised by a thorough understanding of technology coupled with a balanced and appropriate response to the needs of users, context and the environment.

Dr Jacqueline Glass
School of Architecture
Oxford Brookes University

Bibliography

Throughout the encyclopaedia, you will see that most entries are followed by a few specific references of direct interest. These are in addition to the general references listed below, which cover many aspects covered in this book.

Recommended books

Emmitt, S. (2001) *Architectural technology*, Blackwell Science, Oxford, UK.
Watts, A. (2001) *Modern construction handbook*, Springer, Austria.

General reference books

Adler, D. (ed.) (1999) *Metric handbook: planning and design data*, Butterworth-Heinemann, Oxford, UK.
Cowan, H.J. & Smith, P.R. (1998) *Dictionary of architectural and building technology* (3rd edition), E & FN Spon, London, UK.
Hall, K. & Warm, P. (1995) *Green building: products and services directory* (3rd edition), Green Building Press, Carmarthenshire, UK.
Harris, C.M. (2000) *Dictionary of architecture and construction*, McGraw Hill, New York, USA.
Kut, D. (1993) *Illustrated encyclopaedia of building services*, E & FN Spon, London, UK.
Lewis, O. & Goulding, G. (1999) *European directory of sustainable and energy efficient building*, James & James, London, UK.
MacLean, J.H. & Scott, J.S. (1995) *The Penguin dictionary of building*, Penguin, London, UK.
McMullan, R. (1988) *MacMillan dictionary of building*, MacMillan, Basingstoke, UK.
Marsh, P. (1982) *Illustrated dictionary of building*, Longman, Harlow, UK.
Neufert, E. & Neufert, P. (2000) *Architect's data* (3rd edition), Blackwell Science, Oxford, UK.
Philbin, T. (1997) *The illustrated dictionary of building terms*, McGraw Hill, New York, USA.
Powell-Smith, V. & Billington, M.J. (1999) *The Building Regulations explained and illustrated* (11th edition), Blackwell Science, Oxford, UK.
Stein, J.S. (1980) *Construction glossary*, John Wiley & Sons, New York, USA.

Construction and materials

Allen, E. (1999) *Fundamentals of building construction: materials and methods* (3rd edition), John Wiley & Sons, New York, USA.
Ball, P. (1997) *Made to measure: new materials*, Princeton University Press, USA.
Barry, R. (1999) *The construction of buildings: Volume 1 – Foundations, walls, floors, roofs* (7th edition), Blackwell Science, Oxford, UK.
Barry, R. (1999) *The construction of buildings: Volume 2 – Windows, doors, fires, stairs, finishes* (5th edition), Blackwell Science, Oxford, UK.
Barry, R. (1993) *The construction of buildings: Volume 3 – Single storey frames, shells and lightweight coverings* (4th edition), Blackwell Science, Oxford, UK.
Barry, R. (2000) *The construction of buildings: Volume 4 – Multi-storey buildings, foundations, steel frames, concrete frames, floors, wall cladding* (5th edition), Blackwell Science, Oxford, UK.
Barry, R. (1998) *The construction of buildings: Volume 5 – Building services* (3rd edition), Blackwell Science, Oxford, UK.
Brawne, M. (1992) *From idea to building: issues in architecture*, Butterworth-Heinemann, Oxford, UK.
Brookes, A. & Grech, C. (1996) *Building envelope & connections*, Butterworth-Heinemann, Oxford, UK.
Ching, F.D.K. (1995) *A visual dictionary of architecture*, Van Nostrand Reinhold, New York, USA.
Ching, F.D.K. (with Adams, C.) (2001) *Building construction illustrated* (3rd edition), John Wiley & Sons, New York, USA.
Chudley, R. & Greeno, R. (1999) *Construction technology* (3rd edition), Longman, Harlow, UK.
Chudley, R. & Greeno, R. (1999) *Advanced construction technology* (3rd edition), Longman, Harlow, UK.
Dawson, S. (1989 onwards) *Architects working details* (Vols. 1-7), Architects Journal, UK.
Doran, D.K. (ed.) (1992) *Construction materials reference book*, Butterworth-Heinemann, Oxford, UK.
Ford, E.R. (1990) *The details of Modern architecture*, MIT Press, Massachusetts, USA.

Groák, S. (1992) *The idea of building: thought and action in the design and production of buildings*, E & FN Spon, London, UK.

Jackson, N. & Dhir, R.K. (eds.) (1996) *Civil engineering materials*, MacMillan, Basingstoke, UK.

Lyons, A.R. (1997) *Materials for architects and builders*, Arnold, London, UK.

Mitchell's building series

Blanc, A. (1994) *Internal components*, Longman, Harlow, UK.

Burberry, P. (1997) *Environment and services* (8th edition), Longman, Harlow, UK.

Dean, Y. (1996) *Materials technology*, Longman, Harlow, UK.

Everett, A. (with Barritt, C.M.H.) (1994) *Materials* (5th edition), Longman, Harlow, UK.

McEvoy, M. (1994) *External components*, Longman, Harlow, UK.

Stroud Foster, J. (2000) *Structure and fabric Part 1* (6th edition), Longman, Harlow, UK.

Stroud Foster, J. & Harrington, R. (2000) *Structure and fabric Part 2* (6th edition), Longman, Harlow, UK.

Reid, E. (1988) *Understanding buildings*, Longman, Harlow, UK.

Rich, P. & Dean, Y. (1999) *Principles of element design*, Butterworth-Heinemann, Oxford, UK.

Simmons, H.L. & Olin, H.B. (2001) *Construction: principles, materials and methods* (7th edition), John Wiley & Sons, New York, USA.

Taylor, G.D. (2000) *Materials in construction: an introduction* (3rd edition), Longman, Harlow, UK.

Structures

Addis, W. (1990) *Structural engineering: the nature of theory and design*, Ellis Horwood, Chichester, UK.

Addis, B. (1994) *The art of the structural engineer*, Artemis, London, UK.

Gauld, B.J.B. (1991) *Structures for architects*, Longman, Harlow, UK.

Gordon, J.E. (1978) *Structures – or why things don't fall down*, Penguin, London, UK.

Hunt, T. (1997) *Tony Hunt's structures notebook*, Butterworth-Heinemann, Oxford, UK.

MacDonald, A.J. (1997) *Structural design for architecture*, Butterworth-Heinemann, Oxford, UK.

MacDonald, A.J. (2001) *Structure and architecture* (2nd edition), Butterworth-Heinemann, Oxford, UK.

Mainstone, R.J. (1998) *Developments in structural form* (2nd edition), Butterworth-Heinemann, Oxford, UK.

Millais, M. (1997) *Building structures*, E & FN Spon, London, UK.

Moore, F. (1999) *Understanding structures*, McGraw Hill, New York, USA.

Seward, D. (1998) *Understanding structures: analysis, materials and design* (2nd edition), Macmillan, Basingstoke, UK.

History and theory

Elliott, C.D. (1992) *Technics and architecture*, MIT Press, Massachusetts, USA.

Frampton, K. (Cava, J. ed.) (1996) *Studies in tectonic culture: the poetics of construction in nineteenth and twentieth century architecture*, MIT Press, Massachusetts, USA.

Friedman, D. (1995) *Historical building construction: design materials and technology*, Norton, New York, USA.

Jester, T.C. (ed.) *20th century building materials*, McGraw Hill, New York, USA.

Mark, R. (ed.) (1993) *Architectural technology up to the scientific revolution*, MIT Press, Massachusetts, USA.

Peters, T.F. (1996) *Building the 19th century*, MIT Press, Massachusetts, USA.

Sebestyén, G. (1998) *Construction – craft to industry*, E & FN Spon, London, UK.

Strike, J. (1991) *Construction into design*, Butterworth-Heinemann, Oxford, UK.

Yeomans, D. (1997) *Construction since 1900: materials*, Batsford, London, UK.

Aalto, Alvar

Alvar Aalto (1898–1976), the acclaimed Finnish architect, used indigenous materials, particularly timber, in his Modern, yet contextually sensitive brand of architecture.

See also: BESPOKE; BRICKS AND BLOCKS; CASTINGS; CERAMICS; CLADDING; CONCRETE–STRUCTURES; GRIDS FOR STRUCTURE AND LAYOUT; LIGHTING – DAYLIGHTING; TIMBER; TIMBER – HARDWOODS AND SOFTWOODS; TIMBER – PRODUCTION AND FINISHES; TIMBER – LAMINATED TIMBER; WEATHERING.

Alvar Aalto: Vuoksenniska church, Imatra (1956–59). The double layer clerestorey level windows give distinct forms to the external form and interior space. Photograph by Thomas Deckker.

Alvar Aalto grew up in Jyväskalä in central Finland, at a time when Finland was still a province of Russia; it fought for and gained its independence during the Revolution in 1917, and again during the Second World War against both the Soviet Union and Germany. National identity was of particular importance; Aalto started in the nationalistic classical style of his contemporaries but converted to the Modern Movement during the 1920s.

Three buildings established Aalto's credentials as a Modern Movement architect: the competition entry for the Municipal Library, Viipuri (1927; built 1930–35), the Turun Sanomat newspaper offices (1927–29); and the Paimio Sanatorium (1928; built 1929–33) in the culturally independent city of Turku. Even in these early works, however, one can see a divergence from programmatic Modernism in the environmental and constructional adaptations, as well as the aesthetic preferences. The asymmetrical columns in the production hall of the Turun Sanomat building (one of its most famous images) showed Aalto moving towards the formality of the Modern Movement; the double windows in the Paimio Sanatorium acted as a moderating device for incoming air. The ceiling of the concert hall in the Viipuri Library, supposedly justified on acoustic grounds, was an experiment in sensuous wood architecture.

It was experiments with wood (Finland's most abundant natural resource) which signalled a change in direction away from the Modern Movement. The first use was in the open-air bandstand at the *700 Years of Turku* exhibition (1929). Aalto started to use timber screens to relieve the severity of the otherwise white-rendered geometric volumes of the staff housing at the Paimio Sanatorium; these became external screens of larch poles joined with wicker at the workers' housing at Kauttua (1937–40). This expanded into the wholesale use of timber cladding on his house in Munksnäs (built

1935–36). The Finnish Pavilion for the Paris World's Fair (1937) had external walls wrapped in timber sections and columns of larch poles joined with wicker, perhaps as a metaphorical representation of a forest; that for the New York World's Fair (1939) had a four-storey internal curved exhibition wall of timber.

The Villa Mairea, Noormarku (1937–39) is a virtuoso display of Aalto's preoccupations of the period. Floors and ceilings were clad with boards; walls were clad in various timber sections; the columns of the entrance canopy were constructed of rough timber poles; a sauna was made of untreated logs. The internal structure was also highly varied, with groups of steel and concrete columns, some clad in wicker, timber sections or leather, supporting the concrete floor slabs. The double layers of windows were widely mixed in size with ventilators of separate wooden shutters.

Aalto experimented with timber not only in architecture but also in furniture and works of sculpture. His major invention was a joint consisting of thin lamina of wood inserted into saw-cuts in a solid timber section; this technique weakened the cross section which allowed the section to be bent, and then set solid again by gluing the lamina. This was evident not only in the legs of table and chairs he promoted through his furniture company Artek, but also in purely experimental pieces. The sensuousness of the forms and material also found expression in his designs for cast glass and cast bronze door handles.

Aalto had great opportunities in Finland after the Second World War in response to the need for reconstruction and to Finland's economic development. He developed architectural solutions as distinct 'types' in which social, programmatic and technical solutions could be refined. These 'types' included libraries, theatres, museums, churches, town halls, offices and housing. While no common features can be ascribed to such a diverse set of 'types', many common features abound, particularly:

- Informal plan shapes highly responsive to the geography of the context;
- Large internal social spaces intended not only as functional areas but as replacements for outdoor space in the hostile climate;
- Extraordinary attention to the manipulation of light through windows and rooflights.

The Rautatalo Office Building, Helsinki (1951: built 1953–55), the Vuoksenniska church, Imatra (1956; built 1957–59) and the Rovaniemi Library (1963; built 1965–68) epitomised the spatial and material qualities and showed the range of invention of Aalto's 'types'. The Rautatalo Building is noticeable for the highly refined bronze cladding of its very austere façade and the travertine-clad internal atrium lit by round skylights. The Vuoksenniska Church, whose nave is often described as a series of 'hands', has extraordinary double-layered light hoods. The Rovaniemi Library has a fan-shaped plan with light hoods over the reading and stack areas.

At this time Aalto began to regard brick and ceramic tiles as appropriate cladding, and in some cases as structural materials, not least to avoid the problems of the weathering of concrete and render finishes. His own holiday house on the island of Muuratsalo (1953) is an example of the latter, with façades made of varied types and sizes of brick. Brick was also used for the town hall on the adjacent island of Säynatsälo (built 1950–52) and the Pensions Institute, Helsinki (1948–56). In the 'House of Culture', Helsinki (1955–58), concrete was used as a 'plastic' material clad in glazed tiles, similar to Roman roof tiles, which could accommodate the changes in angle.

Aalto's buildings have a profound material presence due to the sensuous use of materials and to the craftsmanship with which they were executed. Most buildings are signalled by his trademark cast bronze door handle; often stacked three high for various heights of user. It is a tribute to Aalto's skill that his buildings still function well without excessive programmes of maintenance or environmental problems.

Further reading

Aalto, E. & Fleig, K. (eds.) *Alvar Aalto* (Volumes 1, 2 and 3), Artemis, Zurich, Switzerland.

Nerdinger, W. (1999) *Alvar Aalto: towards a human modernism*, Prestel, Munich, Germany.

Schildt, G. (1984) *Alvar Aalto: the early years*, Rizzoli, New York, USA.

Schildt, G. (1986) *Alvar Aalto: the decisive years*, Rizzoli, New York, USA.

Schildt, G. (1991) *Alvar Aalto: the mature years*, Rizzoli, New York, USA.

Schildt, G. (1994) *Alvar Aalto: the complete catalogue of architecture, design and art*, Academy Editions, John Wiley & Sons, London, UK.

Schildt, G. (1998) *Alvar Aalto: masterworks*, Thames & Hudson, London, UK.

Weston, R. (1995) *Alvar Aalto*, Phaidon Press, London, UK.

TD

ABS

See: PLASTICS

Access floor

See: FLOORS

Acid – etching

See: GLASS; GLASS – LAMINATED AND COATED GLASS

Acrylic

See: PLASTICS – TYPES

Acoustics

Acoustics is the science of sound. The acoustical environment is important for human comfort and health: sound, noise and vibration control are critical elements in a building.

See also: AIR-CONDITIONING; AIRTIGHTNESS; CEILINGS; ENVIRONMENTAL DESIGN; FABRIC ENERGY STORAGE; HVAC; INSULATION; INTEGRATION; SICK BUILDING SYNDROME.

Common terms

'Sound' is a sensation produced through the ear resulting from fluctuations in the pressure of the air. Normally such fluctuations are set up by some vibrating object, and are in the form of a longitudinal wave motion or frequency.

'Noise' is a sound that is undesired by the recipient. This simple description emphasises the fact that noise is subjective; a noise problem involves people and their feelings and its assessment is a matter of human values and perceived environments rather than precise physical measurement.

'**Vibration**' is a periodic motion of particles of an elastic body or medium in alternately opposite directions. Such oscillations can affect people's wellbeing unfavourably in addition to the functioning of sensitive apparatus such as laboratory equipment. Strong vibrations from traffic, industrial processes, and transportation machinery, both within and outside a building, can cause inappropriate damage.

'**Decibels**' (dB) are the logarithmic mathematical scale of sound pressure. The base is zero (based on the typical human threshold of hearing) and the scale moves upwards, i.e.

- 50 dB is typical of heavy traffic noise;
- 80 dB is where damage to hearing begins;
- 130 dB is the threshold of pain;
- At 150 dB a jet engine 30 metres away can cause noise frequencies that burn the skin.

There is now a greater understanding of the vast range of frequencies that are beyond the hearing range of human beings. New terms have been created to describe these frequencies such as 'blue' and 'white' sound frequencies that are measured in Hertz (Hz) and which, like oscillations, are akin to electromagnetic forces. There is some concern over the use of mobile telephones: although the sound level is low, the frequency is very high and even a very short exposure to the ear and brain is thought to cause damage.

Design considerations

Acoustic measurement of the locality surrounding a building should be undertaken at an early stage of the design process. All the potential impacts must be assessed including perceived future impacts from infrastructure developments such as transport, rail, road and air traffic. There is increasing concern about noise pollution. In 1990, a quarter of the population in England and Wales were exposed to noise levels outside their homes of 60 dB and 5% to levels above 70 dB. These impacts have been addressed in recent amendments to the UK Building Regulations which have increased the requirements for sound insulation to the external envelope of homes and also between adjacent dwellings.

For most normal buildings, i.e. those with no special acoustic requirements, the requirements of Building Regulations provide sufficient guidance on sound insulation. It is typical to use combinations of heavyweight and lightweight materials: the former insulates lower frequency sounds (e.g. traffic) and the latter protects against high frequency sounds (e.g. conversation). It is only really in buildings such as libraries, theatres and other performance spaces that more sophisticated techniques need to be applied at the design stage. Computer modelling of acoustics using chaos theory can be used as a means of testing multiple outcomes for say a symphony hall. Acoustics as a design discipline should be addressed in parallel with other aspects such as buildings services and workplace design. An interesting example is the use of exposed concrete for fabric energy storage, where the hard concrete surfaces can, if not modelled and tested adequately, lead to unwanted echoes and sound reflections. Shaping the soffit and providing areas of sound absorbent panels and mats can prevent this occurring.

Sensitive buildings

Assessment of risk by an acoustics engineer or specialist contractor is based not only on the prediction of vibration levels but also the establishment of an upper safety limit where damage may occur. Everything, be it an oil painting, plaster on a wall, a car, or a human being has its own 'natural' frequency. Determining these frequencies and monitoring both the construction process and the building in-use may be essential. An example was the construction of an underground coach station in Amsterdam, close to the Museumplein (the city's cultural centre). To prevent damage to the valuable paintings above such as Van Goghs and Rembrandts, the construction team carefully adapted their normal tools and techniques to allow heavy piling work to continue without disturbing the museums above.

Concert halls and theatres require architectural solutions that allow a listener to enjoy music and voice in the most perfect conditions. External impacts from adjacent railways or aircraft are a major design problem. When the Royal Festival Hall was built in 1950 in London, potential noise intrusion from a nearby rail viaduct was overcome with the clever notion of insulating the double-shelled auditorium by surrounding it with other ancillary accommodation. Internally, the technical acoustics of the Hall's performance space were designed to a particular reverberation time (the time taken for a sound energy wave to meet a boundary, such as a seat, or overhanging projection). This feature can be adapted to meet the needs of a modern concert hall so that it can fulfil many functions from music to spoken word. In other halls, 'wave field effect' technology can be used to 'move the sound around' (using speakers and adaptable chambers within the fabric of the building) thus enhancing the performance for the audience.

Further reading

Cavanaugh, W.J. & Wilkes, J.A. (eds.) (1997) *Architectural acoustics: principles and practice*, John Wiley & Sons, New York, USA.

Parkin, P.H., Humphreys, H.R. & Cowell, J.R. (1979) *Acoustics, noise and buildings* (4th edition), Faber & Faber, London, UK.

Smith, B.J., Peters, R.J. & Owen, S. (1996) *Acoustics and noise control* (2nd edition), Longman, Harlow, UK.

WH/JG

Adaptability

See: BUILDABILITY; DESIGN LIFE; PERFORMANCE; SPECIFICATION

Adaptive façades

See: INTELLIGENT FAÇADES AND MATERIALS; FAÇADES AND FAÇADE ENGINEERING

Adhesives

See: PLASTICS FOR ADHESIVES AND FINISHES

Adobe

See: EARTH CONSTRUCTION

Aerogels

See: PHASE CHANGE MATERIALS

Air change rate

See: VENTILATION

Air-conditioning

The primary function of air-conditioning is to maintain conditions that are conducive to human comfort or are required by a product or process.

See also: AIRTIGHTNESS AND IAQ; BUILDING MANAGEMENT SYSTEMS; CONSTRUCTION PROGRAMME; ECOLOGICAL DESIGN; ENVIRONMENTAL DESIGN; HVAC; INSULATION; LIFE-CYCLE COSTING; NIGHT VENTILATION; SERVICES; SICK BUILDING SYNDROME; THERMAL COMFORT; THERMOLABYRINTH; VENTILATION.

Introduction

Human beings are adaptable to surrounding environmental conditions, but tend to prefer to live within a limited range of temperatures. The desire to limit the effects of the extremes of hot and cold, or to reduce the effects of high humidity, have occupied human civilisations for thousands of years. For example, the people of Urk on the river Euphrates used adiabatic cooling in 4,000 BC by having water cascade along perimeter troughs on the walls of the city. Earth cooling systems were an integral part of the Palace of Knossos, Crete.

This desire to create comfortable conditions led Frank Lloyd Wright to develop the forerunner of modern air-conditioning systems in the Larkin Building in Buffalo, New York (built in 1906). Corner stair towers were combined with duct boxes to convey forced air via giant centrifugal fans through ductwork, with controllable air grilles at high levels under an edge beam. This simple system developed through the 20th century into 'air-conditioning' (or a/c) using refrigeration to further cool the air temperature. However, this is an energy-intensive technology. Increasing concerns to reduce energy use and remove ozone-depleting refrigerant chemicals have influenced drives towards more 'passive' solutions as a 'green' alternative to what Reyner Banham described as 'the well-tempered environment'.

Types of air-conditioning systems

The most commonly understood type of air-conditioning is 'comfort conditioning'. This is an 'all water' system that can be located locally or centrally in a building. Comfort conditioning involves passing fresh outside air through a series of controllable processes. Air is first passed through water-flushed 'eliminator' plates to remove dirt and grit and then filtered according to the outside conditions. The next step is for the air be pre-heated, taken through a spray washing chamber, passed through a cooling coil and once again pre-heated before being conveyed through ductwork to discharge grilles. A return air system in interconnected (via damper controls) to allow a percentage of mixed air to reduce energy loads. These 'total' a/c systems are used primarily in manufacturing or laboratory spaces that require highly controlled environments, such as tobacco storage and spinning sheds for rayon, nylon and other fabrics. In many buildings, the only spaces that genuinely require such systems are computer rooms. However, comfort conditioning is perceived by letting agents as a mark of prestige and so it is common for it to feature in high quality accommodation such as offices and dealing-rooms, particularly in city centre locations.

- Other types of air-conditioning systems include:
- **Direct expansion** – these are self-contained room cooling units;
- **All air systems** – such as used in the Larkin building (above);

- **Heat pumps** – these are used mainly in the USA and Asia;
- **Induction or air water systems.**

Design considerations

Load estimation for air-conditioning systems is critical in order to select the optimum equipment. As discussed, it is only specialised buildings that really require full comfort cooling; in other instances 'mixed mode' or localised solutions may be more appropriate but the design team should always consider whether air-conditioning is really necessary at all. The final decision should be based on a comprehensive survey of load components, which include:

- Exhausts from other buildings that could be induced into the system (creates overloading);
- External effects from wind, rain and snow;
- Heat from electrical lighting, power equipment and other machinery;
- Heating and cooling gains – e.g. solar gains as well as detailed heat losses;
- Metabolic heat from people (NB: this varies from person to person);
- Shading effects from nearby buildings;
- Ventilation rate and air change rate and relation to airtightness.

Critical design factors to consider are the relationship of the location to solar sun paths; the climatic location, which will affect the local ambient environment giving dry or humid conditions; altitude; and impacts such as traffic, industry etc. Sun path charts are available for all major latitudes. In modern computer-aided-design (CAD) such information is part of the design program. The use of these charts and the understanding of the essential laws of air movement and thermodynamics is essential. During the design process, the development of the physics of the a/c system should go on in parallel with a discussion of a range of other factors, including:

- Construction cost;
- Environmental impacts and carbon dioxide emissions;
- Flexibility of use (e.g. possible future changes or sub-division of spaces);
- Impact of different zoning requirements;
- Integration with other services;
- Interaction with the structural design concept;
- Maintenance contracts or agreements;
- Need for occupants to have personal control (or not);
- Operating costs (i.e. payback time and life-cycle costs);
- Use of control systems/building management systems.

Further reading

Banham, R. (1984) *The architecture of the well-tempered environment* (2nd edition), Architectural Press, London, UK.

Chadderton, D.V. (1997) *Air conditioning: a practical introduction* (2nd edition), E & FN Spon, London, UK.

Chartered Institute of Building Services Engineers (2000) *Mixed mode ventilation: CIBSE Applications Manual 13*, CIBSE, London, UK.

WH/JG

National Space Centre, Leicester (Nicholas Grimshaw & Partners). Two rockets are enclosed in a 42 m high tower within a skin of triple-layer ETFE cushions. Photograph by Graham Beardwell, courtesy of Ove Arup & Partners.

Air-supported structures

This term describes two types of roofing or cladding techniques that use air as a method of inflation or 'support'.

See also: CABLE NETS; ETFE; GRIMSHAW, NICHOLAS; PLASTICS – TYPES; ROOFS; TEXTILE MEMBRANE ROOFS.

There are two main types of what are generically called 'air-supported structures', which are discussed in turn.

Air-supported

This type of structure consists of a space-enclosing membrane anchored continuously to the ground or similar fixed plane. The membrane is patterned and shaped so as to take up a smooth, almost spherical shape once the air inside has been slightly pressurised (typically 400–1,000 Pa). The internal pressure needs to be sufficient to resist any loads that might be externally applied (e.g. wind and snow) to avoid inversion and collapse. Entry into the enclosed space within is via a simple airlock, i.e. a separate chamber. The fabric of the structure uses coated textiles such as PVC, coated polyester and PTFE coated glass cloth together with a network of reinforcing cables providing support to the large membrane panels and anchored to the ground via a perimeter ring beam. The English engineer F W Lanchester is regarded as the inventor of air-supported structures via his patent of 1917. After 1940 Walter Bird, a US engineer, researched and developed the generic design type, which was used initially for Radomes (radar installations) and satellite tracking stations. The development of the plastic coatings and computer analysis of structures meant that air-supported structures are now used commercially for storage, warehousing, sport facilities such as tennis halls. In the USA between 1975 and 1990, a number of large, covered stadia were constructed, seating up to 80,000 people. In very cold working conditions, air-supported domes are used to shelter construction workers. For example, in Canada they are large enough to accommodate vast working areas and allow concrete trucks to enter via the airlocks. These structures enable winter working in comfortable conditions with outside temperatures way below freezing.

Air-inflated

The second type consists of a two layer, self-enclosed membrane inflated with air to form a stiff structural member capable of spanning and taking loads to perimeter points of support. Both high- and low-pressure systems have been developed, but use of the former has been limited to military use and exceptional buildings such as the 50 m diameter Fuji Pavilion at Expo '70 in Osaka, Japan. These high-pressure systems are sometimes referred to as 'pneumatic' structures and generally take the form of closed tubular beams and arches. The low-pressure option typically takes the form of a sealed cushion supported along its sides by a framework or cable network. A striking example of this is used to cover and protect the Roman Arena at Nimes in France through the winter months. The air inflated roof has an elliptic plan of 88 m × 57 m and is installed each year in the autumn and removed in the spring. The roof was designed by German engineers Jorg Schlaich and Partners (renowned for their innovative structural engineering work, particularly bridges).

Contemporary development and applications centre around the use of ETFE cushions developed by Dr Stefan Lehnart et al. ETFE is a transparent foil typically 150 microns thick. Cushions consist of several layers typically spanning 4 m pressured to 250 Pa. Larger spans can be achieved using cable harness reinforcement to support snow loads. This can be seen to good effect in the 'Biomes' of the Eden Project in Cornwall and the National Space Centre in Leicester (both by Nicholas Grimshaw & Partners).

Further reading

Herzog, T. (1976) *Pneumatic structures*, OUP, New York, USA.
Price, C., Newby, F. & Suan, R. (1976) *Air structures*, HMSO, London, UK.

OA

Airtightness and Indoor Air Quality (IAQ)

The balance between providing a building envelope that not only protects against the weather and promotes energy efficiency by being 'airtight', but which also maintains a supply of fresh air to its inhabitants.

See also: AIR-CONDITIONING; CONCRETE; DRY CONSTRUCTION AND WET CONSTRUCTION; ECOLOGICAL DESIGN; 'ECO-POINTS'; ENERGY EFFICIENCY; HVAC; INSULATION; NIGHT VENTILATION; PERFORMANCE; SICK BUILDING SYNDROME; STACK EFFECT.

There is an important relationship between airtightness and indoor air quality. While there is a desire to promote energy efficiency by sealing up a building so that it does not 'leak', there are also growing concerns that the quality of the indoor air cannot be maintained healthily unless there is a steady supply of fresh air into the space. These considerations require the building physicist or services engineer to work with the design team to establish a suitable balance. The health problems associated with 'sick building syndrome' are thus impacting on the design of energy-efficient buildings.

Airtightness

Energy efficiency depends not only on the efficacy of the equipment used for heating and cooling, but also on the overall performance of the building envelope. It is usual to think of insulation values as the primary indicator of energy efficiency in the fabric, but other factors can be equally, if not more important. Airtightness is the degree to which a building permits air to enter and/or heat to escape via 'holes' in its fabric, and can completely alter the performance of a building. The likely areas that can present problems include junctions between elements, connections, service penetrations and gaps between adjacent elements. Some building types are more prone to 'leakiness' such as dry construction (with no wet materials to fill any gaps), where the layers of framing and insulation are riddled with potential problem areas. These construction methods have to be managed well on site to ensure that they meet airtightness standards.

It is only recently that airtightness requirements have started to appear in UK Building Regulations, but other countries have been demanding tighter and tighter buildings for some years. The issue is that of 'the overtight building syndrome', i.e. trying too hard to seal up a building and actually not understanding that this can make it stuffy, humid and unpleasant. This tendency to over-emphasise airtightness is a result of instituting design codes to conserve energy without fully understanding the need for adequate ventilation. Hence, designers should ensure that they meet standards but allow for good air quality via an appropriate air change rate. The UK construction industry is still developing its expertise in this area. Woolley et al. recommend some simple steps to ensure a building is airtight to the external elements (but not too tight), including:

- Consider night purging systems to dilute and clear out pollutants accumulating during the day;
- Define the detail and the method of achieving airtightness at joints between elements such as walls, windows, roofs and floors;
- Design out unwanted ventilation pathways in the structure – use full fill insulation rather than partial fill;
- Design the ventilation system to achieve air change rates sufficient for people and their occupations;
- Design/install an air barrier layer on the inside face;
- For renovation projects, identify and seal as many leakage routes as possible, with fan-testing as a tool to locate leakage areas;
- For new constructions, design and build an airtight shell and confirm its tightness by pressure testing;
- Minimise services penetrations through the fabric;
- Use local, room-sealed appliances wherever possible.

Researchers at the University of Cambridge are developing a 'supply air window' as a means to manage airtightness of the envelope. The window draws in air at cill level, which is warmed passively between the two layers of glass and then passes into the interior via a trickle vent at the top. This should facilitate a good stream of fresh air without draughts.

Indoor air quality

When environmental health problems are found, the cause is often attributed wrongly to external traffic problems rather than the indoor climate. Indoor air is composed of a complex blend of oxygen, carbon monoxide, moisture, combustion gases, fumes from industrial appliances, radioactive gases, dust particles, ions, biological materials, static electric fields, and chemical outgassing from construction materials and furnishings (although most of the above are normally present only in very small amounts). It was recognised, first in 1963, that some chemicals in the indoor air could provoke symptoms of illness. Volatile organic hydrocarbons were known to be a trigger, but increased use of urea-form formaldehyde insulation (UFFI) also contributed towards a dramatic increase in what has become known as Environmental Illnesses (EI). Investigations were then undertaken in the USA and Sweden on a wide scale with formaldehyde as an indicator. A study of a Swedish nursery school in 1998 established that building materials acted like a sponge for Volatile Organic Compounds (VOCs), taking in contaminants and then releasing them at a later point; rougher surfaces absorbed relatively larger amounts of VOCs. In addition, the materials often 'outgassed' in a different chemical form because the contaminants became mixed with chemicals already in the building materials.

Indoor air quality is an important issue for architects, specifiers and facilities managers because changes to the UK Building Regulations and other environmental guidelines mean that designers will not only have to design to airtightness standards, but materials manufacturers will also have to publish data on IAQ characteristics. These requirements are based on what is now standard practice in Sweden and is becoming more of a key design issue in other countries such as the USA and Canada. In the USA, much research has already been carried out into the IAQ properties of various materials; concrete, tiles and other 'hard', inert surfaces appear to be favoured options. Paint, PVC flooring, carpets and timber products do not fare well unless manufactured or processed to very high environmental standards. In a recent survey of US house buyers, 60% said they wanted a 'healthy, green home'.

Conclusion

There is clearly a delicate balance between the need to conserve energy via an efficient, airtight envelope while at the same time maintaining a healthy indoor environment for occupants. Airtightness in a building is essential for energy saving, but good ventilation is essential for people's health. With good, well-managed ventilation and minimal use of contaminating materials, these two elements can be made to work together. This combination of elements must be considered carefully at the design stage and managed well during construction to be effective. Legislative changes suggest this issue will grow in importance in the coming years.

Further reading

Curwell, S., March, C. & Venables, R. (1990) *Buildings and health: the Rosehaugh guide*, RIBA Publications, London, UK.

Hansen, D.L. (1999) *Indoor air quality issues*, Taylor & Francis, New York, USA.

Rogers, S. (1986) *The E.I. (Environmental Illness) syndrome*, Prestige Publishing, USA.

Rogers, S. (1990) *Tired or toxic*, Prestige Publishing, USA.

Rostron, J. (ed.) (1997) *Sick building syndrome: concepts, issues and practice*, E & FN Spon, London, UK.

Woolley, T., Kimmins, S., Harrison, P. & Harrison, R. (2000) *Green buildings handbook: a guide to building products and their impact on the environment*, (2nd edition), E & FN Spon, London, UK.

WH/JG

Aluminium

A metal that is used frequently in buildings, it can be found in roofing, cladding and several other building elements.

See also: CASTINGS; CEILINGS; CLADDING; COPPER; CORROSION; DESIGN LIFE; DURABILITY; LOUVRES AND BRISE SOLEIL; METALS; PROUVÉ, JEAN; ROOFS; STAINLESS STEEL; STANDING SEAM ROOF; SURFACE FINISHES; TIMBER – PRODUCTION AND FINISHES; WEATHERING; WINDOWS AND CURTAIN WALLING.

What is aluminium?

Aluminium is a silvery coloured metal that is used in roofing, cladding, louvres, curtain walling, façade systems and cast features. As a metal, aluminium is versatile – it is very lightweight, strong and ductile, so it is easily drawn into wire, strips and sheets, cast into complex shapes or extruded to form intricate and accurate profiles (e.g. for curtain walling). Although it is three times as flexible as steel, for structural use aluminium is not as stiff and so compared to steel, aluminium section sizes are about half as much again to achieve the same performance. Aluminium has been used in construction since the late 1800s. The metal is manufactured from the naturally occurring and plentiful ore, bauxite. The processes used to derive pure aluminium from the ore are extremely energy intensive, thus production plants are often sited near hydroelectric power stations where electrical power is readily available. However, aluminium can be recycled at a fraction of the energy required to produce it in the first place. Ecological designers are now demanding that recycled aluminium is specified wherever possible.

Uses and applications

It is most common for aluminium to be used in the form of an alloy – several metals can be combined with aluminium to enhance its basic properties and performance.

Alloy description: additional metals	Uses
Pure aluminium	Flashings to be made up in situ; Foil; Sheet roofing (continuously supported).
+ Manganese (adds strength and durability)	Profiled cladding; Profiled roofing (self-supported); Preformed flashings.
+ Magnesium (adds resistance to marine conditions)	Superplastic formed cladding panels; Curved and 3D cladding panels.
+ Magnesium and silicon (adds strength)	Extruded sections for windows, doors, curtain walling, structural glazing and façade systems.
+ Magnesium, silicon and manganese	Loadbearing structural sections.

Standing seam roofing is one of the most common uses for this metal. Sainsbury's superstore at Greenwich in London (designed by Chetwood Associates) features a massive aluminium roof that covers the shop and incorporates wide arrays of roof lights. The building won several awards for its architecture and environmental design. 'Secret fixed' aluminium panels were used to clad 10,600 m^2 of complex curved, interlocking roof shapes on the Scottish Conference Centre in Glasgow designed by Foster and Partners (1995–98). The material is also seen frequently in the work of Erick von Egeraat, the Dutch architect, such as the twin-skin façade extension to the ING bank in Budapest, Hungary (1997). Daniel Libeskind's new Imperial War Museum (North) in Manchester uses 17,000 m^2 of aluminium sheet, profile and extrusions to clad a remarkable configuration of complex curves. The tallest part of the building reaches to 55 m high and is partly open to air; its striking shiny finish will oxidise to a matte silver grey.

Other applications for aluminium include HVAC ducting, interior screens, suspended ceiling systems, luminaires and decorative castings/ironmongery. In the UK after the Second World War, there was a shortage of timber, but a surplus of strategic metals such as aluminium. Hence, around 1945, domestic aluminium furniture appeared for a short time.

Design considerations – finishing

Aluminium forms an oxide film on contact with air, which protects it from corrosion and can actually be thickened artificially in a process called anodising. This process can be used to trap coloured dyes on the surface on the metal such as gold, blue, red and black. Anodising different alloys for different lengths of time will affect the colours and so close colour matching cannot reasonably be expected. A variegated colour distribution is more common and is what designers would anticipate when specifying an anodised aluminium finish, for say cladding or interior screens. As a malleable (easily worked) metal, various textures can also be imparted such as etching and polishing, but a 'natural' finish is also feasible (sometimes called self-finished). Polished aluminium is extremely shiny, producing a highly reflective finish. If a more uniform colour is required, and the natural finish of the aluminium is not a priority, then polyester or PVF_2 coatings can be used. This is typical of the bold curtain walling systems one sees from the 1980s; silver, white or other subtle colour ways are preferred in contemporary architecture. Castings using aluminium are often specified for structural glazing systems, which are normally left with a 'natural' finish. Aluminium is very durable and will last almost indefinitely. Light washing is recommended every three months to remove any surface contaminants.

Compatible materials

In accordance with the galvanic series, designers should exercise caution when using aluminium in combination with a number of materials. If in doubt, the British Standard BS8118 or relevant literature should be consulted, most of which is very informative, showing good practice details for this metal and its alloys.

In general, aluminium can be used alongside the following materials without significant problems:

- Bitumen protective coatings;
- Lacquers;
- (Fixings should be zinc, stainless steel or lead).

The following materials will corrode aluminium:

- Copper and copper alloys (even without direct metal contact);
- Timber preservatives containing copper (under humid conditions);
- Wet cement and concrete.

Further reading

Dwight, J. (1999) *Aluminium design and construction*, E & FN Spon, London, UK.
Wilquin, H. (2001) *Aluminium architecture*, Birkhäuser, Basle, Switzerland.

JG

Ando, Tadao

Tadao Ando is an acclaimed Japanese architect (b.1941). He mastered the vernacular tradition, and brought it to his own brand of Modernism. Ando's work is noted particularly for the simplicity of its design, magical use of concrete and its incredible manipulation of light (artificial and natural).

See also: CONCRETE; CONCRETE – FINISHES; CONCRETE – STRUCTURES; 'HONESTY'; LE CORBUSIER; LIGHTING – DAYLIGHTING; SURFACE FINISHES; WALLS.

Ando is largely self educated. Rather than going to university after finishing high school, he joined a selection of architectural and interior design offices where he gained experience and then, in 1969 at the age of 28, he established Tadao Ando Architects and Associates in Osaka. Initially he struggled to create inhabitable spaces that were autonomous and completely adaptable to ever changing environmental conditions in the heart of urban centres. Finally in 1975–76, he succeeded with the Row House in Sumiyoshi. This was a breakthrough; with this house he won the 1979 award of the Architectural Institute in Japan. For the first time he was able to use his sense of geometry and aesthetic order combined with his implicit understanding of the properties of materials. The exposed concrete walls create a hard, smooth, almost metal-like surface, the polished dark floors reflect light within the built envelope and the timber floors create a sense of luxury on the upper level. Penetration of light into the courtyard in a controlled fashion allows the house to respond to the environment, demonstrating sensitivity to the site while maintaining a strict overall order.

Throughout the 1970s and early 1980s Tadao Ando continued to design houses and shops, creating tranquil living environments on sites neighboured by undesirable features. Ando would erect high concrete walls around the sites to create havens and block out the external influences. Notable examples are The Nakayama House, Suzaka, Nara, 1983–85 and the Kidosaki House, Setagaya, Tokyo 1982–86.

In 1985–88 Ando built the Chapel on the Water and the adjoining Theatre on the Water in Tomamu, Hokkaido. This development marked the next stage of his career. The buildings combine his many skills exquisitely; the knowledge of materials, the desire for minimal design, the comprehensive understanding of the site and its natural environment and most particularly the acute ability to capture the spirit of the place. Having created an artificial pond by diverting water from a nearby stream, the main interior of the Chapel looks out across the pool with its large crucifix looming mysteriously at the centre. The combination of the buildings creates a sense of order through their geometry, accentuating the contrast with the order of nature.

Ando joined many other influential architects of the period with a built contribution to the Vitra complex in Germany in 1993 (Vitra Seminar House, Weil am Rhein). The furniture company Vitra, which uses design classics, both traditional and contemporary, from Charles and Ray Eames to Philippe Stark, had also collected architectural masterpieces from several international architects such as Frank Gehry and Zaha Hadid. It was only fitting therefore that Ando should also be represented.

Ando's use of concrete was based on his desired to 'give concrete, not the coarseness with the material in Le Corbusier's works, but a more refined expression'. His work is now renowned for its deliberate expression of bolt holes used to secure the concrete formwork (steel shutters). These punctuate and order the expanses of exposed concrete walls that one sees throughout his work. Indeed, whichever material is chosen by Ando, it is a fundamental part of his design as much as the dimension of the rooms or the shape of the windows. Ando manipulates space, material and control of the perceptions of the surrounding environment and has won overwhelming praise from his peers, critics and also from the users of his buildings.

Further reading

Anon (1990) *Tadao Ando Architectural Monographs No.14*, Academy Editions, John Wiley & Sons, London, UK.

Blaser, W. (ed.) (2001) *Tadao Ando: architecture of silence*, Birkhäuser, Basle, Switzerland.

Dal Co, F. (1997) *Tadao Ando*, Phaidon Press, London, UK.

Furuyama, M. (1996) *Tadao Ando*, Birkhäuser, Basle, Switzerland.

Jodidio, P. (1999) *Tadao Ando*, Benedikt Taschen, Köln, Germany.

Lloyd Jones, D. & Ando, T. (1998) *Architecture and the environment*, Laurence King Publishing, London, UK.

Pare, R. et al. (2000) *Tadao Ando*, Phaidon Press, London, UK.

MT

Anodising

See: ALUMINIUM; METALS

Artificial lighting

See: LIGHTING – ARTIFICIAL LIGHTING

Arup, Sir Ove Nyquist

The name of the Danish engineer Ove Arup (and the company Ove Arup & Partners) is synonymous with innovation and quality in architectural technology, and civil and structural engineering. Ove Arup (1895–1988) pioneered the integration of architecture, structure and services and his vision lives on in the firm of the same name.

See also: CONCRETE; CONCRETE – STRUCTURES; HAPPOLD, SIR TED & BURO HAPPOLD; INTEGRATION; LUBETKIN, BERTHOLD; RICE, PETER.

Ove Arup

The son of the Danish Consul in Newcastle-upon-Tyne, England, Ove Arup was educated in Germany and later Denmark. His first degree, in philosophy and mathematics, was taken at the University of Copenhagen. Rejecting the idea of studying architecture because he felt unsure of his artistic talents, he moved to the Royal Technical College in Copenhagen to study engineering. He always said that he would rather be a good engineer than a second-rate architect. On graduating in 1922, he joined the Danish civil engineers, Christiani & Nielsen, in their Hamburg office, and a year later transferred to London where he was appointed Chief Designer in 1925. His interest and expertise in marine structures were expressed in several publications on piled jetties, piers and dolphins, but before long he became directly involved with the Modern Movement in architecture. In 1933 Berthold Lubetkin, whose firm Tecton pioneered modern architecture in the United Kingdom, invited him to collaborate on a block of apartments in Highgate, North London, known as 'Highpoint 1'. This gave Arup the opportunity to apply the techniques of reinforced concrete, which he had by then used on many civil engineering projects, to a major modern building. Modern building techniques were to be exploited in the application of what was then a relatively unused material in the building industry. Christiani & Nielsen would not undertake the contract and Arup accepted the post of Chief Designer with J L Kier & Co in London, another firm with Danish roots, on the condition that Kiers would build Highpoint. He designed a system of movable wooden formwork to cast loadbearing reinforced concrete walls on site – an innovation in structural engineering for architecture.

Arup's interest in, and commitment to, what he later called 'Total Architecture' developed and grew. He became a leading figure in the MARS (Modern Architecture

Research Society) group, and worked with Tecton on several more important projects, including, most notably, a second Highpoint block as well as the Penguin Pool at London Zoo, and the Finsbury Health Centre. He formed Arup & Arup Ltd, a firm of engineers and contractors, with his cousin Arne in 1938. Then, in 1946, at an age when many are beginning to think of retirement, he branched out into private practice as a consulting engineer, hoping to realise his dream of 'achieving the perfect union of design and construction'. The firms that bear his name have endeavoured to fulfil this dream over more than half a century's growth and development.

Among the new practice's projects were some significant landmarks in modern architecture. These include Michael Scott's Bus Station in Dublin, the Architects Co-Partnership's Rubber Factory in Brynmawr (the first postwar building to be listed), several innovative housing schemes for the then London County Council, and of course the Sydney Opera House. Since then Arup (as the family of practices is now collectively known) has been associated with a huge number of famous buildings as consulting engineers, as well as constantly extending its activities into new fields. However, the projects which gave Ove Arup personally the greatest pleasure were those in which essentially simple structural concepts were elegantly expressed. An example is the Kingsgate Footbridge over the River Wear at Durham, where he personally spent many hours perfecting every detail of the design.

Ove Arup was always a visionary and an idealist who hated compromise. His writings on architecture and engineering have been seminal in their effect on his collaborators in particular and the industry in general. By example and by his writing, he, probably more than anyone, stopped the divergence between architecture and engineering, which began with the Industrial Revolution in the 19th century. He worked for greater understanding between the professions associated with the creation of buildings, but was never doctrinaire on how this could be achieved. His commitment to real collaboration between them came to its most visible embodiment in 1963 with the formation of Arup Associates, which henceforth would be an identifiable practice of architects, engineers and quantity surveyors working together. Multidisciplinary working became a reality and professional divisions were broken down.

Ove Arup was the recipient of many awards and honorary doctorates. In 1953 he was created a Commander of the Order of the British Empire, and in 1971 a Knight Bachelor. His country of origin honoured him as Chevalier First Class (1965) and Commander First Class (1975) of the Order of Dannebrog. He received the Gold Medals of both the Royal Institute of British Architects (1966) and the Institution of Structural Engineers (1973). He was one of the original Fellows of the Fellowship of Engineering, and in 1987 was elected a Royal Academician.

His partner, Sir Jack Zunz, has written of him: 'looking back over his life and work, one comes back again and again to his passion for quality and his quest for excellence in all that he did – personal and professional. He was one of the greats, if not the greatest of his time'.

Further reading

Anon (1986) *Ove Arup & Partners (1946–1986)*, Academy Editions, John Wiley & Sons, London, UK.

Sommer, D. (1994) *Ove Arup & Partners: engineering the built environment*, Birkhäuser, Basle, Switzerland.

OA

Inside the glazed timber and concrete central atrium of the New Parliamentary Building (Portcullis House), Westminster, London, designed by architect Michael Hopkins & Partners. Photograph by Trevor Jones, courtesy of The Concrete Society.

Atrium

An open space inside a building that is usually covered by glazing: its functions are mainly to enhance the building architecturally and promote natural ventilation.

See also: AIR-CONDITIONING; AIRTIGHTNESS AND IAQ; BUILDING MANAGEMENT SYSTEMS; ENERGY EFFICIENCY; ENVIRONMENTAL DESIGN; FAÇADES AND FAÇADE ENGINEERING; GLASS; GLASS – STRUCTURAL GLAZING; INTEGRATION; INTELLIGENT FAÇADES AND MATERIALS; LIGHTING – DAYLIGHTING; ROGERS, RICHARD; STACK EFFECT; VON GERKAN & MARG; WATER MANAGEMENT AND DRAINAGE; WINDOWS AND CURTAIN WALLING; WRIGHT, FRANK LLOYD.

Introduction

The architectural term atrium (the plural is atria) originates in antiquity, for which it describes an outdoor space within the plan of a building that was open to the sky. The function of the atrium was to give the building a cool, shady, private outdoor space. Water in fountains or rills was also used to cool the air evaporatively and so offer shelter from the hot sun. The atrium was paved at ground level and upper storeys would often have balconies or colonnades overlooking the atrium space. In more recent times, the term has come to mean something rather different in that it is used to describe an open space within a building or adjacent to the building façade that is usually glazed and extends upwards over sometimes many floors. The atrium is used as a climate moderator, often in combination with a natural ventilation strategy, to aid heating and/or cooling (which may differ between countries and climates).

Although Frank Lloyd Wright presaged the architectural use of the atrium in his Larkin office building of 1904, the use of atria grew significantly through the late 20th century. It is used as a means to enhance commercial, residential and leisure buildings to the extent that it is now a very common feature in most large scale, urban architecture. The architectural form of the atrium has developed considerably and there are several generic types including longitudinal indoor 'streets' or single volume entrance plazas. By way of an example, several UK shopping centres are oriented on a longitudinal atrium that runs throughout the building but which is expanded at key points to act as a 'node' for cafés and meeting points.

What's in an atrium?

Although the main volume of the atrium is essentially open space, the floor area at its base offers an architectural opportunity for a high quality space for social interaction and a place to orient oneself. Older examples resembled simple cube-shaped cut-outs in the building fabric, but there is a trend now towards introducing intermediate levels (mezzanine floors) to the atrium to effectively soften the edges of the space. There are hundreds of examples from Europe, North America, Australasia, the Gulf and the Far East countries showing how atria can accommodate a variety of interior styles and patterns of use. The choice of interior may depend on the client's wishes, the needs of the users and/or the function of the building. Some atria feature only a reception desk and a few chairs whereas others have lush planting and water features.

Facilities that can be found in or around atrium spaces include:

- Café or restaurant ·
- Escalators

- Exhibitions
- 'Hot desks'
- ICT equipment
- Lifts
- Public art or sculpture
- Reception areas
- Seating
- Stairs
- Stalls and kiosks
- Telephones

Design considerations

Perhaps the prime consideration for many atria is the need to model thermal performance in use, often using computer simulation. This is vital for designs that aim to use the stack effect to achieve natural, or partly natural, ventilation and can be used to predict and manipulate heat flows in the atrium and surrounding spaces. Different scenarios can be tested to see the effect of seasonal, organisational or other changes on the thermal performance of the atrium. These can be used to inform the building design in plan and section, in addition to programming for the building management system. In larger buildings and in urban areas there is a risk that channelled, high-pressure and turbulent wind flows may cause unpleasant conditions in atria because these extremes are not always modelled sufficiently. The result can be atria that are too breezy and difficult to heat or cool and thus unsatisfactory to users of the building. These problems can be avoided by proper consideration for site-specific conditions in the initial analysis, together with visits to adjacent properties where appropriate. The thermal modelling must also include tests to establish at what temperature overheating will occur (at occupied levels) – this is particularly common in atria with south-facing glazed façades. Other design considerations include:

- Acoustics and noise concerns (very important if an atrium contains a mix of quiet and noisy activities);
- Fire – some atria are fire separated from surrounding areas and upper floors all the way up, depending on the nature of the building;
- Maintenance and cleaning of the glazed areas, inside and outside, in addition to any operable components such as ridge vents;
- Security – again, this is particularly important in buildings with a mix of uses that perhaps share the atrium for access or circulation purposes.

Built examples

PowerGen HQ, Coventry (Bennetts Associates) – a 12,000 m^2 office building with a long, central, indoor street style atrium. The atrium uses the stack effect in combination with fabric energy storage to naturally ventilate and cool the structure.

Central Beheer bank, Apeldoorn, Netherlands (Herman Hertzberger) – an early 1970s example with mini-atria throughout the building. The vertical space is punctuated with platforms and stairs connecting the office floors in an informal way that encourages casual circulation and interaction.

Portcullis House, London (Michael Hopkins & Partners) – this glulam timber and glazed atrium does not extend to the full height of this building for MPs, but sits at low level and is populated by giant fig trees to give the effect of an intimate 'oasis' in the centre of Westminster.

Further reading

Anon (1994) *Passive solar commercial and institutional buildings – a sourcebook of examples*, John Wiley & Sons, Chichester, UK.

Bednar, M.J. (1986) *The new atrium*, McGraw Hill, New York, USA.

Saxon, R. (1993) *The atrium comes of age*, Longman, Harlow, UK.

JG

Automated manufacture and construction

Automation (e.g. robotics) can be used to optimise speed and quality of both manufacturing and construction processes.

See also: BUILDABILITY; BUILDING SYSTEMS; CONSTRUCTION PROGRAMME; CRITICAL PATH ANALYSIS; JUST-IN-TIME CONSTRUCTION; LEAD-TIME; 'LEAN' CONSTRUCTION; MODULES AND MODULAR CONSTRUCTION; OFF-SITE MANUFACTURE; ON-SITE PRODUCTION; PROCUREMENT; RISK MANAGEMENT.

Introduction

Automation is a very specialised area and is not currently used extensively, so this entry focuses on the basic issues underlying the use of automation (e.g. robotics) in the off-site manufacture of goods, products or building modules and in construction operations on site. The reason for using automation is to improve accuracy, productivity, quality and/or speed, often within a context where the employment of people can attract huge long-term investment in facilities, health and safety and on-costs (i.e. pensions etc). However, the installation and operating costs of automated equipment and its output would have to be compared to the equivalent 'human' costs to undertake the same tasks in order to justify the strategic decision to automate. There may also be political pressures brought to bear where there are impacts to local employment from such changes. In industries such as automotive, aerospace, food, pharmaceuticals and others in the manufacturing sector, degrees of automation have been used for decades, but the construction industry has not followed suit. It has certain specific circumstances that could be said to prevent automation such as a high degree of variability in client requirements and in on-site conditions. However there is a growing understanding that some processes in the manufacture and construction of buildings could benefit from automation.

About automated manufacture

Manufacture of construction products, building components or even whole room modules is increasingly being undertaken off site, but automation tends to be used only in mass production for standardised products with a very high production rate and/or large end market e.g. bricks, pipes and structural steel. Computer-numeric-controlled (CNC) manufacture is commonly used in steelwork fabrication for cutting, drilling and folding (the design office CAD systems are linked directly to the CNC machinery). Robots may be used for finishing processes such as paint spraying, galvanising or sealing. Current thought in production engineering suggests that there is scope for further use of automation in the manufacturing side of the construction industry. However the unpredictability of demand 'pull' for such goods in construction and the lack of repetitiveness in many buildings mean that manufacturers are unwilling to take a chance on installing automation. In an attempt to revolutionise the UK housebuilding industry, one particular joint venture developed a proposal for a fully automated factory that would produce modules for a house that could be erected in just a few days. Unfortunately the venture did not receive the necessary support from industry partners to proceed. However should the drive for off-site fabricated goods increase then this position may change.

About automated construction

Construction was undertaken traditionally by legions of skilled site workers, with very few elements produced elsewhere than the site itself. Although aspects of this 'artisan' style of production remain, there are now fewer people on site, more products made off site in the factory and greater use of mechanical or automated means of installing these products. These changes have been driven in the UK mainly by a costly labour force and demands for improvements to productivity and quality of construction products etc. In other countries, with similar influences and market conditions, the drive towards automation in the construction process has been more successful. In Japan the construction and electronics industries have worked closely together in a market that is already focused on off-site production and on-site assembly. The use of robots on site can offer speed and quality benefits but the building design and the construction programme must be developed accordingly to get the maximum advantage. The benefits of using automated or semi-automated robots on site is that they can work quickly and efficiently on repetitive tasks without, for example, the need for all the health and safety considerations that govern the employment of human workers. A robot can be observed closely by site staff or can be controlled remotely, working in areas of the site that are perhaps too risky or exposed for human workers. Examples include welding, steel fixing, reinforcement fixing, painting or installing cladding components.

Further reading

Gibb, A.G.F. (1999) *Off-site fabrication: prefabrication, pre-assembly and modularisation*, Whittles Publishing, Caithness, UK.

Warszawski, A. (1999) *Industrialized and automated building systems* (2nd edition), E & FN Spon, London, UK.

JG

Beams

Beams are horizontal structural members that resist applied loads by bending.

See also: ALUMINIUM; BRACING; CANTILEVER; COLUMN; COMPOSITE MATERIALS; CONCRETE; CONNECTIONS; FIRE PROTECTION; FLOORS; FRAME; STRUCTURAL STEEL; STONE; TIMBER; TIMBER – LAMINATED TIMBER; TIMBER – TIMBER STRUCTURES; WALLS.

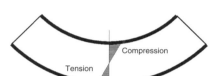

Length of sagging beam. Image provided by Ove Arup & Partners.

Introduction

A beam is a structural member that resists applied loads by bending. Typically it spans between two or more supports, but can cantilever from a single support. The span is usually, but not necessarily, horizontal and the loads usually vertical. Among the earliest beams were tree trunks across rivers, and today many beams, including most of those used in houses, are still made of timber because it is easily available and easily worked. In larger structures beams are made from structural steel or reinforced concrete. Some beams are known by more specific names depending on their use, such as lintels, joists and girders, but, in conversation, it is quite acceptable to use the word beam generically to describe these other types. Note that bending is sometimes referred to as flexure.

How does a beam work?

When a beam bends, the material on the inner side of the curve is squashed into compression while that on the outer side is stretched and goes into tension; material towards the mid-depth of the beam is stressed only a little. If the compressed side is on the top the beam 'sags', if it is on the bottom the beam is said to 'hog'.

Materials used in beams

A beam must be constructed of materials that are able to resist both compressive and tensile stresses.

Reinforced concrete uses the tensile strength of steel combined with the good compressive strength of concrete. Composite steel beams use the supported concrete slab to take compression. Timber has moderate strength for both types of stress, and has been used widely because of its availability and the ease with which it can be worked. Although stone is good at resisting compression its tensile strength is quite poor, and so stone has only been used for minor beams such as short lintels over door openings. Cast iron is again weak in tension, but its successors, wrought iron and steel, are very strong in both compression and tension. Beams can also be made from less common structural materials such as aluminium and plastic composites.

Design of beams

Beams can be of any cross section, i.e. shape or size. Many are rectangular for ease of construction, but since the material near the centre of the beam is little stressed, the best use of material is achieved by having it concentrated where the compressive and tensile stresses are highest. Thus, the cross section of most steel beams is in the shape of an 'I'.

Beams need to be designed to be strong enough to resist the applied loads, with an adequate factor of safety, and stiff enough to be stable and give satisfactory service. Strength checks involve checking both the bending and shear at critical sections and bearing stresses at supports. Walls, columns or other beams are usually used as supports. These supports are described as 'simple' if they allow the beam to rotate and change in length without imparting any force on the beam. Most supports, however, provide some restraint to the beam. Restraint, at and between supports, may be necessary to prevent instability. If a beam has insufficient stability, its strength will be reduced by its tendency to rotate with a sideways displacement.

Additional notes

- Special fabricated steel beams such as castellated or cellular beams (with circular holes in) are useful for threading services through or can be left exposed for aesthetic effect.
- For large open spaces, such as atria, a ring beam may be used, which effectively ties together the floor beams that meet at each storey level.
- Note that structural beams will need to conform to Building Regulations, including the requirements on fire protection.
- Long spans are feasible, e.g. 'glulam' laminated timber beams are attractive and can span over 50 metres.

Further reading

Goodchild, C.H. (1997) *Economic concrete frame elements*, Reinforced Concrete Council, Crowthorne, UK.

Ogden, R.G. et al. (1996) *Architectural teaching resource: studio guide*, SCI Publication 167, The Steel Construction Institute, Ascot, UK.

OA

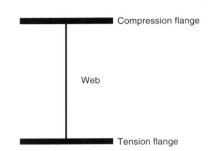

Cross section through I-beam. Image provided by Ove Arup & Partners.

(labels: Compression flange, Web, Tension flange)

Bespoke

This term describes the manufacture of building products or components to specific customer requirements, rather than from a standard range.

See also: BUILDING SYSTEMS; CONSTRUCTION PROGRAMME; DESIGN LIFE; FIT-OUT; LEAD-TIME; OFF-SITE MANUFACTURE; PROCUREMENT; PROPRIETARY GOODS AND STANDARDISATION; SPECIFICATION.

Inside the Plashet School footbridge, London. The sinuous shape is created both by the plan shape and the use of clever bespoke fabricated steel sections, which are fixed in different positions along the length of the structure. Photograph of the Plashet School footbridge (Architects Birds Portchmouth Russum) by Franck Robert, courtesy of Techniker Ltd.

What is meant by 'bespoke'?

Before the advent of industrialisation most buildings and products were made for specific requirements or clients, even though they used some common components. Now, however, most building elements are selected from standard ranges. Methods of mass manufacture enable building components to be made in high volumes, thereby reducing the amount of bespoke work to fewer specific, original applications.

The term 'bespoke' is commonly understood to mean an object that when made is the only one of its type. For example, a bespoke tailor makes individual clothes for clients, specifically to their size and style needed at a particular time. However, this is not the definition used in construction parlance, for which bespoke refers to any product (or a set of products) that is made by request, as required and directed by the client/design team. Requirements may include anything from cladding panels to door handles. In contrast, mass produced items such as bricks, chairs, steel trusses or windows can be selected from a manufacturer's standard range.

The benefit of bespoke work is that the product can be made to the exact design and specification required, and the design team need make no compromise as to materials, shapes, sizes or colours. While this freedom is seductive for architects wishing to indulge in expressive forms and spaces, this must be balanced by the practical limitations of any manufacturing processes, not to mention any additional costs of going down the bespoke route.

Production economies

If a manufacturer offers a standard range then it has already made investment in the production process and these additional costs can be recouped via mass production and marketing. However, for bespoke work, there will be a one-off investment of time and effort, which the manufacturer may or may not recover. This invariably results in a cost premium on bespoke work, which may be acceptable in some instances, but not in others.

In production terms, it is usual to discuss with manufacturers whether products will be mass-produced (a high volume will be made), 'batch' produced (a specified number only will be made) or bespoke (one-off or a small set of one-offs). The inference is that the first will have a low cost, the batch will be mid-range and the last will be expensive. The inference does not necessarily translate directly to 'quality' because this can be specified and can be at whatever level is required by the client whatever scale of production is used.

Examples of bespoke items

Some building elements are produced in a genuinely bespoke way because standard, mass-produced items are either not available or not desirable. For example, a client may wish to replicate a finish that was discontinued, match an existing building or simply express its status in choosing to go bespoke. In most cases, the decision is linked closely to architectural intention, with aesthetics and longevity in mind. It is very common for high quality landmark buildings to use bespoke items where aesthetic and constructional boundaries are being exceeded. Bespoke products include:

- Cast or reconstituted stone;
- Fit-out specifications;
- Interior fittings and finishes;
- Precast concrete cladding;
- Precast concrete frames;
- Structural glazing;
- Textile membrane roofs.

An interesting example is a bespoke bridge (designed by Birds Portchmouth Russum and Techniker) to connect two parts of Plashet School in Newham, London. The 67 m long footbridge crosses the busy A13 road and features a cleverly fabricated bespoke steel section (shown in the Figure). This is placed in different orientations on plan and covered by a PTFE-coated fabric canopy to create an organic shape. Each 'hoop' is galvanised steel, they alternate along the length of the sinuous plan, which also gives the fabric rigidity.

Further reading

Wakita, O.A. & Linde, R.M. (1999) *The professional practice of architectural detailing* (3rd edition) John Wiley & Sons, New York, USA.

CS/JG

Bimetallic corrosion

See: METALS; CORROSION

Biomimetics

See: INTELLIGENT FAÇADES AND MATERIALS

Blastproof design

See: FAÇADES AND FAÇADE ENGINEERING; WINDOWS AND CURTAIN WALLING

BMS

See: BUILDING MANAGEMENT SYSTEMS

Board materials

See: TIMBER – MANUFACTURED BOARDS

Bracing

The term bracing refers to diagonal members that are used to stiffen a structure, by utilising the inherent in-plane stiffness of a triangular framework.

See also: CONCRETE; CONNECTIONS; CORE (STRUCTURAL); FAÇADES AND FAÇADE ENGINEERING; FLOORS; FRAME; STRUCTURAL STEEL; WALLS.

Introduction

In buildings bracing is most commonly found in specific braced bays to resist the horizontal load on steel-framed buildings; as plan bracing (i.e. bracing on plan) to provide in-plane stiffness to timbered or steel framed roofs; and to provide in-plane stiffness to glazed screens.

Consider first the case of a braced bay often used to provide the stiff structural core of a building. Without such a lateral stability system, a building would simply lean sideways under wind or any other horizontal load to its façade. As the walls and columns lean sideways, the weight they support would tend to push them over even further until the building collapses. In each braced bay, the bracing elements are used to form a vertical truss that cantilevers from the ground. The truss resists horizontal load and carries it down to the ground. The truss needs to be not only strong enough to prevent sideways collapse, but also stiff enough to limit the storey height deflection to an acceptable value so that damage to the structure and finishes is avoided.

Design considerations

Several bracing arrangements are possible:

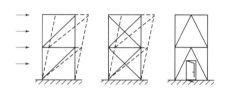

- **Diagonal bracing** – the simplest form. When a horizontal force is applied, the bracing becomes either a tie or a strut – going into either tension or compression depending on the direction of the applied force;
- **Cross bracing** – a variation of the above. Whatever the direction of the lateral force, one of the diagonals will always be put into tension whilst the other buckles and is simply ignored;
- **K-bracing** – this is particularly useful because it enables door openings to be accommodated.

Diagonal, cross and 'K' bracing. Image provided by Ove Arup & Partners.

The location of the braced bays needs to be considered carefully. Braced bays must be provided in two perpendicular directions so that they can resist horizontal loads coming from any direction. To avoid twist of the building, it is also important to place the braced bays fairly symmetrically on plan and generally to have at least two braced bays in each direction. A further requirement is to limit the maximum distance between braced bays in any one direction, so that when the building expands in hot weather it does not force the bays apart, damaging the bracing. In long buildings it may be necessary to provide a movement joint to divide the building into two halves and relieve the thermal expansion forces.

Bracing can also be used to provide in-plane stiffness to roofs and walls. In roofs, diagonal or cross bracing is used conventionally to form a truss that spans horizontally between the stiff structural cores of the building i.e. between the braced bays or shear walls. In glazed screens it is more common to use cross bracing. This is because cross bracing does not have to resist compression (as discussed above) allowing the use of visually slender members such as rods or cables. This is obviously a distinct aesthetic advantage.

The alternatives to braced bays are shear walls and moment frames.

Shear walls rely on the inherent in-plane stiffness or diaphragm action of wall elements. Reinforced concrete shear walls offer a direct alternative to the braced bays discussed above and are used to resist the horizontal loads on both steel and concrete framed buildings. Masonry shear walls are also used, but being much weaker than concrete walls are only appropriate in low-rise masonry construction, such as house construction or cross wall construction.

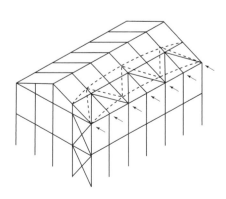

Braced bays in a frame structure. Image provided by Ove Arup & Partners.

Moment frames rely on rigid connections between the beams and columns within the building. They are relatively flexible and are therefore only appropriate in low-rise steel or concrete framed buildings. The most common form of moment frame is the single storey portal used to stabilise factory shed type structures.

Further reading

Institution of Structural Engineers (1988) *Stability of buildings*, Institution of Structural Engineers, London, UK.

OA

Brass

See: COPPER

Bricks and blocks

Bricks and blocks are very common products used in construction of houses and other low to medium rise buildings. Their success lies in the economics of mass production using a cheap and readily available raw material, i.e. clay.

See also: AALTO, ALVAR; BESPOKE; BRICKS AND BLOCKS – FINISHES; CAVITY; CEMENT; EARTH CONSTRUCTION; KAHN, LOUIS; MORTARS – CEMENT AND LIME; RETAINING WALL; SIZA, ALVARO; SURFACE FINISHES; WALLS.

Façade of the Joint Service Command and Staff College, near Swindon, featuring delicately coloured and textured concrete blocks. Photograph by Trevor Jones, courtesy of The Concrete Society.

Introduction and historical development

Bricks and blocks were manufactured originally simply using sun-dried clay. Primitive firing techniques were used only much later and more sophisticated methods of firing were introduced later still. With the development of OPC (Ordinary Portland Cement), concrete block products were introduced from about a hundred years ago. Brick and block are most commonly used in a form, nowadays bound invariably with mortar, which is known as masonry. The individual components, however, are themselves made of different materials, exist in different forms and are used in a variety of ways. In the UK alone, many millions of both bricks and concrete blocks are produced per annum.

The brick is the older building unit. It is basically a small rectangular prism, sometimes made with an indentation in one or both faces known as a 'frog'. The first use of bricks was recorded in Jericho around 8,000 BC. A description has been found of an arch of sun-baked brick constructed in Ur around 4,000 BC, including a reference to the mortar with which the arch was constructed. Chopped straw provided internal reinforcement in these early units. From sun-dried clay the manufacture of bricks progressed to clay hardened by firing, again in the Middle East and from around 1,500 BC. Glazing of bricks, manufactured from clay, is thought to have commenced around 600 BC. Glazed clay tiles are seen in a number of ancient mosques. Hollow clay and concrete blocks have been used in floors since the second half of the 19th century. Brickwork has been used in vaults, in jack-arch construction and for floors.

Non-fired blocks are still used in some developing countries. 'Stabilised soil' is made from clay and a proportion of cement. Blocks are manufactured individually using a lever press and left to cure. The resulting material has good thermal mass, and although variable in strength and finish is strong enough for single storey construction. 'Adobe' or mud bricks are still in use. The principal process today still uses fired clay, although a greater variety of clays is now used and other materials are also employed. Different clays contain varying percentages of minerals, primarily silica and alumina and other materials, which affect the colour of a brick.

The firing process is also more sophisticated and more tightly controlled. Bricks and blocks can be manufactured as solid, cellular or perforated.

About bricks

Clay bricks are broadly of three types:

● Facing brick – these are used where the appearance of the brickwork is important;

- Common brick – these are made of lower quality clays and used for 'normal' construction;
- Refractory brick – used in furnaces and fireplaces and capable of withstanding very high temperatures.

In addition, there is a range of other specialist masonry bricks such as engineering bricks, which are fired almost to vitrification. These are characterised by high strength, low water absorption and good durability. Calcium silicate bricks are manufactured from fine aggregate and lime, pressed mechanically together and combined using steam under pressure. Strengths for use in loadbearing brickwork range from 5 to $100N/mm^2$, although much higher values can be obtained for different types of brick. The durability of different types of brick varies. It is important to specify both strength and durability requirements correctly, depending on the intended use of the material. The standard brick size is $102.5 \times 215 \times 65$ mm. This has varied somewhat over time, but different sizes can still be obtained. There is a healthy market in reclaimed bricks from older properties.

About blocks

Blocks were first manufactured much more recently. They are dimensionally much larger than bricks and are generally made from concrete, either dense or lightweight, or from clay. The manufacture of concrete blocks began with the introduction of Portland cement in the late 19th century. Lightweight concrete blocks are the most commonly used block in the UK. They are handled more easily and have better insulating properties than dense blocks (there is an inverse correlation between density and thermal performance). Concrete blocks are made from cement and aggregate, generally sand, and are available in a range of strengths and sizes. The common face size is 215 mm x 440 mm, with thicknesses varying between 90 and 140 mm Compressive strengths range from 2.8 to $35N/mm^2$. In the UK blocks are most commonly used as the inner leaf of a cavity wall and for internal partitions. However in addition to this, over 2.5 million concrete blocks are used per annum as pavers for external landscaping works. These can include porous blocks such as those used as part of sustainable urban drainage systems (SUDS). In Europe, concrete blocks are used more widely in external loadbearing walls and are finished either by painting or rendering. Clay blocks are more often used in Europe and in the USA. These are generally of voided construction, with the voids filled with mortar or concrete.

Glass blocks

Glass blocks have been a popular architectural choice for decades, perhaps stemming from their use in La Maison de Verre, by Pierre Chareau, built in France (1927–30). These architectural stalwarts are made from two moulded glass halves fused together. The process creates a hollow unit with trapped air that has good sound insulating properties. Construction uses mortar bonding as for ordinary brickwork. Glass blocks are particularly useful in providing acoustic privacy while allowing light to penetrate the wall (although direct visual contact is not possible because the glass is somewhat rippled). The blocks have been used in architecture for many decades; one of the nicest examples is Berthold Lubetkin's Finsbury Health Centre in London, which dates from 1936. A more recent example by Renzo Piano and Arup for Hermes in Tokyo, Japan, uses the largest glass blocks ever made ($450 mm^2$) to clad a new shop.

Bricks and blocks in a structure

When used in walls, bricks are laid in rows, known as courses. The individual bricks are joined using a thin layer of mortar (a mix usually of lime, sand and cement in varying proportions), depending on the requirements for strength and durability. Walls may be loadbearing or non-loadbearing and may be solid, or of cavity construction. In the latter, two separate leaves are separated by a cavity and joined by a series of ties (usually stainless steel) to facilitate a structural connection. Commonly the outer leaf will be of brick and the inner leaf will be of block. When strengthened by reinforcement both brickwork and blockwork can serve as flexural elements such as retaining walls. In countries with seismic design codes, diaphragm masonry walls reinforced with steel bars and filled with concrete are often used.

Loadbearing brick walls are usually laid on the horizontal, but Tim Ronalds Architects adopted a radical approach of laying courses at an 18° incline for the Landmark Theatre in Ilfracombe, Devon (1997). The building features two cone-shaped structures, the largest 23 m high and 20 m diameter at its base. A total of 300,000 white bricks were laid 'off level' in ten months and the building opened to critical acclaim shortly afterwards.

It is also feasible to use bricks in non-loadbearing cladding, cast into precast concrete panels, e.g. the façade of the PowerGen HQ in Coventry (1995, Bennetts Associates) uses pre-tensioned brick cladding panels, with the bricks stack bonded and linked by tension rods.

Further reading

Brickwork Development Association (1994) *The BDA guide to successful brickwork*, Arnold, Windsor, UK.

British Standards Institution (1985) BS 5628-3:1985 *British standard code of practice for use of masonry. Part 3. Materials and components, design and workmanship*, British Standards Institution, London, UK.

Brunskill, R.W. (1990) *Brick building in Britain*, Gollancz, London, UK.

Lynch, G. (1994) *Brickwork: history, technology and practice* (Volume 1), Donhead, London, UK.

Lynch, G. (1994) *Brickwork: history, technology and practice* (Volume 2), Donhead, London, UK.

Plumridge, A. & Meulenkamp, W. (1993) *Brickwork architecture and design*, Studio Vista, London, UK.

OA

Bricks and blocks – finishes

Bricks and blocks have been used for hundreds of years as loadbearing materials and/or as decoration. Bricks can be manufactured from different clays giving a wide range of natural colours; other variations in finishes can be achieved by the addition of artificial colours, glazes, surface textures and the use of units of varied shapes.

See also: AALTO, ALVAR; BESPOKE; BRICKS AND BLOCKS; CAVITY; CEMENT; CONCRETE – FINISHES; EARTH CONSTRUCTION; MORTARS – CEMENT AND LIME; PIANO, RENZO; RETAINING WALL; ROGERS, RICHARD; SIZA, ALVARO; SURFACE FINISHES; WALLS; WRIGHT, FRANK LLOYD.

Introduction

Brick and block can both be used decoratively and for construction purposes. In the former the materials may be used as a veneer, in sculptural form, for roof or wall tiles,

The 19th-century Templeton Carpet Factory in Glasgow – a wonderful example of the decorative potential of brickwork. Photograph courtesy of Ove Arup & Partners.

or for floor tiles. This entry focuses on finishes to bricks because the possibilities are relatively greater than those are for concrete blocks (see final paragraph only).

Highly decorated loadbearing walls can be seen in Mediaeval buildings and in contemporary buildings decoration is also present in the use of different coloured materials and in the detail of the elevations. Clay bricks can be produced in a wide variety of shapes. Variations to the standard rectangular prism are either standard specials, produced regularly and described in a British Standard (BS 4729: 1990 *Specification for dimensions of bricks of special shapes and sizes*), or bespoke 'specials' made to order to meet particular requirements. Standard specials may be curved, flat or a standard brick with a curved or profiled end.

Colour

The colour of bricks varies naturally, depending on the colour of the raw materials used in production. Natural clay colours include white, grey or buff, dark yellow, light to dark reds or even purple. Colour variation occurs through slight differences in the firing or in composition of the material in a given batch, for example:

- Increased iron oxide produces a redder brick;
- Magnesium oxide makes them yellow;
- Normal clay with added chalk produces a creamy colour;
- The above plus manganese dioxide produces brown bricks.

Calcium silicate bricks tend to be more uniformly coloured, generally of pale shades. Colours may also be introduced to these by the use of pigments and glazes. Ceramic glazes may be applied before or after the firing and cooling process; if they are applied afterwards, re-firing is required. The glaze becomes an integral part of the face of the unit. Very rich colours can be produced in this manner, although modern methods cannot reproduce some of the exceptional blue tones found in early mosaics. Other finishes and colours are applied to the unit either fired or unfired, and are only surface coatings. Glazed turquoise bricks form the highly decorative external walls to CZWG's public lavatories and flower stall in Westbourne Grove, London.

Texture

The texture of clay bricks is a function of the manufacturing process. Wire-cut bricks are cut with wires from an extruded column of clay. The process often leaves drag marks on the bed surface; facing bricks may be pressed after cutting to produce a smooth face and sharper arrises (corners). Other varieties in texture are produced by applying a sand facing during manufacture (which also changes the colour), or by imposing a pattern mechanically to produce a 'rustic' brick. The surface may be scored, roughened or have an emblem pressed into the extruded column of clay. Steel moulds produce a very smooth texture and are used for both bricks and tiles. Handmade bricks show some variability in both size and shape but have an attractive, delicately creased surface finish, which distinguishes them from machine-made varieties. Two million hand made bricks were used for the new British Library in London, extracted from the same clay source as those used on the adjacent St Pancras Station.

Bonding

Bricks can be laid in a variety of patterns. Ornamental brickwork has been used for hundreds of years. The pattern in which bricks are laid, known as the bond, can be varied. Different bonds are created by changing the layout of one course in relation to the courses above and below, using bricks laid end to end (stretchers) and end-on (headers). Further decoration can be added by changing the finish to the mortar joints. These may, for example, be finished flush, recessed, 'penny rolled' or keyed ('bucket handle'). The mortar can be coloured with pigments, and joints may be kept particularly narrow to achieve a required appearance. Soft 'rubbed' bricks, generally orange-red in colour were much used with very thin lime mortar joints in the Queen Anne and Edwardian eras. Perhaps the best examples of Victorian decorative, polychromatic brickwork can be found at Keble College, Oxford and the Templeton carpet factory in Glasgow. The former has a recently completed extension, the Arko building by Rick Mather Architects, which uses bonding patterns in a rather more subdued manner, including 'stack' bonding (in which bricks are set directly above one another, rather than horizontally offset).

Other design options

Large terracotta blocks, either applied to a backing skin of brickwork or attached to a steel frame, are commonly seen on the outside of buildings. The blocks themselves may be highly decorated, shaped and hand-carved. A particularly fine example of such work, dating back over a hundred years, is seen at the Natural History Museum in London (Alfred Waterhouse).

Terracotta cladding is particularly popular as a precise 'mathematical' type of finish. The tiles are usually set in an aluminium carrier that can be used as a cladding system to a structural frame. The Monza building by Nicholas Grimshaw & Partners and the Montevetro development by Richard Rogers Partnership (both in London) are modern examples of this form of clayware. The terracotta rainscreen cladding provides a very crisp finish to the façades. Rogers and Piano used this type of terracotta cladding many years ago in the 1980s for the IRCAM building (Offices of the Institute of Acoustic Music) that forms an adjunct to the Centre Pompidou in Paris.

Faience is the term for glazed terracotta, or other glazed ceramic such as tiles. This is often used as a facing over steel framing but was also used extensively in the past as decoration on stone, brick and block structures. The terracotta may be given a clear glaze or an opaque colour. Very intricate patterns may be achieved using a variety of rich colours, exemplified perhaps by some of the religious buildings from the Middle East.

... and for blocks?

Concrete blocks may be made using a variety of crushed rock as coarse aggregate, giving the attractive appearance of natural stone colours when laid with fine mortar joints. Different surface finishes can also be produced on this material, for example polished, exposed aggregate, etched or with an impressed pattern. For highly decorative applications it is more common to specify precast concrete cast stone (or reconstituted stone) units that can be produced to a bespoke specification and include additions such as white cement, mica or dolomite to enhance their aesthetic appearance. In his 'textile block' houses of c.1930, Frank Lloyd Wright used concrete blocks with imprinted patterns, for example the Hollyhock House, which featured a stylised version of the flower imprinted on the blocks.

Further reading

Brickwork Development Association (1994) *The BDA guide to successful brickwork*, Arnold, Windsor, UK.

British Standards Institution (1985) BS 5628-3:1985 *British standard code of practice for use of masonry. Part 3. Materials and components, design and workmanship*, British Standards Institution, London, UK.

Brunskill, R.W. (1990) *Brick building in Britain*, Gollancz, London, UK.

Lynch, G. (1994) *Brickwork: history, technology and practice* (Volume 1), Donhead, London, UK.

Lynch, G. (1994) *Brickwork: history, technology and practice* (Volume 2), Donhead, London, UK.

Plumridge, A. & Meulenkamp, W. (1993) *Brickwork architecture and design*, Studio Vista, London, UK.

Stratton, M. (1993) *The terracotta revival: building innovation and the image of the industrial*, Gollancz, London, UK.

Tunick, S. (1997) *Terra-cotta skyline*, Princeton Architectural Press, USA.

OA

Brise soleil

See: LOUVRES AND BRISE-SOLEIL

Bronze

See: COPPER

Buildability

The consideration of how a building will be constructed before work starts on site, with a view to improving speed and quality when it does.

See also: AUTOMATED MANUFACTURE AND CONSTRUCTION; BUILDING SYSTEMS; CONNECTIONS; CONSTRUCTION PROGRAMME; CRITICAL PATH ANALYSIS; INTEGRATION; 'JUST-IN-TIME' CONSTRUCTION; 'LEAN' CONSTRUCTION; MAINTENANCE; MODULES AND MODULAR CONSTRUCTION; OFF-SITE MANUFACTURE; ON-SITE PRODUCTION; PROCUREMENT; RISK MANAGEMENT; TOLERANCE.

Introduction – what is buildability?

The way in which a building is designed should be informed by the way in which it will be constructed. While this might sound rather 'chicken and egg', there is much sense in considering the practicalities of construction while the design is still being developed and making the design 'buildable'. Hence, buildability is simply a measure of how straightforwardly a building can be constructed, with 'good' buildability being the objective. The aim is to eliminate wasted time, effort and materials. Many people believe that buildability is simply another term for good quality design. In some publications the term buildability has been superseded by 'constructability', but the same principle applies. This entry provides an overview of the concept of buildability, with examples, but more detailed guidance can be found in the references given at the end.

The notion of buildability is intertwined with the need for the design team to have early discussions with contractors, construction managers or specialist contractors to achieve 'better' construction and 'better' buildings. This discussion should take place when sufficient scheme design information is available so that informed and realistic decisions can be made. However, if a building design has already proceeded to a point where input from these specialists is difficult to accommodate (often too late in the tender drawing stage), then it may be much harder to inform and adjust the design to be more buildable.

In Japan, for example, buildability is taken very seriously indeed. No work can start on site until the whole design has been worked through 'on paper' and the construction manager is content to proceed knowing everything has been planned. This gives opportunities to rationalise processes and optimise activities. Hence, time on site, cost, waste and risks can be reduced (the idea of buildability preceded 'lean construction', but many of the outcomes are the same). The key is to establish what has to be done on site to achieve the client's desired outcome, i.e. a building. To do this it is necessary to have a good dialogue between those people with design ideas and those with experience and a very good understanding of construction techniques (and culture). Provided this dialogue is approached with an attitude of co-operation and professional interest, then it can be productive and beneficial.

An informal tip for newly qualified designers: if an experienced constructor uses the phrase 'you don't want to do it like that', then be willing to take note of what they advise. This may be a crucially important piece of information that could have significant benefits to the project. Their practical experience may seem unrelated to the design intention, but could lead to a better building at the end of the day.

What are the critical points?

During the design stage, and particularly during the working up of production schedules and detailed design, the team should take care to address buildability in several areas, some of which are described in the following example. Taking the example of the design of a connection between two different elements in the structure, which also incorporates a hole for pipework (services), the design team might need to consider the impact of the detail on:

- **Timings for different trades** – scheduling arrival and departures so that the detail can be built efficiently. This is particularly important for 'wet trades' and services.
- **Critical path** – are any of these elements or activities on the critical path? What are the up and down stream effects to be addressed?
- **Access** for site workers, plant and equipment must be safe, clean, clear and efficient. Is any specialist equipment needed that would affect the programme or methods used?
- **Production programmes** – avoid trades 'coming back' and having to finish off their work later simply because on and off-site schedules don't work together.

Buildability in practice

There is a general understanding that off-site fabrication of building components or modules will automatically improve buildability, but this is not necessarily the case. Such components often require even more effort than site-based techniques in this respect because accuracy and tolerances assume a greater importance. Indeed buildability for these is a critical factor because it is very difficult and costly to address accuracy problems on site with modules arriving by truck, cranes in use and fixers standing by.

When buildability turns out to be a late discussion there will be a need for much ingenuity on the part of the constructor to 'make it happen'. This may be a high-risk scenario. If the opportunity does not exist to work through buildability issues early on, then there is greater reliance on the constructor to improvise. While this can be exciting and innovative in practice, there are many consequent risks attached that can end in litigation. Thus, buildability should be raised higher on the design agenda.

Further reading

Adams, S. (1989) *Practical buildability*, Butterworth-Heinemann, Oxford, UK.
Construction Industry Research and Information Association (1983) *Buildability: an assessment*, Special Publication 26, CIRIA, London, UK.
Gray, C. (1984) *Buildability: the construction contribution*, Chartered Institute of Building, Ascot, UK.

JG

Building care
See: MAINTENANCE

Building management systems
The often computer-controlled management of services, mechanical or other ICT components (within a building), with a view to optimising performance.

See also: AIRTIGHTNESS AND IAQ; CORE (SERVICES); ENERGY EFFICIENCY; ENVIRONMENTAL DESIGN; FABRIC ENERGY STORAGE; FAÇADES AND FAÇADE ENGINEERING; FIT-OUT; HVAC; ICT IN BUILDINGS; INSULATION; INTEGRATION; INTELLIGENT FAÇADES AND MATERIALS; MAINTENANCE; NIGHT VENTILATION; RISERS AND TRUNKING; SERVICES; SICK BUILDING SYNDROME; THERMAL COMFORT; VENTILATION.

Introduction

The complex nature of some buildings' services is such that, since the 1980s there has been an increasing trend to install what are called building management systems (BMS) or building energy management systems (BEMS). In truth, the prime function of most of these management systems is to run heating and cooling plant, but the abbreviation BMS is more often used. The trend towards using such systems has grown in parallel with the growth of facilities management as a discipline, whereby owners hand over responsibility for the upkeep of the building. However BMS are specialised and require services engineers' involvement. Indeed, they support the notion of such systems because, for example, complex ventilation strategies have to be managed holistically to perform efficiently – this can only be done using IT monitoring and control; no one person can perform such a task. In smaller, simpler or less critical spaces there would be no significant long-term gain from installing a BMS. This is particularly so in buildings with natural ventilation strategies that have been designed to maximise occupant control (i.e. giving the building users control of windows, vents or thermostats so they can autonomously control their own conditions). Although it is feasible to combine some occupant control with a BMS this is difficult as the action of one can cancel out the action of the other (in energy efficiency terms). This would need to be considered carefully at an early stage if occupant control was an important client requirement.

What is in a BMS?

A BMS might consist of a central computer, which basically operates a range of switches and controls, turning plant on and off etc as its program instructs. The computer is connected to a number of data gathering points (e.g. thermostats) and uses this data to make decisions on how parts of the building's services should react. An engineer would usually carry out at least the initial programming. Long-term monitoring of the operation of the BMS can be carried out either by on-site staff or a visiting contractor. The flexibility and scale of a BMS will depend on the building function, the needs of the users and the actual service elements that have been installed. Web-based BMS software is developing rapidly. However, the lack of common industry standards in terms of information presentation and analysis is restricting its widespread use.

Some examples

Using temperature and humidity sensors throughout a building (and with appropriate programming), the BMS judges when and where to open ridge vents above an atrium space to maintain comfort conditions or perhaps switch on radiant panels around the building perimeter. In more complex BMS installations the computer program is linked to aspects of the façade engineering design where louvres or 'intelligent materials' may be used. For buildings using fabric energy storage the BMS is particularly valuable in opening and closing vents at night for purging (bringing down the indoor air temperature to a certain point to cool the structure).

Other examples:

- Single switches to control lighting over a large floor area;
- Temperature sensors to raise or lower blinds to prevent heat loss or avoid unnecessary use of air-conditioning;
- HVAC systems in hotels that switch room units on or off as guests check in or out.

Other functions

In addition to operating heating and cooling plant, a BMS can also monitor and control any of the following:

- Doors and windows;
- Fire exits;
- ICT servers;
- Lighting equipment;
- Mechanical services and movement of goods;
- Security of gates and doors.

Endnote

The capital and operational costs of installing and running a BMS can be considerable. The costs of the IT, staffing and operation need to be exceeded by the potential energy and maintenance cost savings to make a good case for installation. For this reason BMS tend to be used in larger buildings, perhaps with a range of different activities (and thus temperature zones) and sensitive areas e.g. laboratories. The most benefit can perhaps be gained in an owner-occupied building where the owner can reap cost savings from long term improvements in energy and operational efficiency. Where BMS are installed, it is vital that occupants understand the basic operation of the system if there are any autonomous controls.

Further reading

Baird, G. (2001) *The architectural expression of environmental control systems*, E & FN Spon, London, UK.

Chartered Institute of Building Services Engineers (2000) *CIBSE Guide H: Building control systems*, Butterworth-Heinemann, Oxford UK.

Levermore, G.J. (2000) *Building energy management systems* (2nd edition), E & FN Spon, London, UK.

JG

Building systems

This is the development of holistic, standard 'systems' that can be assembled to make buildings. It is quite different from the alternative definition, in which 'building systems' means the various systems within a building such as services.

See also: BUILDABILITY; CONCRETE; CONCRETE – STRUCTURES; FRAME; LEAD-TIME; LIGHT STEEL FRAME; MODULES AND MODULAR CONSTRUCTION; OFF-SITE MANUFACTURE; PLASTICS; PODS; PROPRIETARY GOODS AND STANDARDISATION; SPECIFICATION; STRUCTURAL STEEL; TIMBER; TIMBER – STRUCTURES.

Introduction

Building systems can be said to represent the bringing together (assembling) of a number of pre-designed, pre-manufactured components to produce a building that is then built to a pre-determined format. This is the logical next step from 'system building', where construction follows a pre-determined method, but uses mostly normal mass-produced construction materials. However, the distinction between **'system building'** (i.e. building to a system or method) and **'building systems'** (i.e. building using a pre manufactured system) has become rather blurred by the increasing use of building systems throughout the industry.

The manufacture of prefabricated components, or the extensive standardisation of traditional methods, are equally valid, especially for low and medium volume output, where commodity products are delivered and assembled in a pre-determined, carefully specified way. This level of standardisation is developed typically in response to the need for:

- Reduced design time;
- Reduced site time;
- Reduced long term costs;
- Consistent quality;
- Repeatability.

To achieve all these benefits in practice, off-site manufacture (previously called prefabrication) is utilised widely and building systems tend, therefore, to use materials and technologies that lend themselves to factory production techniques. Building systems have tended to rise in popularity and undergo rapid development, at times when market need and perhaps limited availability of goods have coincided to create market conditions that favour off-site working. However the economics are now quite difficult: the cost of establishing a design, production process, factory facilities and distribution network must be justified by the potential returns. Such a balance is difficult to achieve without having either guaranteed orders early on or having an existing manufacturer underwrite the facility.

Historical note

The need to produce standardised buildings quickly has generated systems for meeting that need, seeking speed, economy and consistent quality by use of a system approach. This approach can be applied to traditional construction methods, demonstrated effectively in major market sectors such as schools, hospitals and housing. However, a systems approach to achieving speed and economy is far from being a new idea. The seminal application of a building system still remains Joseph Paxton's Crystal Palace for the 1851 Great Exhibition in London. Due to bureaucratic delays, the project had a very short lead-time, and in June 1850 Paxton was given nine days to produce designs and details, and subsequently a further week for working drawings and tenders. The resulting system of glazed cast iron frames enabled his contractors to complete a superstructure enclosing almost 92,000 m^2 of exhibition space in just five months. At the end of the exhibition the building was dismantled successfully and re-erected on another site, and the system went on to be used as the basis for other similar structures. Around the same time engineer Eugenius Birch constructed 16 piers around the UK coast between 1853 and 1884, using mass produced cast iron and glazing products extensively.

The use, in the 1930s, of a universal plan form for three bedroom semi-detached houses paved the way for standardised designs, suitable not only for the many prefabricated systems of the 1950s, but also for methods such as 'no fines' in-situ concrete. 'Parker Morris' space standards, and centralised funding, encouraged a system approach to new homes in all construction methods, particularly from major housing providers. In the UK, the school and housing systems that rose to fame in the 1950s were a response to population growth at a time of materials shortages. A variety of systems resulted where speed and economy were the key criteria. A set of different circumstances developing since the 1980s (including a shortage of traditional building skills and government initiatives to improve quality and value) have enabled the building systems industry to make further progress with improved manufacturing technology and a strong market presence.

Materials

The primary structural materials used in building systems are determined by availability and transportation limits (i.e. height and weight). Connection details are also important – there would be little point in investing in off-site production facilities without investigating the on-site buildability aspects. The list below gives an overview of the typical materials used in building systems.

Cast Iron – many early systems used cast iron, and are worthy of mention as they require careful treatment in refurbishment;

Concrete – precast and site-cast precast (tilt-up) reinforced concrete panels are used either in unitary panel systems or as cladding elements to steel or concrete structural frame systems; they are often supplied pre-finished;

Plastics – GRP (glass reinforced plastics) are used in small cabins and storage buildings; plastics cladding panels are sometimes used in conjunction with structural systems in other materials (steel or timber);

Structural steel – (hot rolled) Use of standard size hot rolled sections and lattice beams occurs in several systems for schools, hospitals, and light industrial use; these often incorporate concrete plank or composite decking for floor and roof;

Structural steel – (cold formed) Light steel galvanised sections are used widely in panel or modular systems for housing, schools, offices and light industrial use;

Timber – prefabricated timber frame panel systems are used for housing, small/medium commercial and modular systems.

How are the benefits achieved?

Standard designs and CAD/CAM techniques can be used to reduce design time. Designs, manufacturing schedules and site information can thus be produced very quickly. By assembling fewer, larger, factory-made units on site, construction times for the main structure can be shortened and allow simultaneous working for fit-out trades, although this is usually preceded by a lengthier lead-time. Optimised design procedures, supported by testing, result in efficient structural design and planned factory production thereby reducing materials wastage. There may also be financing and preliminaries savings from shortened build programmes. Off-site manufacture under controlled conditions gives an opportunity for better accuracy in components, quality controlled assembly, and improved standards of finishes. Consistent design, manufacture, and assembly procedures enable universal compatibility with other components (doors, windows, internal fit-out etc).

Further reading

Construction Industry Research and Information Association (1997) *Standardisation and pre-assembly*, CIRIA Report 176, CIRIA, London, UK.
Vale, B. (1995) *Prefabs: a history of the UK temporary housing programme*, E & FN Spon, London, UK.
Warszawski, A. (1999) *Industrialized and automated building systems* (2nd edition), E & FN Spon, London, UK.

GW/JG

Buro Happold
See: HAPPOLD, SIR TED AND BURO HAPPOLD

Cable nets

A roof type that uses cables and a roofing membrane to shelter sometimes vast areas in a seemingly effortless manner.

See also: CONNECTIONS; OTTO, FREI; PLASTICS; ROOFS; TEXTILE MEMBRANE ROOFS.

Net design and construction

Cable nets are a type of tension structure employed in long span roof construction. These are often extensive structures that are architecturally inspiring because they are both clever yet effortless at the same time. Cable nets tend to be used in buildings and structures in which shelter is required but in which clear views are also important, such as sports stadia. The technology of cable net structures has developed rapidly since structural engineering has embraced IT programs.

Nets are generally built-up from cables running in two directions. Since individual cables are highly flexible elements with the capacity to transmit tensile forces only they need to be organised into curved surfaces that give them both structural stiffness and load carrying capacity. In this way they are not reliant on mass or beam-stiffness for their stability. In so called 'anti-clastic' surfaces the two principal curvatures mutually oppose one another making the surface prestressable, while providing resistance to laterally applied loads such as wind (upwards) and snow (downwards). Nets are generally prefabricated off-site using long individual lengths of cable marked with the position of each node point. These are built-up and assembled on site by clamping individual cables together at the node points (clamping pressure is required to prevent cable slippage). The nodes have to allow for changes of cable angle brought about by external loading from wind and snow. Allowance for this movement needs to be made in the connection to the cladding/roofing system (usually transparent plastic or a textile membrane).

Historical note and built examples

The development of cable net roofs was stimulated by the completion in 1953 of the Raleigh Arena in North Carolina, USA designed by Matthew Nowicki (Architect) and Fred Severud (Engineer). A saddle-shaped network of 30 mm diameter steel cables span 95 m between a pair of concrete arches inclined away from one another at 20° to the horizontal. This project became the archetype for a large number of prestressed cable net roofs throughout the world. The Raleigh Arena also inspired Frei Otto to undertake a systematic study of tensile surface structures (using physical models), which lead eventually to the design of the roof of the German Pavilion at the Montreal Expo in 1967 (with Rolf Gutbrod). This was a free-form cable net suspended from masts of varying heights and inclinations and covering 10,000 m². The design was developed through a sequence of physical models each becoming more detailed and sophisticated. The engineering design of this Pavilion was lead by Leonhardt and Andra who with Otto, continued to realise such roofs via the 1976 Olympic Games in Munich. Like Montreal these are free form, mast-supported cable nets covering both the stadium seating and the enclosed swimming and gymnastic halls. The roof was covered with plexi-glass sheets which, to allow for the geometric distortion of the cable nets under snow and wind loading, were supported by flexible mountings from the cable nets. Gaps between individual sheets are closed with a flexible lattice of rubber gaskets, which take up the in-plane shear distortions of the cable net under snow loading.

In contrast to this the 180 m high cooling tower at Schmehausen in Germany by Jorg Schlaich is a three-way cable-net clad in rigid metal panels permitting a simpler joint sealing system. The 'bicycle wheel' roof in which tensioned spokes react against a continuous compression ring can be found in a variety of examples combined with a textile membrane covering – for instance the recent Gottlieb-Daimler Stadium at Stuttgart by Jorg Schlaich.

In the 'Cable-Dome' developed by David Geiger, the structure consists of a series of single panel cable trusses, each one sitting on top of the next, rising in elevation towards the centre of the roof with the feet of the posts linked circumferentially with closed hoop cables. In this way, instead of the roof structure getting deeper towards the centre of the roof and thus projecting down into the space, the underside of the rings rises towards the centre. The largest roof of this type is at St Petersburg in Florida: it has a diameter of 230 m and is covered with a PTFE/glass membrane skin. An elegant elliptical derivative of this by Weidlinger covers the Georgia Dome in Atlanta, USA.

Further reading

Vandenburg, M. (1998) *Cable nets*, Academy Editions, John Wiley & Sons, London, UK.

OA

Calatrava, Santiago

Santiago Calatrava (b. 1951) is one of the world's foremost structural designers. Best known perhaps for his bridges, Calatrava's work also offers genuine architectural inspiration.

See also: CONCRETE – STRUCTURES; GLASS – STRUCTURAL GLAZING; ROOFS; STRUCTURAL STEEL; TIMBER – LAMINATED TIMBER.

A brilliant architect and engineer, Calatrava has reinterpreted the organic strand in engineering and, at his best, can blend the undulating forms of Gaudi with the structural genius of Nervi, Candela and Saarinen. He is responsible for the return of the expressionistic to engineering and also for a remarkable renaissance in bridge design. He first came to international attention with the Bach de Roda bridge, Barcelona (1984–87), a 140 m structure spanning over a railway and linking two areas of the city. The bridge swells in the centre beneath a pair of canted suspension arches creating a pair of suspended public spaces, linked by stairs to a park below. A series of innovative bridges followed including Merida (1988), Valencia (1995) and Salford (1995) and a strikingly beautiful design for Seville with a single 142 m high, 58° inclined pylon. The weight of the concrete-filled steel pylon counterbalances the weight of the deck (constructed from a hexagonal steel box beam) dispensing with the necessity for back stays and providing a perfect visual solution as the pylon leans back to support the weight of the 250 m bridge.

The building of stations at Lucerne (1989), Zurich (1990) and Lyons-Satloas (1994) reinforced Calatrava's reputation as the foremost architect-engineer of his generation. For these buildings, Calatrava took inspiration from animal skeletons. The delicacy and economy of the buildings made the architect a sought-after designer of transport buildings which culminated in the Oriente station built for the 1998 Expo in Lisbon, a major transport interchange incorporating train, bus and metro stations. A striking, heavy undercroft of in-situ concrete arches is set in great contrast to a steel and glass structure of immense delicacy above ground. This station structure is carried above ground on a bridge spanning 238 m with a width of 78 m. A grid of steel 'trees' forms the station canopy; the undulating roof supported between their branches is intended to emulate the waves of the sea nearby, which was the theme of the Expo.

Calatrava has an enduring fascination with movement and in the visual expression of the forces inherent in structure, thus his interest in sculpture can feed into his architecture. He has designed kinetic buildings based on sculptural ideas including the Kuwaiti pavilion for the Seville 1992 Expo. In this structure two opposing rows of attenuated curving ribs of timber supported on reinforced concrete columns, counterbalanced at the bottom and each 25 m in length, can be independently hydraulically lifted into a vertical position. In this manner a number of different permutations can be achieved from a kind of gothic arcade to a gently vaulting roof. For the Ernstings warehouse in Coesfeld, Germany (1983–85), Calatrava introduced an ingenious set of doors which open in a sculptural eye-shape, a series of individual metal strips pivoting at various heights to define a broad curve in the lifting door.

Among Calatrava's other buildings the following are particularly noteworthy. The High School at Wohlen, Switzerland (1988) has a fascinating folded roof structure; BCE Place, Gallery and Heritage Square in Toronto (1992) creates an atrium from an existing street via the insertion of an ambitious steel and glass parabolic arcade; a 250 m high communications tower, the Torre de Montjuic in Barcelona (1989–92) is also worthy of note. Dramatic schemes for the regeneration of St John the Divine in New York with the addition of a crystalline roof garden and spire and the unsuccessful entry to the Reichstag competition have unfortunately been lost to history.

Further reading

Jodidio, P. (2001) *Calatrava*, Benedikt Taschen, Köln, Germany.

Sharp, D. (ed.) (1992) *Santiago Calatrava*, Book Art, London, UK.

Sharp, D. (ed.) (1994) *Santiago Calatrava*, Routledge, London, UK.

Sharp, D. (ed.) (1996) *Santiago Calatrava: Architectural Monographs*, Academy Editions, John Wiley & Sons, London, UK.

Tischhauser, A. (ed.) (1998) *Calatrava: Public Buildings*, Birkhäuser, Basle, Switzerland

Tzonis, A. (2001) *Santiago Calatrava*, Thames & Hudson, London, UK.

EH

Canopy roofs

See: TEXTILE MEMBRANE ROOFS; AIR-SUPPORTED STRUCTURES; GRASS ('GREEN') ROOFS

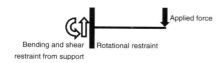

Bending and shear restraint from support | Rotational restraint | Applied force

Cantilever with rotational restraint. Image provided by Ove Arup & Partners.

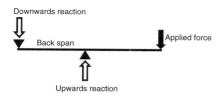

Downwards reaction

Back span | Applied force

Upwards reaction

Cantilever with back span. Image provided by Ove Arup & Partners.

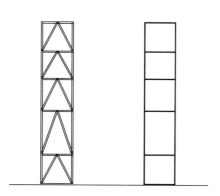

Cantilever truss. Cantilever frame. Image provided by Ove Arup & Partners.

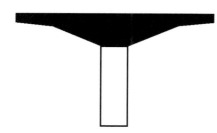

Balanced cantilever. Image provided by Ove Arup & Partners.

Cantilevers

Cantilevers are structural elements or systems that are supported only at one end.

See also: BEAM; BRACING; CALATRAVA, SANTIAGO; CONCRETE; CORE (STRUCTURAL); FLOORS; FOUNDATION; FRAME; NERVI, PIER LUIGI; NOUVEL, JEAN; RETAINING WALL; STRUCTURAL STEEL; WALLS; WRIGHT, FRANK LLOYD.

What is a cantilever?

A cantilever is a structural element or system that is supported at one end only with sufficient fixity to resist the applied loads. Although usually considered as projecting horizontally, like a diving-board or balcony, many cantilevers actually project vertically, such as chimneys and the cores of high-rise buildings, which must resist wind and seismic loads. A cantilever may be a beam, slab, truss or frame; corbels and nibs can also be considered as cantilevers. In its horizontal form, cantilevers can be very architecturally exciting – structural elements that project out for sometimes several metres offer a means to make a hugely dynamic expression or statement in a building. The cantilevered planes of concrete that characterise Frank Lloyd Wright's Fallingwater House (Pennsylvania, USA; 1936) are certainly the single most important architectural motif that designers associate with his work.

How do cantilevers work?

Although beams can have rotational stiffness at their supports, a cantilever must have a support that can resist both the applied force and moment. A moment is the turning effect of a force about a given point and is equal to the product of the force and the shortest distance between the line of action of the force and the support. A rotational restraint can be achieved by:

• Connecting the cantilever to a stiff element (e.g. a wall in the same plane as the cantilever, a raft or a piled foundation);
• Providing a back span;
• Balancing a pair of similar cantilevers on a support that needs only take the reaction force and any out-of-balance moments.

Where the tip of a cantilever is supported it is known as a propped cantilever. Cantilever beams resist applied forces by bending in a similar way to ordinary beams, with the bending moment, shear force and resulting stresses being greatest at the supported end and reducing to nothing at the free end. The cores of buildings act as large cellular beams in a similar way, with the reaction forces and moments provided by the foundations. Cantilever trusses, such as electricity transmission pylons, have discrete chord elements to take the compression and tension forces that resist the overall bending. The chord elements are triangulated by bracing members, which take the shear force. Cantilever frames are similar but rely on the flexural, rather than axial, stiffness of the elements to take shear.

Built examples

The Forth Railway Bridge in Scotland (1890) and the Quebec Bridge in Canada (1917) are examples of balanced cantilever steel trusses and there are many examples of modern balanced cantilever concrete bridges. Although balanced cantilever bridges are constructed as true cantilevers, reducing the need for temporary support during construction, the tips of the cantilevers are normally joined in the completed bridge to create a more robust structure that can also span and provide a continuous deck. Retaining walls are usually designed as cantilever or propped cantilever walls.

Architectural examples of cantilevers abound, including Frank Lloyd Wright's Fallingwater House (Pennsylvania, USA; 1936), as mentioned above, in which the floor planes extend out to various distances over the river running beneath the house. The aesthetic impact is significant and this still remains a key example of what can be achieved, but it also demonstrates the durability problems of having these exposed elements immediately adjacent to a water course (corrosion has always been a difficulty). More recent examples include the cantilevered roof planes that protrude from Jean Nouvel's structure overlooking Lake Zurich in Switzerland and several of Zaha Hadid's projects.

OA

Canvas roof
See: TEXTILE MEMBRANE ROOFS; AIR-SUPPORTED STRUCTURES; GRASS ('GREEN') ROOFS

Carbon dioxide (CO$_2$)
This colourless gas is produced by burning fossil fuels to make energy and has been linked to global warming. Aims are afoot to reduce its production (i.e. the Kyoto protocol), which affects building design, construction and in particular operation.

See also: ECOLOGICAL DESIGN; 'ECO-POINTS'; ENERGY EFFICIENCY; HEAT RECOVERY; INSULATION; LIFE-CYCLE ANALYSIS; PHOTOVOLTAICS; SUSTAINABILITY.

Introduction
Carbon dioxide is a heavy colourless gas that does not support combustion, is formed by the both the combustion and decomposition of organic substances, and is absorbed from the air by plants in photosynthesis. All animals and plants respire by taking in oxygen and giving out carbon dioxide, making these two gases vital to all forms of life. These natural processes tend to sustain a constant amount of CO$_2$ in the atmosphere, but burning of fossil fuels, such as oil, coal and gas has artificially increased the proportion of carbon dioxide. For 160,000 years, CO$_2$ stayed in a range of 200–300 parts per million by volume (ppm). However, following the Industrial Revolution in about 1750, a steady rise has taken place: during 250 years the level rose twice as much as during the previous 160,000 years. In respect to climate, carbon dioxide has additional importance in its effect on the Earth's radiation balance. Carbon dioxide is transparent to incoming solar radiation and so any change in the amount of atmospheric carbon dioxide has a detrimental effect on the climate of the Earth. These changes lead to a shift in climatic zones with consequences that will affect the way people live, work and build. Already, large areas of Southern Spain, Italy and Turkey are suffering from becoming more arid. This is all in combination with the rise in concentration of the gas ozone, mostly in the stratosphere. In response to all this, the international Kyoto conference in 1997 agreed a global target of a 20% reductions in carbon dioxide emissions (based on 1990 levels), with each country now having specific goals of its own to pursue (e.g. the UK government has a binding legal agreement to achieve 12.5% reduction and an aspirational target of 20%).

What does this mean for buildings?

In the UK alone, the occupancy (i.e. heating, lighting and cooling) and construction of buildings account for 50% of total UK CO$_2$ emissions, with transport at about 25% and various industries and other activities the remainder. By way of an example, for every person working in an office building about six tonnes of carbon dioxide is generated per annum. This means that designers, clients and building occupiers must act responsibly to prevent unnecessary energy use. UK government is gradually introducing changes to the Building Regulations and other statutory instruments to facilitate this step-change. To demonstrate the impact of producing 100 MWh heat, using fossil fuel sources, the data below shows the resultant emissions (for the UK):

Source	SO$_2$	NO$_x$	Dust	CO$_2$
	kg	kg	kg	kg
Electricity	81	67	8.3	80,400
Oil	40	30	1.4	37,200
Gas	3	16	0.4	27,200
District Htg.	10	10	6.7	11,500

- Electricity: 80% coal, 20% nuclear;
- District heating: coal and oil.

(Source: Building Research Establishment, 1991)

What can designers do to reduce CO$_2$?

The first step that designers should take when designing a building is to recognise that the in-use impacts from buildings coming from heating, cooling and lighting are very important. After that, consideration should be given to design for better use of transport. There are two main methods of accounting for energy use in buildings, which can be used as indicators of carbon dioxide emissions; these are embodied energy and operational energy.

Embodied energy (EE) – this is the energy notionally embodied in a product (or amount of construction material) that equates to the energy required for extraction of raw materials, processing, manufacture and transport between those stages (i.e. up to 'factory gate'). It may also include transport to site. Clearly those materials manufactured via energy intensive methods (e.g. aluminium, steel, cement and plastics), particularly if they are transported some distance, will have a relatively high embodied energy value (in GJ/tonne). If a material is recycled, then the embodied energy for its 'second life' will be lower. Values for EE may be more appropriately expressed in GJ/m^2, which is the embodied energy per unit area of a completed building (comparisons are thus far easier). Timber, earth, stone, aggregates and other natural materials usually have a very low embodied energy value.

Operational energy (OE) – this is a far more important factor in terms of carbon dioxide emissions. With 50% of the UK's total CO$_2$ arising from the heating, cooling and lighting of buildings, it is clear that energy efficiency in these areas is of significance to designers. Operational energy is the sum of these parts and to put it into perspective, for a four storey office building with mixed mode ventilation, over a 60-year life, the OE value is something in the order of 30–50 times greater than the EE value associated with the building's structure. It is clear that devices such as fabric energy storage, wind towers, good insulation and natural ventilation, which aim to reduce operational energy, will therefore have very long-term benefits for the building owner.

Built examples

While there are many technical and practical solutions available, the greatest success comes from a more integrated approach to building design that considers energy use, people and the local environment. Hence, true sustainability in terms of CO_2 in particular lies in working with infrastructure and local planning.

Solar active and passive systems – these use a variety of techniques and technologies and have gained widespread acceptance in Europe. Germany, The Netherlands, Denmark, Sweden, France and Spain have proved that the building energy demand can be reduced by up to 80%. Solar architecture results in lower energy use and in turn lower carbon dioxide emissions.

Zero energy housing – this is being pioneered where high insulation is combined with solar passive systems and photovoltaic solar panels. A major development of 100 homes and 30 businesses (BedZed) is to be completed at Beddington in Surrey. Another 'zero emission' development is an autonomous group of houses, the Hockerton Housing Project in Nottingham.

Heat recovery – in The Netherlands solar induced roads (in which water is piped below the asphalted road surface), collect direct solar energy which is then stored. The road is then cooled in summer and heated in winter. Road life increases by 20 years. For every kilometre of road enough energy is collected to heat/cool 100 family houses.

Other options – photovoltaic cells are now being produced at economic rates and are becoming part of external building fabrics. Wind turbines, wave and water energy, ground heat sources, bore holes, heat pumps, clay and straw baling techniques are just some of many options available, and the range is increasing steadily.

WH/JG

Carbon fibre
See: COMPOSITE MATERIALS

Cardboard

Waste paper formed into cardboard tubes and panels provides an ecological alternative to common building materials for light structural and non-structural applications.

See also: BESPOKE; CONDENSATION; CONNECTIONS; ECOLOGICAL DESIGN; 'ECO-POINTS'; TECHNOLOGY TRANSFER; TIMBER; TIMBER – MANUFACTURED BOARDS.

Introduction

Cardboard may seem a rather unusual construction material, but it has already been used in a handful of projects throughout the world and has significant potential for future development. Originating from wood pulp, cardboard and other paper-based products are usually manufactured for use as packaging materials such as boxes, but are also used in furniture and doors. Cardboard tubes are now used frequently as formwork for circular concrete columns. However, cardboard also offers designers an alternative to common building materials for other structural and non-structural applications in buildings.

Use of paper products in buildings

Paper has actually been a fundamental part of Japanese vernacular architecture for centuries being utilised as a screening material in homes, temples and workplaces. It is used in combination with timber frames. The paper sheeting is used to create walls and screens because it is lightweight, easy to produce and repair. It also gives a wonderful quality of light inside and offers visual, if not acoustic, privacy. However it was not until recently that board and manufactured paper products have offered rigidity and strength as well. Japanese architect Shigeru Ban has been experimenting with cardboard products for some years. His work includes a structural arch in the garden of the Museum of Modern Art (MoMa) in New York using eight 600 mm cardboard arch trusses spanning 27 metres. He also undertook the Japanese Pavilion at Expo 2000, and a series of quick assembly refugee shelters for Rwanda and Turkey. In a more recent project, Europe's first permanent cardboard building was erected in Essex (completed in 2001). The after-school club at Westborough Primary School in Westcliff-on-Sea used cardboard tubes and cardboard panels in a government funded initiative to find out more about the potential of the material. Although larger buildings may be feasible, it is thought that the smaller, domestic-scale buildings market offers better possibilities.

Generic advantages of cardboard:

- Can be formed into a wide range of shapes;
- Cheap to produce;
- Easy to handle, move and cut;
- Excellent environmental credentials;
- Good thermal insulation;
- Lightweight;
- Recyclable at end of use;
- Uses waste paper;
- Very adaptable/flexible in its use.

Generic disadvantages of cardboard:

- Creep – it deforms over time;
- Damage from rodents etc;
- Fixing can be difficult;
- Flammability (reduced by applying a retardant);
- Moisture – cardboard attracts and absorbs moisture;
- Perceptions of the material;
- Surface damage from wear and tear.

Cardboard components

Cardboard tubes offer structural (compressive) strength, and so can act as columns to support roof trusses or lintels. To avoid creep, Buro Happold and Cottrell & Vermeulen Architecture suggest that cardboard be designed to carry just 10% of its maximum possible load. In Westborough School, a fire retardant was used and a chemical was added during manufacture to help prevent moisture absorption (cardboard acts hydroscopically, attracting moisture from the air). Vapour barriers can also be installed. Connections between tubes need to be considered carefully.

Cardboard panels can be used internally or as part of an external wall construction. Exposed parts need to be treated with a fire retardant. The wall construction should include a vapour barrier on the inside and a breathable membrane on the outside. Using a lacquered panel system on the exterior prevented deterioration and wear and tear of the Westborough School panels. Connections between adjacent panels is made easier by setting square-edged timber inserts at the ends of the panels, allowing conventional joinery details to be used. To increase structural capacity and rigidity the School's panels used a composite layering of three 50 mm thick honeycomb boards edged with 15 mm solid card layers. The construction programme at Essex's largest primary school was rapid. However, the costs were comparable to conventional construction due to Building Regulations compliance.

JG

Cassette Panels
See: CLADDING; COMPOSITE PANELS; OVERCLADDING

Castings
A production method used to form materials into structural connectors, glazing components and other building products, often bespoke.

See also: ALUMINIUM; BESPOKE; CLADDING; CONNECTIONS; CONSTRUCTION PROGRAMME; COPPER; GLASS – STRUCTURAL GLAZING; GRIMSHAW, NICHOLAS; LEAD-TIME; METALS; OFF-SITE MANUFACTURE; PIANO, RENZO; PLASTICS; PROPRIETARY GOODS AND STANDARDISATION; PROUVÉ, JEAN; ROGERS, RICHARD; STAINLESS STEEL; WINDOWS AND CURTAIN WALLING.

Introduction
There are a number of specialised production and fabrication techniques which are used to make metal and plastic components. The following is a brief overview with particular emphasis on castings using metals.

Extrusion means simply to force, or push through. In production terms it describes a method by which plastic or metal is forced through a die to form a shape (which is often thin and complicated in section).

Pultrusion is about pulling the material through the die (this is often used for plastic components where molecular orientation is important).

Although these methods are commonly used to produce standard building products such as cladding panels and curtain walling profiles there is much scope at the bespoke end of the market to employ the production skills of the specialist fabricator to create exquisite architectural components. It is useful to understand a little about these methods because the design of a component often determines the production method, but the production method in turn will also affect the detailed design of the component.

The bespoke option can be expensive for structural and non-structural applications, but it is very effective in creating building elements with special architectural interest. Although many production techniques date back thousands of years, architects and engineers have employed them more recently on some of the most prestigious projects where detailed design can be explored in depth and there is freedom to create objects of real beauty. In general however such attention to detail is unfortunately now more of a luxury than a necessity and so these may be rare opportunities to grasp as and when they arise. Castings offer the best opportunity for architectural expression via bespoke items, rather than mass-produced standard units.

What are castings?

This term describes a group of production methods whereby metals such as bronze, steel, and stainless steel are placed molten into a mould with a cavity shaped to make the component. The metal is allowed to harden in the mould, which is stripped off when the metal has cooled. There should be no need to do any further work to the component because the process, properties and surface finish required, determines which casting method is used. Casting is advantageous because it offers:

- High dimensional accuracy;
- Range of high quality surface finishes;
- Sculptural solutions to details with difficult geometries;
- Simple to install components;
- Wide range of sizes and shapes.

Architects, in particular, benefit from the ability to create curved shapes that are difficult to form in any other way. The high quality surface finishes are very appropriate for visible, aesthetic components. Structural castings especially are one part of a building where the structural and architectural intentions of the design team can come together in a very visual expression. Although costs can be relatively high, increased re-use of the mould will improve overall value. It is important to work with the foundry from an early stage, particularly for structural castings because the production/construction programme may need to incorporate various tests in addition to the usual samples being created.

Built examples

There are many buildings that feature elegant and expressive castings as a key feature of the architecture. A few are described below.

In their elegant portfolio of steel and glass structures, Nicholas Grimshaw & Partners have used castings for the Western Morning News building, Plymouth (stainless steel and cast iron glazing components) and in the prestigious Waterloo International rail terminal in London (steel castings for truss connectors). Gunmetal façade components (for Bracken House, London) and steel roof forks for the Inland Revenue HQ in Nottingham have been cast for Michael Hopkins & Partners. Alan Brookes Associates used bronze castings for counter supports at East Croydon rail station, just south of London.

These examples were preceded by the work of Renzo Piano, who has used castings throughout his work including (as part of the well-known brise soleil array) at the Menil Collection in Houston, Texas. The massive steel castings called 'gerberettes' used by Piano and Rogers for the Pompidou Centre in Paris have been highly influential since their construction in the early 1970s. These castings are about nine metres long and can be seen clearly on the end façades of the building connecting the main structure with the façade systems.

Further reading

Baddoo, N.R. (1996) *Castings in construction*, SCI Publication 172, Steel Construction Institute, Ascot, UK.

Brookes, A. & Grech, C. (1996) *Building envelope & connections*, Butterworth-Heinemann, Oxford, UK.

JG

Cast stone
See: CONCRETE – FINISHES

Cavity

A void in the building fabric, introduced to achieve a functional separation between elements.

See also: ACOUSTICS; AIRTIGHTNESS AND IAQ; BRICKS AND BLOCKS; CLADDING; CONDENSATION; CONNECTIONS; ENERGY EFFICIENCY; FIRE PROTECTION; FLOORS; INSULATION; OVERCLADDING; PERFORMANCE; ROOFS; VENTILATION; WALLS; WEATHERING; WINDOWS AND CURTAIN WALLING.

Introduction

Designers may seek to enhance building performance by establishing discontinuity between building elements, or by introducing a cavity with particular qualities. The introduction of a void, gap or cavity can fulfil a range of functions. As such, it may have an 'exclusive effect' (by merely keeping two components apart, as in, say, a masonry cavity wall) or a 'supplementary effect' (by providing a physical benefit, such as the thermal resistance of a cavity and its surface resistances in assessing thermal transmittance). The reasons for using a cavity are discussed below.

Weathering

Conventional detailing uses a cavity to isolate the outer skin of a wall from its inner skin, so that moisture penetrating the outer leaf cannot cross to the inner skin. This is particularly important in locations susceptible to wind driven rain, such as many parts of the UK. This is based on the assumption that even an outer skin designed and constructed to be impervious might not make a 100% sealed face as a result of factors such as poor workmanship or extreme weather conditions. In a masonry cavity wall, the cavity is usually 50 mm, with the two skins (e.g. brick, block or timber) linked by wall ties. In non-masonry cladding, the cavity is usually narrower (around 20 mm), and formed by a spacer system. The latter often constitutes a 'rainscreen' cladding, where the void is ventilated in order to be pressure equalised, thus discouraging the movement of moisture through the system.

Thermal

The pocket of air provided by a cavity in roofs, walls, or floors can make a contribution to the overall thermal performance of the element, particularly at the cavity interface where materials with optimum surface resistance can be specified (such as foil faced insulation boards). These principles apply just as well to sealed double glazed units, where the total sealing of the cavity permits performance to be improved by the use of gases other than air (e.g. argon), and where the interfaces are enhanced with low emissivity coatings to the glass. Air movement within wider cavities can reduce thermal effectiveness, where convection currents can set up heat transfer and cooling conditions.

Acoustic

The introduction of a cavity improves acoustic performance by separation and discontinuity, considerably reducing the transmission of sound. In practice the effect is also an arithmetical increase in sound insulation in relation to the ratings of individual elements (rather than just their mass), enabling a build up of components to achieve good separation. This principle is used widely in timber frame and lightweight steel construction.

Ventilation

Improved standards of heating and airtightness increase the likelihood of warm moist air from inside meeting cold dry air from outside, leading to condensation. The use of a ventilated cavity is a key feature in control of this, particularly in roofs, where the tendency of warm moist air to rise increases the risk. For example, the provision of a ventilated cavity in the batten/felt zone of pitched roofs gives effective moisture control.

Design note

The purpose of a cavity in the building fabric needs to be defined as ventilated, unventilated, or sealed, and then detailed and specified accordingly. Where moisture (from weather or condensation) is anticipated, provision must be made for vapour checks, membranes, damp proof courses and adequate drainage. Cavity barriers are introduced to compartmentalise the cavity and to control the spread of fire within it. They are also used to control sound transmission along cavities.

GW

Ceilings

These are the zones at the underside of upper floors. These may be exposed, or have suspended systems to provide space for services.

See also: ALUMINIUM; BUILDING MANAGEMENT SYSTEMS; CONCRETE – FINISHES; CONNECTIONS; FABRIC ENERGY STORAGE; FIT-OUT; FLOORS; FRAME; GRIDS FOR STRUCTURE AND LAYOUT; HVAC; LIGHTING – ARTIFICIAL LIGHTING; SERVICES; SURFACE FINISHES.

Introduction

In domestic architecture, the ceiling is most commonly a smooth plaster or plasterboard finish to conceal the structure of the upper floor. There may be a hole for electrical cabling to a light fitting, together with simple coving details around the edge to make good. This is how simplistic ceilings can be, but there have been many developments, which have affected their design, construction and use in other building types such as offices and hospitals and it is these more complex systems that are focussed on.

Historical note

The change from natural ventilation to air-conditioning and the development of information and communication technology (ICT) equipment in the 1960s and 1970s both led to significant architectural changes relating to building design. Not only did there need to be more space in the building for plant generally, but local space was also needed to accommodate more cabling and ducting. Therefore the designs changed from simple, often cellular loadbearing structures to open plan layouts with deeper ceiling zones (beneath upper floors) within which services could be distributed, and floor-floor depths increased, making buildings taller. Hence, the development of suspended ceiling systems that were designed to hang below the upper floors offering concealment, better flexibility, access and architectural appearance to the office interiors. On a structural note, the 1970s open plan layouts called for more widely spaced columns, which at that time often meant 'downstand beams' were used to support upper floors. These were problematic for services distribution at ceiling level and it is more common now to see concrete 'flat slab' structures that allow the overall depth of the ceiling zone to be reduced.

Ceilings today

The trend to use suspended ceiling systems continues today as a convenient, safe and attractive method of distributing services and concealing them from view. The systems tend to use slender aluminium profiles in a grid layout (usually 600 mm modules) as a carrier system for plasterboard, plastic or metal ceiling tiles. The advantage of this approach is that it is a lightweight system that is easy to access at any point and can be refurbished easily by choosing different tiles. Despite there being some very sleek metal systems on the market, they do not always appeal to architects preferring 'honest' and pure expression of materials; the architect Louis Kahn was particularly disparaging about suspended ceilings, saying he would hate to die looking up at one! The trend towards exposing services (begun by the Pompidou Centre in Paris in the 1970s) has also influenced ceiling design in industrial, commercial and leisure buildings.

The alternative approach to managing services around floor level is a raised floor (above the floor slab), which offers easy access and can be combined with exposed soffits for fabric energy storage. Therefore contemporary, naturally ventilated offices, for example, would tend to use raised floors in preference to ceiling systems. Although the access floors have replaced suspended ceilings in some building types, the most heavily serviced structures (e.g. hospitals and laboratories) may use both ceiling and floor systems in tandem to accommodate all the necessary ICT, air-conditioning, detection devices and telecommunication servicing. Indeed, the ceiling zone is now a major area for integration of structure and services. With the advent of chilled beams and other active fabric energy storage systems, the forward planning of structure and services has become more important. The ceiling can now provide much more than a simple interior finish.

The Lloyds Register of Shipping building in London by Richard Rogers Partnership provides an excellent example of integrated design in its offices and trading floors. It has precast concrete soffit units, chilled beams for cooling purposes, integrated luminaires and elegant in-situ concrete beams.

JG

View of the University of East London Docklands Campus (Edward Cullinan Architects). Coloured cement renders were used as the external finish to these cylindrical student accommodation buildings. Photograph by the author.

Cement

The generic name for cementitious (binder) materials used in concrete, which is a commonly used building material. Cement is made from a range of natural materials such as limestone.

See also: BRICKS AND BLOCKS; CONCRETE; CONCRETE – FINISHES; CONCRETE – STRUCTURES; DRY CONSTRUCTION AND WET CONSTRUCTION; GRC; MORTARS, CEMENT AND LIME; SURFACE FINISHES.

Introduction

What is the difference between cement and concrete? Many people mistakenly use the term 'cement' when they actually mean concrete. Concrete is made from cement, aggregates (fine and coarse) and water.

Cement is produced from chalk or limestone, and clay or shale in a sophisticated, energy intensive process that takes place in specially designed kilns. These typically operate at 1400 °C, the heat at which limestone becomes molten. The high operating temperatures require significant quantities of fuel to be burnt, but this need not be environmentally harmful because the fuel can include waste tyres, paper, or even some industrial solvents. Cement is usually made from the cooled clinker from the kiln, which is ground down to a dry, grey coloured powder. This is commonly called OPC (Ordinary Portland cement) and is supplied in bulk to large customers, such as precast concrete works or ready-mix depots, or in bags to small customers, such as builders or DIY stores.

Use of cement in concrete

In concrete, cement acts as a binder material, which causes the concrete to harden when water is added due to a chemical reaction (hydration). About 10% of the mass of concrete is taken up by cementitious materials, the major performance property of which is to give strength to the concrete in its hardened state. In addition, the manipulation of the cement content and type can also affect construction factors such as curing time and rate of gain of strength as well as performance attributes such as durability and serviceability.

There are several types of cement that are used for different applications. The basic 'Ordinary Portland Cement' appears in the majority of concrete mixes, but this may be substituted by other specialist blends such as sulfate-resisting cement. Of particular interest to designers is the use of white cement, which affects the colour properties of the concrete. Although this is much more expensive than OPC it is used in most architectural work such as cast stone, cladding and sculpture work. Cement companies also supply specialist products such as ready-blended cement with glass-fibres that are suitable for use as renders. A good architectural example of renders is the University of East London Docklands campus (by Ted Cullinan Architects). The cylindrical student residences that line the dockside have a colourful and stimulating presence. Green, blue, yellow and white renders form the exterior finish backed by insulation, in-situ concrete and blockwork. Cement renders were used to provide a consistent surface for the green, blue and white painted buildings. In a nearby project at Greenwich, architect Ralph Erskine has used a wide range of coloured renders (green, red, orange, blue, black, gold and crimson) to enliven the façades of the 'Greenwich Millennium Village' sustainable development.

Alternative binder materials, such as ground granulated blastfurnace slag (GGBS) and pulverised fuel ash (PFA) can be used to replace a fraction of the cement content.

These potential waste materials offer performance improvements in the concrete mix as a whole, but have to be used in combination with OPC for structural concrete.

Now, over 14 million tonnes of cementitious materials are used in the UK every year. Further information is available from the British Cement Association.

JG

Ceramics

Ceramics are hard, durable materials formed from clays and fired at high temperatures. They are used widely in construction in elements such as brick, tiles, pipes, terracotta and faience and whiteware.

See also: BRICKS AND BLOCKS; BRICKS AND BLOCKS – FINISHES; GLASS; SURFACE FINISHES.

Introduction

A ceramic is a hard, brittle, heat-resistant and corrosion-resistant material made by shaping and then firing a non-metallic mineral (e.g. clay) at a high temperature. The word ceramic derives from the Greek 'Keramos' which means 'burnt stuff' or pottery. Ceramics, in the form of earth-based bricks and earthenware were most likely the earliest man-made materials; they provide archaeologists with one of the most reliable means to date new finds. Ceramics as defined actually encompasses many more materials than usually realised and includes pottery, whiteware, or vitreous china, (sinks, baths etc), bricks, pipes and tiles, glass, porcelain and engineering ceramics such as alumina or silicon nitride. It is often not fully appreciated that ceramics have important engineering applications in addition to the more commonly associated decorative function. Thus, these materials can actually be found within buildings in a wide range of uses. Perhaps the most decorative use of ceramics and glass can be seen in the work of Spanish architect Antoni Gaudi.

How are ceramics made?

The raw materials used to make ceramics are predominantly clays, of which there are many types with differing composition and properties. It is the clay minerals, such as kaolinite ($Al_2O_3.2SiO_2.2H_2O$), montmorillonite and illite which are present in varying quantities (typically between 30% and 90%) and give bulk clays their properties. All clay minerals are composed predominantly of metal oxides, have a sheet-like atomic structure and are able to absorb water on the surfaces of these sheets. The consequence of this is that clay is malleable and can easily be formed into shapes when wet. The other main components of clay are quartz sand, which acts as filler, other minerals and various impurities. There are several forming processes to produce a ceramic object:

- Extruding through a die (for pipes and bricks);
- Powder pressing (for purer engineering ceramics);
- Pressing into a mould (for bricks and tiles);
- Slip-casting in a mould (for whiteware, some pottery and porcelain).

Once the object has been formed it must be allowed to dry under controlled conditions so that it does not warp or crack as the evaporating water causes considerable shrinkage. The dry object is then fired at elevated temperature to densify the clay particles. Two processes called sintering and vitrification (i.e. making glass-like) occur. During sintering the clay particles are drawn together, by their high overall surface energy. Vitrification involves the formation of a viscous liquid phase, which coats the particles and fills voids. The mechanical properties of the fired ceramic are very dependent on the firing process, which controls their microstructure such as porosity and crystal size. Some ceramics are fired a second time at a lower temperature to apply a glaze. **Glaze** is essentially a glass, which is applied to the object as a suspension of ground glass and pigment particles in water. During firing these particles coalesce to form a continuous layer bonded to the ceramic substrate. It fills surface porosity and is virtually impervious to water, thereby preventing absorption by the bulk ceramic. Because it is also brittle it will craze with time particularly if the object is subjected to large temperature or moisture fluctuations and the thermal properties of the ceramic and glaze are not well matched.

Ceramics in use

Ceramics are inherently resistant to chemical attack and oxidation. Their resistance to weathering by freeze-thawing, thermal cycling and salt crystallisation depends on their structure and properties. They are strong and hard and dimensionally stable and can withstand high service temperatures. All of the ceramics used in construction behave in a brittle manner. Apart from the use of ceramics in public art, mosaics and sculpture, more typical applications for ceramics in buildings include:

Bricks, tiles and pipes – these are made from fireclays and shales, which comprise clayey shales, quartz and feldspar. These constituents are often found together in the ground, such as London clay. Brick is the most common form of ceramic in construction.

Terracotta – this is made from yellow to brownish red clays and has been used since Victorian times for details such as cornices and chimney pots. It was also produced as hollow blocks, filled with concrete and used in wall construction. Today, terracotta is used for detail work and as tiles in cladding systems.

Faience – this is a glazed form of terracotta and can be used to give a durable coloured surface. It is produced in standard sized slabs, but can also be made to order.

Whiteware – most sanitary fittings are made from whiteware, which has a higher glass content than earthenware (used for pottery) so has low water absorption. This is important for sanitary fittings; if the glaze cracks, only minimal damage results.

Further reading

Ashurst, J. & Ashurst, A. (1988) *Practical building conservation, English Heritage Technical Handbook Volume 2, Brick, terracotta and earth* (Chapters 5 and 6), Gower Technical Press, UK.

Hamilton, D. (1978) *The Thames & Hudson manual of architectural ceramics*, Thames & Hudson, London, UK.

Herbert, T. & Huggins, K. (1995) *The decorative tile in architecture and interiors*, Phaidon Press, London, UK.

Stratton, M. (1993) *The terracotta revival: building innovation and the image of the industrial*, Gollancz, London, UK.

Tunick, S. (1997) *Terra-cotta skyline*, Princeton Architectural Press, USA.

OA

Chasings

See: RISERS AND TRUNKING; CORE (SERVICES)

Chipboard

See: TIMBER – MANUFACTURED BOARDS

Cladding

In external walls, the separation of decorative, weather resistant elements from structural, loadbearing elements defines cladding as an element of enclosure.

See also: ALUMINIUM; BESPOKE; BRICKS AND BLOCKS; CLADDING COMPONENTS; COMPOSITE PANELS; CONCRETE – FINISHES; CONCRETE – STRUCTURES; CONNECTIONS; DURABILITY; FAÇADES AND FAÇADE ENGINEERING; GLASS – STRUCTURAL GLAZING; GRC; HIGH TECH; 'HONESTY'; INSULATION; METALS; NEUTRA, RICHARD; OVERCLADDING; PLASTICS; PROUVÉ, JEAN; STAINLESS STEEL; TIMBER – PRODUCTION AND FINISHES; TOLERANCE; WEATHERING; WINDOWS AND CURTAIN WALLING; ZINC.

Introduction

It is tempting to regard cladding as a 20th century concept (or possibly 19th century, if early corrugated iron applications are included), yet the Georgian fashion for brickwork resulted in 'mathematical tiles' as a brick slip cladding method, often in the refurbishment of older buildings. Shiplap boarding and similar timber products have always, of course, acted as cladding for (usually) timber frame structures. The application of mass production techniques in off-site manufacture launched cladding materials as competitors to traditional building materials such as loadbearing brickwork, by promoting their ease of assembly as a cost and time advantage.

It could be said that the 'high-tech' architecture movement really brought cladding to life in its use of plastics and metals in the building envelope. Precision-formed components were seen as highly efficient and indicative of a higher degree of sophistication for the building. The work of Grimshaw, Foster and Rogers throughout the 1980s made use of an ever-developing expertise in cladding technology. Such product development has continued to the current day, to the point where there is an overwhelming choice of small modular components such as tiles, larger components such as boards and planks, sheets, and fully finished panels for use as a cladding 'envelope' to the main structural frame.

With the continuing investigation by façade engineers into cladding as an 'intelligent skin' there seem now to be even more possibilities for the design team. This said however, cladding poses a philosophical problem for architects with a Modernist perspective on the 'honest' use of materials, cladding being seen by some as a trivial overcoat rather than 'real' architecture with an appropriate use of materials.

What materials are used?

The application of cladding to new build projects, and to refurbishment, uses essentially identical products, but differentiated by the type of support system used. In addition to this, some methods are suitable not just for walls, but for roofs and other areas as well (technical details are described in the following entry). Cladding materials and products in common usage include:

- **Clay products** – terracotta tiles and brick slips;
- **Concrete panels** – precast reinforced concrete or glass reinforced concrete (GRC);
- **Fibre cement** – profiled sheet and coated flat panels;
- **Insulated composites** – a bonded assembly of metal outer sheet and liner with insulation core;
- **Metals** (steel, aluminium, etc) – profiled sheet, flat panels and plank systems;
- **Metal composites** – lead-faced steel, coated aluminium faced plastics;
- **Plastics** – GRP composites and preformed thermoplastics;
- **Shiplap and plank products** – timber (treated softwood or specialist timbers like cedar), metal 'sidings' (coated steel or aluminium), plastic extrusions and coated wood particle board.

Design considerations

In addition to architectural requirements, client needs and other considerations such as airtightness, insulation and energy efficiency, cladding systems need to fulfil three typical functional criteria.

Structure: wind loads and other live loads are transferred to the supporting structure, with the cladding supporting only its own dead loads. Movement control is an integral part of maintaining appearance and weathertightness. Span characteristics and deflection under load should be determined in the specification.

Weathertightness: conventional cladding systems exclude the weather by complete enclosure, sealing joints and openings with flashings, soakers, gaskets, and sealants. Rainscreen cladding systems exclude only the worst of the weather, but use a ventilated cavity to separate the outer leaf from the weather-sealed inner leaf.

Durability: facing materials are generally specified with a design life, or period to first maintenance, in mind. Traditional fairfaced brickwork, for example, can last a very long time (100 years or more) before maintenance (re-pointing), while coated steels might require maintenance at much less than 40 year intervals, and site painted timber at around 5 years. The durability of the substrate may also be a factor, especially on exposed sites.

Further reading

Brookes, A. & Grech, C. (1996) *Building envelope & connections*, Butterworth-Heinemann, Oxford, UK.
Brookes, A. (1998) *Cladding of buildings* (3rd edition), E & FN Spon, London, UK.
Hislop, P. (2001) *External timber cladding*, TRADA, High Wycombe, UK.

Ryan, P.A., Wolstenholme, R.P & Howell, D.M. (1992) *Durability of cladding*, Thomas Telford, London, UK.

Ogden, R.G. et al. (1996) *Architectural teaching resource: studio guide*, SCI Publication 167, The Steel Construction Institute, Ascot, UK.

GW

Cladding – components

Cladding uses a wealth of structural and non-structural components to provide a weatherproof, durable envelope to a building.

See also: ALUMINIUM; BESPOKE; BRICKS AND BLOCKS; CLADDING COMPONENTS; COMPOSITE PANELS; CONCRETE – FINISHES; CONCRETE – STRUCTURES; CONNECTIONS; DURABILITY; FAÇADES AND FAÇADE ENGINEERING; GLASS – STRUCTURAL GLAZING; GRC; INSULATION; METALS; OVERCLADDING; PLASTICS; STAINLESS STEEL; WEATHERING; WINDOWS AND CURTAIN WALLING; ZINC.

Introduction

Cladding is a non-loadbearing building envelope, which is comprised of primary enclosure components (e.g. tiles, planks, sheets and panels) together with a diverse assembly of secondary components that enable the enclosure to fulfil its main functions of structural performance, weathertightness, insulation, and durability. Each component part plays a crucial role in the effectiveness of the whole, in accordance with manufacturers' specifications and in the case of bespoke installations, the façade engineers' recommendations. It is important to note that the intricacy and detailed nature of cladding installation requires particular attention to detail, not only in design but also in workmanship. Good practice on site will produce durable and long-lasting installations, but this should be monitored carefully for optimum results.

The following offers an overview of the principal elements that make up a typical cladding assembly. In this instance, the text focuses on metal cladding, but the basic issues are the same for most materials.

Panels

The cladding panels themselves, of course, form the major part of any assembly. The typical materials used are listed in the previous entry. Most cladding panels are specified from manufacturer's standard ranges, but some prestigious projects will use bespoke work. The wide range of panels available are such that designers have an almost unlimited choice of colours, shapes and textures, with the major metals all offering slightly different options. In essence all panels must be sufficiently durable to last to the required design life and the design team must be made aware of relevant maintenance intervals. Exposure ratings in terms of weathering will determine the choice of cladding panel as will architectural and client requirements. In general, smooth, flat panels offer a sleek aesthetic, but are less stiff (and thus more vulnerable to damage) than profiled panels. Complex or curved panels are a more expensive option. Panels can be simply plain metal, composite or insulated.

Connections and fasteners

Besides the act of fixing the cladding to the secondary structure, fastener systems also form an engineered route for load transfer from the cladding face. Performance of bolted fixings is well documented in standards and codes, and these are often used in conjunction with specialist cleats as part of the cladding system. However, since there is normally a need in practice to fix from one side only, self-drill fasteners are the most common method. These consist of a drill point and thread designed specifically for the material to which the fixing is made, driven by a hexagonal, colour matched head. For example the thread can be specially designed to drill and tap even hot rolled steel up to 16 mm thick (which covers most structural steel sections), or to maintain inner and outer cladding faces at a constant spacing ('stand off' threads).

Fastener suppliers publish data to supporting specification criteria such as performance in shear, pullout, and pull over (ultimate failure being when the fastener pulls through the cladding material). It is important to specify the fasteners as well as the rest of the cladding system. Cladding fasteners often feature a washered head to spread the clamping loads, and a washer may be added to form an airtight seal or achieve an effective separation between dissimilar metals. By way of contrast, fixings and connections for precast concrete cladding tend to be fewer, but more robust, as they have to deal with heavier panels. It is common to see cast-in connectors in the back of panels or nibs (protruding sections) ready to connect direct to the main structural frame, corbels or hanger systems.

Secondary structure

It is unusual for the fixing centres for cladding systems to coincide with the main structural grid. Thus, it is usual to see a secondary structure to act as an interface, connecting the cladding to the frame. Traditionally, purlins or cladding rails have been used (typically cold rolled galvanised steel channels or 'zed' sections); major manufacturers also produce additional components such as wind posts, sag bars, braces, and struts. For built-up cladding systems (as distinct from panel systems), it is common to use a spacer system to accommodate insulation or to create a cavity between the outer leaf and the secondary structure as part of the weathertightness strategy. At its simplest, a light gauge metal zed section or a treated timber batten is used, but the need to minimise thermal bridging has generated a number of specialised spacer bar systems, spanning further between supports. Additional benefits are a better continuity of insulation, and the ability to accommodate thicker insulation whilst providing an economical solution to the potential problem of structural eccentricity created by the width of the cavity.

Membranes

Vapour barriers are used to control the movement of moisture through the cladding system, principally to prevent moisture-laden air penetrating to the position of the dew point to cause interstitial condensation. Breather membranes are used as an interlayer that is vapour permeable and breathable, yet water resistant, to prevent a vapour build up within the cladding.

Insulation can be included as a separate component (e.g. boards and quilts), manufactured as part of the envelope component (i.e. in composite panels), or as an integrated component (e.g. insulated brick slip systems).

Other components

These are used to make cladding systems weathertight and airtight.

Flashings – these are press formed or extruded sections usually made from the same material as the cladding (e.g. colour-coated steel), fixed to the cladding with self-drill fasteners or rivets. Their purpose is to finish/cover open or cut edges, corners and junctions, to prevent ingress of water and throw water out from the cladding face by forming drips and water bars.

Soakers – these are metal, plastic, or damp-proof course (DPC) sections fixed behind cladding to check the ingress of water behind the cladding and shaped so as to channel it back out to the cladding face. The purpose of these is to block penetration of wind driven rain, provide a 'second line' of defence against weathering and to direct moisture outwards.

Gaskets – preformed sealing sections (face gaskets and joint gaskets: strip or pre formed shapes) inserted into a cladding joint to prevent ingress of water at cladding face and seal panel to panel details.

Sealants – mastics and other formless materials used for sealing cladding joints, supplied both in gun grade or strip form. Common uses include bedding under flashings, behind panels, around window/door frames, and to seal cladding sheet laps.

Further reading

Brookes, A. & Grech, C. (1996) *Building envelope & connections*, Butterworth-Heinemann, Oxford, UK.
Brookes, A. (1998) *Cladding of buildings* (3rd edition), E & FN Spon, London, UK.
Hislop, P. (2001) *External timber cladding*, TRADA, High Wycombe, UK.

GW

Cold bridging
See: THERMAL BRIDGING

Columns

Columns are isolated elements that carry mainly vertical loads through a structure to the foundations. Although normally structural, these elements may be constructed for purely aesthetic reasons, e.g. as free standing monuments.

See also: BEAM; BRACING; BRICKS AND BLOCKS; CONCRETE; CORE (STRUCTURAL); FLOORS; FOUNDATIONS; FRAME; GRIDS FOR STRUCTURE AND LAYOUT; STRUCTURAL STEEL; STONE; TIMBER – LAMINATED TIMBER; TIMBER – STRUCTURES; WALLS.

Why use columns?

The self-weight of a structure and the weight of anything it carries need to be transferred safely to the foundations. This can be achieved by the use of loadbearing walls, but these can interrupt the enclosed space. Columns are isolated elements and therefore far less intrusive. In addition, where floors are supported on beams the vertical loads are concentrated at their ends. It is more efficient to then transfer these loads down the building through a column than to disperse them through a wall. Columns are part of the structural frame. As well as carrying vertical loads, columns may carry horizontal loads such as those due

The main atrium of the Lloyd's headquarters building in the City of London (Richard Rogers Partnership, 1986). The columns can be seen clearly in this well-articulated concrete frame design. Photograph courtesy of Ove Arup & Partners and Richard Rogers Partnership.

to wind (in conjunction with the rest of the structural frame), and provide the stability for the whole building. Where this is the case a structural core is no longer necessary and this increases the space use flexibility of the building. The carrying of the horizontal loads will introduce additional bending into the column, which may affect both its size and the choice of materials with which it can be constructed.

Column design and construction

There is little restriction on the shape of columns; typically they are round or rectangular but they may also be oval, or any form of polygon. Generally the costs will increase with greater complexity of shape, regardless of the material employed. Decorative forms may be added as cladding around a structural centre. For example, decorative concrete blocks which are assembled and then filled in-situ with concrete. Columns may also be constructed within the thickness of a wall for thickening (i.e. strengthening) purposes. Columns can be constructed in most structural materials (e.g. concrete, masonry, steel, stone, and timber). They are often the most visible part of the loadbearing structure and therefore the choice of material, and indeed to some degree their form, may be dictated by the architectural intention. The choice of material will however affect the design of the rest of the structural frame (and its constituent materials) and this requires careful consideration.

The architectural possibilities of columns have been realised for as long as columns have been used as, for example, the '*caryatids*' of antiquity (columns in the shape of human figures carved as if they themselves are bearing the weight of the building). The contemporary construction of columns for purely aesthetic purposes is probably best demonstrated in their use for monuments, e.g. Nelson's Column, Trafalgar Square in London. It is interesting that many architectural concepts stem from principally structural design requirements. This can be seen in the decoration of the classical Greek orders, Mediaeval church construction and even the tapering '*pilotis*' used by Le Corbusier in the 20th century. The Greek capitals are beneficial in distributing the loads concentrated at the top of the column, and tapered columns give stiffer columns whilst minimising the size at ground level.

Further reading

Adams, J. (1998) *Columns*, Academy Editions, John Wiley & Sons, London, UK.

Goodchild, C.H. (1997) *Economic concrete frame elements*, Reinforced Concrete Council, Crowthorne, UK.

Ogden, R.G. et al. (1996) *Architectural teaching resource: studio guide*, SCI Publication 167, The Steel Construction Institute, Ascot, UK.

OA

Composite decking

A popular floor system using profiled steel sheeting, an in-situ concrete topping and shear connectors to supporting beams (usually for medium- to long-span floors). Supporting beams may be separate or within the depth of the slab.

See also: BUILDABILITY; CEILINGS; CONCRETE – STRUCTURES; CONSTRUCTION PROGRAMME; FABRIC ENERGY STORAGE; FLOORS; FRAME; METALS; OFF-SITE MANUFACTURE; ON-SITE PRODUCTION; PROFILED METAL DECKING; STRUCTURAL STEEL.

Introduction

Composite decking is the combination of a profiled steel sheet, and an in-situ reinforced concrete topping, used mainly in the construction of medium- and long-span floors. The profiled sheet acts as permanent formwork, and is often similar to conventional metal decking sections, but modified by embossing so that it also achieves composite action with the concrete. This is a structural term meaning that the concrete and steel components are working together in unison. Composite action between the deck and the supporting steel beams is achieved by the use of shear connectors (studs welded to the beam via the decking) before placement of concrete. The efficiency of this system is such that it has become the preferred method of floor construction for many building types, but most commonly in offices and medium to high-rise apartment buildings. The main reasons for this widespread use are the relatively speedy construction programmes and the reduced floor depth (because composite action results in slimmer floors). Other building types that are suitable for composite decking include:

Steel fixing underway for the HSBC European HQ, Canary Wharf, in London's Docklands. Photograph courtesy of Richard Lees, Derbyshire.

- Car parks;
- Cinemas and auditoria;
- Hospitals and health care;
- Housing;
- Industrial;
- Recreational;
- Roof decks;
- Schools and colleges.

Spans of up to nine metres are possible, although six to seven metre spans are more commonly specified. Providing temporary propping to the deck during curing extends the maximum spans. Composite decks using profiles in the range of 46 mm to 70 mm are typically suitable for spans of about three metres, without temporary propping. Deep deck profiles from 210 mm to 225 mm can give spans of up to 6.5 metres unpropped, or up to nine metres with temporary propping. The overall depth depends on design factors, a 60 mm minimum cover over the crown of the profiled sheet gives a slab depth from 100–295 mm, depending on the profile. Many profiles feature a dovetail section in the crown for insertion of special services hangers, so these floor options normally have to be used in combination with a suspended ceiling system, particularly as they are not architecturally acceptable to building occupants. The composite decks are also not quite as effective for fabric energy storage as exposed concrete soffits because the concrete is 'behind' the steel profile.

The steel in composite decking

The prefabricated steel profiles allow fast construction and an early working platform for following trades. They are manufactured from hot dipped galvanised steel, galvanised in the flat by the steel manufacturer prior to delivery to the profiler. Profiled sheet is available in depths 46–70 mm for shallow decking, with 'deep deck' sections 210–225 mm (these sections are used in the deeper systems, sitting within the depth of special steel beams).

The concrete in composite decking

The concrete strength is specified by the structural designer, typically from C30–50 and suitable for placement by pumping. Both normal and lightweight concrete can be used, with lightweight concrete offering a weight saving and better thermal performance in this situation. Reinforcement is usually limited to a simple anti-crack mesh, but some designs specify a single reinforcement bar in each trough of the profile.

'Slim floors'

This method of using composite decking further reduces the overall depth of the floor zone (typically 290–340 mm deep) by containing the support steelwork within the slab depth thus avoiding or reducing downstand depth. There are also benefits in performance and services integration. Special section beams are produced as fabricated, asymmetric, or rectangular hollow sections designed to support profiled decking on the bottom flange. Long spans are achieved with deep profiled decking (usually 225 mm deep).

Further reading

Couchman, G. et al. (2000) *Composite slabs and beams using steel decking*, SCI Publication 300, The Steel Construction Institute/MCRMA, Ascot, UK.

Johnson, R.P. (1994) *Composite structures of steel and concrete*, Blackwell Science, Oxford, UK.

Lawson, R.M. (1989) *Design of composite slabs and beams with steel decking*, SCI Publication 055, The Steel Construction Institute, Ascot, UK.

Lawson, R.M., Mullett, D.L. & Ward, F.P.D. (1990) *Good practice in composite floor construction*, SCI Publication 090, The Steel Construction Institute, Ascot, UK.

Mullett, D.L. (1992) *Slim floor design and construction*, SCI Publication 110, The Steel Construction Institute, Ascot, UK.

Mullett, D.L. (1998) *Composite floor systems*, Blackwell Science, Oxford, UK.

Mullett, D.L. & Lawson, R.M. (1993) *Slim floor construction using deep decking*, SCI Publication 127, The Steel Construction Institute, Ascot, UK.

GW

Composite materials

Composite materials are those consisting of a combination of two or more distinct materials, together yielding superior characteristics to those of the individual constituents.

See also: BESPOKE; CLADDING; EPOXY; FAÇADES AND FAÇADE ENGINEERING; PLASTICS – FABRICATION; PLASTICS – TYPES.

Introduction

A wide array of materials can be termed composite materials. In the context of construction, they range simplistically from reinforced concrete to polymer composites. Polymer composites themselves can be subdivided further into two categories: fibre-reinforced polymers and particle-reinforced polymers. The latter are typically used as high compressive strength, quick-setting mortars. They are similar in nature to concrete in that they are composed of hard aggregates, but incorporated in a polymer rather than a cementitious matrix. Of more technological importance are fibre-reinforced polymer (FRP) composites such as glass fibre reinforced plastic, or GRP. The polymer matrix of an FRP is reinforced with lightweight fibres with outstanding tensile mechanical properties. That said, polymer composites have inherent limitations such as their relatively low compressive strength and poor fire performance. Their key attributes are high strength to weight ratio; high stiffness to weight ratio; durability and flexibility of form and finish.

About FRP

For both categories of FRP, the matrix acts as a medium through which externally applied stress can be transmitted to the reinforcement. The second function of the matrix is to protect the reinforcement from surface damage as a result of mechanical abrasion or chemical reactions with the environment. By virtue of the relative softness and ductility of the matrix, the propagation of cracks through the material is hindered, giving polymer composites very good fatigue resistance and toughness. It is essential for FRP materials that the bond strength between the fibres and the matrix is very high to maximise the stress transmittance from the weak matrix to the strong reinforcement. The polymer matrix of FRP materials is typically a thermoset polymer such as polyester, epoxy or phenolic resin. Thermoset polymers generally have superior mechanical and thermal properties (they will not melt when heated) than thermoplastic polymers. As a result, an FRP material will char rather than melt or burn in a fire. Phenolic matrix FRPs perform particularly well in fire. Nevertheless, the mechanical properties of a thermoset will reduce dramatically above a distinct temperature, known as the glass transition temperature (Tg) – typically 60–120 °C, depending upon the resin type. Consequently the properties of an FRP will also reduce dramatically.

Production and applications

FRPs may be fabricated using a variety of fibre types, orientations and lengths. Fibres may be included as short and randomly orientated or continuous and aligned (such as straight woven or wound). By orientating the fibres, the material can be tailored so that it has the desired mechanical properties in particular directions. Different fibre types may be used together to further customise the material. Glass fibres typically have a similar tensile strength to steel, but have about a third of the tensile modulus. Carbon fibres have superior mechanical properties, typically having a tensile strength similar to or greater than steel. Aramid fibres (commonly known by the trade name Kevlar™) have outstanding toughness and are used to impart impact resistance, hence their use in body armour.

FRP composites have been used since the 1960s. However, so far they have failed to achieve significant use in structural applications. This is due largely to a lack of understanding within the construction industry of their behaviour and design together with the relatively high materials cost. They have mainly found use in decorative features, façade panels and niche structures such as bespoke footbridges. Indeed, advanced pultruded composite profiles for bridges using FRP are to be tested in Spain. The 225 mm × 520 mm profile is already under production in Denmark. Such bridge sections weigh 70% less than conventional solutions. Recently, progress has been made with the development of useful design guidance. Materials costs are also falling and an awareness of the potential for project cost savings through ease of construction (owing chiefly to the lighter weight of FRP) is being realised.

Further reading

Birley, A.W. (1988) *Plastics materials, properties & applications*, Blackie & Sons, UK.

Brydson, J.A. (1999) *Plastics materials*, Butterworth-Heinemann, Oxford, UK.
Bunsell, A.R. (1988) *Fibre reinforcements for composite materials*, Elsevier, Oxford, UK.

OA

Composite panels

Panels that are a bonded assembly of three layers – outer layer, insulation and inner liner, most commonly used in metal cladding systems.

See also: CLADDING; CLADDING – COMPONENTS; CONCRETE; CONCRETE – STRUCTURES; DURABILITY; FAÇADES AND FAÇADE ENGINEERING; GRC; INSULATION; MODULES AND MODULAR CONSTRUCTION; OVERCLADDING; THERMAL BRIDGING; WINDOWS AND CURTAIN WALLING.

Introduction

Conventional double skin (or built-up) cladding systems use separate layers of outer face, insulation and liner. Composite panels are comprised of the same components, but instead they are a bonded assembly, enabling the enclosure and insulation of the building in one operation/element. The principle makes use of the fact that two rigid skins separated by, and bonded to a core, gain rigidity from the composite action thus attained. A recent development in the area of composite panels is 'SIPS' (structural insulated panel systems). This term is now used to describe any metal, timber or concrete panel options that form a major component part of the external envelope of a building. This could be an insulated timber panel that will be faced with a brick skin, or precast concrete panels used for basements. Nevertheless, the generic description of composite panels most usually applies to metal faced panels (covered below), but a wider variety of bonded composites is manufactured with facings such as colour-coated fibre cement and wood particle board in addition to concrete options such as insulated precast panels. The basic issues are the same for most materials.

Product types and applications

All manufacturers publish load span tables and U value data for their panels. Maximum spans vary according to wind loads and span conditions, but are typically 3–12 m depending on panel specification. Panels are available in standard modules, or in special sizes (300–1200 mm wide). Comprehensive assembly and opening details are usually provided in manufacturers' literature. Insulation thickness should be selected on the basis of the U value required for the building type being designed. The main application for composite panels is for external walls/façades in high quality commercial and industrial projects, where high standards of fit, flatness, and finish are required. Composite panel systems often include integrated glazing systems. Some systems are also suitable for roofs and other non-vertical features. The key aspects are outlined below.

Profiled panels – these are essentially an 'all in one' method of installing the profiled sheet cladding used in built-up systems, consisting of a profiled outer sheet and liner panel bonded over insulation. Fixing is through the panel, as for double skin systems, and panel joints are sealed with conventional side/end lap details. This configuration is suitable for roofs as well as walls.

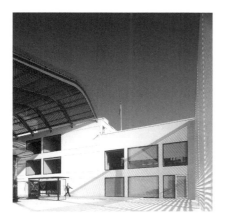

Insulated precast concrete cladding panels form the pure, white façade to Foster & Partners' UK headquarters building for French street furniture company JC Decaux in West London. Photograph courtesy of The Concrete Society.

Flat panels – these combine a flat or micro-profiled outer sheet and liner with an insulation core to form panels which fit together using interlocking, weathered and gasketted joints. A concealed fixing is generally achieved with self-drill fasteners through the inner section of the interlocking joint, which is faced with a gasket or capping section.

Bonding – some manufacturers rely on autohesive bonding where the adhesive qualities of the foam (polyurethane), before and during curing, achieve a bond in a continuous process. Others bond the steel facing adhesively on to insulation board (mineral wool or expanded polystyrene) in a discontinuous process.

Finishes – facing materials are generally colour coated steel, stainless steel, or aluminium, in flat sheet and profiled or micro-profiled sheet (flat sheet formed with a very fine ribbed finish). The increased rigidity gained from composite action often enables a thinner outer sheet to be used, especially when micro-profiled.

Insulation – this is usually polyurethane foam for autohesively bonded systems, and mineral wool or expanded polystyrene for adhesive bonded.

Built examples

There are many composite, bonded metal panels available in the UK and Europe. An alternative to metal composite panels is the Hardwall™ precast concrete cladding system that uses insulation and composite connectors to form an insulated sandwich panel for exterior applications. The system offers the choice of a bespoke exterior concrete leaf, and the added benefit of thermal mass from the interior concrete leaf. Hardwall™ was used by Norman Foster for the JC Decaux UK Headquarters at Brentford in West London and features an envelope of elegant white precast concrete panels.

Further reading

Davies, J.M. (ed.) (2001) *Lightweight sandwich construction*, Blackwell Science, Oxford, UK.

GW/JG

Concrete

Concrete is a commonly used construction material composed mainly of cement, crushed rock or gravel, sand and water. It is used in buildings to form foundations, frames, walls, floors and many other architectural elements.

See also: ANDO, TADAO; BEAMS; CALATRAVA, SANTIAGO; CANTILEVERS; CEMENT; CLADDING; COLUMNS; CONCRETE – FINISHES; CONCRETE – STRUCTURES; CORE (STRUCTURAL); DURABILITY; FABRIC ENERGY STORAGE; FIRE PROTECTION; FLOORS; FOUNDATIONS; FRAME; GRC; KAHN, LOUIS; LE CORBUSIER; MORTARS, CEMENT AND LIME; NERVI, PIER LUIGI; NIEMEYER, OSCAR; RETAINING WALLS; SIZA, ALVARO; SURFACE FINISHES; WEATHERING; WRIGHT, FRANK LLOYD.

What is concrete?

Concrete is made from cement, aggregates (fine and coarse) and water (about 10% of the mix). Sometimes other chemicals (called admixtures and additives, up to about 1% of the mix) are added to alter the performance of the concrete, for example to make it set faster or flow more easily. Concrete mixes are specified according to their strength, appearance and long-term performance. The relative proportions of the constituent materials are adjusted accordingly to suit, to the extent that concrete can be made so light that it can float or so smooth that it feels like glass.

Night-time view of the massive concrete 'hangar' at RAF Duxford American Air Museum, near Cambridge (Foster & Partners with Ove Arup & Partners). The building has no internal columns and houses a B-52 bomber and other aircraft. Photograph by Trevor Jones, courtesy of The Concrete Society.

Cement: this is produced from chalk or limestone, and clay or shale in a sophisticated, energy intensive process: cement kilns typically operate at 1400 °C. Cement is a binder material, which will cause the concrete to harden when water is added due to a chemical reaction. There are several types of cement from 'Ordinary Portland Cement' (OPC) to white cement, which is very popular in 'architectural' concrete mixes. Cement usually accounts for 10–20% of the concrete mix.

Aggregates: these are coarse and fine particles of sand, gravel or crushed rock that make up the majority (75–85%) of the volume of a typical concrete mix. These give robustness to the concrete. Waste materials such as pulverised fuel ash and ground blast-furnace slag may also be added in the form of aggregates. These lightweight materials have insulating properties and are often used in the concrete blocks seen in housing.

Reinforcement: about half of all concrete used in the UK is 'reinforced concrete'. Concrete is strong in compression, but relatively weak in tension; adding reinforcement (usually in the form of steel bars) overcomes this weakness in tension and controls cracking. Reinforcement includes bars or mesh (steel), placed in the mould or form before the concrete is poured. Alternatively, steel or plastic fibres may be introduced to the concrete during mixing to improve its tensile strength. The British Standard for concrete (BS8110) specifies 'cover' to reinforcement for different exposure conditions. All UK-produced steel reinforcement uses 100% recycled steel scrap.

Concrete in architecture

Concrete was known to the Romans and may have been used as early as 7,000 BC. 'Ordinary Portland Cement' (the most important constituent of concrete), was first patented in 1824 by Joseph Aspdin. Since then there have been many developments in the material, its use and applications, not least the advent of reinforced concrete in the mid 1800s, which revolutionised concrete's structural use in buildings. In 1898 the first multi-storey reinforced concrete framed building was erected in the UK using the Mouchel/Hennebique system.

Concrete can be used in most areas of building construction: foundations, ground slabs, structural frames, cladding, walls, floors, roofs and external landscaping. Almost every building has at least some concrete in it and there are many ways in which concrete can be used – for example, it can be cast monolithically, sprayed, continually 'slip' formed or precast off site in moulds. Designers best known for their concrete include Norman Foster, Frank Lloyd Wright, Louis Kahn, Carlo Scarpa and engineers Ove Arup and Santiago Calatrava.

Practical matters

In most cases, concrete is used in two basic forms: either it is formed into 'units' in a factory (precast) and then delivered to site or it is formed on site (in situ) at its desired location. It is also feasible to combine in situ and precast construction methods to suit a particular project. This 'hybrid' concrete construction can increase speed of construction dramatically (See *Concrete – structures* for more details).

Concrete has the benefits of strength, durability, flexibility of the mix design, and architectural and sculptural potential for fabric energy storage. However, the constituent materials of concrete are predominantly natural, so its appearance will change over time if it is exposed to rain, atmospheric pollution or mechanical damage. This feature can be managed or even made a feature, provided designers understand the weathering mechanisms involved. Buildings that date from the mid-20th century may have staining and deposits on their façades, which can be unsightly and detract from the desired architectural effect. However, better guidance is now available on mix design and architectural detailing so that weathering can be prevented in contemporary architecture. Designers need to be aware that structural engineers will follow BS 8110 (soon Eurocode 2) on structural concrete, particularly with respect to cover for reinforcement. Again, with older buildings one often sees 'spalling' of the surface layers of concrete. This is caused by water penetration to the steel reinforcement, which rusts and pushes the concrete away from the steel. Careful consideration of types of exposure, location, cover and surface finishes together with mix consistency will help prevent such premature ageing.

Further reading

British Cement Association (1999) *Concrete through the ages*, British Cement Association, Crowthorne, UK. ISBN 0 7210 1547 6.

British Standards Institution, BS 8110: *Structural concrete*, BSI, London, UK

JG

Concrete – finishes

Concrete is a commonly used construction material composed of cement, crushed rock or gravel, sand and water. The ability to 'design' the concrete mix and use a range of surface finishing techniques gives designers significant potential for architectural expression.

See also: ANDO, TADAO; BEAMS; CANTILEVERS; CEMENT; CLADDING; COLUMNS; CONCRETE; CONCRETE – STRUCTURES; CORE (STRUCTURAL); DURABILITY; FABRIC ENERGY STORAGE; FIRE PROTECTION; FLOORS; FOUNDATIONS; FRAME; GRC; HERZOG AND DE MEURON; MORTARS, CEMENT AND LIME; RETAINING WALLS; SCARPA, CARLO; SURFACE FINISHES; WEATHERING.

Introduction

Concrete is made from cement, aggregates and water. Other chemicals may be added to change the properties or performance of the material. Where concrete is used for structural purposes only, there is little need to consider the quality of finish in any great detail. This is why much structural concrete is often called 'structural grey', because it uses a normal mix design of locally available, economic materials and

Façade of the Eberswalde Technical Library in Germany (Herzog & De Meuron). The precast concrete cladding features images created in the concrete by exposing aggregates in the mix. Photograph by Margherita Spiluttini.

the chief concern is one of ensuring structural, not aesthetic performance. However, where concrete is 'exposed' and seen by people, i.e. it has an architectural purpose as well, then there is scope to consider the full range of surface colours and textures available (hence 'architectural concrete'). There is a wide range of possible finishes, but these will tend to go in and out of fashion from time to time. For example, exposed aggregates and board marked concrete were very popular in the 1960s and 1970s, whereas contemporary architects have a preference for white or pale concrete with a smooth finish. Finishes can be applied to both interior and exterior concrete, but careful consideration should be given to the latter as it is subject to the effects of weathering. Interior concrete surfaces may simply be subjected to wear-and-tear in heavy circulation areas.

About finishes

Concrete can be cast so that the 'as-struck' appearance is its final finish (a direct finish). Architects often prefer this option because it is more 'structurally honest' to the material. However it is also feasible to complete the finishing process after the concrete is struck from the formwork or mould. This is necessary for highly textured finishes such as sand or grit blasting and tooling. In any case, when concrete hardens, it takes on the appearance of the surface against which it has been poured i.e. it reflects that finish. These surfaces, on the inside of forms/moulds, can be timber, sheet plywood, steel, GRP or other moulded plastics called formliners (these come in a range of patterns). It is possible to use standard patterns or bespoke designs for a particular company logo. The degree to which any finishing technique is employed may depend on the type of building, cost, client requirements and construction programme (time).

It is usual that the specification for a concrete element will contain reference to the desired qualities of the finish under two broad categories: surface consistency and colour consistency. The Concrete Society's Technical Report TR52 on plain-formed concrete finishes offers extensive guidance on architectural finishes.

Surface consistency

This is a means of specifying the quality of surface finish required that is acceptable to the designer. Surface consistency is defined by the number, distribution and size of surface defects, such as hairline cracks or blowholes (caused by air settling against formwork) as discerned from a specified distance. For example, the designer of an exposed slab above an office space might specify that blowholes up to 0.5 mm are acceptable. For floor slabs, it is more common to see specifications refer to surface flatness. A sample panel is useful, but it is wiser to do a full-size trial panel for very high quality specifications. To achieve very fine, smooth finishes, the mix design may include microsilica or metakaolin. For exposed aggregate finishes, the mix design, relative proportion and grading of the fine and coarse aggregates becomes particularly important in achieving the desired aesthetic effect. Aggregates can also be specified to enhance surface qualities e.g. adding mica or dolomite will produce a sparkly effect.

Colour consistency

Colour consistency is again a matter of defining what is acceptable to the designer and stating this in the specification. Acceptability is often verified visually by visiting comparable buildings or erecting sample panels. Time and budget should be set aside to reach agreement where colour consistency is likely to be a critical design issue. Although it is feasible to produce almost any colour, white, buff and natural coloured concretes appear to be the most popular. White cement is often specified in architectural concrete as a base, but the colour of aggregates will also affect the overall aesthetic impression. For example, a white architectural concrete mix might include the very pale and finely graded Hepworth sands and Ballidon aggregates, in addition to white cement. Chemical stains, dyes and pigments are also used. The more complex the mix and the more closely-matched the concrete, the more expensive it is, sometimes 5 to 10 times the cost of normal structural concrete. For some projects, colour matching of adjacent concrete elements is important, but allowance should be made for minor natural inconsistencies and for lime bloom (efflorescence) to settle down.

Other special finishes

The technologies of mix design, formwork preparation and chemicals are such that specialist companies offer particular aesthetic effects. Polished concrete and pattern-imprinted floors are popular in retail and leisure buildings and inlaid materials such as bricks, stone, flints, marble or mosaic may also be used to enliven a façade. Cast stone and reconstituted stone (i.e. stone dust or fine aggregates bound with a cement matrix) are used extensively in conservation work and for decorative elements on modern buildings such as lintels and cills. Of particular interest is a technique for screen-printing graphics, images or designs onto concrete (called Serilith) which was used by Swiss architects Herzog & De Meuron to great effect on the Eberswalde technical library. The façades featured horizontal bands of concrete cladding panels, with each band featuring a repeated image that represented something of Eberswalde's history.

Built examples

A few architects are very well known for their work with concrete. The range of architectural styles is very broad: from the elegant and restrained work of Foster and Partners, Tadao Ando and David Chipperfield to the more colourful and outspoken work of John Outram, Piers Gough and Ricardo Bofill. Indeed, there are many more outstanding designers across the world, who are well documented in the references given below.

Further reading

Bennett, D. (2001) *Exploring concrete architecture – tone, texture and form*, Birkhäuser, Basle, Switzerland.
Concrete Society TR52 (1999) *Plain formed concrete finishes*, Concrete Society, Crowthorne, UK.
Slessor, C. (2001) *Concrete regionalism*, Thames & Hudson, London, UK.

JG

Concrete – structures

Concrete is a commonly used construction material, much of which is used in building structures and civil engineering works. In buildings, concrete can be used in various elements such as foundations, walls, floors, structural frames and architectural features.

Schematic diagram of the concrete frame for the Lloyd's Register of Shipping in London (Richard Rogers Partnership). Photograph courtesy of Anthony Hunt Associates Ltd & Richard Rogers Partnership.

See also: AALTO, ALVAR; ARUP, OVE; BEAMS; CALATRAVA, SANTIAGO; CANTILEVERS; CEMENT; CLADDING; COLUMNS; CONCRETE – FINISHES; CORE (STRUCTURAL); CONSTRUCTION PROGRAMME; DRY CONSTRUCTION AND WET CONSTRUCTION; DURABILITY; FABRIC ENERGY STORAGE; FIRE PROTECTION; FLOORS; FOUNDATIONS; FRAME; GRC; GRIDS FOR STRUCTURE AND LAYOUT; KAHN, LOUIS; LUBETKIN, BERTHOLD; MORTARS, CEMENT AND LIME; NERVI, PIER LUIGI; NIEMEYER, OSCAR; RETAINING WALLS; SCHINDLER, R M; SIZA, ALVARO; SURFACE FINISHES; WEATHERING; WRIGHT, FRANK LLOYD.

Introduction

The basic processes used to produce structural concrete elements on or off site are described below. Detailed guidance on structural design, concrete construction plant and equipment is available in other publications. The descriptions here apply to the use of structural concrete in the majority of building types, but specialist applications (e.g. radiation protection) would require more specific, further reading.

Concrete is used in two basic forms; either it is formed into 'units' in a factory (**precast**) and then delivered to site or it is formed on site (**in situ**) at its desired location. The criteria by which the construction method is chosen may include cost, time, access to site, client requirements or architectural design. Each method has its own advantages that need to be evaluated during the design and construction planning stages and the choice will depend on the relative importance of any of the factors listed above. Perhaps the one aspect that distinguishes concrete from other common construction materials is the sheer range of options open to the design team. This portfolio is extensive and in many respects means that 'anything is possible' but this is dependent, of course, on the design skills and practical expertise available. Hence, it is only feasible to present an overview in this entry.

In-situ construction

Keeping all concreting operations on site can be a good idea because everything can be undertaken and managed by one specialist contractor. This one-stop procurement route is helpful because it simplifies construction programming and enables plenty of flexibility in the way site activities are carried out. In-situ concrete is often the one key material that 'stitches' together discrete structural concrete or steel elements. However in-situ construction can be vulnerable to weather conditions and the availability of short-term concretors (i.e. specialist site staff).

For in-situ construction, timber or steel formwork is erected on site as a 'box' within which wet concrete can be poured. This formwork is usually designed and erected by the specialist trade contractor undertaking the work. Formwork materials, finishing techniques, dimensional accuracy are all determined in the specification to be appropriate to the size and characteristics of the element, the end-use and architectural intention for the building. In a structure, concrete has good compressive properties but has little tensile strength so reinforcement is used to make up this shortfall. Steel reinforcing (bars, fabric or mesh) is commonly used in building and civil engineering (vertical) structures, but metal or plastic reinforcement may be suitable for floors or other horizontal elements. Reinforcement takes time to set out and is fixed in accordance with the structural engineer's drawings. There is now a greater use of specialist reinforcing products such as stud rails and shear ladders, which perform the same structural task as bars and links, but speed up the fixing process and weigh less. Flat work such as ground slabs, floors or car-parking areas may use fibres for reinforcement – these are mixed with the concrete and disperse throughout the mix to provide tensile strength.

Fresh concrete can be either delivered to site as ready-mixed by truck, or actually batched and mixed on site. The latter is more common for major infrastructure works (with high usage) or work in remote areas without a local ready-mixed concrete supply. In the UK alone, 25 million m^3 of ready-mixed concrete is supplied per annum. Following pouring or pumping the concrete into the formwork, most concrete is then vibrated to ensure consistency and good compaction. More use is now being made in the UK (Japan has been using it for years) of self-compacting concrete which does not require vibration. Although mass concrete pours of several thousand cubic metres at a time are feasible, concrete creates heat when it starts to cure (or hydrate), and this heat should not really exceed 70 °C otherwise the durability of the concrete may be affected. The concrete is left to cure, during which time it gains strength and becomes hard. The formwork around the concrete element is typically stripped (removed) after 3–7 days. Protection may be installed thereafter unless there are any finishing works to carry out. This general process of activities is repeated until the concrete works in the building are complete. In construction programming, there is a conscious attempt to schedule these types of 'wet' trades as early as possible to allow drying out time.

In the last five years the UK cement and concrete industry has undertaken a major research programme on in-situ building techniques, the results of which can be found on a series of Best Practice leaflets. These leaflets include advice on early striking of formwork, reinforcement, strength testing and acceptance of ready-mixed concrete. Useful information on floor types, construction methods, research projects and innovations in in-situ concrete can also be obtained from the Reinforced Concrete Council.

Precast production

Precast concrete elements are made principally in the same way as in-situ concrete, but off site, in a factory. Working off site means that the concrete can be produced under cover, on a 24-hour cycle in controlled conditions to high degrees of accuracy. While this brings durability and architectural quality benefits, there can be a cost premium associated with precast concrete owing to the upkeep of the factory and its staff. However this initial capital increase can be significantly offset by long-term performance benefits. In non-architectural precast concrete work, repeat production of standard units helps to keep costs down. Mould making for architectural concrete (sometimes called pattern making) is a skilled job and precasters tend to look for high numbers of re-use from each mould to gain economies of scale. Moulds can be made from timber, steel or GRP. Some are used only once, but wherever possible precasters aim to get as many possible re-uses as they can from a mould. Hence, early discussions between the precaster and the architect would be directed at striking a balance between architectural intention and production efficiency.

Like in-situ concrete, most precast concrete units require reinforcing to be set out in the mould before pouring the concrete, which is batched at the factory. The factory operates on a production line with the final stages being given over mould stripping and finishing methods such as acid etching. The completed units are stored on the premises until they are taken for delivery to site. Non-architectural precast might use a simpler set of processes because it requires no specialist finishes. Precast units are designed to fit on a truck (for transport to site) and because they are produced off-site are not considered as 'wet' construction. Hence, the products of this dry concrete construction method are often installed later than in-situ concrete.

Precast concrete products include columns, beams, floor and wall panels, blocks and cladding. Many companies also produce precast concrete modules for residential and other types of accommodation such as prisons. In Europe, it is very typical to see fully fitted, precast concrete prefabricated bathroom 'pods' arriving on site. These save time on the construction programme and reduce the need for follow-on trades on site. Modular or panelised precast concrete units can also be used for hotel, student or residential accommodation where there are high degrees of repetition and a market for the high quality direct surface finishes offered by precasters. Information on precast concrete can be obtained from the British Precast Concrete Federation.

Hybrid construction

It is also feasible to combine in situ and precast construction methods to suit a particular project. This 'hybrid' concrete construction can increase speed of construction dramatically as it helps to streamline the construction programme. However, as we have seen above, these techniques are very different and so planning the construction of a hybrid structure must take these differences into account to maximise the possible speed and quality benefits. Research on the business case for hybrid concrete construction shows that there are long-term value benefits of combining in situ and precast, but these are not necessarily reflected in the initial capital costs, indeed a whole-life costing approach is more suitable in this case. Hybrid concrete structures in the UK include:

- Toyota HQ, Epsom, Surrey;
- Bracken House, City of London;
- Broadwalk House, City of London;
- Princess Margaret Hospital, Swindon.

There are many examples of hybrid concrete construction throughout the world, which can be found in the publications listed below.

Further reading

Bennett, D. (2001) *Exploring concrete architecture – tone, texture and form*, Birkhäuser, Basle, Switzerland.

British Standards Institution, BS8110: *Structural concrete*, BSI, London, UK

Building Research Establishment/CONSTRUCT (2001) *National structural concrete specification*, BRE, Watford, UK.

Glass, J. (1999) *The future for precast concrete in low rise housing*, British Precast Concrete Federation, Leicester, UK.

Glass, J. (2001) *Ecoconcrete: the contribution of cement and concrete to a more sustainable environment*, Reinforced Concrete Council, Crowthorne, UK.

Goodchild, C.H. (1995) *Hybrid concrete construction*, Reinforced Concrete Council, Crowthorne, UK.

Goodchild, C.H. (1997) *Economic concrete frame elements*, Reinforced Concrete Council, Crowthorne, UK.

JG

Condensation

Where two materials, elements or layers of air meet, there may be differences in their thermal transmittance, which can lead to the formation of water droplets (condensation).

See also: AIRTIGHTNESS; CONNECTIONS; CORROSION; ENERGY EFFICIENCY; INSULATION; MAINTENANCE; ROOFS; THERMAL BRIDGING; THERMAL COMFORT; VENTILATION; WINDOWS AND CURTAIN WALLING.

What is condensation?

Condensation (i.e. the forming of water droplets as a condensate) is caused at edge or boundary conditions between materials or layers of air at different temperatures. If the drop in temperature causes water in the air or material to drop below its 'dew' point it will condense to form droplets. Air carries moisture naturally, and inside buildings the level of moisture is sometimes high due to people cooking and breathing. In this case, condensation is likely to occur at points in and around the building envelope where the warm moist air of the interior meets the cooler drier air outside or the cooler elements in the building fabric. The first indication of condensation is slight dampness, progressing through visible water droplets and finally running streams of condensate (e.g. on a single glazed window in a kitchen in winter).

Types of condensation

The roof of a building is a particularly vulnerable area for condensation because warm, moist air in the building rises naturally to this point. Walls and floors may be less susceptible, unless there is any thermal bridging. Windows and other openings are the most likely places to see condensation as the number of layers (interstices) between interior and exterior are minimised so the dew point is reached on the glass itself. The key to preventing condensation in a building is usually to adhere to Building Regulations by providing adequate ventilation (and thereby also preventing sick building syndrome), which removes warm moist air from the problem area.

Thermal bridging – this occurs where elements of the building run continuously between interior and exterior, effectively forming a bridge. Exposed or expressed structural elements are very vulnerable. Condensation can form easily and in any season. Hence the Building Regulations require thermal breaks and appropriate insulation details to prevent problems occurring (for more detail see *Thermal bridging*).

Interstitial condensation – this unseen and dangerous form of condensation occurs within the fabric of the building, and so is invisible to the occupants. Here, the dew point occurs physically at a point within the fabric and so damage may go on unnoticed in a building for some years. Interstitial condensation is found on or around walls, insulation, a cold roof, or in double-glazing. The layer of moisture that forms initially provides an easy route for heat loss, and then could go on to freeze, cause corrosion or rot the insulation. Ideally to prevent interstitial condensation a vapour barrier should be incorporated to exclude moist air from getting in contact with the warm side of the fabric and using ventilation plus breather gaps on the cold face of the envelope. This type of condensation demands particular care as unless it is prevented, it may develop unseen prior to the onset of serious material damage that is visible to occupants.

It should be noted however, that in cavity wall construction, interstitial condensation may form naturally (and is designed to do so) on the cavity side of the inside leaf and drains down the cavity harmlessly or is cleared by trickle ventilation.

JG

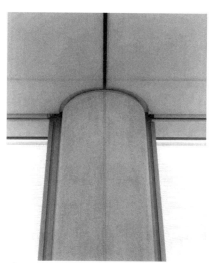

Column to floor connection detail in the offices of the Toyota GB Headquarters (Sheppard Robson Architects). The precast concrete elements have been designed carefully to create a crisp, elegant connection. Photograph by Barry Bulley, courtesy of Trent Precast Concrete Ltd.

Connections

The materials and methods by which structural or non-structural elements are connected, part of detailed design.

See also: BESPOKE; CASTINGS; CLADDING; CONCRETE; DESIGN LIFE; DURABILITY; FAÇADES AND FAÇADE ENGINEERING; FRAME; 'HONESTY'; PLASTICS; SEALANTS; STRUCTURAL STEEL; SURFACE FINISHES; TIMBER; TOLERANCE.

Definitions

A 'connection' or 'interface' describes any instance where different structural elements or materials are joined, sealed, fastened together, jointed, meet or where structural forces are transferred.

Although 'joint' is the more traditional terminology, this is now more commonly used to describe timber connections or the mortar layers between adjacent layers of brickwork, except for movement joints and expansion joints, which are special cases. The former is a connection that allows some degree of movement between elements, for example a hinged connection to allow a façade to 'flex' a little under strong wind loads without being restrained unnecessarily by the primary structure. The generic 'control' joint is an expansion (movement) joint. This is used for example in bridge construction to allow the road surface to expand and contract with temperature changes. However, this entry looks at connections in a generic sense, i.e. the many and varied interfaces within a building where the design team has an opportunity to 'make its mark'. To quote Mies van der Rohe, 'God is in the detail', simply meaning that detail design is where the opportunity for genuine exploration and flair exists for the architect.

Architectural note

The art of designing, specifying and detailing high quality architectural connections is a book in its own right and one needs only to look at the architectural 'greats' of the 20th century to see what can be achieved via even the simplest door handle. Indeed, the scale of connections varies from the detailing of a metal balustrade to the structural design of a concrete column-beam connector. In many instances, the connections, joints or interfaces that are used throughout buildings are commonplace, simple to install and not usually seen by people. The connections between structural elements often go unseen, as do most details in domestic construction unless one lives in a converted barn, where the timber jointing is exposed as standard practice.

However, in landmark buildings, or ones in which the designer wishes to make a particular statement in the way materials are used, then we might expect to see connections between elements of structure shown, expressed and detailed for this purpose. The Modernist principle of 'honesty' is explained in a separate entry, but it is clear that the notion of expressing different structural elements or materials in a structure is key to achieving this sort of crisp, clean architecture. Connections provide architects with a marvellous opportunity to demonstrate their skills in this regard.

Functions of a connection

Although the prime consideration for a connection from the designer's point of view is its aesthetics, this may be only one factor to be addressed. In structural connections the transfer or forces, environmental movements and thermal expansion coefficients may determine design to a greater extent. Depending on the materials used, then production techniques such as casting will also influence the design.

It is vital that both architect and engineer are aware that the creation of a 'bespoke' (tailor-made) connection will have cost and time implications. Standardised connections may be feasible for domestic scale construction. However, where the designer wishes to make an architectural statement by creating a unique and bespoke fitting for structural glazing connectors for example, the items may need to be designed from first principles. The cost implications of doing this for every element or connection within a building are usually too onerous to be considered, and so one might expect to see only particular details highlighted and considered in more depth. However, it is feasible to design exciting connections without going down the bespoke route.

Connection design checklist

A number of issues need to be considered if a bespoke connection or fitting is being designed from first principles, these include the following:

- Appropriate materials and particular characteristics (e.g. metals, plastics or other;)
- Cost to produce (and/or replicate at a later date);
- Dimensional tolerance;
- Installation constraints or conditions;
- Likely need for structural movement;
- Likely replacement interval;
- Need for resistance to damage from traffic or impact;
- Number of units/repetition (for manufacturing economy);
- Options for gaskets (e.g. materials like neoprene and 'Compriband');
- Predicted design life of the elements and connection;
- Production methods;
- Thermal expansion compatibility.

Built examples

Many buildings exhibit excellent practice in the design of connections. Carlo Scarpa's Castelvecchio Museum in Verona, Italy demonstrates perhaps the greatest extent to which the majority of connections in any one building can be designed with care and utmost attention to detail. The works of Herman Hertzberger, Norman Foster and Alvar Aalto are also particularly worth looking at; notice especially the connections between elements of structure, where the architects have chosen to visually emphasise the structural hierarchies in the building.

Further reading

Brookes, A. (1998) *Cladding of buildings* (3ʳᵈ edition), E & FN Spon, London, UK.

Brookes, A. & Grech, C. (1996) *Building envelope & connections*, Butterworth-Heinemann, Oxford, UK.

Dawson, S. *Architect's Journal working details*, Volumes 1–7, EMAP Construct, London, UK.

Wakita, O.A. & Linde, R.M. (1999) *The professional practice of architectural detailing* (3ʳᵈ edition) John Wiley & Sons, New York, USA.

JG

Construction programme

A 'plan of work' showing various construction activities from mobilisation on site to hand-over, which are described in terms of timing and sometimes the resources allocated to the activities.

See also: BESPOKE; BUILDABILITY; CRITICAL PATH ANALYSIS; INTEGRATION; 'JUST-IN-TIME' CONSTRUCTION; LEAD-TIME; 'LEAN' CONSTRUCTION; OFF-SITE MANUFACTURE; ON-SITE PRODUCTION; PROCUREMENT; RISK MANAGEMENT; VALUE ENGINEERING.

What is a construction programme?

The successful organisation of the many activities that are undertaken on a construction site is vitally important, but this cannot happen by chance – it is totally dependent on pre-planning before any work begins on site. At an early stage of design it will be possible to sketch the approximate amount of time to complete the project and as more details are agreed, this rough idea can be formalised into a timetable of activities. This timetable becomes the 'construction programme' when contracts are let to those companies that will manufacture, install or erect parts of the new building. All construction products or packages of work need to be timetabled: items produced off site must be integrated with those activities that will be based on site. The careful 'choreographing' of these activities (on and off site) is a skilled job and takes experience. Contractual matters and other requirements (such as those listed below) need to be taken into account from an early stage in the project.

Factors to be taken into account

- Availability of labour;
- Client requirements e.g. on completion dates;
- Contingency plans;
- Contracts and procurement routes;
- Delivery schedules;
- Health and safety aspects;
- Lead-times on products and materials;
- Site access (restrictions such as power lines etc);
- Statutory holidays;
- Union requirements.

If we take, for example, a simple warehouse project, the construction programme would show many activities with some degree of overlap as different trades start and finish on site. These include groundworks, foundations, structural frame, cladding, landscaping and interior fit-out. Clearly it is necessary to have completed at least part of the foundations before the structural steel for the frame arrives, but the foundations can be ongoing and the tasks can overlap. When the basic envelope is complete both external landscaping and internal finishing can go on at the same time, as they are independent of one another. Even for this simple building, there will be a 'critical path' through the construction programme (i.e. a 'map' of activities on which the progress of others is totally dependent).

The role of the construction manager

For some projects, it may be necessary to organise the procurement process to include a project manager and/or a construction manager. The latter is responsible in particular for the more practical aspects of the project. Large projects such as high-rise offices, shopping centres, airports or railway stations may have a construction management company in charge of managing the whole construction process (and its many attendant specialist sub-contractors). An experienced construction manager will be an invaluable member of the project team in advising on different programming scenarios, for example overcoming restrictions on site access or working hours. There may be alternative approaches that could save weeks from the overall programme and the manager should also have a 'toolkit' of strategies to deal with unexpected delays or problems when the project does get underway on site. The construction manager should also have a good appreciation of the relative trade-offs that can be made between construction costs and the cost of time. For example, the erection of steelwork, plant and cladding for a high-rise building may be streamlined if the 'hook time' on tower cranes is optimised. Manipulation of programmes is now easier with IT: some construction programmes will show tasks, time on site and allocated resources (staff and equipment). There are a number of computer packages that can help co-ordinate all these aspects together e.g. Primavera.

Further reading

Allinson, K. (1998) *Getting there by design: an architect's guide to project and design management*, Butterworth-Heinemann, Oxford, UK.

Gray, C. & Hughes, W. (2000) *Building design management*, Butterworth-Heinemann, Oxford, UK.

Harris, F. & McCaffer, R. (2000) *Modern construction management* (5th edition), Blackwell Science, Oxford, UK.

JG

Cooling

See: AIR-CONDITIONING; FABRIC ENERGY STORAGE; HVAC; NIGHT VENTILATION; VENTILATION

Copper

A commonly used metal found in roofing, cladding and plumbing.

See also: ALUMINIUM; CEILINGS; CLADDING; CORROSION; DESIGN LIFE; DURABILITY; ECOLOGICAL DESIGN; GALVANISING; HERZOG & DE MEURON; LOUVRES AND BRISE SOLEIL; METALS; ROOFS; SERVICES; STAINLESS STEEL; STANDING SEAM ROOF; SURFACE FINISHES; TIMBER – PRODUCTION AND FINISHES; WEATHERING; WINDOWS AND CURTAIN WALLING; ZINC.

What is copper?

Copper is a common reddish metallic element that is durable, ductile and malleable and one of the best conductors of heat and electricity. It can be found in buildings being used for roofing and cladding, but it has also been used extensively for plumbing pipework, although this has been superseded somewhat by the development of plastic pipework. Copper has been worked for thousands of years, perhaps as early as 7,000 BC but its use grew immeasurably when it was found that the addition of tin (to make bronze) made it much stronger.

The metal occurs as a sulphide ore with only a tiny fraction of copper present; hence it has to be concentrated through about five separate processes, until purification produces 99.9% pure copper. This extraction and processing yields large amounts of heavy metal contaminated waste and toxic emissions to air. Production of copper from the ore is energy intensive. Its embodied energy is estimated at 70 MJ/kg and about seven tonnes of carbon dioxide are produced per tonne of copper produced from ore. However, copper is recyclable: carbon dioxide emissions drop significantly when recycled copper is utilised. About 40% of copper used in the UK comes from recycled scrap.

Types of copper and its alloys

Copper is produced in sheets, foil, wire and rod forms, which can be supplied to varying degrees of hardness, although it can always be worked and re-worked, even at room temperature. There are four main grades of copper, which are designated by their uses, i.e.

- C101 – this is a very pure grade suitable for electrical work or roof sheeting;
- C102 – this is similar but contains more impurities;
- C104 – this can be used for any building purpose;
- C106 – this is used for plumbing, hot water tanks and roofing, but not electrical work.

A range of alloys can be made from copper with the additions of zinc, tin, aluminium and nickel; the alloys are termed brasses or bronzes. Brass is an alloy of copper with zinc and is typically used for small building components such as door furniture, balustrades and handrails. **Bronze** is an alloy of copper with tin, is slightly harder than brass and is used for stone fixings and decorative work such as castings. Other alloys include **gunmetals**, made from copper, tin and zinc, which tend to be very strong and durable e.g. castings on Bracken House in the City of London by Michael Hopkins & Partners.

Uses and applications

Copper is a durable material that is worked easily, making it a valuable material for roofing and ornamental work. Copper roofing can last up to 100 years or more and has a high degree of resistance to corrosion. Copper is used in continuously supported sheets no larger than 1.3 m^2 and 0.4–0.7 mm thick, with specification depending on the exposure and atmospheric pollution conditions and required design life. The roofing can be installed as a standing seam system for roof pitches from 3° to 45°, with different fixing configurations. The four main finish types are: normal copper, pre-oxidised (dark brown), pre-patinated (green) and tinned (matte grey).

Copper roofing changes attractively upon exposure, taking on a green patina that protects the metal sheeting. The characteristic patina develops in five to ten years, depending on the atmospheric conditions. Heavy air pollution eventually turns the metal very dark brown. On vertical surfaces, the rainwater run-off prevents the patina building up, so one might chose pre-patinated copper instead (i.e. where the development of the patina has been accelerated in the factory). Copper roofing can be found on many buildings in its normal or pre-patinated forms e.g. the Hammersmith Ark building in London, by Ralph Erskine. Standing seam copper sheets clad the Dutch National Heritage Museum at Arnheim by Mecanoo: a half-sunker, egg-shaped volume that would be difficult to clad in anything else!

The use of copper to convey water goes back to Egyptian times, 5,000 years ago. Copper pipework was used extensively in buildings for hot water and cold water installations. The material is durable and has a long life. Until the 1960s copper pipe-work systems for drainage and sanitation was widespread. Two factors helped in the demise of what was an essential craft of plumbers and hot water engineers. The introduction of plastic pipework, which could be cut with a saw, and the demise of skilled workers who had the art and patience to sand or lead fill large pipes prior to annealing and bending in special machines. Plastic pipework also replaced copper in floors (e.g. for underfloor heating) because the presence of phosphorus in the copper and ammonia in the concrete can cause the copper to crack.

Copper can also be used to preserve timber in what are known as CCAs (copper-chromium-arsenic formulations), which are poisonous to insects and fungi. These compounds are actually found in many paints and varnishes and although they have been linked to human nervous disorders as well as damage to liver and kidneys, there are no UK regulations governing use. Despite their effectiveness in performance terms, their relative toxicity has meant that they are 'blacklisted' by the more ecologically conscious designers.

Compatible materials

In accordance with the galvanic series, designers should exercise caution when using copper in combination with a number of materials. If in doubt, the British Standards BS2870, BS2874 and BS2875 or relevant literature should be consulted, most of which is very informative, showing good practice details for this metal.

In most instances, copper is the aggressive element and causes other materials to corrode (because it is at the opposite end of the galvanic series to most other metals used in construction). As copper is used as a roofing material there is high risk of corrosion via rainwater runoff onto other materials. Although very resistant to corrosion, copper itself can be corroded by bitumen, bitumen paint and acidic runoff from western red cedar. It may be damaged locally by splashes of wet cement or mortar, but this can be made good.

The following materials will be corroded by copper (depending on individual circumstances):

- Aluminium;
- Galvanised steel;
- Iron;
- Stainless steel;
- Steel;
- Zinc.

WH/JG

Core (services)

Spaces within a building that are designated for the distribution of services, usually enclosed and often used in partial fulfilment of the structural requirement for bracing.

See also: AIR-CONDITIONING; BRACING; CORE (STRUCTURAL); ENVIRONMENTAL DESIGN; FIRE ENGINEERING; FABRIC ENERGY STORAGE; FRAME; HVAC; ICT IN BUILDINGS; INTEGRATION; MAINTENANCE; PHOTOVOLTAICS; RISERS AND TRUNKING; SERVICES; VENTILATION; YEANG, KEN.

What is a service core?

In large, complex and highly serviced buildings, there is a need to consider carefully both the horizontal and vertical distribution routes for services such as power, HVAC ducting and ICT cabling. HVAC, electrical & water systems usually require some 6–9% of the gross floor area of a building (based on CIBSE guidance). In some instances, the size of the building or pattern of occupancy may allow very localised siting of plant and equipment. However, deep plan forms and heavy servicing demands usually dictate that 'cores' are designated for primary service routing. While this allows total flexibility of design, it can have implications for cost, maintenance and long-term patterns of use. Hence, the discussion arises whether services should be designed as autonomous cores or, whether a bespoke arrangement (in which services and structures are more integrated) is most appropriate. This is a complex decision-making process, which will invariably depend on the individual circumstances of a project, but the following information provides some general guidance.

Autonomous service cores

If we take the example of office buildings, then the main reason for their existence is to generate rental income per unit area. Thus the aim in terms of servicing is to maximise the floor area, keeping services (and structure) isolated from the main occupied spaces. As such, it is common to see enclosed concrete shafts at the centre (or at evenly distributed points) on the plan, which contain the lifts, stairs and servicing elements, together with plant rooms at top, base and sometimes intermediate floor levels. In high-rise buildings the vertical core elements are also used as structural stiffening against wind forces, but this is not always the case. Central lift cores are a commonplace element of all deep-plan offices as well as high-rise skyscraper buildings (e.g. Seagram Building, Mies van der Rohe, 1958; Broadgate Centre, London, SOM & Arup Associates, 1988). Some of the earliest examples can be seen in US skyscrapers from the turn of the 20th century, such as Frank Lloyd Wright's Larkin building in Buffalo (1904). In these cases, there is a strong business case for maximising the floor area, but they run a risk of increasing life-cycle costs (e.g. maintenance) if the services strategy does not allow for sufficient flexibility in occupancy. Thus, there is a delicate balance between achieving long term 'lettability' and providing service core(s) with long-term flexibility. Some developers would probably anticipate over-charging to cover what they would consider inevitable refurbishment costs.

Bespoke service cores

This option is based on the assumption that centralised or autonomous cores simply do not allow the building to fulfil its long term design, energy or environmental potential. If greater effort is put into a project-specific solution at the design stage, then there is a chance that a better building may result. For example, during the Industrial Revolution cast iron columns became conduits for steam heating; their contemporary equivalent Termodeck™ uses structural concrete hollowcore floor units to convey air as a heating and cooling medium. These types of solution mean that servicing can be less centralised and less reliant on cores – in a way an 'incremental' step change for servicing strategies. The Lloyds Building in London (1986) and its predecessor the Pompidou Centre in Paris (Renzo Piano & Richard Rogers, 1973), both raised awareness of the opportunities for taking services out of cores and putting them 'on show'. The lifts, escalators and even bathroom pods are situated on the outside, allowing maximum use of space at the centre of the building. However, these buildings were both for 'owner-occupiers', unlike the previous example.

An alternative approach

In the new generation of ecological buildings, as seen in Malaysian architect Ken Yeang's work, energy generation is local and part of the skin of the building, e.g. using photovoltaic arrays. Water distribution can also be based on the façade using recycling of 'greywater'. This type of approach actually removes the need for service cores altogether because their only function is to carry services from a plant room to an end point. Conceptual designs by Battle McCarthy for a courthouse project in the USA do not feature large service cores, because a huge PV wall will produce more energy than required, coupled to a natural stack ventilation system and a thermolabyrinth device. This example is more than an incremental change, it is a cultural shift in services design!

Endnote

The decision about the allocation of space to services on plan and in section is often left too late and taken without adequate input from a building services engineer. In successful buildings, particularly those taking a more forward-looking approach to services provision, the close involvement of these engineers has been the key to achieving the design/environmental intention. Therefore, this collaboration is to be recommended.

Whatever strategy is used, it is vital that adequate space to repair, clean and maintain any plant or engineering services is provided, and in all routes certain services must be separated such as electrical from water, riser ducts for fire purposes.

Further reading

Baird, G. (2001) *The architectural expression of environmental control systems*, E & FN Spon, London, UK.
Yeang, K. (2000) *Service cores in buildings*, Academy Editions, John Wiley & Sons, London, UK.

WH/JG

Core (structural)

A structural core includes elements of structure that provide the lateral stability to the building.

See also: BRACING; CANTILEVERS; CONCRETE; CORE (SERVICES); FRAMES; GRIDS FOR STRUCTURE AND LAYOUT; INTEGRATION; RISERS AND TRUNKING.

Introduction

The need for service cores is discussed in the previous entry (*see* Core (services)). This entry is a structural account of the role that cores can play, particularly in relation to buildings of different heights. It goes without saying that the decision-making process for the structural frame and overall structural solution for a high-rise building will go on in parallel with the discussion regarding services strategy.

The need for stability

As well as supporting vertical load due to self-weight and occupants, all buildings must have a system to resist horizontal loads and provide stability to the building. The most common horizontal loads are from the wind; though in some parts of the world seismic loads from earthquakes will be more important. The system must also provide stability so that the vertical load does not excessively magnify any out-of-plumb of the building or deflections due to horizontal loads. The frame can resist horizontal loads by relying on the rigidity of the connections between beams and columns. However an efficient way of providing the strength and stiffness that is required is to use walls or

In-situ concrete cores under construction – this example shows how major elements such as lift shafts and staircases can be erected early on in the construction programme. The main structural frame usually follows on shortly afterwards. Common applications are residential accommodation, offices and hospitals. Photo courtesy of the Reinforced Concrete Council.

pairs of columns connected by bracing. Connecting the pairs of columns together by bracing forms a 'braced bay'. Although the walls or braced bays can have some holes (e.g. for doorways), these will be limited. They therefore need to be located where they will not hinder the use of the building by the occupants. The logical location for these elements is around fixed items such as lifts, staircases and service risers, i.e. around the service cores of the buildings. Often the walls can be arranged to form a box, which will increase the structural efficiency. When the core includes structural elements that provide the stability of the building it is termed a 'structural core'.

Cores and building height

In many low- and medium-rise buildings there will be more than one structural core. The main banks of lifts are obvious locations and usually provide the largest core. Other service cores (e.g. fire escape stairs) can also be used to provide perimeter structural cores. Because these will be distributed around the building this technique gives a good distribution of horizontal load-resisting elements. This factor can be important to resist torsional forces, i.e. to prevent the building from twisting. For taller buildings, the main core will usually increase in size relative to the floor plan. Because the perimeter cores do not increase in size the main core provides most of the structure and the perimeter cores become non-structural. The torsional stiffness is provided by the large main core. It is generally preferable to give the occupants the perimeter spaces on the floors so the main core is usually in the centre of the building. This type of building can be referred to as a 'central core' building. The strength, and more importantly, the stiffness required of the stability system increases at a greater rate than its height. Above a certain height of building a central core by itself cannot efficiently provide what is required. A totally different system can be used or the core can be helped by adding outriggers, which are stiff arms attached to the core that reach out to the columns at the perimeter of the building. As the core tries to bend they reduce the rotation at the outrigger locations and therefore increase the stiffness.

Further reading

Institution of Structural Engineers (1988) *Stability of buildings*, Institution of Structural Engineers, London, UK.

OA

Corrosion

Metals generally have a tendency to combine with oxygen and atmospheric pollutants to form oxides and salts. This is referred to as corrosion, and is a property that designers usually seek to control or eliminate.

See also: ALUMINIUM; CONCRETE; CONNECTIONS; COPPER; COR-TEN; DESIGN LIFE; DURABILITY; EPOXY; GALVANISING; LEAD; METALS; PERFORMANCE; STAINLESS STEEL; STRUCTURAL STEEL; SURFACE FINISHES; TIMBER – PRODUCTION AND FINISHES; WEATHERING; ZINC.

Corrosion is one aspect within the umbrella term 'building pathology' (see references below). There are two broad types of corrosion, which are to some extent inter-related. These are discussed in turn.

Atmospheric corrosion

Most metals will combine easily with moisture and the oxygen in the air to revert towards their unrefined state. In practice, this is a complex electrochemical process, and can be aggravated by the presence of acidic or alkaline compounds in the atmosphere, or in adjacent materials. Generally, the more effort required in extraction of a metal from its ore, the less stable it is likely to be in corrosive environments. Some 'noble' metals are found naturally in their metallic state. For some metals, the first formation of an oxide film is sufficient to arrest or prevent further corrosion. The widespread use of aluminium, zinc, lead, copper, and stainless steel rely largely on this factor. Nevertheless, repeated wetting and drying cycles in exposed conditions can cause repeated loss and renewal of these oxide films on some metals, which will cause degradation, but at a slower rate. If oxidisation does not result in a stable and continuous film, successive layers of the unprotected metal can become exposed and corrosion will continue. Structural steel corrodes in this way, and therefore usually requires a regime of protection to suit particular uses and applications.

Bimetallic corrosion

A major source of concern in building is bimetallic corrosion, where dissimilar metals come into contact with each other through a conductive medium or, indeed, direct contact aided by the presence of moisture. A 'galvanic cell' is formed between the metals, the severity of which depends on their relative positions in the **galvanic series** (and the differential polarity causing the movement of ions between the two). The farther apart the metals are on the list below (i.e. the greater the polarity), the greater the potential for corrosion.

Anode (negative, −ive end): Base metals

Magnesium
Zinc
Aluminium
Cadmium
Iron, mild steel
Chromium
Lead
Tin
Nickel
Brass
Stainless steel
Bronze
Copper
Silver

Cathode (positive, + ive end): Noble metals

In practical terms there are a number of common situations that should be avoided (or specialist advice sought) due to bimetallic corrosion. Among these are stainless steel with galvanised steel, and copper with iron or steel, aluminium, or zinc. Contact area is a key factor, with a small anode/large cathode being the worst case. The use of galvanised steel fasteners with stainless steel cladding, for example, can lead to localised corrosion around the contact.

Conditions of corrosion are invariably aggravated by a number of environmental factors:

- Acid runoff (e.g. some timbers, atmospheric pollutants);
- Alkaline runoff (e.g. cements and plasters, atmospheric pollutants);

- High temperatures;
- Marine locations (i.e. salt atmosphere);
- Metallic salt runoff (e.g. from copper roofs into aluminium gutters);
- Some timber treatments (e.g. tanalising is not suitable for use with galvanised steel fittings);
- Sulphates and chlorides in surface water run-off and ground water;
- Warm, moist atmosphere can increase corrosion rates tenfold, especially in tropical/marine locations.

Prevention and protection

The following strategies and techniques are commonly used:

Care in specification: The adjacency of dissimilar metals relative to their position in the galvanic series should be considered, and expert advice sought from manufacturers and suppliers.

Coatings: Paints, epoxy powder coating, and similar are applied to the bare metal during manufacture or on site, in order to protect the metal from atmospheric corrosion. The durability of epoxy coatings makes them suitable for limiting bimetallic corrosion in some cases.

Isolation gaskets: Neoprene washers and gaskets are used for bimetallic risk in contact areas, especially with fasteners and brackets.

Plating and anodising: Protective metallic layers (plating) or oxide films (anodising) are applied to the metal. Metallic layers are also applied to aluminium (sacrificial alloys) or steel (lead) by a rolling/bonding process.

Sacrificial anode (cathodic protection): The use of galvanising forms in effect a layer that corrodes preferentially to the substrate metal. This is particularly effective around damaged areas on galvanised steel, to the extent that an exposed cut edge on a light gauge galvanised steel component will be protected for some time by the zinc that surrounds it. The principle is also used in the protection of concrete encased steelwork in damp conditions, and specialist techniques have been developed arresting deterioration of cast iron frame structures.

Further reading

Harris, S.Y. (2001) *Building pathology: deterioration, diagnostics and intervention*, John Wiley & Sons, New York, USA.

Parnham, P. (1997) *Prevention of premature staining of new buildings*, E &FN Spon, London, UK.

Watt, D. (1999) *Building pathology: principles and practice*, Blackwell Science, Oxford, UK.

GW

COR-TEN® (weathering steel)

This is a particular type of steel that has greater resistance to atmospheric corrosion than normal grades of steel. Its architectural opportunities lie in the fact that it is designed to corrode to a deep russet colour.

A major application of COR-TEN steel on the Shanks Millennium bridge, over the River Nene at Peterborough. Photograph courtesy of Fairfield Mabey, Chepstow.

See also: CLADDING; CORROSION; DESIGN LIFE; FAÇADES AND FAÇADE ENGINEERING; 'HONESTY'; METALS; STRUCTURAL STEEL; SURFACE FINISHES; WEATHERING.

Introduction

COR-TEN® is a high strength, low alloy weathering steel. The original formulation was patented in 1933 by US Steel, based on an observation that copper-bearing steel offered improved corrosion resistance. Altering the chemical composition of carbon steel by increasing the percentage of certain trace elements (phosphorus, silicon, nickel, chromium, and notably copper), produces a steel alloy that offers greater resistance to atmospheric corrosion, and significantly higher yield strength. This material (now referred to as COR-TEN 'A') was used first for coal hopper railway wagons, where its higher resistance to impact damage and the corrosive effects of sulphur in the coal extended the useful life of the wagons considerably.

About the surface finish

Under corrosive conditions the composition of the COR-TEN alloy creates an oxide film that adheres to the metal substrate so as to discourage its further oxidation in normal wetting/drying cycles. By comparison, the oxide film on conventional steels is penetrated by water at each successive wetting, causing repeated corrosion of the metal. COR-TEN's corrosion resistant characteristics in conditions that are continuously wet are comparable to that of carbon steels.

COR-TEN comes in plate sizes of up to about 8 mm thick. It can be used bare or painted, according to the environment in which it is to be placed. When used bare, the oxide layer takes on a rich colour varying from russet to deep purple (depending on its environment). This is the feature that makes designers choose this type of steel. COR-TEN gives designers the option to use steel in an 'honest' way, allowing it to corrode naturally while remaining structurally intact. When painted finishes are specified (e.g. in highly corrosive atmospheres), the surface finish provides good adhesion for the paint, and its own surface characteristics reduce the extent of corrosion where the paint finish is damaged.

There are a few design conditions that govern the use of this metal. Rainwater run-off from bare COR-TEN can cause staining, at first, from insoluble iron oxide on certain adjacent surfaces. In addition, cathodic action (between dissimilar metals) makes it necessary to specify fasteners and other components with care.

Uses for COR-TEN

The weathering and corrosion resistant properties of COR-TEN make it popular for architectural and structural use, and also for other exposed applications such as:

- Bridges;
- Cargo containers;
- Communications masts;
- Construction in industrial settings;
- Motorway crash barriers;
- Lamp posts;
- Storage tanks.

As with all specialist materials, guidance in specification will ensure that correct use is made of its finish and environmental behaviour. It is recommended that for architectural use of COR-TEN the manufacturer or licensee should be consulted over matters of usage and detailing.

Recently built examples in the UK include the Crystal Palace concert platform in London by Ian Ritchie Architects and a footbridge over the River Nene at Peterborough by engineers Whitby Bird & Partners. The latter uses COR-TEN as a response to the rural context to provide a stimulating crossing for pedestrians and cyclists using the town's sustainable transport network, the 'Green Wheel'.

Notes

COR-TEN® is a registered trademark of USX Corporation.

GW

Critical path analysis

Planning of important construction activities, on which other activities are dependent.

See also: CONSTRUCTION PROGRAMME; 'JUST-IN-TIME' CONSTRUCTION; LEAD-TIME; 'LEAN' CONSTRUCTION; OFF-SITE MANUFACTURE; ON-SITE PRODUCTION; PROCUREMENT; RISK MANAGEMENT; VALUE ENGINEERING.

Introduction – about planning

In construction programming, time is taken to plan out all the various activities that need to be undertaken both on and off site, for example groundworks, steel fabrication, installation of cladding and fit-out. These activities are set out against a time-scale so the construction manager has an overall picture of what should be happening and when, in order for the building to be completed/delivered on time. By setting out these activities it becomes clear that some are very much more important than others because future progress depends on their completion.

Any activities that directly affect the completion date for a project are called 'critical activities'. It is usual to find that there is a chain of these occurring along the time-scale of the construction programme – this is called the '**critical path**' and it represents the shortest possible time in which the project can be completed. The manipulation and management of the critical path is usually called critical path analysis, but the terms critical path method and critical path scheduling are also used. Typical activities on the critical path include:

- Foundations;
- Ground works;
- Lift shafts;
- Roofs;
- Services;
- Shear walls/service cores;
- Structural frames.

Some examples are given above of activities that quite literally underpin continued progress on site. Most are as expected; the foundations are needed to begin progress on the structural frame and the roof can be vital to permit follow-on trades (e.g. electrical and mechanical services contractors) to begin work. In some projects however, the path may turn out to be dependent on a rather unexpected item. For example:

- A footbridge linking two wings of a building, without which access is difficult;
- A large sculpture that has to be placed in an atrium before all glazing work is completed;

- Refrigeration equipment for a cold store that has to be installed early on;
- Major lighting installations in a football ground without which games cannot be played.

The critical activities effectively control the progress of the whole project; they need to be carried out successfully or there may be knock-on effects on other subsequent tasks. It is common for main contractors and construction managers to have considerable expertise in analysing construction programmes and manipulating the activities and their scheduling to better manage the critical path. Such expertise can help to deliver a building quickly and efficiently.

Managing the critical path

There is now much emphasis on trying to take activities off the critical path where possible, keeping it limited to just a few manageable tasks and therefore minimising the risk of time and cost over-runs. This is one of the major reasons for the recent drive towards a greater use of off-site fabrication, taking these activities off site and usually off the critical path. Nevertheless, site-based construction techniques such as in-situ concrete work are still used because they offer flexibility and the opportunity of working in parallel. Take the example of high-rise offices at Canary Wharf in London: slip-formed in-situ concrete structural service cores were being cast on site at the same time steelwork for the frame was being fabricated. When the concrete was a few weeks ahead, the steelwork was installed on site in parallel, the two activities meeting at the top of the building. Although the slip forms were on the critical path, the speed of erection and ability to work in parallel helped the contractors shorten the overall construction programme.

Computer software is available (e.g. Primavera) that manages the construction programme, costs, resources and critical path analysis. Such programs will test the critical path and allied activities, testing both forward and backward. It is important to keep updating and running these models during construction, particularly if any slippage (i.e. delay) has occurred.

Further reading

Allinson, K. (1998) *Getting there by design: an architect's guide to project and design management*, Butterworth-Heinemann, Oxford, UK.

Gray, C. & Hughes, W. (2000) *Building design management*, Butterworth-Heinemann, Oxford, UK.

Harris, F. & McCaffer, R. (2000) *Modern construction management* (5th edition), Blackwell Science, Oxford, UK.

Lockyer, K.G. (1984) *Critical path analysis and other project network technologies* (4th edition), Pitman, London, UK.

JG

Cross bracing
See: BRACING

Cross ventilation
See: NIGHT VENTILATION

Curtain walls
See: WINDOWS AND CURTAIN WALLING

Data cabling
See: ICT IN BUILDINGS

Daylighting
See: LIGHTING – DAYLIGHTING

Decking
See: COMPOSITE DECKING

De Meuron, Pierre
See: HERZOG AND DE MEURON

Design life
The predicted life of a building or component that defines the longevity and durability of the materials specified therein.

See also: BUILDABILITY; DURABILITY; LIFE-CYCLE COSTING; PERFORMANCE; SPECIFICATION.

Introduction
Buildings can be described as having a 'design life' of anything between a few weeks and hundreds of years. This design life is the notional life span of a building or component as predicted before it is designed, specified and constructed. Ascribing a design life of x amount of time to a building design effectively determines the type and quality of materials that will be used in it. The design life is therefore the period intended by the designer that, subject to normal maintenance, an element or structure should last for without the need for replacement or significant repair. Design life is also known in some documents by other terms such as design working life or intended working life.

How long is design life?
The design life of a structure should be at least equal to the required service life, i.e. the lifetime required by the client. This could be specified for the structure,

fittings, furnishing and services based on what the client intends. For example, clients developing a 'serviced office' might be very specific about the structure, services and major fittings they require, expecting them to be long lasting, as they will have to maintain them in the future. However, speculative housebuilders might simply wish to conform to the 10 year NHBC standard and offer the most basic design life for fittings etc. as they know the house purchaser may change them. For local authority and public sector work, design life may be specified exactly for particular types of buildings such as leisure centres, sheltered housing or offices. Private Finance Initiative (PFI) jobs require a 60-year design life. To illustrate how complex 'design life' can be, a temporary site office might only have a notional life on site of a few weeks, but the cabin can be re-used many times and so may have a total design life of 10–20 years.

For all these reasons, design life in the past has rarely been specified explicitly, but this is changing with the advent of service life design techniques and the birth of a new generation of standards and codes of practice. Classes of design life have been introduced into a number of recent standards. An example of design life classification [from ENV 1991-1: 1994] is given below.

Class	Required design life (years)	Example
1	1–5	Temporary structures.
2	25	Replaceable structural parts, e.g. girders, bearings.
3	50	Building structures and other common structures.
4	100	Monumental building structures, bridges, and other civil engineering structures.

By way of a specific example, houses are generally designed for a 60-year life, but it may be more useful to break this down into separate elements that might be replaced or refurbished at about the following intervals:

- Finishes 5 years
- Internal fittings 10 years
- Services 20 years
- Structure 50–60 years

Design life expectancy and service life

Design life is 'a building's life as predicted', but circumstances may change during the course of a building's life. This is why it may be more appropriate to use the term 'design life expectancy'. Although the deterioration processes of most materials are time-dependent it is not generally possible to predict reliably when the end of its service life will occur. The service life of an element or structure is the actual time in use before it has to be replaced or subjected to significant repair. Thus, the service life may in some cases be much shorter than the design life because of, say, obsolescence or redundancy. In other cases, the actual service life may well exceed design life as, for example, is the case for much domestic housing.

The design life of individual elements within a structure may actually be less than the required service life in which case they need to be replaceable. Thus the design life of the foundations and structural frame of a building needs to be at least equal to the required service life, whereas the window frames, cladding or roof tiles, for example, may be designed to be replaced. In considering design life the designer should also consider whether elements should be replaceable, maintainable or life-long. It is likely to be uneconomic or even impossible for all parts of a structure to have a design life equal to that of the structure itself. An example of suggested minimum design lives for components of buildings is given below (suggested minimum design lives for components from ISO 15686-1 (*Building and constructed assets – Service life planning – General principles*)).

Design life of building	Inaccessible or structural elements	Components where replacement is expensive or difficult	Major replaceable components	Building services services
Unlimited	Unlimited	100	40	25
150	150	100	40	25
100	100	100	40	25
60	60	60	40	25
25	25	25	25	25
15	15	15	15	15
10	10	10	10	10

NOTE 1 'Easy to replace' components may have design lives of 3 or 6 years
NOTE 2 An unlimited design life should very rarely be used, as it significantly reduces design options

There are examples of buildings being in service for much longer than was originally anticipated for many different reasons. Perhaps the most widespread in the UK were the 'prefabs' built as emergency housing during and after the Second World War. These modest prefabricated bungalows and houses were erected in many towns and cities as a rapid means of housing families who were made homeless during the War and as a stopgap while more traditional forms of housing were built. Despite being designed to last only a few years, many prefabs still exist today and some are Listed Buildings (i.e. protected by English Heritage as buildings with particular historical and/or architectural value).

What does design life mean for technology?

The impact of specifying a design life is that architecture should be designed accordingly, which may compromise or conflict with other agendas in the design process. Here are two rather extreme examples as a way of illustrating the implications of design life: a temporary exhibition centre and a university hall of residence.

1. Shortened life

For a temporary structure to house an exhibition, the specified design life expectancy might be just a few weeks. For the Cardiff Bay exhibition centre, architects Alsop & Stormer designed a lightweight timber structure using small, easily handled and transported components that could be both assembled and demounted quickly, without need for much equipment or labour. Construction details were simple but effective and although cost was limited the structure was of such significant architectural interest that it attracted visitors in its own right. For this reason the exhibition centre remained in place for some time after it was due to be dismantled. Fortunately, the structure and materials survived this time extension and the form of the building has inspired many designers since.

2. Extended life

In a significant new addition to Magdalen College Oxford, Demetri Porphyrios Architects designed a new range of buildings including student accommodation and a theatre (the Grove Buildings). The stone built structures complement the existing buildings and further develop the masterplan for the college, which began life in the late 15th century. The student accommodation in particular is of note because a design life of 200 years was specified. To achieve such longevity the materials and workmanship were of the highest quality to the extent that this was, at the time, the most expensive hall of residence for a UK university by a considerable margin. Carefully matched stonework construction, in addition to extensive bespoke hardwood joinery to the interiors, are clear indicators of quality and durability. That this building will last a very long time we can be sure as the construction materials are the same as those used in many Oxford buildings dating from 500 years ago.

Conclusion

Design for a specific life is difficult because of the generally large number of unknown factors, or factors such as environmental exposure, which are difficult to quantify. Study of performance of materials, elements and structures has shown repeatedly that nominally identical items can vary widely in service life in the same environment. As it is not possible to accurately predict actual service life, the design life can rarely be stated with certainty and should be considered as the life that can be expected with a high degree of probability. Statement of design life for a given element or structure, or selection or design of materials for a specific design life, must rely on one of a number of different approaches:

- Known performance over that lifetime;
- Extrapolation from performance over shorter periods;
- Judgement based on performance of similar items;
- Fundamental understanding of behaviour;
- Mathematical modelling based on degradation processes and known, measured or assumed properties.

Further reading

ENV 1991-1:1994, *Eurocode 1 – Basis of design and actions on structures* – Part 1: Basis of Design, European Pre-standard.
Housing Association Property Mutual (1991) *HAPM property component life manual*, E & FN Spon, London, UK.
ISO 15686-1:2000, *Buildings and constructed assets – service life planning* – Part 1: General principles.

OA/JG

Diagonal bracing
See: BRACING

Dimensional stability
See: BRACING

Dimensional tolerance
See: TOLERANCE

Dissimilar metals
See: CORROSION; METALS

DPC: damp proof course
See: FLOORS; RETAINING WALLS

DPM: damp proof membrane
See: FLOORS; RETAINING WALLS

Dry construction and wet construction

The categorisation of construction materials and components according to the moisture levels that they contain, release and/or absorb before, during and after construction.

See also: BRICKS AND BLOCKS; BUILDING SYSTEMS; CERAMICS; CONCRETE; CONSTRUCTION PROGRAMME; DESIGN LIFE; DURABILITY; EARTH CONSTRUCTION; FABRIC ENERGY STORAGE; METALS; MODULES AND MODULAR CONSTRUCTION; MORTAR, CEMENT AND LIME; OFF-SITE MANUFACTURE; ON-SITE PRODUCTION; PLASTERBOARD; PLASTICS; STONE; STRUCTURAL STEEL; TIMBER.

There are two basic categories that can be applied to construction materials and processes:

1. Dry construction

Those materials which are 'dry' and neither require water to be added during installation nor do they release any significant amounts of moisture during their service life. For example:

- Canvas roofs;
- Metal cladding;
- Metals;
- Plasterboard;
- Plastics;
- Precast concrete;
- Sheet insulation;
- Structural steelwork;
- Timber (NB: not all species).

2. Wet construction

Those materials that are 'wet' because they release moisture during service, require water for their installation or require a period of time to dry out. For example:

- Brickwork and blockwork;
- Earth construction;

Both dry and wet construction methods can be seen on this housing project. Traditional 'wet' masonry construction in the form of brick and block walls is combined with 'dry' precast concrete hollowcore units. Photograph courtesy of Bison Concrete Products Ltd.

- In-situ concrete;
- Mortar;
- Paint;
- Plastering;
- Renders and screeds;
- Stone work;
- Tiling.

It is usual for the construction programme to reflect these types of materials – dry trades will follow on from wet trades after drying out is complete. Drying out can be a lengthy process often involving ventilation and/or heaters to remove excess moisture from the building fabric. During cold and wet periods this may be very problematic, hence there is now a tendency to adopt 'dry' forms of construction where possible to reduce the overall construction programme by removing the need for drying out.

The change from wet to dry

Traditional methods of construction using natural materials such as brick and stone (and some timbers) coupled with traditional processes such as plastering tend to be described as 'wet' because not only do the materials contain moisture, but water is also often required during the construction process. Hence, there needs to be a period of drying out before the building can be occupied. This generic type of construction has been effective for hundreds of years in providing satisfactory protection, airtightness, sound insulation and durability. The heavyweight 'wet' construction materials also offer good levels of thermal mass.

However, the growing pressure on construction to achieve faster build programmes using fewer materials, at lower cost and using fewer skilled workers means that interest in alternative materials and methods has grown steadily. This pressure is such that the traditional forms of construction and the 'wet trades' that accompany them are under threat from materials and methods that reduce the time taken to construct a building by eradicating drying out time and using fewer skilled workers.

Alternatives are generally described by the term 'dry construction'. This includes materials and methods that tend not to rely on skilled workers and tend not to contain, require or release significant moisture levels. Materials such as plasterboard and structural steel, in addition to certain timber frame construction methods can be used to replace 'wet trades'. These 'dry' materials may be highly beneficial in a fast programme as they are quick and simple to install on site and obviously do not require a drying out period. Many are handled easily and can be factory-produced, thus offering high quality (sometimes bespoke) products. The lightweight nature of the products means future adaptations and changes to the fabric of the building are very straightforward. However, concerns have been raised over long-term durability of these lighter weight materials, which can be damaged easily. There are also doubts about airtightness and sound insulation, unless construction is managed carefully.

Conclusion

Despite the move away from traditional 'wet' trades, there are advantages and disadvantages to both 'wet' and 'dry' construction materials and methods, which will have different weightings depending on the type of building and architectural intention. Therefore it is not possible to globally recommend one or the other. Rather a decision could be made on the basis of the following type of questions:

- How important is fast completion and early occupancy?
- How important is overall longevity/design life?

- How important is thermal mass?
- How important is adaptability?
- How important is the architectural style of the materials?

JG

Durability

Durability is the ability of a material, element or structure to perform its intended function for its required life without the need for replacement or significant repair, but subject to normal maintenance.

See also: CONNECTIONS; DESIGN LIFE; MAINTENANCE; PERFORMANCE; SPECIFICATION.

Introduction

Durability is a function of, at least, the exposure environment, the design and detailing of the element or structure, material properties, quality of manufacture and installation, maintenance and the conditions of use. Thus durability, or lack of it, is not necessarily an inherent characteristic of a material, element or structure. A particular softwood, building stone or grade of reinforced concrete may thus be durable in a benign indoor environment but may have an unacceptably short life, or lack of durability, when subject to the ravages of, say, wind, rain, frost or splashing by sea water.

What affects durability?

Durability in a given environment will be dependent on the degradation factors arising from that exposure and the severity of those factors. The degradation factors that are relevant and the severity of a given environment may be specific to the particular material under consideration. For example, chlorides from sea water or road de-icing salts can be detrimental to steel and reinforced concrete but not to unreinforced concrete or some plastics. Durability of an element or whole structure will depend not only on the materials used in the construction but also on the interfaces and possible interactions between different materials.

Design or selection for durability must take account of the required life, the required function, the operating or service conditions and the minimum acceptable level of performance. The inherent durability-related properties of some materials cannot be changed in themselves, such as timber or stone, but a wide variety of these materials is available, each with its own unique properties. Other materials such as plastics, metal alloys and reinforced concrete can be designed to provide particular durability-related properties. Durability of some materials in particular environments may be enhanced by, or even rely upon, special treatments or protection such as painting of timber or metal, or the use of stainless steel instead of normal steel for reinforcement in concrete. Achievement of the potential durability of such materials may thus also be dependent on maintenance, which might include measures such as repainting.

Predicting and designing for durability

Prediction of durability of a particular material, element or structure in a given exposure environment will need to be based on one or more of a number of different approaches:

- Known performance over that lifetime;
- Extrapolation from performance over shorter periods;
- Judgement based on performance of similar materials or items;
- Fundamental understanding of behaviour;
- Mathematical modelling based on degradation processes and known, measured or assumed properties.

As lack of durability means that an unacceptable state has been reached within the required life, it is necessary to have a good idea of what that state is, i.e. what constitutes the end of its life. In some cases this could be related to structural capacity, inability to perform its required function, marred appearance, or an unacceptably high maintenance burden. For certain components it may be impossible, impractical, inappropriate or simply too costly to provide a material or design that will be durable for the required life of the whole structure. In these cases, components should be designed with replacement in mind. On the other hand some components or structures may only be required to have a short design life and materials which are less durable under the particular exposure and service conditions may be appropriate.

Further reading

British Standards Institution *BS 7543: 1992, Guide to durability of buildings and building elements, products and components*, BSI, London, UK

OA

Dynamic thermal simulation

Computational fluid dynamics (CFD) is at the heart of most dynamic thermal simulation techniques. In essence the computer uses the same algorithms that engineers have used traditionally, but can calculate larger numbers of them, faster and in greater detail.

See also: AIR-CONDITIONING; AIRTIGHTNESS AND IAQ; BUILDING MANAGEMENT SYSTEM; ENERGY EFFICIENCY; ENVIRONMENTAL DESIGN; FABRIC ENERGY STORAGE; HVAC; INSULATION; NIGHT VENTILATION; SERVICES; STACK EFFECT; THERMAL BRIDGING; THERMAL COMFORT; VENTILATION; WIND TOWERS; WINDOWS AND CURTAIN WALLING.

What is dynamic thermal simulation?

The development of good thermal modelling software has been a real benefit to design teams, building services engineers and building physicists seeking to achieve both a better understanding of how heat flows in buildings can be predicted and how they can be monitored. Traditionally algorithms (calculation methods) for energy flows in buildings were carried out by hand, which was a laborious process. IT solutions meant that a larger number of calculations could be performed at a faster rate to investigate a series of scenarios. This has revolutionised thermal modelling and there are now several commercial software packages on the market such as 'Apache'. A broad range of analyses is possible using different packages, from simple fabric analysis to combined dynamic thermal simulation and bulk airflow.

The dynamic thermal simulation packages use computational fluid dynamics (CFD) to model heat flows in a building. This is particularly useful for design strategies that use natural ventilation, stack effect and/or fabric energy storage. The programs produce a graphical output (visualisation), which is excellent for communicating the impacts of a design decision. With dynamic thermal simulation the picture of heat transfer, seen flowing in animation, can be of great service in communicating important characteristics or principles to other members of a design team and client body. 'Seeing' heat flows can be of real value to engineers and architects in assessing both the strategic and detail aspects of an evolving design.

CFD methods can be used to track heat fluctuations over time, which can be important in assessing the effectiveness of new technology. It also enables designers to model day and night time modes of operation for say, fabric energy storage systems. Alternative atrium designs can be investigated to test stack effects together with options for soffit systems and louvres for night ventilation.

Limitations

As with any computer model, it is necessarily a simplification – a representation of reality – and so users should be aware of the limitations of CFD for thermal modelling. A few phenomena are known to fall short of complete representations, but may still, in favourable circumstances, permit useful predictions to be made. These are: turbulence; chemical reaction; multi-phase flow; and radiation. The latter two cause particular problems because a number of important influences such as wavelength, angle of reflectivity and surface finish cannot currently be included as they require significant tranches of additional investment in computer power. As a consequence, inability to model radiation properly is often the main cause of inaccuracy in CFD predictions, especially in living accommodation, where convective, conductive and radiative modes of heat transfer may have similar orders of magnitude.

Further reading

Clarke, J.A. (2001) *Energy simulation in building design*, Butterworth-Heinemann, Oxford, UK.

WH/JG

Earth construction*

Earth building is an age-old process that is being re-developed for our modern world. In the UK alone there are nearly 50,000 earth buildings still in use. Earth construction has a low environmental impact compared to conventional building techniques.

See also: DESIGN LIFE; DURABILITY; DRY CONSTRUCTION AND WET CONSTRUCTION; ECOLOGICAL DESIGN; 'ECO-POINTS'; ENVIRONMENTAL DESIGN; SUSTAINABILITY; WEATHERING.

Earth is an abundant material extracted easily and at little cost. A properly built earth construction is durable as well as fire, rot and termite proof. Such a building has a self-regulating indoor climate, in particular with moisture, and helps to absorb polluted air. However, in its natural state earth is vulnerable to damage by water and has low resistance to impact or earthquakes. As a 'toolkit' of construction methods, earth has formed the basis of the vernacular architectural tradition of many countries for hundreds, sometimes thousands of years and is receiving more interest now because it has very low environmental impacts. As an indication of this interest, the use of earth-based products has increased by about 3,000% in the last five years in Germany and The Netherlands alone.

Techniques

Older techniques found in the UK include wattle and daub, with mud applied to a light wooden framework; as well as **cob**, where a mud and straw mix is packed by hand to form a thick wall (found in Devon and Cornwall). The method of laying hand-made earth blocks in the sun to dry is called **adobe**. Modern versions include earth blocks made in a form or press, which are then laid like conventional blocks in mud or mortar These are usually made in similar shapes and sizes to conventional bricks. Earth may also be rammed into formwork, similar to in-situ cast concrete. Small amounts of cement, lime or even bitumen are sometimes used to stabilise the soil. **Rammed earth**, a dry technique consisting of clay and sand, was used for the construction of foundations of many of London's houses built in the 18th and 19th century. Even during the Second World War bombing, the houses 'bounced' on these

* With thanks to Professor Tom Woolley of Queen's University, Belfast and Dr David Webb.

stable, yet pliable foundations and resisted collapse, unlike those built on more rigid brick stepped foundations.

The houses of American architect Frank Lloyd Wright embodied the principle of natural building. He intended them to be at home in nature and grow, 'out of the ground and into the light'. Wright was thinking organically where architecture not only worked with the natural conditions, but the building itself was also organic. In California earth buildings have been constructed where the earth mix was put into canvas bags and then built into walls with barbed wire as a bonding element; then the whole wall placed on impervious slate foundations. This technique is found throughout Ireland (plus Australia and South Africa where Irish immigrants had settled).

Design considerations

A few general observations can be made. To prevent unnecessary damage from moisture, the site must be well drained and any construction should have a good damp-proof course. Protection from rain damage is a primary design issue, with large roof overhangs and good detailing being the key. For stabilised soil blocks, designers should be aware that there is linear shrinkage on drying out, e.g. about 15 mm over 600 mm length for a block with 12% cement content. On a practical note, earth construction should use soil from below topsoil level, from the sub-soil, which is a stickier but more consistent material, with a more effective composition of sand, clay and silt for building construction. Earth construction has a much lower environmental impact than conventional techniques. Even when mechanical digging is used the embodied energy is much less than conventional construction.

Built examples

Obtaining building regulations approval for earth built structures, as well as mortgage finance and insurance, may present some interesting hurdles to overcome. Nevertheless there are a number of examples of earth buildings that have laid down a foundation for a new direction in sustainable architecture. A settlement of houses built at Amesbury, Wiltshire after the First World War by the Ministry of Agriculture investigated methods that would save scarce and expensive materials. Several different materials were used and the houses were still occupied in recent years and are regarded as being of high quality. A good example can be found at Isle d'Abeau, France, where rammed earth was used to construct social housing (1982–84); Jourda & Perraudin used a plain finish without render. Other than housing, the Centre for Alternative Technology (CAT) in Wales includes a new information centre, which uses rammed earth construction. Here, 450 mm thick walls standing 4 m high are free-standing and visually very attractive with their striated red earth finish.

Further reading

Easton, D. (1996) *The rammed earth house*, Chelsea Green Publishing Company, Vermont, USA.

Elizabeth, L. & Adams, C. (eds.) (2000) *Alternative construction: contemporary natural building materials*, John Wiley & Sons, New York, USA.

King, B. (1996) *Buildings of earth and straw*, Ecological Design Press, California, USA.

Lunt, M.G. (1980) *Stabilised soil blocks for building (overseas) Note 197*, Building Research Establishment, Watford, UK.

WH/JG

Ecological design

Ecological design requires the architect to regard and to understand the environment as a functioning natural system and to recognise the dependence of the built environment.

See also: AIRTIGHTNESS AND IAQ; ENVIRONMENTAL DESIGN; 'ECO-POINTS'; RECYCLING; SICK BUILDING SYNDROME; SUSTAINABILITY.

What is ecological design?

Ecological design is essentially about applied ecology. It is based on the concept of the eco-system, which requires an analytical understanding of the macro, meso and micro-climatic environment and the particular site in question. Ecological design acknowledges that:

- The built environment is dependent upon the earth as a supplier of energy and material resources;
- Renewable resources should be utilised ideally at rates less than the natural rate at which they are generated;
- The efficiency with which non-renewable sources are used should be optimised;
- All design has a global impact because of the inter-relationship of the ecosystem;
- An anticipatory and multidisciplinary design approach is preferred.

Based on these statements, it is clear that conventional methods of design, construction and use may be ill-equipped to perform successfully. Furthermore, the mechanistic use of computer software for analysing energy conservation, lighting levels and acoustic factors etc., does not typically take into consideration biological components, the *genius loci* (sense of place), geographic location, land and habitat. Thus these design methods are not deemed wholly ecological, rather the designer is required to acknowledge the resilience of the natural environment and its limits by using a different starting point and evaluating:

- If a building should be constructed;
- Where it is to be built;
- What is to be built;
- How it is to be built.

Malaysian architect Ken Yeang defines ecological design as a means of creating buildings with positive, reparative and productive consequences for the natural environment, and at the same time integrating the built structure with all aspects of the ecological systems of the biosphere over its life-cycle. This more contributory approach is clearly a step forward from simply 'respecting the natural environment'. However, there are many design and technical issues to be overcome to achieve this goal, many of which remain unresolved and yet to be invented. But this does not mean that a technological 'fix' is the preferred solution for comprehensive holistic ecological design.

An alternative approach for the design team

ECHOES (Environmentally Controlled Human Operational External – Enclosed Space), is an ecological design methodology first developed from energy saving design methods by environmental engineer Bill Holdsworth in 1972. It was upgraded in 1980 and 1992 (see reference below). This methodology considers building design as part of a complete circle, with wholeness and a sense of balance at its core. A sample of the design considerations in ECHOES is listed below as an indicator of the breadth of analysis required.

Outside: micro-climate, land, water table, air quality, roads, walking, cycling, safety, waste, relationship and use of other buildings, industries, infrastructure, elements of pollution, solar, wind, rain, shade and openness, visual appetisers: plants, water.

Inside: people's needs, space needs, machine needs, operational polluters, daylighting, illumination, thermo-control, ventilation, stimulation, colour, services, building materials, maintenance, waste, recycling, visual appetisers: plants, water.

The ECHOES design method can be extended with a client's briefing document, sustainable strategies of construction, commissioning and maintenance as well as interacting with human ecology in strengthening the local environment and encouraging community and individual participation.

While some would say issues like those above should be considered as a matter of course, in reality they rarely form part of the key design criteria for a project. For this reason, these types of design tools are essential to address the full range of factors that need to be part and parcel of ecological design.

Further reading

Daniels, K. (1995) *The technology of ecological buildings*, Birkhäuser, Basle, Switzerland.

Edwards, B. (1998) *Green buildings pay*, E&FN Spon, London, UK.

Farmer, J. (1996) *Green shift: towards a green sensibility in architecture*, Butterworth-Heinemann, Oxford, UK.

Holdsworth, B. & Sealey, A.F. (1992) *Healthy buildings: a design primer for a living environment*, Longman, Harlow, UK.

Roaf, S., Fuentes, M. & Thomas, S. (2001) *EcoHouse: a design guide*, Butterworth-Heinemann, Oxford, UK.

Slessor, C. (2001) *Eco-Tech: sustainable architecture and high technology*, Thames & Hudson, London, UK.

Wines, J. (2000) *Green architecture*, Benedikt Taschen, Koln, Germany.

Woolley, T., Kimmins, S., Harrison, P. & Harrison, R. (2000) *Green buildings handbook: a guide to building products and their impact on the environment* (2nd edition), E & FN Spon, London, UK.

WH/JG

'Eco-points'

The use of methods for environmental assessment and eco-labelling of building materials and products is increasing. This includes thermal performance standards in buildings and the increased monitoring of the performance of buildings in use.

See also: CARBON DIOXIDE; ECOLOGICAL DESIGN; ENVIRONMENTAL DESIGN; ENERGY EFFICIENCY; RECYCLING; SPECIFICATION; SUSTAINABILITY.

Introduction

Environmental assessments, the creation of diagnostic lists, and international guidelines and methodologies for environmental and ecological design arose from a combination of scientific research and knowledge gained and codified by professional engineers, architects and others from as early as 1970. The tendency towards league tables and performance monitoring has driven the many industries to improve their environmental accounting methods such that credentials can be easily understood, assessed and compared. By way of an example, washing machines now display eco-scores for both energy and water consumption. While this is said to give consumers ecological peace of mind, criticisms have been aimed at the lack of robustness or critical depth to such measures. This said, they are better than no indicators at all!

In 1987, the US Environmental Protection Agency compiled a statutory regulatory diagnostic list of tests to reduce radon intrusion into existing and new dwellings. In the same year, the Nordic Seminar on Healthy Building Design established new sets of building codes, now common in Sweden and Denmark. These included clear guidelines for:

- Building location and local climate;
- Building physics and construction engineering;
- Climate engineering;
- Building materials;
- Maintenance and administration building process.

Sweden, Denmark, the USA and the Netherlands were the early prime movers in the creation of such assessments, which in turn led to eco-labelling and eco-points. The introduction of 'league tables' and 'green scores' did not appear until about 1990. In recent years, the UK situation has changed so that there are several schemes in existence such as BREEAM (described below) and environmental indicators for sustainable construction from the Movement for Innovation, via which designers and clients can assess eco/environmental performance. The *Green guide to specification* has been particularly influential in its presentation of materials in terms of life-cycle impacts with simple ratings of A, B or C. The Building Research Establishment (BRE) also maintains an extensive database on construction materials data called *Environmental Profiles*.

However, these schemes are only as good as the choice of indicators and data that is included (e.g. amount of carbon dioxide emitted) and the benchmark against which performance is judged. Given these issues, it comes as no surprise that the various eco-point schemes are being updated constantly as and when new information becomes available. It has to be said that data is lacking for UK performance for a number of key indicators and the government is now addressing this problem.

BREEAM

This is probably the one eco-point scheme of which most designers will be aware; the Building Research Establishment Environmental Assessment Method (BREEAM) was released in 1990. It is an environmental assessment tool for office designs developed by the Building Research Establishment (BRE) and the ECD Partnership, specialists in energy conscious design. It was the first of a proposed series of simple design goals for the UK to facilitate reduction of CO_2 and CFC emissions from buildings. A credit system was established for reducing the predicted carbon dioxide emission (in $kg/m^2/year$) compared with CO_2 emissions from a typical office, using standard assumptions about the building's use and occupancy. Further credits are given for:

- Reduction or removal of CFCs, HCFCs in refrigeration systems;
- Recycling of materials;
- Air-conditioning systems where wet cooling towers have been designed out;
- Minimal use of formaldehyde, lead based paints and asbestos.

Even so, both BREEAM (version 1/90) and BREEAM (New Homes version 3/91), which awards credits for masonry containing fly-ash and blast furnace slag, still fall short of the Japanese Ecomark standard. New versions of BREEAM have been developed for other building types.

Other eco-point schemes

Eco-labelling has been adopted commercially in the UK as a voluntary scheme. However, there is a significant body of literature, which is critical of current attempts to develop standardised systems of environmental criteria. If something has an eco-label or eco-points, consumers may assume it is 'OK', although full awareness of the impact of the product or installation may be questionable. The European Community has now agreed the criteria for the first two of its new eco-label scheme; one covers interior decorative paints and varnishes with a much stricter limit on VOCs. There is also a list of substances not allowed, which includes lead, cadmium, dibutyls and also processes supplying any titanium dioxide. Germany has its own 'Blue Angel' eco-label for paints low in lead and chromates and for low-pollutant varnishes, which covers 3,000 products. Canada has 'cradle-to-the-grave' 'Environmental Choice' label, but the USA leads the field with a 'Green Seal Award' that includes a long list of toxic chemicals and is much stricter than the EC equivalent.

Further reading

Howard, N. & Shiers, D. (1996) *The green guide to specification*, Post Office Property Holdings, UK.

Liddell, H. (ed.) (1995) *Eco-labelling in Europe: conference report*, Robert Gordon University, Aberdeen, Scotland.

Woolley, T., Kimmins, S., Harrison, P. & Harrison, R. (2000) *Green buildings handbook: a guide to building products and their impact on the environment* (2nd edition), E & FN Spon, London, UK.

WH/JG

Electrochromic glass

See: GLASS – LAMINATED AND COATED GLASS; INTELLIGENT FAÇADES AND MATERIALS

Embodied energy

See: CARBON DIOXIDE (CO_2); 'ECO-POINTS'; INSULATION

Enamel

See: CERAMICS; GLASS

Encasement

See: FIRE PROTECTION; CONCRETE; PLASTERBOARD; STRUCTURAL STEEL

Energy efficiency

Methods, systems and technologies that reduce the amount of fossil fuel energy used, in addition to conservation techniques for all energy systems.

See also: AIR-CONDITIONING; AIRTIGHTNESS; BUILDING MANAGEMENT SYSTEMS; DYNAMIC THERMAL SIMULATION; 'ECO-POINTS'; ENVIRONMENTAL DESIGN; FABRIC ENERGY STORAGE; FAÇADES AND FAÇADE ENGINEERING; HEAT RECOVERY; HVAC; INSULATION; LIGHTING – DAYLIGHTING; LIGHTING – ARTIFICIAL LIGHTING; NIGHT VENTILATION; PHASE CHANGE MATERIALS; PHOTOVOLTAICS; SOLAR PANELS; SUSTAINABILITY; THERMOLABYRINTHS; TROMBE WALLS; VENTILATION; WIND TOWERS.

Introduction

Until the world oil crisis in the early 1970s, the terms 'energy efficiency', 'energy saving' and 'energy conservation' simply meant the most profitable ways that coal, oil and gas were burnt to provide energy for the UK population. However, that period changed the emphasis, so that energy efficiency has now come to mean ways of reducing our dependence on fossil fuels by reducing energy needs and conserving the energy that is used. Energy efficiency became part of UK government policy after 1973, with recommended guidelines for standardised thermal conductivity (U values), ventilation rates, daylighting, driving rain and the effect of winds on tall buildings – all having to be accounted for in the calculation of heat loads for new buildings.

As energy consciousness gradually developed, relatively inexpensive, step-by-step, conservation applications were undertaken in housing (mainly through DIY schemes) as well as other existing buildings. These included installation of double-glazing, better thermal insulation, sealing up buildings to reduce draughts as well as simple control systems on energy plant to reduce the running costs.

In 1995 the Building Regulations for the conservation of fuel and power and for ventilation laid down indicative U values for material, determination of the thickness for thermal insulation and a Standard Assessment Procedure (SAP rating). SAP is a step-by-step series of calculations based on the annual energy cost for space and hot water heating to produce the overall energy rating for dwellings. The 2000 amendments to the Building Regulations include a further increase in energy efficiency requirements for buildings in a bid to reduce the UK's total carbon dioxide emissions (where buildings in use account for almost 50% of the total).

Design options

In addition to changes in design standards and assessment methods, there are many practical measures that can be used within buildings to reduce energy consumption in use. Detailing for insulation, airtightness and ventilation will play an important part, but it is also feasible to address energy conservation on a bigger scale; for example:

- **Passive solar heating** including fabric energy storage, trombe walls, sunspaces, conductive air loops or **passive solar cooling**: ventilation, radiation, evaporation and dehumidification.
- **Mechanical heating and cooling systems**: dual and single duct all air systems with inclusive heat/energy recovery systems, air-water systems with zoned and individual heat/cooling terminals, co-regeneration systems, heat pumps and energy derived from deep ground wells.

- **Luminance and lighting systems**: critical installations where energy efficiency techniques should be employed as a matter of normal design. Light switches fitted with timers, human heat-sensitive switches, daylight sensors that interact with light fittings, re-circulation of heat energy from light fittings and the correct luminosity required for task lighting.

Further developments

Climate does not actually determine form, but it does influence it. This truism is taking designers back to vernacular traditions in architecture, in which passive forms of cooling for example have been used for hundreds, if not thousands of years. A recent EC research project into Passive Downdraught Evaporative Cooling (PDEC) undertaken within the JOULE programme found that this technique has the potential to replace conventional air-conditioning in locations where global warming is causing climate change. Using 'wind tower' technology, the technique provides substantial energy savings and avoids the need for ductwork, fans and suspended ceilings. Free standing 'cooling towers' using PDEC were used on the campus of the Expo in Seville, Spain to give visitors a place to escape from the heat of the day.

Providing cooling without air-conditioning and providing significant energy savings were also key drivers in the design of the ING Bank building in Amsterdam in 1990. In this series of linked office towers Dutch architect, Ton Alberts, used a plan related to the sunpath and stack ventilation combined with adiabatic cooling from water flowing down flow-form balustrades. These innovations are now easier to achieve with the advent of 'dynamic thermal simulation', in which the complex heat flows in a building can be modelled. CFD computer programmes offer highly sophisticated methods of creating new energy saving and climate-responsive architectural technologies to improve energy efficiency.

Further reading

Baker, N. & Steemers, K. (2000) *Energy and environment in architecture: a technical design guide*, E & FN Spon, London, UK.

Chartered Institute of Building Services Engineers (1998) *Energy efficiency in buildings*, CIBSE, London, UK.

Goulding, J.R., Lewis, J.O. & Steemers, T.C. (eds.) (1992) *Energy conscious design: a primer for architects*, Batsford, London, UK.

Roaf, S. & Hancock, M. (eds.) (1992) *Energy efficient building*, Blackwell Science, Oxford, UK.

WH/JG

Envelope

See: FAÇADES AND FAÇADE ENGINEERING; WINDOWS AND CURTAIN WALLING

Environmental design

The word 'environment' in design terms took on a greater significance as our realisation of the impacts of fossil fuels interacted with the way we built and planned our urban and rural habitats. It is seen as a step towards 'sustainable' or 'ecological' design.

See also: AIR-CONDITIONING; AIRTIGHTNESS; BUILDING
MANAGEMENT SYSTEMS; DYNAMIC THERMAL SIMULATION;
ECOLOGICAL DESIGN; 'ECO-POINTS'; ENERGY EFFICIENCY;
FABRIC ENERGY STORAGE; FAÇADES AND FAÇADE
ENGINEERING; HEAT RECOVERY; HVAC; INSULATION; NIGHT
VENTILATION; PHOTOVOLTAICS; SOLAR PANELS;
SUSTAINABILITY; THERMOLABYRINTHS; TROMBE WALLS;
VENTILATION; WIND TOWERS.

Introduction

The term 'environmental design' has two meanings in architectural technology. The most used (and what is considered here) is what is colloquially known as 'green' design, i.e. architecture designed with environmental or ecological concerns in mind. The other use of the phrase is to describe the general activity of designing a building's environment (including heating, ventilating, acoustics and daylighting design). 'Green' and 'ecological' are words that have expanded the meaning of the phrase 'environmental design' which now takes account of the relationship of design to fossil fuel use, natural eco-systems, food production, ways of travel, the health and safety of the human race and biodiversity. Hence, environmental design is sometimes a 'catch all' term to represent this type of design approach.

Key aspects of environmental design

If we consider that building design was based previously on a rather mechanical understanding of construction, building physics etc., then it is not surprising that we look back on these as unsatisfactory methods because our current design standpoint is much more holistic. Traditional approaches to the design of a building were based on generalised weather information, temperature and humidity, which resulted in large variations between predicted and actual performance. There was also a tendency to under-estimate the importance of indoor air quality and ventilation. The worst case scenario is a building with poor health and energy performance.

Environmental design now requires that designers adopt a different attitude that pays more regard to energy efficiency and health aspects, thus taking a step towards more sustainable buildings. However, this is not an easy step to take because it calls for a different approach that is much more holistic. In a bid to help designers understand and use environmental design criteria, an 'environmental design matrix for the creation of a well tempered environment' was developed in 1970*. This became an educational tool, which inspired many subsequent variations.

Practical solutions

Although environmental design is a discipline in its own right, certain technologies have become closely associated with it including solar, wind and wave (i.e. renewable energy) technologies. These have developed and expanded in Europe and the USA, but wind energy has only recently been developed in the UK as a large-scale enterprise. Construction with straw bales, earth construction and reed bed water cleaning systems have until recently been seen as rather eccentric, with no commercial applications. However the recycled rainwater system used at the Millennium Dome in Greenwich, London provided a much-needed PR boost. These, and other environmental design solutions, can increase people's health and well being when combined with ways to reduce noise, vibration and chemical emissions, as well as improved ventilation and illumination.

---

* By engineer Bill Holdsworth (see reference in *Ecological design*).

Environmental standards

There is a drive to establish both European and international standards to enable better enforcement of environmental design. In the UK, Building Regulations have been improved to reduce energy consumption and more regulations are coming into force to reduce toxic emissions from building materials. Unfortunately such standards can be undermined as a result of commercial pressures or failure to enforce them. Nevertheless, assessment methods such as BREEAM are well regarded by architects, services engineers and building occupiers alike (See *Eco-points*). International scoring systems are being developed by the EC, based on practice in countries such as the Netherlands, Germany, Italy and Sweden. These will help to raise awareness of environmental design and enable performance measurement and benchmarking.

Further reading

Baird, G. (2001) *The architectural expression of environmental control systems*, E & FN Spon, London, UK.

Mackenzie, D. (1997) *Green design: design for the environment*, Laurence King, London, UK.

McMullan, R. (1998) *Environmental science in building* (4th edition), MacMillan, Basingstoke, UK.

Olgyay, V. (1992) *Design with climate: a bioclimatic approach to architectural regionalism*, Van Nostrand Reinhold, New York, USA.

Thomas, R. (ed.) (1999) *Environmental design* (2nd edition), E&FN Spon, London, UK.

Vale, B. & Vale, R. (2000) *The new autonomous house*, Thames & Hudson, London, UK.

WH/JG

Epoxy

This petro-chemically derived material is used, usually as a glue, or in paints where a high standard of resistance is required to wear or chemical attack.

See also: COMPOSITE MATERIALS; COMPOSITE PANELS; CONNECTIONS; ECOLOGICAL DESIGN; INTUMESCENT PAINT; NIGHT VENTILATION; PLASTICS – TYPES; PLASTICS – FABRICATION; PLASTICS FOR ADHESIVES AND FINISHES; CORROSION; TIMBER – LAMINATED TIMBER; VENTILATION; WEATHERING.

Introduction – what is epoxy?

Epoxy is best known as a twin-component glue, but it can also act as a hardener or resin. It has excellent wearing properties and can be designed to fulfil a variety of functional requirements. Epoxy is seen commonly in construction as an adhesive or jointing material and within certain paints (to provide better weathering performance). It was also used previously as a base ingredient for intumescent (fire-protecting) paint before other water-based mixes were developed. Although it is used regularly on site and in some manufacturing situations, epoxy is harmful to health and should therefore be used only by trained, responsible and appropriately protected workers.

Uses for epoxy

When properly applied, epoxy produces a vapour-proof coating and is virtually impermeable to water-vapour. This makes it particularly useful for timber, for which the epoxy helps maintain original moisture content and structural characteristics, but in addition makes it virtually rot-proof. Epoxy is subject to degradation under UV light and needs to be coated with UV-inhibiting varnish. Hence, epoxy is applied under controlled conditions to make timber a long-life building component. Epoxy is also used as a compound with chlorine in adhesives for manufacture of timber boards and 'glulam'. On site, mixed with cotton-fibre thickening, epoxy makes a suitable adhesive, which in turn gives superior strength and 'bridging' capacity to internal joints. With phenolic additives, it also becomes a good structural and strong filler agent that is easily sanded. Epoxy resins can be found in floor hardeners, plasticisers, fillers and dyes.

Health and safety

Epoxy and associated epoxides and compounds can, without stringent safety measures, cause hypersensitivity, allergies, carcinogenic illnesses and poison the immune system. Many countries, especially Sweden, have laid down rules concerning the use of epoxy products at work. These require that workers receive special training in such a way as to avoid skin contact. Epoxy eczema very often affects not only the hands but the face as well. Swedish research has shown that very small quantities of epoxy are sufficient for the eczema to flare up. A link has been established in the electrical industry between the use of epoxy in cabling/fixing and incidence of workplace stress illnesses. In the UK regulations for its use are not as stringent as in Sweden and the USA. New EC rules are being drawn up to ensure greater control of both manufacture and use and the World Health Organisation has established a standard for all epoxy compounds under its International Programme for Chemical Safety (IPCS).

Further reading

Curwell, S., March, C. & Venables, R. (1990) *Buildings and health: the Rosehaugh guide*, RIBA Publications, London, UK.

Ledbetter, S.R., Hurley, S. & Sheehan, A. (1998) *Sealant joints in the external envelope of buildings: a guide on design, specification and construction*, CIRIA Report 178, CIRIA, London, UK.

WH/JG

EPS: expanded polystyrene

See: INSULATION; PLASTICS – TYPES

ETFE

Ethylene-Tetrafluoroethylene copolymer (ETFE) is a thermoplastic polymer, chemically similar to PTFE (Teflon™). Typically processed into transparent film, ETFE is used as a lightweight and versatile plastics glazing material.

See also: AIR SUPPORTED STRUCTURES; FAÇADES AND FAÇADE ENGINEERING; GLASS AND GLAZING; GRIMSHAW, NICHOLAS; PLASTICS – TYPES; ROOFS; TEXTILE MEMBRANE ROOFS; WEATHERING.

ETFE covered, air filled cushions form the roof of the biomes at the Eden project in Cornwall (by Nicholas Grimshaw). Photograph by Trevor Jones, courtesy of The Concrete Society.

Introduction

Excellent optical properties coupled with lightweight and flexibility makes ETFE suitable for use as a novel glazing material. ETFE has found widespread use as glazing for large horticultural structures, leisure and recreation centres as well as rooflights for office and hospital buildings. The material is used typically in the form of air filled pillows, formed by thermally welding sheets together. They are supported in a frame incorporating an inflation system to maintain the air pressure within them. By inflating the pillows they can offer thermal insulation to the structure and also form a stable, free draining shape. The pillows are often multi-skinned to maintain integrity should a skin be punctured. ETFE is a fluoropolymer like Polytetrafluoroethylene (PTFE, otherwise known as Teflon™) and has a similarly low surface energy, giving it desirable dirt repellent properties. However, this can make it awkward to print coloured patterns on the surface. To enable pigments to stick to the film, the surface of the film needs to be prepared using an ion-plasma etching technique to activate it. Once prepared, a wide range of coloured pigments can be applied.

Properties

ETFE has particularly good mechanical properties for a thin thermoplastic film. It is resistant to tears and punctures and has a relatively high tensile modulus. Its high tensile modulus enables the glazing to maintain its form and dimensions well when inflated, even under wind loads. However, due to its relative stiffness it can crease easily – this can be a problem during installation. ETFE film has excellent optical transparency, characteristically transmitting 90% of incident light. Although the film transmits the majority of incident light, ETFE glazing can appear milky, particularly when observed from a distance. This is because light is scattered by the internal microstructure of the film. ETFE is also highly transparent to ultra-violet (UV) light, making it suitable for use over plants and trees, since they require UV light to perform photosynthesis. Fluoropolymers such as PTFE and ETFE are chemically quite inert materials, giving them very good fire performance. Although ETFE will melt in a fire, it does not support combustion. In addition, as a thin film it rapidly melts and contracts in a fire, forming a vent to allow smoke and fumes to escape. Their inertness also imparts them with very good resistance to the ageing effects of UV light from the sun. Glazing exposed to UV light for over 20 years has shown insignificant yellowing or loss of transparency. By the same token, ETFE has excellent resistance to chemicals and solvent. Together, these properties confer ETFE with moderately good durability – ETFE glazing installed 25 years ago is still performing well.

Built examples

The Eden Project in Cornwall is the largest single use of ETFE cushions. Here, a cluster of 'biomes' nestles at the base of a disused quarry enclosing several climate zones with plants and wildlife from all over the world. Architects Nicholas Grimshaw & Partners have also recently completed the National Space Centre in Leicester. The main building houses two rockets and stands 42 m high. It is clad with triple layered ETFE air cushions, tailored to the geometry of the complex frame of curved CHS steel beams and girders. The ETFE cushions are less than 1% of the weight of an equivalent glazed façade and their architectural image alludes appropriately to the content of the rocket tower and the 'space race'.

OA

Expansion joint
See: CONNECTIONS

Extrusion
See: ALUMINIUM; CASTINGS; METALS

Fabric energy storage

Fabric energy storage refers to the utilisation of building materials to reduce and delay peak internal temperatures. It is associated with heavyweight building materials such as concrete.

See also: AIRTIGHTNESS AND IAQ; BUILDING MANAGEMENT SYSTEMS; CONCRETE; CONCRETE – FINISHES; CONCRETE – STRUCTURES; DYNAMIC THERMAL SIMULATION; ENERGY EFFICIENCY; FLOORS; HOPKINS, SIR MICHAEL AND PATTY; HVAC; NIGHT VENTILATION; STONE; THERMAL COMFORT; THERMOLABYRINTHS.

Introduction

The thermal mass of heavyweight building materials enables them to store and re-radiate heat provided they are 'exposed' to the heat source. This property can be optimised in design to address solar gain and/or heat gains from people and equipment. This is called fabric energy storage (FES). It can reduce or even eliminate the need for air-conditioning in buildings, which results in savings in capital and running costs, and in some instances means a significant reduction in the carbon dioxide emissions associated with energy use. The materials typically used for FES are concrete, stone and masonry. These dense, heavyweight materials have a high conductivity value (i.e. they have an enhanced capacity to admit heat or coolth). Utilising this property effectively 'irons out' the peaks and troughs of external temperature swings and internal heat gains from people, computers, equipment and lighting. Fabric energy storage can be employed usefully in many building types, but is most helpful in buildings where the peak external temperature coincides with the period of maximum occupancy (e.g. offices and schools). However, other buildings such as houses and factories may also benefit.

How does FES work?

During the day a heavyweight material exposed to the internal environment gradually absorbs heat, offsetting uncomfortable heat gains. At night, a period of ventilation or 'purging' is usually needed to cool it, which effectively primes the material for the same cycle the next day. The onset of peak temperatures in a building can be delayed by up to six hours and reduced by 3–4 °C. Although any part of a structure can be used for FES (façades, floors, frames, walls etc.), the inside or undersides of

Interior view of the Toyota GB headquarters in Epsom, Surrey (Sheppard Robson Architects). The precast concrete soffit units can be seen clearly throughout the office space, illustrating the architectural qualities of this concept for energy storage in the structure. Photograph by Barry Bulley, courtesy of Trent Precast Concrete Ltd.

floors (soffits) are particularly suitable because these form a large surface area and are distributed evenly throughout the building. There are many built examples that use the soffits of the frame structure in this way to reduce or even eliminate the need for air-conditioning. Older buildings can be refurbished to take advantage of their thermal mass. By removing any suspended ceilings, just exposing existing heavyweight material can be helpful.

FES can be designed according to the building's orientation and predicted internal heat gains. In some instances it may be necessary only to provide a few internal exposed elements, for example in a circulation area. However in areas such as offices or meeting rooms it may be advisable to expose the soffits of a structural frame. Soffits can be shaped (coffered or troughed) to provide the largest possible 'heat exchange' area. A normal slab thickness of 200–300 mm of concrete is very effective; any extra mass provides free 'heatwave insurance'. Consideration should be given to the aesthetic qualities of the exposed soffit, both surface texture and colour. FES soffits are most effective (for daylighting purposes) if they have a white or pale coloured finish which 'bounces' light into the building. Fabric energy storage may play a key part of the overall services strategy for the building, so thermal modelling using dynamic thermal simulation (CFD) may be very useful in manipulating the design and communicating the results.

Types of FES

A 'passive' FES design is one in which soffits are exposed to allow heat exchange between the air volume and surrounding surfaces. Here, the material provides up to $25W/m^2$ of passive cooling capacity, which is more than adequate to cater for heat loading of a typical commercial building (a building using lightweight materials might achieve $6-8W/m^2$ of passive cooling). The exposed 'passive' slabs are designed with flat, contoured or troughed surfaces (with a raised floor system rather than a suspended ceiling). The PowerGen HQ, in Coventry (Bennetts Associates) was an early example of the architectural potential of exposed, shaped and sculpted concrete soffits. The Toyota HQ in Epsom, Surrey (Sheppard Robson Architects) uses exposed precast concrete soffit units as part of a hybrid precast and in-situ concrete frame.

An 'active' FES system is suitable for buildings with higher heat loads and/or cooling requirements such as lecture halls, theatres and hospitals. Enhanced heat transfer and thus extra cooling is achieved by forced ventilation through a floor, or across the floor surface by means of a plenum. Hollowcore floor panels and similar systems offer about $40W/m^2$ of cooling and a major reduction in capital costs compared to air-conditioning. Active FES (in this case 'Termodeck™') was used in the University of East London Dockland campus as a means of providing controllable heating and cooling for student accommodation. Another example is a curved bespoke, precast concrete floor system in the Building Research Establishment's 'Environmental Building' in Garston, Watford.

Further reading

Glass, J. (2001) *Fabric energy storage*, Reinforced Concrete Council, Berkshire, UK.
Santamouris, M. & Asimakapolous, D. (eds.) (1996) *Passive cooling of buildings*, James & James, London, UK.

JG

Façades and façade engineering

This describes the discipline behind the design, construction and operational characteristics of the building envelope. The façade is the 'skin' of a building and performs many useful functions.

See also: CLADDING; CLADDING COMPONENTS; COMPOSITE PANELS; CONCRETE; CONNECTIONS; DESIGN LIFE; ENERGY EFFICIENCY; ENVIRONMENTAL DESIGN; FOSTER, NORMAN; GLASS; GLASS – LAMINATED AND COATED; GLASS – STRUCTURAL GLAZING; GRIDS FOR STRUCTURE AND LAYOUT; GROPIUS, WALTER; HAPPOLD, SIR TED AND BURO HAPPOLD; INTEGRATION; INTELLIGENT FAÇADES AND MATERIALS; LIFE-CYCLE COSTING; LOUVRES AND BRISE SOLEIL; MAINTENANCE; NOUVEL, JEAN; PHOTOVOLTAICS; PLASTICS; PROUVÉ, JEAN; RITCHIE, IAN; SOLAR PANELS; WEATHERING; WINDOWS AND CURTAIN WALLING; YEANG, KEN.

Introduction

Façade engineering is a relatively new field and the following entry sets it in the context of façade design in its own right. As a means of distinguishing between the various terms used here, the following definitions are suggested:

Façades are different to windows. The term façade is understood usually to mean a 'skin' or envelope that wraps around a framed structure. It is not part of a loadbearing structure, and usually bears only part of its own weight. This frees up the designer to use different materials such as steel and glass. It is usual for a façade to be considered as a system in its own right and related to other aspects of design such as services strategy and planning grids within the building.

Windows are found more usually in buildings with loadbearing walls or curtain walling as discrete openings in the wall itself. Windows tend to be small as the loads within the wall need to be re-distributed around the opening using a lintel. It is more typical for windows to be part of a natural ventilation strategy than façades (which tend to be associated with mechanical ventilation, although this is not always the case).

Historical note

A façade forms a skin around a framed structure as the 'building envelope' and there are many design issues that relate to the detailing, materials and structural nature of the façade. In some respects the façade offers the architect the potential of a 'highly-designable' element, which can be very expressive and exciting. This opportunity has arisen over time. Since the structural frame facilitated the move away from fully loadbearing façades for large buildings, it has been common to see fully enclosed buildings in the 1970s (hermetically sealed, air conditioned, glass-clad towers). However, these have since fallen from favour because research has established a link between the symptoms of sick building syndrome and sealed buildings with low levels of daylight and fresh air. Thus the modern approach to façade design (since the 1980s) is to improve occupant comfort by using the façade as a climate moderator with some inherent 'adaptivity' such that changes in interior conditions are feasible. The discipline of façade engineering has developed in response to this trend because it is vital to approach façade design with integration in mind, moving towards what can be termed 'total façade solutions'.

Issues in façade engineering

Some of the basic issues discussed in façade engineering are outlined below:

Structure – a vital part of the design of a façade is its structural design. This must take into account a number of factors relating to the question 'what does the façade need to do?' including:

- Architectural intention – where is the structure in relation to the façade? Exposed or hidden? Within the plane of the façade or not?
- Climate – precipitation levels, wind pressures, temperature range, solar gain;
- Environmental conditions such air pollution and noise;
- Extreme design – monsoons, cyclones, bomb/blast-proofing;
- Interior requirements – daylighting, security, access, views etc.;
- Performance issues – insulation, acoustics, fire safety, design life and movement (expansion etc.).

Materials – those associated currently with façade engineering are aluminium, steel and glass. These are lightweight and relatively thin materials (and fashionable), but others are used too. Although standard façade systems are available (some of the best originate from the EC countries, Germany and Italy), many are bespoke designs developed in collaboration with façade system manufacturers.

Cost – this is a major issue; the cost of façades can account for 15–30% and more of the total construction costs and is also linked to operational costs of running the building. The capital cost of a façade with some adaptive (say, ventilation) elements can be in excess of ten times the cost of a simply clad façade i.e. £2000+/m^2 compared to say £200–300/m^2. However, a client may be prepared to pay such a cost if the life-cycle benefits of installing such a façade system are convincing. For this reason façade specification is often discussed in terms of life-cycle costs and energy efficiency.

Intelligence – this is the capacity of the façade to incorporate materials or components that 'think' or respond to stimuli, such as light, wind, sun or rain levels. Intelligence is linked clearly to the façade's need to provide an environmental function. Also referred to as 'smart' buildings, the designer may choose to install photovoltaic panels (PV), photochromic glass or other similar materials. These give the façade added value in that it is better equipped to respond to external conditions and thereby temper the internal environment, e.g. prevent overheating. Many such materials are computer-controlled and linked to the building's energy management system (BMS). Adaptive façades is a term related to intelligence, but is more commonly associated with say louvre systems, which allow the façade to adapt to the external conditions.

One example is the 'twin skin' (environmental modifier) system whereby a void between two layers of the envelope becomes a managed interface environment between interior and exterior. In this instance a combination of fixed and adaptive elements provide flexibility of operations: control is either manual or via a BMS. Note that the design of such façades should therefore be linked closely to floorplate depth and other factors related to natural ventilation. In addition, the terms 'thermal chimney' or wind tower may be applied. There are two broad categories of twin-skin façades; thin and thick, with heating and ventilating mechanisms for each varying considerably. Foster and Partners' Business Promotion Centre at the Duisberg Microelectronics Park in Germany is a good example of a (thin) twin-skin façade, as is their Commerzbank in Frankfurt with its 'sky gardens' set into the façades. The Swiss Re tower in London will continue to build on these façade concepts. The Helicon building in London by Sheppard Robson Architects is an example of a thick, wider 'flue'. Research indicates that, in comparison to single leaf façades, many multiple-skin options offer:

- 65% reduction in energy consumption;
- 50% reduction in carbon dioxide emissions;
- 65% reduction in operating costs (approx.).

Maintenance – this includes routine checking, replacement and cleaning routines. Any façade system needs a known maintenance regime, which should be developed in relation to its predicted behaviour under weathering. As discussed under *Weathering*, there are several approaches depending on how much the designer wants the building to change. Water run-off, rainfall patterns and local atmospheric conditions will determine the outcome, but whatever approach is taken it should be realistic for the client and its attitude to design life. Access systems for cleaning and maintenance are often provided from roof level.

Built examples

Although there are many excellent examples of façade design to be found throughout mainland Europe, a few buildings stand out as particular examples. Jean Nouvel's L'Institut du Monde Arabe in Paris was designed with a whole façade of tiny mechanical devices like camera shutters that act to manipulate lighting conditions within the building. Foster and Partners 1970s Willis Faber Corroon building is simple but effective. The glass façade predates many high tech examples and it is now a Listed Building. Although there are no adaptive elements to the façade, its qualities stem from the simple way the building comes alive at night when one can see through the glass.

Ken Yeang's work demonstrates the bioclimatic approach to building design and features façades broken by gardens and adaptive elements. Two further examples in Riyadh, the Al Faisaliah centre and the Kingdom Centre Project have become the two tallest structures in the Arab world (267 m and 300 m high respectively). Both have highly articulated façade systems that have been designed to withstand high wind pressures and sandstorms (the former building was designed by Foster and Partners and Buro Happold, and the second by Ellerbe Becket and Ove Arup (New York). For these two buildings the capacity of modern IT programs to hone structural design and environmental performance proved invaluable.

Further reading

Compagno, A. (1999) *Intelligent glass façades: materials, practice, design* (4th edition), Birkhäuser, Basle, Switzerland.

Davies, C. & Lambot, I. (1997) *Commerzbank Frankfurt*, Watermark/Birkhäuser, Basle, Switzerland.

Oesterle, E., Lieb, R-D, Lutz, M. & Heusler, W. (2001) *Double-skin façades: integrated planning*, Prestel-Verlag, Munich, Germany.

Shittich, C. (ed.) (2001) *In detail: building skins*, Birkhäuser, Basle, Switzerland.

JG

Faience

See: CERAMICS; BRICKS AND BLOCKS – FINISHES

Finishes
See: SURFACE FINISHES

Fire engineering

Fire engineering combines the knowledge of scientific and engineering principles, standards and guidelines as well as the understanding of an expert, to contribute to the design of a building.

See also: CONCRETE – STRUCTURES; FIRE PROTECTION; FRAME; INTUMESCENT PAINT; PLASTERBOARD; RISK MANAGEMENT; STRUCTURAL STEEL.

What is fire engineering?

Fire engineering is the application of scientific and engineering principles to the protection of people, property and the environment from fire. Fire safety considerations can have a major impact on building design and use. The issues were traditionally dealt with through rule-based systems of regulations and standards, developed over time on the basis of experience of real (usually disastrous) fire incidents. The rules were generally prescriptive, conservative and rarely flexible enough to address all the issues that arose on any new project. This situation resulted in extra expense without necessarily addressing the safety issues inherent in a new building and which may occur during its lifetime.

Applying fire engineering

Fire engineering takes an 'on first principles' approach to establish the conditions that might develop as a result of fire, and analyses how people and structure might respond. It embraces a wide range of sub-specialisms, from materials behaviour and toxicology, to design of systems for fire detection or suppression. Buildings are rarely designed wholly on a fire engineering basis. Much of the design will follow the traditional codes, with engineering methods deployed to solve specific areas of difficulty. For example innovative designs of large complex spaces containing a mixture of uses can fall outside the limits of the general code guidelines. In these situations a **fire strategy** should be developed that demonstrates how the combination of code-based and engineering design will satisfy the safety (or property protection etc.) objectives. A fire strategy is developed using the fire engineering principles as a framework. Some of the factors affecting a fire-engineered design are:

- Building geometry, layout and use;
- Building location in relation to adjacent properties;
- Building management, i.e. how it will be used;
- Fire service – access and advice;
- Fuel load and distribution;
- Occupants;
- Probability of a fire occurring.

Fire engineering methods include probabilistic and deterministic analysis, physical modelling and larger-scale (occasionally full-scale) testing. The availability of powerful desktop computers has helped the discipline to develop techniques for modelling fire behaviour, including smoke movement and heat transfer, and for analysing crowd movement in escape routes. One area where further development effort is being concentrated is the composite behaviour of structural frames in response to heating. This promises to produce savings in both the structure and its protection against fire. Another field for development, where limited knowledge constrains engineering methods, is that of human behaviour. For example, how people respond on discovering a fire, being warned of a fire and what they do during their escape.

Further reading

Chartered Institution of Building Services Engineers (1997) *CIBSE Guide E: Fire Engineering*, CIBSE, London, UK.

Stollard, P. & Johnston, L. (1994) *Design against fire: an introduction to fire safety engineering design*, E & FN Spon, London, UK.

OA

Fire protection

Fire protection methods are intended to achieve desired levels of safety and property protection from the effects of a fire.

See also: CONCRETE – STRUCTURES; FIRE PROTECTION; FRAME; GLASS – LAMINATED AND COATED; INTUMESCENT PAINT; MINERAL FIBRES; PLASTERBOARD; RISK MANAGEMENT; STRUCTURAL STEEL; TIMBER.

Introduction

During the design of any building it is important to understand that fire prevention cannot be relied on to be 100% successful. If it is critical that a fire should be limited and that subsequent damage from fire or smoke should be mitigated, then some form of fire protection is necessary. There are however occasions where the fire protection strategy is to allow people to escape, but the building (and the property within) to be destroyed. The 'protection' strategy here may be financial e.g. by having some form of insurance. Normally physical protection measures are also taken. Fire protection systems include:

- Compartmentation (using walls and fire-breaks);
- Fire resistant construction (e.g. concrete);
- Fire load control (e.g. limiting amounts of stock);
- Fire detection systems;
- Fire suppression systems;
- Means of escape for occupants;
- Smoke control systems.

Active fire protection

Active fire protection systems respond to the effects of a fire in a way that should suppress the fire, control combustion products or facilitate safe movement of occupants. Automatic fire alarm systems alert the occupants of a possible incident and initiate the investigation of the cause of the alarm and enable the evacuation of the building. They may also trigger the operation of other protection systems, such as smoke control fans. Automatic sprinkler/suppression systems are normally activated by heat, and are designed to limit the fire growth and spread. Automatic smoke ventilation systems prevent the build-up of hot combustion products within an area. Depending on the design objective they can also reduce the temperature increase within the fire compartment, prevent smoke from affecting evacuation routes, or make conditions easier for the fire fighters operating inside the building.

Passive fire protection

Another line of defence, passive fire protection, is intended both to contain the fire within a room or compartment of origin and also to avoid structural collapse. In order to achieve effective compartmentation, careful attention should be given to any walls, windows, doorways or any other openings through which fire and smoke could potentially escape. To prevent rapid fire growth in both horizontal and vertical directions, the choice of materials used in the construction, contents and finishes of the building is important. In some instances fire-resisting construction is specified as a barrier to fire spread. For example, in most buildings floors are designed to do this. To avoid rapid fire growth within a space the surface linings may be specified to have low flame propagation and a low rate of heat release. Concrete generally has inherently good performance in fire and is used in structures either in its own right or as an encasement to, say, structural steel which will fail under continued exposure to fire (at temperatures $>550\,°C$). Plasterboard can also undertake this function, although applied coatings such as intumescent paint are also useful. Thick timber sections will protect themselves by charring in a fire. An unusual example is the Centre Georges Pompidou in Paris, which features water-filled steel columns.

Endnote

The protection of property and maintenance of business continuity are increasingly important issues for building owners. The use of fire engineering methods as discussed in the previous entry is being used more often in the analysis of possible fire scenarios, and the response of the building to them.

Further reading

Chartered Institution of Building Services Engineers (1997) *CIBSE Guide E: Fire Engineering*, CIBSE, London, UK.

Stollard, P. & Abrahams, J. (1999) *Fire from first principles: a design guide to building fire safety* (3rd edition), E & FN Spon, London, UK.

Lawson, R.M. & Newman, G.M. (1990) *Fire resistant design of steel structures*, SCI publication 080, The Steel Construction Institute, Ascot, UK.

OA

Fit-out

Activities that follow on from the major construction works to a building – usually including some electrics, fittings and furnishings etc. The fit-out activities complete a building ready for occupation.

See also: BESPOKE; BUILDING MANAGEMENT SYSTEMS; CEILINGS; CONSTRUCTION PROGRAMME; CRITICAL PATH ANALYSIS; DESIGN LIFE; FLOORS; GRIDS FOR STRUCTURE AND LAYOUT; HVAC; ICT IN BUILDINGS.

Introduction

The client requirements that define the way in which a building is designed and 'delivered' will affect the construction programme, the relationship and number of parties involved and the relative importance of different stages of the construction activities. It is in the latter stages of the process where the client may have particular influence on 'fit-out' activities. These are the final touches – servicing, fittings, and furnishings – that can be defined by the client or alternatively, the occupier or architect. These tend to define the character of a building and can set one building apart from another. Items covered in the fit-out specification may include the following:

- Art and sculpture;
- Catering equipment;
- Communications and data cabling;
- Control systems;
- Disabled access equipment;
- Display/information screens;
- Doors and ironmongery;
- Fire detection and alarms;
- Flooring finishes;
- Furniture;
- ICT equipment, TV, telephones etc.;
- Lighting;
- Non-loadbearing partitions or screens;
- Planting;
- Security and access equipment;
- Signage;
- Some aspects of HVAC;
- Storage.

The type of fit-out activities that are undertaken, and their cost, quality and specifications, will depend on the needs of the end-user, but they can also be influenced by the letting arrangements that will be used. The following sections explain the basic differences.

Owner-occupier

In owner-occupied buildings, the client is known from the outset and is also the final user of the building. This type of client would therefore expect to have significant input in the design and selection of all the above items, usually with advice and guidance from the architect. In some instances the owner-occupier may have very particular needs and a specialist contract (e.g. for laboratory equipment) may need to be let. In many respects, this is the simplest fit-out to provide because details can be discussed easily at any stage.

Speculative development

Where the building is being delivered to a client that is a speculative developer (i.e. a firm that lets out the building to others), then it may be difficult to provide a highly defined brief for the fit-out. Indeed, such is the case that a 'developer's fit-out' may be generic, responding to the basic requirements for a general market sector such as office occupiers. Some fit-out requirements will not be known until the final occupier and their activities are known, but the speculative developer would tend to avoid providing specialist items. Further options are described below.

Developer's fit out – this is common for speculative offices where the end requirements of the tenant can be predicted within reason. For example, typical office occupiers with no particular need for specialist equipment can easily be accommodated by a basic fit-out specified by the developer. There is no need for specialist input where such simple accommodation and facilities are expected and are easily lettable. The 'shell' and 'core' of the building would usually be let as a separate contract.

Turnkey contract – this example of a more sophisticated fit-out is where a building is provided either by a developer to any client or a known client. The principle is that the building is delivered to exacting requirements and the occupier can move in by 'turning the key' – everything is provided and is ready to use. It is more common for this to be handed over to a client for purchase otherwise there is a risk that the requirements may not fulfil the needs of a speculative occupier.

Serviced offices – in a similar example, the fit-out is designed to be managed in the long term by the developer. The developer takes on the responsibility of maintaining the entire office environment including all the fit-out items, and the occupier needs only to move in almost literally a few boxes of 'personal' items or specific equipment. Although this is a higher cost option for the occupier it is increasing in popularity for short and long term lets as it allows them total flexibility to pick and move their operations at short notice. In recent years it has been a popular option for IT 'start-ups' – small IT companies just starting out.

Endnote

The size and scale of fit-out will vary considerably according to the client, occupier, developer and each of their core businesses. In large buildings, separate contracts for the interior design of the building, the facilities management, the provision of planting or even management of pieces of art may be let as separate contracts. Such arrangements will influence the design and maintenance of the fit-out. This is of course related to refurbishment strategy and design life for the various elements of the interior of a building. Refurbishment intervals should be determined on the basis of likely functions and intensity of use that the building will experience in its lifetime. This could be less than five years for, say, retail refurbishments, up to 15 years for major office refurbishments.

Further reading

British Council for Offices (2000) *Guide to best practice in specification for offices*, BCO, London, UK.

McGregor, W. & Shiem-Shen Then, D. (1999) *Facilities management and the business of space*, Butterworth-Heinemann, Oxford UK.

Worthington, J. (1997) *Reinventing the workplace*, Butterworth-Heinemann, Oxford, UK.

JG

Flat roof
See: ROOFS

Installing a concrete beam and block system as the ground floor for a housing development. Photograph courtesy of the British Precast Concrete Federation.

Floors

Horizontal elements in a building, that span between beams or walls to provide space for occupation or circulation.

See also: ACOUSTICS; BEAM; CEILINGS; COMPOSITE DECKING; CONCRETE – STRUCTURES; DESIGN LIFE; FABRIC ENERGY STORAGE; FIT-OUT; ICT IN BUILDINGS; INTEGRATION; STRUCTURAL STEEL; SURFACE FINISHES; THERMAL BRIDGING; THERMOLABYRINTHS; TIMBER.

Materials and structure

A floor is an area of level structure within a building that can be used for circulation, living or working. Apart from the ground floor of a building (which may be a concrete slab on the ground) all floors are suspended, i.e. not in contact with the ground, rather they are supported by horizontal structural elements (beams) or span between loadbearing walls. Most floors consist of a wearing surface and structural elements beneath e.g. timber joists and floorboards (planks). Ground floor construction includes at least some perimeter (edge) insulation and a DPC or DPM (damp proof course or membrane) to prevent thermal bridging. Intermediate floors within buildings usually only require sound insulation.

Timber, concrete and steel are used in floor structures and there is a wealth of different floor configurations, designs, spans and attributes to choose from. In domestic construction, simple timber or concrete structures span short distances whereas in larger framed structures, floors and beams become integrated in flat slabs or steel 'Slimdek' solutions. Steel and concrete tend to be used to span longer distances, but laminated timber is an alternative. In the UK the Building Regulations govern the structure, thermal, fire and acoustic performance of floors.

Floor finishes

The building use and function of a space will usually determine the most appropriate type of floor finish in terms of material, flatness and colour. Natural timber, plastics (linoleum or PVC), concrete, stone, tiling, mosaic, carpet or even glass can be used. Heavy circulation areas for example demand a hardwearing finish such as concrete, marble or terrazzo. Less trafficked areas will clearly require surfaces with less wear resistance such as carpet. For buildings with large expanses of flooring such as warehouses and retail parks it may be appropriate to consider surface flatness in some detail. This is a measure of accuracy for floors and can be critical for buildings with high bay racking systems. In these facilities, laser-levelled concrete screeds are used to ensure 'very flat' floor levels (e.g. +/−1 mm in 3 m). In shopping centres and hospitals self-levelling screeds are often used: over 10,000 m^2 can be poured in just a few days with no need for manual finishing afterwards. Floor finishes cover a significant area of internal surfaces and so the materials specified will affect indoor air quality. The general understanding is that people with allergies and asthma etc. suffer less in buildings with hard and/or inert surfaces such as terracotta tiles, concrete, marble, terrazzo and some forms of natural timber flooring (depending on the timber treatment used). These are cleaned easily and do not withhold dust and dirt. In areas such as kitchens, bathrooms and laboratories, it is common to see floor surfaces that are easy to clean and are non-slip for hygiene and safety reasons.

Integrated design of floor systems

The cost of building structures is such that a reduction in height of even 500 mm overall can mean significant savings (i.e. in cladding, structure and foundation costs). For this reason, there has been a trend towards more careful co-ordination of structure and servicing in order to reduce overall building height. This integrated approach demands great effort at the working drawing stage on the part of the architect and building services engineer, but will reap dividends in overall costs (see also *Integration*). The integrated approach considers typically the close inter-linking of floor structure and:

- Air handling ducts;
- Electrics;
- Fire protection systems;
- ICT and data cabling;
- PA systems;
- Telecommunications;
- Wet services.

In some types of construction there is considerable scope to utilise the space between the floor finish and the floor structure (sometimes called a plenum). In Roman buildings the floor surface was stacked on piles of stone or tiling to create a void through which warm air would circulate (a hypocaust). This was an early form of underfloor heating – in modern buildings the space between floors is more often used for data cabling, electrics and air-conditioning ducts. Underfloor heating is now more typically a system of pipes embedded in a concrete screed through which heated or cooled water is circulated; thermolabyrinths work on a similar principle.

In many buildings that use a frame structure the plenum space is utilised for ICT cabling etc., and it is usual to see 'raised floor systems' or 'access floor systems' with adjustable aluminium props supporting a tiled or carpeted floor finish. The 600 mm square modules allow easy access and are very flexible for the commercial occupier. In sports centres and dance studios it is common practice to have a sprung timber floor, which prevents jarring to the body on impact. In a similar application a 'floating floor' is sometimes used to acoustically isolate machinery from the building structure to reduce noise transmission.

Built examples

It is not difficult to find ingenious examples of floor designs in contemporary architecture.

- An innovative approach to a heavily serviced laboratory building is the Salk Institute in California, USA (1959–65) by American architect Louis Kahn. To maximise the floor area available for lab space, Kahn used intermediate mezzanine floors with integrated structure (Vierendeel trusses) and servicing.
- In Renzo Piano's temporary wooden interior structure for the performance of *Prometeo* (1983, Venice and Milan, Italy) he used a raised floor of expressive laminated timber that curved upwards into screen walls. The entrance to the space was at the base of the timber floor structure, heightening the experience of the performance. The scale and craftsmanship were likened to that of boats or musical instruments.
- In the UK, commercial raised floor systems were not common until after 1974, following the first application in the Willis Faber Corroon building in Ipswich by Foster and Partners. This building set the standard for many UK office developments and is still revered architecturally for its façade and innovative approach to office design.

Further reading

Goodchild, C.H. (1997) *Economic concrete frame elements*, Reinforced Concrete Council, Crowthorne, UK.

Ogden, R.G. et al. (1996) *Architectural teaching resource: studio guide*, SCI Publication 167, The Steel Construction Institute, Ascot, UK.

JG

Foster, Norman (Lord Foster of Thames Bank)

An internationally renowned architect, Norman Foster (b.1935) leads the UK 'high-tech' movement with his rigorous approach to quality and detailing. Foster's buildings share a common theme of stunning visual architecture coupled with cutting edge technological innovation.

See also: ALUMINIUM; ATRIUM; CLADDING; CONCRETE; CONNECTIONS; FAÇADES AND FAÇADE ENGINEERING; FLOORS; GRIMSHAW, NICHOLAS; 'HIGH TECH'; HVAC; INTEGRATION; INTELLIGENT FAÇADES AND MATERIALS; LOUVRES AND BRISE SOLEIL; RITCHIE, IAN; ROGERS, RICHARD; STACK EFFECT; STRUCTURAL STEEL; SURFACE FINISHES; TECHNOLOGY TRANSFER; VAN DER ROHE, MIES; WINDOWS AND CURTAIN WALLING.

The leading British architect of his generation, Foster began in practice with the other prophet of High Tech, Richard Rogers in 'Team 4' until 1967. His first important solo building was the Willis Faber Dumas Insurance Offices in Ipswich, Suffolk (1970–75; now Willis Faber Corroon) in which an undulating, glazed, hung curtain wall follows exactly the contours of the site, the structural columns set well back from the skin. The floor plans are left completely free in a radical realisation of the flexibility and flowing space anticipated by Mies van der Rohe. The high proportion of glazing to floor area also contributed to the building, which was extensively naturally lit. The Sainsbury Centre for the Visual Arts at the University of East Anglia, Norwich (1976–78) is an ingenious and impressive shed for art, a radical engineering take on the preciousness of traditional museum architecture. The structure is hangar-like, in the form of continuous trusses for both walls and roof within the depth of which the services are housed. The industrial, engineering aesthetic was moved forward with the dramatically suspended roof of the Renault Distribution Centre in Swindon, Wiltshire (1980–83). However it was the remarkable Hong Kong and Shanghai Bank (1979–86) which made Norman Foster an international name and seemed to define the role of the international banks in the consumerist 1980s as machines for the production of money. The huge cross braces which strengthen the exposed steel structure became the building's aesthetic expression and are echoed internally in the overwhelming atrium criss-crossed with escalators leading to a public plaza and thoroughfare running beneath the structure.

Foster's subsequent buildings included Stansted Airport Terminal in Essex (1981–91), one of the clearest, most readable and most enjoyable of transport interchanges with its elegant tubular steel 'trees' and slender roof. Based on a series of modules that are both structural columns and contain the building's servicing, the extensively glazed roof is supported on struts emerging from the top of these modules.

The building's clarity has been spoilt somewhat by subsequent interventions although it still reveals Foster's love for aeronautical structures (when asked to choose his favourite building he famously declared it to be the Boeing 747). The designs for Hong Kong International Airport (1992–96) also represented a significant landmark in the planning of complex, functional transport structures. The ITN Headquarters building in London (1989), Century Tower Tokyo (1992), Business Promotion Centre, Duisberg, Germany (1993) compounded his reputation but it was another bank, the Commerzbank in Frankfurt-am-Main (1994–97), which reaffirmed him as one of the few innovators consistently concerned with the crossover between technology and architecture. An apparently 'eco-friendly skyscraper', the building boasts a series of gardens in atria rising up through its floors which allow the building to breathe and create internal parks. The Commerzbank also uses a twin-skin façade system with integral louvres and shading.

Despite being widely known for the design of megastructures, Foster's smaller buildings, including the Sackler Galleries atop the Royal Academy in London (1989–91) and the Mediatheque in Nîmes, France (1984–93) demonstrate a subtlety and ability to work with historic buildings, contexts and a smaller scale of intervention which is sometimes surprising and often delightful. The Mediatheque in particular, is a delicate concrete and aluminium response to the Roman temple which is its neighbour. Foster's work with context and history led to a remarkable victory in the competition to rebuild the Reichstag Parliament building in Berlin (1995–99), a scheme which centred around the construction of a new glass dome above Berlin's most iconic government building. At the centre of the dome a cone clad in mirror glass acts both as a funnel to extract exhaust air from the heart of the building and as a device to reflect natural light back into the spaces below. Excess heat produced from the building is also transferred to a natural aquifer 300 m below the building where it is stored; warm water can be pumped back up to the building when required.

The Scottish Conference Centre on the bank of the River Clyde in Glasgow (1995–98) is another notable example of Foster's skill with landmark buildings with its interlocking curved volumes and shiny aluminium cladding. Other recent buildings include the controversial Millennium Bridge (1996–2000) and the GLA headquarters building (1999) both in London. Foster remains one of the most influential and successful architects currently working and one of the few who is genuinely and passionately involved in the aesthetic dialogue between engineering, technology and architecture.

Further reading

Davies, C. (1997) *Commerzbank Frankfurt*, Watermark/Birkhäuser, Basle, Switzerland.

Jenkins, D. (ed.) (2000) *On Foster… Foster On*, Prestel Verlag, Munich, Germany.

Lambot, I. (ed.) (1990) *Norman Foster, Foster Associates, Buildings and Projects* (Volume 1: 1964–1971),Watermark, Surrey, UK.

Lambot, I. (ed.) (1989) *Norman Foster, Foster Associates, Buildings and Projects* (Volume 2: 1971–1978), Watermark, Surrey, UK.

Lambot, I. (ed.) (1989) *Norman Foster, Foster Associates, Buildings and Projects* (Volume 3: 1978–1985), Watermark, Surrey, UK.

Lambot, I. (ed.) (1990) *Norman Foster, Foster Associates, Buildings and Projects* (Volume 4: 1982–1989), Watermark, Surrey, UK.

Papadakis, A. et al. (eds.) (1992) *Foster Associates, Architectural Monographs No.20* Academy Editions, John Wiley & Sons, London, UK.

Pawley, M. (1999) *Norman Foster – a global architecture*, Thames & Hudson, London, UK.

EH

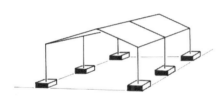

Pad foundations supporting a portal frame structure. Image provided by Ove Arup & Partners.

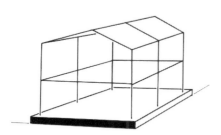

Raft foundations – typical for houses and other small, light structures. Image provided by Ove Arup & Partners.

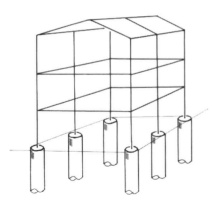

Pile foundations – used in weak ground and for taller structures. Image provided by Ove Arup & Partners.

Foundations

There are two basic types: 'shallow', which includes pad footings, strip footings and rafts and 'deep' i.e. piles. The choice is a function of the strength and stiffness of the underlying strata and the load to be carried, the aim being to limit differential settlement on the structure and more importantly the finishes.

See also: BRACING; CANTILEVERS; COLUMN; CONCRETE; CONNECTIONS; CONSTRUCTION PROGRAMME; CORE (STRUCTURAL); CRITICAL PATH ANALYSIS; DESIGN LIFE; DURABILITY; FRAME; STRUCTURAL STEEL; WALLS.

What is a foundation?

The purpose of a foundation is to spread the weight of the building onto the ground below without undue settlement or collapse. The ground will always tend to compress or settle when additional weight is placed upon it. Foundation design is usually governed by the need to limit the relative or differential settlement between adjacent walls or columns and thus limit the risk of damage, particularly to any brittle internal or external finishes.

Broadly speaking, most foundations are made with concrete, either as a mass material, or using reinforcement. Nevertheless, masonry, stone and sometimes steel have a part to play in some instances.

Shallow foundations

The simplest and cheapest form of foundation is a shallow concrete **pad or strip footing** – individual pad footings being used to support columns and continuous strip footings for walls. The footing simply spreads the wall or column load over a sufficient area, as a 'bulb' of pressure, to limit the settlement to an acceptable value. The size of the footing depends on the load to be carried and the stiffness of the ground below. Clays and sands tend to be more compressible than gravel or rock, so larger footings will be needed to keep the settlement within acceptable limits. The depth of the footing is chosen to avoid any seasonal movements due to expansion of the ground when it freezes or shrinkage of the ground in dry weather (a particular problem in clays). In the UK this implies a minimum depth of about 750–1000 mm.

Where the upper strata are too soft or variable, it may be necessary to adopt a **raft foundation**. In its simplest form a raft is a thick concrete slab which extends under the building. A raft foundation has two advantages. First, it spreads the load onto the ground over the full area of the building, rather than the smaller area of individual pad footings. The pressure applied to the ground and hence the amount of settlement is therefore reduced – a particular advantage on soft ground. Second, a raft is able to span over any localised soft spots under the building, evening out any differential settlement; an advantage on variable ground such as man-made fill.

Deep foundations

Where a stiff enough founding strata does not exist within about 2–3 m of the surface, or where there is a high local water table, a shallow foundation becomes uneconomic to construct. In this case, it may be necessary to use piles to carry the weight of the building onto deeper stiffer strata below. The most common piles are **bored cast-in-place concrete piles** varying in diameter from about 0.2–2 m and in depth from perhaps 10–40 m. **Driven piles**, though also used, are less common, driven referring to the manner in which the steel, concrete or timber shaft is hammered into the ground. All piles work in more or less the same way – load applied to the top of the pile is resisted in a combination of bearing on the base of the pile and friction between the side of the pile and the ground. Where two or more piles are required to support the load on a single column, a pilecap is used to spread the column load onto the group of piles below.

Before the form and cost of a building's foundations can be determined with any certainty, there will need to be a geotechnical site investigation – trial pits and boreholes are dug to find the thickness of the underlying strata, which are then tested for strength and stiffness. Sometimes, the underlying strata may even determine the form of superstructure. For example on relatively weak ground, it might be sensible to optimise the frame to limit the load on the foundations, enabling a pad or raft type foundation to be used, rather than adopt a solution that might require a piled and therefore costlier foundation. The site investigation might also detect the presence of man-made fills, hazardous materials, underground obstructions or a high local water table. If these are known about in advance then appropriate allowance can be made in the programme and cost plan and remediation techniques can be used.

Further reading

Tomlinson, M.J. with Boorman, R. (2001) *Foundation design and construction* (7th edition), Prentice Hall, Harlow, UK.

OA

Frame

The structural frame is the skeleton that supports the building above foundation level. Normally consisting of beams, columns and walls, the structural frame takes the loading on the building to the foundations.

See also: BEAM; BRACING; CANTILEVER; COLUMN; CONCRETE; CONSTRUCTION PROGRAMME; CORE (STRUCTURAL); CRITICAL PATH ANALYSIS; FOUNDATIONS; STRUCTURAL STEEL; TIMBER – STRUCTURES; VAN DER ROHE, MIES; WALLS.

What is a frame?

Frames support the loads applied to a building via beams and columns, thus differentiating themselves from other forms of construction such as loadbearing walls. The frame may be stabilised by bracing or a structural core. The use of frame construction minimises the amount of structure within the used space, maximising flexibility of the enclosed space. Columns are arranged typically on an orthogonal grid and connected by beams. Either secondary beams and/or a slab then connect these beams. The orthogonal grid normally produces the most economic frame, but it is possible to construct frames to suit any practical grid layout. Whilst the overall building frame is clearly three-dimensional, it is often convenient to consider the parts of the frame in the orthogonal directions as independent. These independent frames only have stability in two directions and rely on their orthogonal frames for stability in the third. These types of frame are known as **plane** frames. Alternatively the frame

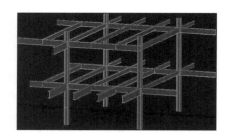

Extract of a three dimensional model of a typical steel frame. Image provided by Ove Arup & Partners.

may be designed such that the behaviour in all directions is related and the three dimensions require consideration together. This type of frame is known as a **space frame**. The stability to the frame may be provided by the rigidity of the connections between the columns and the beams (or slab): this is known as a **moment frame**. Alternatively the horizontal loads may be carried through the floor to a structural core: this is known as a **braced frame**. Whilst moment frames remove the need for structural cores, they may lead to larger column and beam sizes.

Design and material selection

The normal materials for frame construction are concrete, steel and timber. Whilst generally the frame includes the columns, beams and their stability system the slab may be included, more commonly in in-situ and hybrid concrete construction where it forms an integral part of the frame. A particular example of this is concrete flat slab frame construction where there are no beams. Traditionally steel frame structures require a significant amount of factory fabrication before work starts on site but are quick to erect, whilst concrete frame structures are quick to start on site but may be slower to construct. Steel frames are lighter, which can help in foundation design, whilst concrete structures have inherent fire and corrosion protection. There are exceptions to these general rules and it is likely that in the future environmental issues such as material use and energy efficiency (e.g. fabric energy storage) will dictate increasingly the choice of frame material.

Architectural note

Historically, timber frames were used for medieval housing with the walls constructed from local non-loadbearing materials. Cast iron was also used in the 19th century but this was often to provide additional framing to loadbearing masonry structures. Cast iron was superseded by the use of structural steel, and its principal rival during the last century has been reinforced concrete. Although concrete and steel framing techniques dominate the market for commercial buildings and larger structures, the use of timber remains popular for smaller structures or bespoke architecture. Laminated timber frame elements, 'green' oak and other built-up timber beams and columns are particularly attractive.

Further reading

Chilton, J. (2000) *Space grid structures*, Butterworth-Heinemann, Oxford, UK.

Goodchild, C.H. (1997) *Economic concrete frame elements*, Reinforced Concrete Council, Crowthorne, UK.

Ogden, R.G. et al (1996) *Architectural teaching resource: studio guide*, SCI Publication 167, The Steel Construction Institute, Ascot, UK.

OA

Lloyds Register of Shipping in the City of London. This Richard Rogers Partnership design features an innovative 'hybrid' concrete frame structure, shown here during construction. Photograph courtesy of The Concrete Society.

FRP

See: COMPOSITE MATERIALS; PLASTICS

Galvanic series
See: CORROSION; METALS

Galvanising

Steel is vulnerable to corrosion but can be treated with a protective layer. The protection afforded by zinc is very effective. The application of a zinc layer is called galvanising.

See also: CLADDING; CORROSION; COR-TEN®; DESIGN LIFE; DURABILITY; EPOXY; METALS; ROOFS; STAINLESS STEEL; STANDING SEAM ROOF; STRUCTURAL STEEL; SURFACE FINISHES; WEATHERING; ZINC.

What is galvanising?

Zinc coatings protect steel by acting as a physical barrier, isolating the steel from the atmosphere, and corroding more slowly than the steel. They also self-heal to protect the steel, even if the coating is cut or damaged – the corrosion products of zinc include an oxide film that forms over the cut. The best protection is provided by hot dip galvanising which produces a coating which is metallurgically bonded to the steel, forming zinc/iron alloys at the prepared face of the steel, with an outer layer of pure zinc. This outer layer is relatively soft, protecting the surface from damage during handling and fixing, whilst the hardness of the alloy layer continues to protect the steel itself. The products of corrosion of the zinc itself add to the protective layer (typically an oxide skin), unless washed off by repeated wetting and drying. The bright metallic appearance of galvanising changes with exposure to a uniform grey. Some products (e.g. continuous galvanised strip or sheet) can be specified with a range of either smooth or spangle (i.e. crystalline pattern) finishes.

In terms of design life, galvanising dramatically improves the durability of steel. The period of effective protection is determined by coating mass (usually expressed in grammes/m^2), and the environmental conditions of exposure. Testing by accelerated weathering demonstrates that the period to first maintenance can be up to hundreds of years when correctly designed and installed (average annual corrosion rates are indicated in BS EN ISO 14713, with corrosivity categories from ISO 9223).

Alternative protection methods for steel include the use of stainless steel, protective surface coatings or the use of weathering steel (COR-TEN®).

Types of galvanising

A range of galvanising techniques exist to cater for architectural, engineering and specialist manufacturing applications.

- **Hot dip** – this is applied to steel of at least 6 mm thickness, giving a metallurgically bonded coating typically 600 g/m². After preparation, components are dipped in molten zinc.
- **Centrifuge** – this is used for complex shapes like threaded bolts.
- **Zinc spraying** – heated, atomised zinc is sprayed on to components.
- **Continuous galvanised sheet** – light gauge steel strip is passed through a hot dip as part of a continuous process for coating steels about 3 mm thick, giving a range of coatings from 100–600 g/m² (275 g/m², Z275 is often used in construction).
- **Electroplating** – the component acts as a cathode in a plating bath, metal being deposited electrolytically to give a lighter coating than with hot dip.
- **Sherardising** – smaller components like screws and ironmongery are tumbled with zinc dust and heated. This gives a closely controlled coating of uniform thickness particularly suitable for screw fasteners.
- **Painting** – zinc rich paints can afford some protection when applied to bare steel, or used as a remedial treatment to damaged areas or cut edges.

Practical matters

Mechanical fixings (e.g. bolts, self-drill screws, rivets and clinches) should be specified carefully to minimise damage to the coating. Welding employs a number of techniques for effective joints, and specialist advice should be sought regarding safe and effective methods. Damage to the coating would normally need to be made good afterwards. Adhesives are used increasingly, especially in conjunction with mechanical fixing, where epoxy adhesives tend to perform well, and some PVC based formulations cope well with surface contaminants such as rolling oil (from the manufacturing process). Specialist advice should be sought for particular applications. Heavy gauge components for hot dip are fully worked and finished, where possible, before galvanising. Forming pre-galvanised components (such as cold formed galvanised strip) takes account of the effect of coating thickness/bend radius on final design, and the consequences of cutting and drilling. Detailed guidelines are available from industry specialists.

GW

Gasket
See: CONNECTIONS

Gerberette
See: CASTINGS; PIANO, RENZO

Glass

Glass is a very common construction material, used in windows, doors, façades and curtain walling. It is the principal material in glazed assemblies and can be ordered from a wide variety of different specifications.

View of the glazed bridge between adjacent shops in the Arndale Centre, Manchester city centre. Such dynamic glass structures are now more easily designed with the aid of computers. Photograph courtest of Ove Arup & Partners.

See also: CLADDING; FAÇADES AND FAÇADE ENGINEERING; GLASS – LAMINATED AND COATED; GLASS – STRUCTURAL GLAZING; INTELLIGENT FAÇADES AND MATERIALS; GRIMSHAW, NICHOLAS; JIRICNA, EVA; MINERAL FIBRES; SEALANTS; VON GERKAN AND MARG; WINDOWS AND CURTAIN WALLING.

Definitions

The term *glass* denotes a wide range of ceramics that have been cooled from a melt to a rigid state without crystallisation.

The term *glazing* is used to denote:

- Glass or transparent plastic material that covers a building or fills an opening;
- Process of placing glass into a frame or onto a building;
- Process and/or materials used in bonding glass to a frame, as in structural silicone glazing or structural sealant glazing.

Glass types and manufacture

The majority of glass used in buildings is a type called soda lime glass, the exception being low thermal expansion borosilicate glass, which is used for some fire resisting applications. Soda lime glass is used in a variety of tinted forms, which are achieved by the addition of metal oxides, to decrease its absorption of solar energy. Soda lime glass is also available as low iron glass with reduced levels of iron oxide for increased clarity and absence of the common green tint. The majority of glasses are transparent, but mixtures of glassy phases or a degree of crystallisation provides translucency in some glasses. The term 'super cooled liquid' is misleading because, at typical usage temperatures, they are solids and do not flow. However, like liquids, glasses have an amorphous, macroscopically homogeneous microstructure.

Glass has been in use for about 7,000 years, but the material that we associate with buildings today has only been produced for the last hundred years or so. The availability of better production technology (and that of iron and steel etc.) led to such buildings as the palm houses at Kew gardens, London (c.1845) and the Crystal Palace in London (1851) together with a series of glazed railway station roofs across the capital. Until the 1920s, all glass was "blown" – the Crystal Palace featured some 270,000 individually hand-blown panes.

Flat glass of various types is now the most common product for use in the construction industry – millions of square kilometres are specified every year. Historically, this was produced by a number of processes, many of which are now used rarely but whose capacity and characteristics influenced architecture in their time. Designers should be aware of the differences between the techniques – in conservation work it may be necessary to specify both the material and the method of production.

Crown glass was produced by spinning a disc of hot glass on the end of an iron rod in front of a furnace. The surfaces had a fire polished finish but small pane sizes.

Cylinder glass was manufactured by hand blowing a cylinder of glass and then cutting it open and flattening it in a kiln. The process was incrementally mechanised leading to increased pane sizes and cost reduction. The surface quality was only moderate owing to contact of the hot glass with an iron surface while flattening.

Plate glass was made by pouring molten glass onto an iron table, rolling it roughly flat and then grinding and polishing both surfaces to achieve transparency. The optical quality and cost of plate glass were both high and it was generally used for large shop windows prior to the advent of float glass.

Drawn sheet glass is produced continuously by drawing a ribbon of molten glass from a tank by means of rollers on the edges. The surfaces are of high clarity because they are fire polished but minor variations in thickness produce ripples, which are visible in transmission.

Rolled sheet is generally patterned and is produced by continuously rolling molten glass between cooled metal rollers. Rolling two streams of molten glass together, with a steel mesh in between, produces wired glass (used for fire safety purposes).

The generic glass: 'float glass'

Devised by Sir Alastair Pilkington, circa 1955, this now makes up the majority of flat glass production with about 180 operating lines worldwide. Molten glass flows continuously onto a bath of molten tin where it forms a flat pool as it cools and is drawn across the tin and onto rollers. The ribbon of glass is continuously annealed and automatically cut and off-loaded. The surface quality approaches that of plate glass and the process has been automated progressively to reach very low production costs. Float glass is available in a range of thickness from 3–25 mm, although the majority of production is 3 and 4 mm with 6, 8, 10 and 12 mm commonly used in architecture. The maximum width of float glass is 3.21 m and the largest 'jumbo' sheets are 6 m long. Longer pieces of float glass have been manufactured by special arrangement with certain glass producers.

Annealed glass, usually float, can be **toughened** by heating it to about 600 °C and quenching it evenly with air. The surfaces of the pane solidify while the core continues to contract because it cools more slowly, producing a system of residual stress, which is compressive at the surface and tensile in the core. The compressive stress in the surface of toughened glass increases its strength by a factor of about four. When toughened glass is fractured, the stored strain energy is released by shattering the pane into thousands of fragments. If the fragmentation meets approved standards, toughened glass may be classified as 'toughened safety glass' because it reduces the risk of serious injury in the event of breakage. Good quality conditions in the oven make for good quality glass. A recent spate of breakages has been attributed to nickel sulphide inclusions, which can be detected easily by heat-soaking the glass to 300 °C.

Enamelled or fritted glass is used for decoration, shading and spandrel applications. Decorative enamel is applied to glass as a frit by screen-printing or roller. The coloured glass particles in the frit fuse to the surface of the glass during the heating stage of toughening.

Interested readers should consider a visit to the National Glass Centre in Sunderland, which showcases the use of many types of glass and glazing products. The building uses glass extensively in its construction, including a glass roof that visitors can traverse.

Further reading

Behling, S. & Behling, S. (eds.) (1999) *Glass: structure and technology in architecture*, Prestel Verlag, Munich, Germany.

Button, D. & Pye, B. (eds.) (1993) *Glass in building: a guide to modern architectural glass performance*, Butterworth-Heinemann, Oxford, UK.

Cerver, F. (1997) *The architecture of glass: shaping light*, Hearts Books International, USA.

Compagno, A. (1999) *Intelligent glass façades: materials, practice, design* (4th edition), Birkhäuser, Basle, Switzerland.

Institution of Structural Engineers (1999) *Structural use of glass in buildings*, ISE, London, UK.

Knaack, U. (1998) *Konstrucktiver Glasbau*, Rudolf Müller, Köln, Germany.

Krampen, M. & Schempp, D. (1999) *Glass architects*, AVEdition, Germany.

Krewinkel, H.W. (1998) *Glass buildings: material, structure and detail*, Birkhäuser, Basle, Switzerland.

Rice, P. & Dutton, H. (1997) *Structural glass* (2nd edition), E & FN Spon, London, UK.

Schittich et al. (1999) *Glass construction manual*, Birkhäuser, Basle, Switzerland.

Vandenburg, M. (1997) *Glass canopies*, Academy Editions, John Wiley & Sons, London, UK.

Wigginton, M. (1996) *Glass in architecture*, Phaidon Press Limited, London, UK.

OA

Glass – laminated and coated glass

These two types of glass provide designers with a remarkable array of options for the building envelope from improved energy efficiency to holographic imaging.

See also: DESIGN LIFE; ENERGY EFFICIENCY; FAÇADES AND FAÇADE ENGINEERING; GLASS; GLASS – STRUCTURAL GLAZING; GRIMSHAW, NICHOLAS; INTELLIGENT FAÇADES AND MATERIALS; JIRICNA, EVA; PLASTICS; RICE, PETER; RITCHIE, IAN; WINDOWS AND CURTAIN WALLING.

The potential of toughened, laminated glass – a glass walkway. Many such examples exist now, inspiring architects to push glass technology even further. Photograph courtesy of Ove Arup & Partners.

Introduction

These two groups of glass products form a vast range of materials, which are suitable for use in architecture. The developing technology of glass production is resulting in a continually evolving range of specialist glasses that offer new opportunities for designers seeking perhaps 'smart' materials, intelligent façades or even just an interior glass screen. In parallel with drives for 'lean construction', we now expect building materials to deliver much more added value. In the case of glass products, this means we expect more than just a glazing material. The two types, laminated and coated glasses are explained in turn.

Laminated glass

The term laminated glass refers to a range of products which comprise two or more layers of glass bonded with another material, usually a more ductile plastic. In common usage, laminated glass commonly denotes laminated annealed glass, which is two layers of float glass bonded with polyvinyl-butyral (PVB). Laminates may also be made with glass that is tempered, heat-strengthened, chemically strengthened, coated or otherwise processed. Laminated glass of various types can be used in differing situations to provide:

- Containment of people or broken glass;
- Human impact safety;
- Resistance to break-in;
- Resistance to firearm attack (bulletproof glass is about six layers thick);
- Resistance to explosive blast;
- Robustness where glass carries structural loads.

Toughened laminated glass is twice the cost of normal toughened glass, but it is safer for overhead applications (the glass breaks, but sticks to the interlayer, rather than falling).

Polyvinyl-butyral (PVB) is the most widely used interlayer material owing to its high ductility at room temperature and its large capacity to absorb impact energy. Several other interlayers are in use, giving a range of specialised benefits. Chemical curing polymethyl methacrylate (PMMA) will accommodate variations in flatness when laminating heat treated glass and can be formulated to enhance the sound attenuation of laminated glass. Chemical curing polyester resin requires minimal capital equipment for laminate production and offers improved toughness compared with PMMA. Polyester resin cured by ultra-violet light has extended working time and faster cure. High strength transparent films of drawn polyester may be laminated between panes of glass using resin systems to give enhanced penetration resistance. Polyurethane (PU) interlayers have improved clarity and temperature resistance compared with PVB and are also used to laminate glass with layers of polycarbonate for ballistic protection. A sheet interlayer of ionomer (a polymer containing ionic bonds between long chain molecules) was first introduced in 1999 and offers increased resistance to penetration in addition to higher shear stiffness and useable temperature range.

A number of other special purpose interlayers are in use or under development:

- **Electrochromic glazing** that changes the depth of its colour with application of a voltage;
- **Holographic glazing** that redirects or manipulates light in unusual ways;
- **Intumescent fire resistant glazing** that foams under intense heat to provide integrity and insulation against fire;
- **Liquid crystal privacy glazing** that is switchable between clear and diffusing states;
- **Selective vision glazing** that obscures the view through selected ranges of angle;
- **Thermotropic glazing** that reversibly changes its appearance with temperature.

An interesting example of the structural potential of simple laminated glass can be seen in Rick Mather's extension to a house in Hampstead, London. The single storey extension is made almost entirely of laminated glass, including façade, beams and columns (it was built in 1992).

Coated glass

Glass may be coated to change its reflectivity to visible light and infrared radiation. This can change its appearance and improve its performance in regulating the flow of energy into or out of a building. The surface of glass can be modified during production by the float process to achieve a number of benefits, including:

- Conductivity for electromagnetic shielding;
- Reflection of visible light for solar control or use as a mirror;
- Reflection of near-infrared radiation to reduce the transmission of solar energy into a building (clear solar control);
- Reflection of far-infrared to reduce heat loss from a building (low emissivity);
- Cancelling interference between incident and reflected light to reduce reflectivity;
- Super-hydrophilicity and photo-catalisation to minimise the need for cleaning (super-hydrophilicity is the property of attracting water very strongly and consequently repelling oily droplets. It makes water spread out into a film on the surface rather than forming droplets).

Coatings produced directly onto the ribbon of hot glass as it floats on the tin bath are known as on-line, pyrolitic or hard coatings and are generally sufficiently durable to be stocked, transported, cut tempered, bent or laminated. The production cost is minimised by the level of automation and scale of production on a limited range of thickness. An 'on-line' coating is typically a single, precisely controlled, layer of a metal or silicon oxide or nitride.

Improved performance in most of the above benefits, notably clear solar control and increased choice of substrate glass, can be obtained by off-line coating techniques where the coating is applied under vacuum conditions. The coatings are commonly systems of several layers of metals and metal oxides and nitrides, deposited to controlled thicknesses. Vacuum deposition or soft coatings tend to be more readily scratched and attacked by the environment so subsequent processing is limited. For these reasons soft coatings are generally used only in sealed insulating units such as double and triple glazing.

The combination of coated glasses in a laminate is under development.

Further reading

Behling, S. & Behling, S. (eds.) (1999) *Glass: structure and technology in architecture*, Prestel Verlag, Munich, Germany.

Button, D. & Pye, B. (eds.) (1993) *Glass in building: a guide to modern architectural glass performance*, Butterworth-Heinemann, Oxford, UK.

Cerver, F. (1997) *The architecture of glass: shaping light*, Hearts Books Intl, USA.

Compagno, A. (1999) *Intelligent glass façades: materials, practice, design* (4th edition), Birkhäuser, Basle, Switzerland.

Institution of Structural Engineers (1999) *Structural use of glass in buildings*, ISE, London, UK.

Knaack, U. (1998) *Konstrucktiver Glasbau*, Rudolf Müller, Köln, Germany.

Krampen, M. & Schempp, D. (1999) *Glass architects*, AVEdition, Germany.

Krewinkel, H.W. (1998) *Glass buildings: material, structure and detail*, Birkhäuser, Basle, Switzerland.

Rice, P. & Dutton, H. (1997) *Structural glass* (2nd edition), E & FN Spon, London, UK.

Schittich et al. (1999) *Glass construction manual*, Birkhäuser, Basle, Switzerland.

Vandenburg, M. (1997) *Glass canopies*, Academy Editions, John Wiley & Sons, UK.

Wigginton, M. (1996) *Glass in architecture*, Phaidon Press Limited, London, UK.

OA

Glass – structural glazing

Glass can be used in an expressive way in structural elements. Toughened laminated glass panes can be installed with minimal fixings and in some instances used as beams to support all-glass structures.

See also: ALUMINIUM; BESPOKE; CASTINGS; CLADDING; CONNECTIONS; FAÇADES AND FAÇADE ENGINEERING; FOSTER, NORMAN; GLASS; GLASS – LAMINATED AND COATED GLASS; GRIMSHAW, NICHOLAS; JIRICNA, EVA; RICE, PETER; RITCHIE, IAN; SEALANTS; STAINLESS STEEL; STRUCTURAL STEEL; VON GERKAN & MARG; WINDOWS AND CURTAIN WALLING.

Introduction

The use of glass in the design of structural elements (i.e. façades, floors and roofs) is now a substantial subject area (readers should refer to the references given at the end for comprehensive guidance). This discussion is not about windows, rather it is about using glass as a material in its own right with a minimum of supporting structure to meet modern architectural expectations relating to achieving maximum transparency, while at the same time creating a robust building envelope. The use of glass in this way is now very popular and is a highly fashionable design solution for a range of building types including commercial, leisure and individual residences. The transparency and finely detailed nature of structural glazing enables architects to develop the concept of reducing the physical separation between interior and exterior spaces without compromising the need for performance.

Historical development

Glass has been in use for thousands of years, but it was only fairly recently that large panes, and appropriate connection details, allowed the structural possibilities of the material to be capitalised upon. The Great Exhibition Pavilion at the Crystal Palace in 1851, and several London railway stations, indicated what could be achieved with a glazed cast iron structure. After the Modernist movement and the widespread fashion for 'picture' windows in the 1930s, there was a dip in popularity but this changed in the 1980s. The high-tech movement brought back glass into the architectural idiom again. However, this was presaged as early as 1975 when Foster & Partners used frameless glass panels (12 mm thick, and 2000 mm wide) for the façade of the Willis Faber building in Ipswich.

The real revolution for 'structural' glazing was in the use of toughened glass because it maintains its integrity even when perforated at the corners. This was demonstrated elegantly and manifestly in the Parc de la Villette Science Museum in Paris, completed in 1986. The ingenious engineer Peter Rice was behind the design for the façade system, with colleagues Martin Francis and Ian Ritchie (RFR). The system of steel struts and tie rods that support the large glass sheets were a significant step forward; this building re-defined the way that glass could be used in modern buildings.

It was not long before the first patents appeared for the now familiar spider-like connectors and structural glazing soon became the façade material of choice for many prestigious projects. Engineers Dewhurst Macfarlane have also provided influential expertise in this area. Their portfolio includes Eva Jiricna's early glass staircases (London, late 1980s), glass beams for a number of Rick Mather's designs and the amazing cantilevered subway station canopy by architect Rafael Vinoly (Tokyo, 1996). This project used a series of 19 mm thick toughened glass beams to create a canopy 11 m in length and 5 m wide. With plans afoot to create 30 m high glass towers, there is no stopping the progressive development of structural glazing.

Design options

There are four principal design options within structural glazing, as described below:

- **Point fixing** – this term describes glass panels that are connected directly to primary structure either via the joints between panels or by perforating the glass panel itself. This is commonly called 'planar' glazing (now a Pilkingtons trademark). The use of toughened glass that can be drilled near its corners was combined with a point-fixing system that could be connected at the nodal points of pre-tensioned cable structures. Hence, the weight of each pane is taken up by the structure incrementally. Panes of up to 4 m x 2 m are typical, with examples since the early 1980s (e.g. the façade of Foster's Renault Centre, Swindon of 1982). This option is perceived as the most transparent and usually the most architecturally desirable solution. The first fastening system with articulated fixings – now called 'spider' connectors (a Saint Gobain trademark) was the Parc de la Villette structure described above. Massive double-curved glazed roof structures can now be realised via computer-aided design (CAD) and computer-numeric-controlled (CNC) manufacture of steel nodes or bars to carry the glass (e.g. Foster & Partners 2001 glazed courtyard at the British Museum, London). In a break from the metal-based fixings, Bucholz McEvoy Architects incorporated laminated timber elements in their glazed façade design for the Fingal County Hall in Dublin.

- **Suspended glazing** – if we consider that glass can be hung (suspended) then another option emerges, which was developed in the 1960s, but has been in common use since the Willis Faber building by Foster & Partners (Ipswich, 1975). In many examples, the upper edge of each pane is held by a clamp (which is fastened to the primary structure); pane lengths of up to 13 m are feasible. The use of 'patch' (bolted corner fittings), i.e. friction grip fittings, enables pane sizes to extend to 15 m. This option has been somewhat overtaken by point fixing systems, which offer greater overall transparency. However, the method of suspension from primary structure rather than cable nets can mean that this option has a much shallower overall depth on plan. An easy way to identify this option is to look for a set of springs (shock absorbers) at the base fixing to allow some limited degree of movement.

- **Glass fins for wind bracing (stiffening)** – rather than use cables or rely on the primary structure, it is also feasible to use glass fins set at 90° to the façade to provide restraint, wind bracing and some degree of support. Foster & Partners' 1978 Sainsbury Centre at the University of East Anglia featured toughened glass panes (2400 mm × 7500 mm) stiffened by 600 mm deep glass fins. This option also led to the development of toughened glass for beams to support horizontal elements such as floors and roofs. Bentham & Crouwel's sculpture pavilion in Arnhem (built 1986, but dismantled the same year) was an excellent demonstration of this opportunity with its 12 mm thick toughened glass panes and almost complete aesthetic of transparency.

- **All glass structures** – given that it is feasible for structural glazing to be used for façades, floors and roofs, then it is no surprise that some structures have been erected that are almost 100% glass. Most UK architects would be familiar with Rick Mather's 1992 glass house extension in Hampstead (engineered by Dewhurst Macfarlane), but there have been significant advances since then, including the highly influential glass bridge at the offices of Kraaijvanger and Urbis Architects in Rotterdam, installed in 1993. The Dutch architects have a 3.2 m toughened, laminated glass bridge between their second floor offices, which uses point fixings. The image of people marvelling at the glazed structure under their feet has been a massive influence on designers seeking a contemporarily transparent aesthetic.

Indicative design considerations

The choice and design of structural glazing typically takes into account a number of factors such as self-weight, predicted environmental loads (from wind and snow), effect of temperature change and resulting degrees of movement. It is common for a façade to take major horizontal and vertical loads via a connection to the support structure and then to the building frame or within a pre-tensioned cable structure. Capacity for movement is provided by the sealant between adjacent panes and within the components of a spider-type connector. These must not allow unacceptable stresses to build up and care must be taken with regard to rotational stresses on the glass at bolted connections. Clearly, in locations exposed to severe weather conditions such as typhoons, large expanses of glazing should be designed with a high inherent degree of robustness.

The initial cost and life-cycle aspects of design life, durability and replacement should also be considered. It is common for the initial cost of structural glass façades, for example, to cost 5–10 times the cost of a conventional loadbearing wall with typical windows. However, the architectural cachet associated with these high-tech design options is considerable and despite the need for regular inspection/silicone replacement, many clients will choose to make the long-term investment in the elegant aesthetic.

Practical matters such as installation and construction tolerances (typically +/−2–5 mm) are critical. Sophisticated glazing systems require experienced installation engineers to ensure accuracy and quality of work. For example, inexperienced workers may be tempted to flex a glass pane to fit; this can be dangerous – misalignment can cause unpredicted stresses to build up, causing cracking after a time. Indeed, the UK's Health & Safety Executive has made specific recommendations that toughened laminated glass should be used in all overhead applications to prevent such cracking causing a structural failure.

The Institution of Structural Engineers has produced a comprehensive guide to the structural use of glass, which covers all the relevant design issues together with a wealth of case studies, specification guidance and worked examples of typical calculations (see reference below).

Built examples

Many examples exist and are very well covered in the references below. Foster & Partners, Nicholas Grimshaw, Eva Jiricna and Ian Ritchie are renowned for their work in this area. Selected precedents worth investigating are as follows.

- Von Gerkan Marg and Partners, together with Ian Ritchie Architects were responsible for the staggering Leipzig Messe, a massive trade fair hall (80 m wide, 244 m long and 30 m high at apex). Built in 1996, some 26,000 m² of glazing (5,526 panes) was erected in just seven months. The glass panes of 1524 mm x 3105 mm are suspended 500 mm from the single layer steel grid shell in a barrel vault structure. The Messe is the largest single glazed volume of the 20th century. Each pane is held at four points via articulated fixings, joints are sealed with silicone and some panes are coated with ceramic to reduce solar gain/glare.
- Ian Ritchie and Arup's 1992 suspended glazed façade at the Centro de Arte Reina Sofia in Madrid still provides an excellent example of an elegant support system. The 35 m high lift towers use glazing suspended from the top and supported on springs at the base. Movement on the vertical arrays of glass panes was restricted by using metals with different coefficients of thermal expansion in the main vertical rods and individual hangers.
- Richard Rogers Partnership's Channel 4 Headquarters has a prominent glazed entrance hall (London, 1994). The structural frame lies on a semi-circle on plan, which cantilevers a short distance as balconies at each storey level. A point fixed glass curtain is suspended from intermediate points from the structural frame. Silicone joints keep it weatherproof and allow sufficient movement due to wind loading.

Further reading

Behling, S. & Behling, S. (eds.) (1999) *Glass: structure and technology in architecture*, Prestel Verlag, Munich, Germany.

The Institution of Structural Engineers (1999) *Structural use of glass in buildings*, Institution of Structural Engineers, London, UK.

Knaack, U. (1998) *Konstrucktiver Glasbau*, Rudolf Müller, Köln, Germany.

Krampen, M. & Schempp, D. (1999) *Glass architects*, AVEdition, Germany.

Krewinkel, H.W. (1998) *Glass buildings: material, structure and detail*, Birkhäuser, Basle, Switzerland.

Rice, P. & Dutton, H. (1997) *Structural glass* (2nd edition), E & FN Spon, London, UK.

Ryan, P., Otlet, M. & Ogden, R.G. (1997) *Steel supported glazing systems* (SCI Publication 193), The Steel Construction Institute, Ascot, Berkshire, UK.

Schittich et al. (1999) *Glass construction manual*, Birkhäuser, Basle, Switzerland.

Vandenburg, M. (1997) *Glass canopies*, Academy Editions, John Wiley & Sons, London, UK.

Wigginton, M. (1996) *Glass in architecture*, Phaidon Press Limited, London, UK.

JG

Glass fibre
See: MINERAL FIBRES

GMP (Von Gerkan Marg & Partner)
See: VON GERKAN & MARG

GRC – glass fibre reinforced concrete

Concrete is a commonly used construction material composed of cement, crushed rock or gravel, sand and water. GRC is a highly adaptable and lightweight alternative to conventionally reinforced concrete.

See also: CEMENT; CLADDING; CONCRETE; CONCRETE – FINISHES; MINERAL FIBRES; PLASTICS; SURFACE FINISHES.

About GRC

Fibres of plastics or metal are often used in concrete. Glass fibre reinforced concrete (GRC) describes a range of cement-based materials that include the usual cement and aggregates that are found in concrete, but rather than using conventional forms of reinforcement (such as steel mesh or bars), GRC uses glass fibres. GRC was developed in the 1970s but was used more widely when alkali-resistant glass fibres became commercially available. Other forms of glass fibre are unsuitable for use in concrete because these will deteriorate on contact with cement, which is alkaline.

Production processes

There are five ways in which GRC can be produced:

- By mixing the fibres into the concrete before pouring into a mould;
- Spraying (the fibres are chopped and mixed by the spray gun and simultaneously mixed with the concrete);
- Applying in sheet form (woven glass textiles) for flatwork such as floors;
- Extruding or injection moulding, for smaller components;
- Using bagged cement products for renders, screeds and specialist mortars (especially on site).

For architectural elements, GRC is usually produced off site in a factory, where quality control is easier to manage. In this instance the considerations for surface and colour consistency described in *Concrete–finishes* are also relevant. For GRC, sulfate resisting cement and additives such as fly-ash and metakaolin can be particularly useful for long-term performance of the material. For very crisply detailed GRC units (e.g. decorative architectural mouldings), elastomeric formliners are a good choice for maintaining accuracy over a high number of mould re-uses.

Properties of GRC

Research into the durability of such thin section concretes is ongoing, but the results show that GRC remains stable even after long periods of exposure to weathering. It is generally less permeable to moisture and is less vulnerable to freeze-thaw action than normal concrete. These properties may be due in part to the combination of high cement content, lack of corrodible materials in the mix and good dispersion of the glass fibres. Compared to 'normal' concrete, GRC products are generally:

- Lightweight (easy to handle and cheap to transport);
- Thin in section (8–20 mm);
- Fire resistant;
- Impact resistant;
- Highly versatile in appearance.

Built examples

GRC can be used for rather different applications compared to normal concrete. Architectural uses include cladding panels, permanent formwork for in-situ concrete, service conduits and channels, street furniture, decorative mouldings and roofing tiles. The material is often used for restoration projects because it can be made to mimic original features at a fraction of the cost of natural stone and other materials.

GRC cladding is popular because it is lightweight and easy to handle. In particular, the intricate Islamic decorations characteristic of the Middle Eastern countries can be reproduced quickly and economically on a large scale. Although GRC is used in the USA, Hong Kong and many other countries, it is not used commonly in the UK although its use is growing as an alternative to normal concrete for delicate architectural cladding panels.

Further reading

Glass Reinforced Concrete Association (2000) *Specification for the manufacture, curing and testing of GRC products*, GRCA, Crowthorne, UK.

JG

GRP
See: COMPOSITE MATERIALS; PLASTICS – TYPES

'Glulam'
See: TIMBER – LAMINATED TIMBER

Granite
See: STONE

Grass ('green') roofs

Roofs typically with grass or low growing plants used to ecological and/or visual effect.

See also: DESIGN LIFE; ECOLOGICAL DESIGN; ENERGY EFFICIENCY; ENVIRONMENTAL DESIGN; LIFE-CYCLE COSTING; MAINTENANCE; ROOFS; SINGLE-PLY MEMBRANE; WATER MANAGEMENT AND DRAINAGE.

Introduction

Green roofs have a wide range of benefits; they are visually appealing, ecologically and technically effective and financially beneficial with very reasonable maintenance costs. Although grass is most typically used (e.g. pitched turf roofs), it is feasible to plant low growing shrubs and even trees, but these will clearly require rather more in the way of structural support, most probably a flat, concrete roof slab. Houses in Alpine regions of Europe have used turf roofs for hundreds of years, some seeded with wild flowers to make an attractive display in spring. For larger buildings, a flat roof can be transformed into a roof garden with areas of planting and hard landscaping. Grass roofs are also used on contemporary large-scale office and museum buildings, as well as housing. Commercial interest in 'green' roofs and product development began in parallel with energy efficiency drives in the 1970s and was spurred on by environmental and ecological design approaches. In the past 12 years grass roof construction has become widespread in Germany, the Netherlands and Scandinavia. In Germany alone, there are now over 2,000,000 m^2 of low maintenance grass roofs. This was helped in 1989, for example when it became building law in Stuttgart that all flat roofs were grassed.

Why use a 'green' roof?

The first major reason to use this technology is based on ecological grounds. The roof reduces storm water runoff, absorbs airborne pollutants and carbon dioxide, provides a degree of cooling and offers a better habitat for insects and flora. The technical performance of the roof is the second reason. It can provide improved thermal insulation, thermal mass (for cooling) and sound insulation compared to a conventional roof design. For householders and building clients, 'green' roofs improve amenity values – there is a psychological benefit from seeing greenery, and in a roof that improves the architectural appearance and sense of place. Of course, there is also the amenity value of having access to a roof garden. The financial reasons for specifying these roofs is based on the potential for reduced maintenance costs and the added prestige value to occupiers and building owners.

Practical matters – design considerations

'Green' roof design basically divides into two main categories; the light touch turf-type roofs and the rather more intensive roof gardens. Green turf-type roofs require thin soil with little or no irrigation and are suitable for large areas with roofs from 0–30° slope. They are low in maintenance, but cannot be used by inhabitants of the building. Roof gardens on the other hand require deep soil, extensive irrigation systems and more favourable conditions for trees, shrubs and plants. Although they allow greater diversity and are suitable for growing food, the soil can add substantially to weight loading on the roof, and have a higher cost in use. In either case, the soil is of particular concern; it needs to exhibit a range of properties, including:

- An excellent rooting medium;
- Good air retention;

- Good moisture retaining capabilities;
- Good nutrient status;
- Good plant anchorage properties;
- Good water permeability;
- Minimal organic decay and shrinking;
- Resistance to rot and frost.

The amount of soil in a 'green' roof will vary according to the type of planting that is used, from grass, camomile, heathers, and sedums to shrubs and trees. Hence, loads on the supporting structure vary also, with weights from $5-150$ kg/m^2 and more. This can mean the difference between a domestic timber trussed roof being quite sufficient and a reinforced concrete roof slab being needed. Approximate soil depths are:

- Grass 200–250 mm
- Herbaceous plants 500–600 mm
- Trees 800–1300 mm

The configuration of the interlayers within the roof will also vary according to the planting used. It is typical to see the soil interleaved with several layers of membrane to control and distribute moisture in the soil, with insulation in addition to at least one layer of waterproofing membrane at the base. Single-ply roofing membranes are essential in ensuring long-life waterproofing, e.g. EPDM, a rubber compound with tensile strengths of $4-9$ MPa.

Built examples

Mecanoo's Library building at the University of Delft in the Netherlands, is a particularly exciting example with a gently undulating grassed roof, pierced by a massive metal and glass conical skylight that brings light into the centre of the space. UK examples of large scale 'green' roofs can be found at The Scottish Widows Assurance HQ in Edinburgh, Cannon Street Railway Station in London, the Willis Faber building in Ipswich and the ecological demonstration building 'Integer' at the BRE campus in Garston, Watford. The Hockerton Housing Project near Nottingham is an earth-sheltered housing scheme with a grassed roof. The Centre for Understanding the Environment at the Horniman Museum in Dulwich, London shows how a green roof works very well in a public building. Hopkins' University of Nottingham extension features a green roof planted with sedums. The plants provide a colourful display, protect the roof materials and offer 'on the spot' water recycling.

A detailed, first-hand description of turf roof construction can be found in the 'Self-build book' (see below), in which an architect explains how it was used on his own home in Hertfordshire to reduce temperature extremes and arrest decay.

Further reading

Broome, J. & Richardson, B. (1991) *The self-build book*, Green Books, UK.

Johnston, J. (1993) *Building green: a guide to using plants on roofs, walls and pavements*, London Ecology Unit, London, UK.

WH/JG

Green oak

See: TIMBER – PRODUCTION AND FINISHES

Green timber

See: TIMBER – PRODUCTION AND FINISHES

Interior view in the Toyota GB headquarters offices, Epsom. The column grid can be seen, but this does not impact on the inherent flexibility of the space. Photograph by Barry Bulley, courtesy of Trent Precast Concrete Ltd.

Grids for structure and layout

Consideration for the layout of the structure and non-structural elements in a building such that dimensions are co-ordinated and the interior spaces can be used efficiently.

See also: BRACING; BUILDABILITY; BUILDING SYSTEMS; CEILINGS; CLADDING; COLUMNS; CONCRETE – STRUCTURES; CORE (SERVICES); CORE (STRUCTURAL); FLOORS; FOUNDATIONS; FRAME; HVAC; INTEGRATION; MODULES AND MODULAR CONSTRUCTION; SERVICES; STRUCTURAL STEEL; TIMBER – STRUCTURES; TOLERANCE; VAN DER ROHE; MIES.

Introduction

In discussing the close relationship between structural elements, space use efficiency and the need for sustainable buildings, there is a need to address the design of structural frames and the ways these interact with a building's users. In this entry, the term 'grid' is used to describe the arrangement of elements within a building on plan. Ideally, this grid is set out so as to optimise the way in which that building is used (also described as dimensional or modular co-ordination). Hence the term structural grid refers to the arrangement of structural elements on plan, and the term planning grid describes the way partitions, furniture and other items are arranged on plan.

It is feasible to devise simple orthogonal grids that lead to effective structural designs, use of space, foundation design and longevity for the building. This intention is particularly important in the layout of larger structures such as commercial offices and retail developments where space is at a premium and rental value per unit (useable) area is the key criterion for income generation. However in many instances, designers are faced with a non-orthogonal site with other constraints that force them to balance up space use and grid arrangements to optimise space efficiency.

Grids for industrial projects tend to be planned around the dimensions of racking systems (for storage buildings), cladding dimensions (because of the expanses of wall area) or the constraints of process machinery. It is usually the case that designers will opt for orthogonal grids at large column intervals in relation to these criteria. Column sizes and distances between columns can be larger as the structure tends only to support roof loads. For domestic scale construction, layout is usually determined not by grid (as these rarely use frames), but by optimal use of the space available to provide living space and accommodate standard sizes of furniture and fittings. The grid in this instance is often simply a graphical method for layout of the key fittings such as the kitchen and bathroom.

Historical note

The use of 'modules' i.e. dimensionally co-ordinated building elements, fittings and furniture can be traced back many centuries. The Japanese system of dimensioning for buildings based on their tatami mats was a particularly rigorous example of the way in which dimensional consistency could be used to provide architectural 'order' in even the simplest structures. The walls, floors, roof, fittings, furniture and ephemera of the Japanese household was all laid out according to the tatami system.

Planning grid

The British Council for Offices (BCO) guidelines explain how the structural grid of a building relates closely to what they call the 'planning grid', i.e. sub-division and layout of the interiors in plan. The BCO supports a planning grid of 1500 mm and multiples thereof; for example, cellular offices are rarely narrower than 3000 mm and external cladding may well co-ordinate with this dimension. BCO suggests that a 1.5 m grid will provide good flexibility in terms of layout. However, a grid of 1350 mm may be used in some European countries (this relates to parking bays and brickwork dimensions and gives a tighter grid of cellular offices). As mentioned above, the 1500 mm grid in plan may also be expressed in other structural and non-structural elements such as partitioning, cladding, services, lift cores, furniture and ceilings. Clearly there are efficiencies to be gained from this type of dimensional co-ordination.

Structural grid

The structural frame (and its column grid) is often designed as a multiple of the dimension of the internal planning grid, i.e. 1500 mm. For offices, the general understanding is that column to column distances of 7500–9000 mm are efficient in terms of structure, capital costs, floor-to-floor heights and interior layouts. In some instances, such as complex sites, curved plans and particular business working practices, these dimensions may be larger. Buildings using natural ventilation strategies may be just 15 m wide, so the central column may be omitted and a clear-span solution selected to span between the external walls. Specialist buildings such as dealing floors, banking and trading companies may also have very specific planning requirements, which will affect structural grids. The issue of tolerance must be part of the discussion of a structural grid. These 'permissible deviations' must be accounted for so there should be a little flexibility in dimensional planning at the concept stage. Although tolerances within the structure itself should only account for a few millimetres here and there when complete, when design analyses are still in progress, the interiors design team should resist the temptation to rush ahead with their layouts.

Endnote

A regular orthogonal grid definitely makes planning an easier task, both in terms of structure and internal layouts. However for many UK projects, either the site or the architectural intention determines that a non-orthogonal grid will be used. While this offers opportunities for architectural and structural ingenuity, it provides interior, fit-out and M&E trades with a challenge. This challenge is precisely the point at which the truly inspirational buildings are separated from the average, because the former tend to go through many design iterations to resolve grids and planning layouts. It has to be said that the best examples have used more integrated approaches to the planning structure and services, such as the first Lloyds building and the later Lloyds Register of Shipping building in the City of London (both by Richard Rogers Partnership). Floor structures, lighting, HVAC, ICT, frame and layouts work together in both buildings, yet they share similarly difficult site conditions and geometries. These buildings prove that effort spent in resolving grids is a good architectural investment.

Further reading

British Council for Offices (2000) *Guide to best practice in specification for offices*, BCO, London, UK.

McGregor, W. & Shiem-Shen Then, D. (1999) *Facilities management and the business of space*, Butterworth-Heinemann, Oxford UK.

Worthington, J. (1997) *Reinventing the workplace*, Butterworth-Heinemann, Oxford, UK.

JG

Grimshaw, Nicholas

One of the key proponents of 'high-tech'
architecture, Nick Grimshaw (b.1939) is
renowned for his expressive, yet rational
approach to design – his work embodies the
architecture-meets-engineering concept.

See also: AIR SUPPORTED STRUCTURES; ALUMINIUM; BRICKS
AND BLOCKS – FINISHES; CASTINGS; ETFE; FOSTER, NORMAN;
GLASS – LAMINATED AND COATED; GLASS – STRUCTURAL
GLAZING; HIGH TECH; ROGERS, RICHARD; ROOFS;
TECHNOLOGY TRANSFER.

A member of the triumvirate of leading British High Tech architects along with
Norman Foster and Richard Rogers, Nicholas Grimshaw is one of the most successful
exporters of the British brand of the crossover between architecture and engineering.
Although his career stretches back into the 1960s, it was the complex and exquisitely
elegant Waterloo International Railway Terminal in London (1988–93) which assured
him exposure world-wide. There is no differentiation between architecture and
structure – the serpentine glass roof, a complex construction of slender steel trusses
and myriad different sections, is a stunning technical achievement recalling London's
great station roofs of the Victorian era.

Grimshaw's earlier works include an assembly plant for Herman Miller in Bath
(1977), the very fine sports hall for IBM, Hampshire (1980–82) and the Financial
Times printing works, London (1987–89). The latter is a wonderfully transparent
building in which the services and printing machinery were made entirely visible in
the finest functional tradition; the metal cladding completed the mechanistic aesthetic.
The British Pavilion at Expo in Seville, Spain (1992) gave Grimshaw an international
platform. The steel and glass box was cooled by a constantly flowing wall of water
and was well received internationally, the building overshadowing its typically bland
contents in a precedent of the problems of the later Rogers' Millennium Dome. The
Igus GmbH factory in Cologne (1993), Western Morning News Building, Plymouth
(1990–93) and the RAC Regional Centre in Bristol (1995) followed. All of these
buildings used materials in an expressive and visually exciting manner.

In the Ludwig Erhard Haus (containing the Berlin stock exchange and chamber
of commerce, 1999), Grimshaw took some of the ideas which made the Waterloo
International Terminal such a success and transposed them to a major urban building
in Berlin. A complex arcuated structure (shaped like a bow), the upper storeys are
suspended on steel hangers from a series of variously sized reinforced concrete arches
leaving the lower floors entirely free of structure and, in theory, highly adaptable. It
is an innovative and striking blend of theatrical structure and clever spatial planning.
Grimshaw compounded his success in Germany recently with the Messehalle in
Frankfurt (2001), a curvaceously organic, folded roof structure clad with aluminium.
The roof covers a column free volume 165 m wide beneath it, almost certainly the
largest such span in Europe.

Grimshaw's most extensive structure is the incredible Eden project in Cornwall
(2000). Built in a disused quarry, the structure is composed of a series of interlocking
glazed geodesic domes held together by tubular steel members meeting in standardised
spherical nodes. The domes (or biomes) contain simulations of plant habitats from
throughout the world. These domes are dissimilar to those promoted evangelically by
Buckminster Fuller in that they act both in compression and tension through a double
grid, the outer being compressive, the inner in tension. The building is undoubtedly

one of the most daring and fascinating testaments to the potential in the combination of engineering and architecture. It has attracted a staggering number of visitors in the first few months of opening, many of whom are probably unaware that the roof is the largest application for air-inflated ETFE covered foil cushions to date.

Further reading

Amery, C. (1995) *Architecture, industry and innovation: the early work of Nicholas Grimshaw & Partners*, Phaidon Press, London, UK.

Moore, R. (1993) *Structure, space and skin: the work of Nicholas Grimshaw & Partners*, Phaidon Press, London, UK.

Pearman, H. (2000) *Equilibrium: the work of Nicholas Grimshaw & Partners*, Phaidon Press, London, UK.

EH

Gropius, Walter

Walter Gropius (1883–1969) played an immensely important role in the development of technology within the Modern movement. His most well known building is the Bauhaus at Dessau in Germany.

See also: CONCRETE; CONCRETE – STRUCTURES; FAÇADES AND FAÇADES ENGINEERING; GLASS; HIGH TECH; STRUCTURAL STEEL; VAN DER ROHE, MIES; WRIGHT, FRANK LLOYD.

One of the key figures in the development of modern architecture and design, Gropius started his career in the offices of Peter Behrens. There, he spent the years between 1907–10 soaking up Behrens's attitude to design as an all-encompassing idea, which should be applied equally to architecture, to household goods and graphics and to everything else. Gropius's most radical innovations in architecture came in his brilliant designs for industrial buildings and his passion for social housing. His first masterpiece was the Fagus factory in Alfeld an der Leine (designed with Adolf Meyer, 1911). The building was constructed around a steel frame, which supported the floors so that the corners and walls were glazed virtually from floor to ceiling and left free of columns, making the structure appear light and airy and affording the interiors the maximum possible natural light. It is often credited as the first recognisably Modern movement building. At the Deutsche Werkbund Exhibition Building in Cologne (1914), Gropius created a building, which blended the solid, even massive masonry of Frank Lloyd Wright, and the lightness of his glazed walls at the Fagus factory using delicate curving glass walls wrapped around serpentine spiral stairs.

After the First World War Gropius was made head of the Weimar School of Arts and Crafts and he quickly went about transforming it into the Bauhaus. The new school was set up on the model of the medieval guilds, which Gropius admired, and the Gothic cathedral. This was Gropius's exemplar of mankind's ability to co-operate and create a truly corporate work of art within which the individual is subsumed into a greater system for the benefit of all, and was taken as the ultimate artistic paradigm. To this end the Bauhaus (translated as 'house of building') was set up to ensure that all students, artists, architects and craftspeople would learn about all the crafts. The early years of the Bauhaus and the corresponding phase of Gropius's architecture was dominated by the influence of expressionism. Impressed by the success of the De Stijl group of artists working in the Netherlands, Gropius returned to his earlier functionalist aesthetic with a remarkably prescient design for the Chicago Tribune Tower competition in 1922, a design which has barely dated. The Bauhaus did not actually boast an architecture course, but the zenith of Gropius's achievements at the school was the creation of a new building for the Bauhaus at Dessau (1925–26). The workshops at the new building were enveloped in a glass screen wall, up to an unprecedented four storeys, which allowed for a brilliantly naturally lit series of interiors. The structure (a simple frame) is contained well within the footprint of the building allowing this uninterrupted screen wall to achieve a level of purity which had not been seen before and which later became the trademark of the International Style.

Gropius left the Bauhaus in 1928 and the following year saw the completion of the huge social housing project at Siemensstadt in Berlin (1929), the fruition of Gropius's commitment to providing the proletariat with at least a minimum standard of space and light. After Hitler's rise to power Gropius left Germany, arriving in England in 1934. Here he formed a partnership with Maxwell Fry and together they built Impington Village College near Cambridge and a number of other small schemes. However, it was in the receptive atmosphere of the post-war USA that Gropius really made his mark. As professor at Harvard, Gropius was able to proselytise American architecture students from Beaux Arts to international modern. His most important buildings during this period were his own house in Lincoln, Massachusetts (1937), the Harvard Graduate Center (1949) and the Pan Am Building in New York (1958–63). During this period Gropius set up and worked with TAC (The Architects' Collaborative), a group of young architects working in a co-operative. It was a development of Gropius's ideas about teamwork which remained remarkably consistent throughout his career in contrast to many other figures in contemporary architecture. His dedication to the development of standardised elements, to the accommodation of function and economy also marked him out from many other Modernists. At the end of his career he returned to factory design with a very fine, functional building for Rosenthal porcelain.

Further reading

Berdini, P. (1996) *Walter Gropius*, Gustavo Gili, Barcelona, Spain.

Herbert, G. (1984) *The dream of the factory made house: Walter Gropius and Konrad Wachsmann*, MIT Press, Massachusetts, USA.

Sharp, D. (1993) *Bauhaus Dessau: Walter Gropius* (Architecture in Detail), Phaidon Press, London, UK.

Sharp, D. (1999) *20th century classics: Walter Gropius, Le Corbusier & Louis Kahn*, Phaidon Press, London, UK.

EH

Gunmetal
See: COPPER

Gypsum
See: PLASTERBOARD

Happold, Sir Ted and Buro Happold

The design office of Buro Happold, founded by Ted Happold (1930–1996), has often been the technical powerhouse behind some of the most advanced and challenging buildings of recent years. This multidisciplinary practice provides an integrated and sophisticated response to architectural technology, working in close harmony with the architectural intention.

See also: ARUP, OVE; FOSTER, NORMAN; HIGH-TECH; HOPKINS, MICHAEL & PATTY; INTEGRATION; PIANO, RENZO; ROGERS, RICHARD; TEXTILE MEMBRANE ROOFS.

'I believe that everyone has within them a desire to create something – an object, relationship, or what you will – and that it is a basic urge which if stifled leads to unhappiness.'

Ted Happold speaking at an RIBA address (1984)

Ted Happold went to Leeds University (Department of Geology) to read Physics Maths and Geology in 1949. He assisted on archaeological digs in the UK and Cyprus then undertook his National Service, during which time he switched his interest to engineering. From 1954 to 1957 he returned to Leeds, but this time to the department of Civil Engineering. By this point he became friendly with Sir Basil Spence and Alvar Aalto and from 1957 had begun to work with Ove Arup & Partners. In 1976, after some time in the USA and following many successful projects with Arup, Happold took the position of Chair of Building Engineering at Bath. On moving there with a group of colleagues (principally from Ove Arup & Partners), the collective design office 'Buro Happold' was founded. He became known affectionately as Sir Ted after his knighthood in 1994.

'Be patterns, be examples in all countries, places, islands, nations, wherever you come, that your carriage and life may preach among all sorts of people, and to them: then

you will come to walk cheerfully over the world, answering that of God in every-one'.

George Fox (1624–1691)

Derek Walker writes that these words strike a chord for those who have observed the 'Happold phenomenon'. Ted Happold was governed by his faith, his vision for society as a whole and his profession in particular. He believed that the best work is done by the most diverse group of talents who can still live together. The multi-disciplinary ethos espoused by Happold is perhaps the key factor for the success of Buro Happold. In his work in collaboration with Ove Arup & Partners and within the design office, Ted Happold had the pleasure of working on many spectacular buildings, with well-known architects to an increasing agenda of design and technology integration. It was in this regard that he excelled as a designer and so is Buro Happold as a design office still renowned.

Selected projects

With Ove Arup & Partners:

- Coventry Cathedral, West Midlands, 1955–60 (Architect: Sir Basil Spence);
- British Embassy, Rome, 1961–70 (Architect: Sir Basil Spence);
- Centre Pompidou, Beauborg, Paris, France 1971–75 (Architect: Renzo Piano & Richard Rogers);

With Buro Happold:

- Katherine Hamnett shop, Brompton Road, London 1988 (Architects: Foster Associates);
- Globe Theatre, Southwark, London 1989–96 (Architects: Pentagram);
- Offices and extensions to the research laboratories of Schlumberger, Cambridge, 1990–92 (Architects: Michael Hopkins & Partners);
- Millennium Dome, Greenwich, London 1996–2000 (Architects: Richard Rogers Partnership).

Further reading

Allen, W.A., Courtney, R.G., Happold, E. & Wood, A.M. (eds.) (1992) *A global strategy for housing in the third millennium*, E & FN Spon, London, UK.

Walker, D. & Addis, B. (1998) *Happold: the confidence to build*, E & FN Spon, London, UK.

MT

Hardboard
See: TIMBER – MANUFACTURED BOARDS

Hardwoods
See: TIMBER – HARDWOODS AND SOFTWOODS

Heating
See: AIR-CONDITIONING; FABRIC ENERGY STORAGE; HVAC;
NIGHT VENTILATION; NIGHT VENTILATION

HVAC

The primary mechanical sciences used to manage the internal environment of buildings.

See also: AIR-CONDITIONING; AIRTIGHTNESS AND IAQ; BUILDING MANAGEMENT SYSTEMS; CORE (SERVICES); ENERGY EFFICIENCY; ENVIRONMENTAL DESIGN; FIT-OUT; HEAT RECOVERY; INSULATION; INTEGRATION; LIFE-CYCLE COSTING; MAINTENANCE; NIGHT VENTILATION; SERVICES; SICK BUILDING SYNDROME; STACK EFFECT; THERMAL COMFORT; THERMOLABYRINTHS; TROMBE WALL; VENTILATION; WIND TOWERS.

Introduction

The term HVAC is used as shorthand for heating, ventilating and air-conditioning, although in truth it also includes the following: pipework services associated with hot water systems for heating and domestic hot water; cooling and chilling as well as associated pneumatic; gas, fire, and cold water systems.

Heating

Most buildings in the northerly latitudes have a long heating season that extends from September to April. Subsequently there are very few structures in these regions that do not incorporate some form of heating systems (e.g. earth sheltered houses). Heating systems are therefore a major part of HVAC design and are configured on the basis of requirements for use/demand and energy efficiency (i.e. Building Regulations). Heating requires that designers have an appreciation of:

- The physics of heat – the nature of heat and temperature; units of measurement; definition of concepts, i.e.: mean radiant temperature, sol-air temperature, absolute and relative humidity;
- Psychothermics – the heat exchange process between humans and the environment; the physiological responses;
- Thermal environment – elements of climate, solar, wind, precipitation, and humidity.

Building services engineers will have knowledge of local heaters and heat emitting units (radiators, convectors – natural and forced), central heating systems, boilers, and pumping and distribution systems, combined with hot water supply generation and distribution. The design team can contribute towards the discussion and calculation of heat losses and gains, fuel requirements, fuel/energy source and running costs. In particular, some types of building will have occupants who are dependent on heating, such as health care facilities, residential nursing homes and hospitals. There may also need to be clarification about occupant control, thermal comfort and the relative scope for energy efficiency measures.

Ventilating

Ventilation is a means by which comfort conditions can be improved by the better management of air changes within a space, and is often provided in tandem with heating systems. Ventilation can be provided naturally (e.g. opening windows) or via mechanical systems. The latter is usually required for buildings with deep floor plans, no opening windows or, for example, factories and laboratories with a need for faster air change rates to maintain good indoor air quality. However, with the increasing use of stack effect and natural ventilation systems it is essential that the theoretical knowledge of ventilation and air treatment is not forgotten. This requires knowledge of fan laws for exhaust, plenum and balanced systems, in addition to the physics of air movement and knowledge of duct sizing for low and high velocity systems. There is also a need to consider vibration damping and acoustic control of noise from ventilation equipment. Night time ventilation is an important part of fabric energy storage systems, in which the thermal mass, usually concrete, is cooled and recharged by fresh air passing over it at night.

Heating and ventilation equipment can actually become elements of expression in architectural design, especially where the building or its façades are active components in this regard. Atria are often used as working components in the stack effect, together with wind towers or ventilating lanterns at ridge level e.g. Foster and Partners' Parliament building in Berlin. However, without competent advice from building services engineers to fully test these types of innovative designs, the 'intelligent arrows' indicating ventilation routes on a drawing will not come to life.

Air-conditioning (see also *Air-conditioning*)

The primary function of air-conditioning is to maintain conditions that are conducive to human comfort or are required by a product or process. However, air-conditioning is not needed in all buildings – it is energy intensive, so is typically used only where needed in computer rooms, deep plan offices etc. A good knowledge of air-conditioning design should include refrigeration, cooling plant, heat pumps and cold storage for industrial applications. In addition there are different mechanisms for cooling, i.e. adaptive, absorption, adiabatic and evaporative cooling.

In this part of HVAC systems, the issue of 'space for services' is more important, with discussion between architects and building services engineers, as well as other associated disciplines from an early stage. Space is needed for mechanical and electrical equipment to allow adequate and proper commissioning and maintenance.

One novel form of ventilation, which can also act in an air-conditioning capacity, but actually saves energy in the long term is 'Termodeck™'. This Swedish system has been used in the UK at many locations, including lecture and seminar spaces at the University of East Anglia (Elizabeth Fry building) in Norwich and for student residences at the University of East London Dockland campus. 'Termodeck' uses concrete hollowcore flooring units through which fresh, heated or cooled air can be circulated.

Further reading

Chartered Institute of Building Services Engineers *CIBSE Guides : Volumes A, B and C*, CIBSE, London, UK.

Markus, T.A. & Morris, E.N. (1980) *Buildings, climate and energy*, Pitman, UK.

Moore, F. (1993) *Environmental control systems: heating, cooling, lighting* (International Edition), McGraw Hill, New York, USA.

WH/JG

Heat recovery

Applications for the effective utilisation of heat energy generated by machines, buildings, human beings and other sources of latent heat energy.

See also: ENERGY EFFICIENCY; ENVIRONMENTAL DESIGN;
FABRIC ENERGY STORAGE; FAÇADES AND FAÇADE
ENGINEERING; HVAC; INSULATION; INTEGRATION;
INTELLIGENT FAÇADES AND MATERIALS; INTUMESCENT PAINT;
LIGHTING – ARTIFICIAL LIGHTING; PHASE CHANGE MATERIALS;
RECYCLING; THERMOLABYRINTHS; TROMBE WALL;
VENTILATION.

What is heat recovery?

All machinery generates heat energy. In many instances, this heat goes to waste because it must be removed to ensure continued operation of equipment e.g. computers require expended heat energy to be removed, so they have an integral fan. This heat could be recovered, even if it is not clean. Heat can be reused effectively by the application of a 'heat pump' to transfer it to another part of a building. In ventilation systems the higher temperature of exhaust air can be recycled for transfer by devices such as 'heat wheels'.

The potential for the recovery of 'low grade heat' before it escapes from a building is extremely beneficial in economic terms and has been the focus for efforts to apply the technology to larger buildings where there are significant benefits to be gained. In factories, heat produced by machines can be high enough to affect both workers and the process. Industrial processes with hot flue gases can use the available 'latent' or hidden energy through heat exchangers to heat water etc. In buildings such as office blocks, schools and other public buildings, unwanted heat generated by lighting, people and computers can be soaked up by fabric energy storage or via phase change materials. The combination of passive thermal mass and active recovery from ventilation offers a complete solution to heat recovery.

Heat recovery can be an extremely useful solution to managing large, multi-zoned buildings such as conference centres, educational and cultural buildings. For example, the Royal Academy of Music in London has theatres, recital and rehearsal studios, music carrels, offices, boardrooms and canteens. Different conditions were required at different times and for differing populations, so heat recovery enabled energy to be saved by diverting flows as appropriate using simple, but effective control systems.

Examples of heat recovery mechanisms

Heat pumps – the heat pump can offer significant big advantages in energy terms. A system first invented by Kelvin (1824–1907) was used to great advantage for heating and cooling the Royal Festival Hall in London, in which low grade latent heat energy in the water of the River Thames was used as a prime heat recovery source.

Heat pipes – these are normally constructed from short lengths of copper tubing, sealed tightly at the ends with wicks or capillaries containing a charge of refrigerant. Transfer moves by conductive transmission between the hot and cold surfaces.

Rotary heat exchangers – otherwise known as thermal wheels or heat wheels, resemble turbine blades packed with heat-absorbing material such as aluminium or stainless steel wool, allowing transfer of heat from say a hot flue gas to a cooler air stream.

Further reading

Moore, F. (1993) *Environmental control systems: heating, cooling and lighting* (International Edition), McGraw-Hill, New York, USA.

Reay, D.A. & MacMichael, D.B.A. (1979) *Heat pumps: design and applications: a practical handbook for engineers, architects and designers*, Pergamon Press, Oxford, UK.

WH/JG

Herzog and De Meuron

The Modern masters of minimal architecture, Herzog and De Meuron have proved their strong alliance throughout the last few decades. Although the practice shot to fame in the late 1990s as a result of renovation of the Bankside power station in London into the 'Tate Modern' art gallery, their oeuvre has always been characterised by beautiful expression of materials via exquisitely simple designs.

See also: CONCRETE – FINISHES; CONCRETE – STRUCTURES; COPPER; HONESTY.

Jacques Herzog and Pierre de Meuron were both born in Basle, Switzerland in 1950, graduated from ETH Zurich in 1975 and worked with Professor Dolf Schnebli in 1977. They formed the practice Herzog & De Meuron in 1978 and have since then risen steadily through the ranks of revered European architects.

Although they claim to prefer art to architecture, their structures also demonstrate a comprehensive understanding of the building process in addition to a determination to express it as art. The architects emphasise that they spend a considerable amount of time on research, including work on building materials. One particular innovation of note (with Pieri), Serilith is the use of screen-printing photographs onto concrete using selective retardation of the concrete's surface. This can be seen to great effect on the Eberswalde technical library in Germany where the precast concrete cladding features potent local and historical imagery. The practice is looking constantly for the science and technology that can bring their architecture to life – even noting that 'invention enables (their) architectural vision'.

The first building of theirs to genuinely capture the imagination of an international architectural audience was the signal box in Basle, Switzerland (1992–95). The absolute simplicity of this small structure is combined with practicality to demonstrate an exquisite talent. The six-storey signal box is wrapped in 200 mm wide copper strips, gently tilted by degrees to allow daylight to penetrate in a sophisticated manner. The façade operates as a copper coil: a Faraday cage that protects the electronic equipment inside.

A building whose texture and aesthetic have often been imitated is the Dominus Vinery, Yountville, Napa Valley, USA (1994–97). The external wall of this building is created by rough layers of stone, filling a strong metal mesh i.e. a gabion, a technique used in civil engineering. In this instance, the gabion walls are filled with differing densities of stones according to the necessity for internal light. The resulting interior light seeps through in a random fashion, creating an unexpectedly soft visual effect.

The most well-known of Herzog and De Meuron's portfolio is their biggest and one of the most recent projects. The Tate Gallery of Modern Art (1994–2000) was the result of an international design competition. Herzog & De Meuron transformed a beautiful utilitarian power station by Sir Giles Scott, a landmark building on the River Thames in London, into a fully functioning art gallery. In addition to attracting some of the largest numbers of visitors ever seen in the UK, the Tate Modern has proved to be an architectural masterpiece. The large turbine hall acts as a central street where crowds of people can congregate having slipped down into the building via a wide but appropriately scaled concrete ramp. The gallery is arranged by theme rather than chronologically and with each level featuring a different floor finish, the themes are delineated in a subtle vertical order.

Further reading

Herzog, J. & De Meuron, P. (2000) *Herzog & De Meuron*, Birkhäuser, Basle, Switzerland.

Mack, G. (1997) *Herzog & De Meuron, The complete works*, (Volume 1: 1978–1988), Birkhäuser, Basle, Switzerland.

Mack, G. (1998) *Herzog & De Meuron, The complete works*, (Volume 2: 1989–91), Birkhäuser, Basle, Switzerland.

Mack, G. (2000) *Herzog & De Meuron, The complete works*, (Volume 3: 1992–96), Birkhäuser, Basle, Switzerland.

Wang, W. (1998) *Herzog & De Meuron* (2nd edition), Birkhäuser, Basle, Switzerland.

Readers may also wish to refer to the special edition on Herzog & De Meuron featured in the architectural magazine *El Croquis* (no. 84, Spain, 1997).

MT

High tech

An architectural style that started in the 1970s and 1980s using high precision structural and non-structural components to create lightweight, non-traditional buildings.

See also: ALUMINIUM; BESPOKE; BUILDING SYSTEMS; CLADDING; COMPOSITE PANELS; FOSTER, NORMAN; GLASS – STRUCTURAL GLAZING; GRIDS FOR STRUCTURE AND LAYOUT; GRIMSHAW, NICHOLAS; GROPIUS; WALTER; 'HONESTY'; INTELLIGENT FAÇADES AND MATERIALS; JIRICNA, EVA; MODULES AND MODULAR CONSTRUCTION; PIANO, RENZO; PLASTICS; RICE, PETER; RITCHIE, IAN; ROGERS, RICHARD; STRUCTURAL STEEL; TOLERANCE; VON GERKAN & MARG; WINDOWS AND CURTAIN WALLING.

Introduction

High-tech architecture describes a particular style of buildings that arose in the 1970s and 1980s from architects such as Renzo Piano, Norman Foster, Nick Grimshaw and Richard Rogers. The buildings are characterised by rigorously laid out exposed structures, metal cladding panels and a tendency towards technical prowess over contextual exploration. The term high-tech is now often used to describe any architecture that has a visibly obvious technological bias in its detailing.

Key features

The materials usually associated with high-tech architecture are steel (and other metals such as aluminium), glass and sometimes plastics. Such buildings often feature exposed structures designed for viewing – architectural steelwork using tubular sections and cellular beams for example. Cladding is a common feature for the external envelope (a systematic way of dealing with the walls, roof and windows). The structure and cladding are conceived in parallel with the aim of articulating elements clearly, constructing efficiently and precisely. Lightweight, precisely manufactured components and new composite materials were popular. The more traditional materials (e.g. brick, stone, concrete and timber) are not conventionally associated with high-tech architecture, although there is a trend now towards using even these in a more 'technical' manner.

Building layouts are characterised by a fairly strict adherence to a structural grid, cladding modules, etc. (the layout here is definitely based on structure, rather than function). High tech tends to be repetitive, regular and rigorously planned – perhaps based on the 'production aesthetic' described below. The buildings are simple, orthogonal boxes with minimal variations in plan, elevation or material use. For this reason, high-tech architecture is not popular with architects who are driven towards contextual, regional or organic solutions to design. There is more than a little influence from the International Style.

Construction methods are based on the premise that the only activities to take place on site will be the assembly of components or elements manufactured off site. Hence, high tech is associated with off-site manufacture of structure, cladding and other components that are made in high quality manufacturing environments with very accurate product tolerances. For this reason, dimensional accuracy and setting-out on site is critical for high-tech architecture – there is little room for manoeuvre. Such levels of accuracy were not found commonly on construction sites in the 1970s and 1980s and the trade of the specialist erector/fixer developed alongside high-tech buildings. Nowadays, these specialist trade contractors are more common.

Architectural style

There is certainly visual consistency in the materials used in high-tech architecture and the ways in which these materials are combined. However, some critics argue that high tech is not a consistent architectural 'school', rather it is a collection of buildings that happen to share the same visual imagery. The argument is that a shared desire to use 'modern' materials does not reflect any similarity in architectural intention or underlying theory. Rather the various high-tech architects each have their own drivers to adopt this type of approach. In addition to visual image, many high-tech buildings are also noted for their qualities as 'object buildings' i.e. they are conceived in their own right, without particular reference to contextual cues.

Historical note

The history of high tech can be traced back to the early Modernist's 'machine aesthetic' espoused by Prouvé, Gropius and others and even further back to the Crystal Palace of 1851. The fascination with using manufacturing methods to produce building components continued throughout the 20th century. However, the rise of computer controlled and robot production revolutionised many manufacturing industries. Thus architects in the 1970s were able to take advantage of the technology transfer of high-tech manufacturing of cars etc. into manufacture of building components—structural steel and cladding panels etc. From then on, building designers had more options open to them and were able to engage with the opportunities offered by high-tech architecture.

Pioneers began to develop ideas of high quality, demountable structures, lightweight structures, modular buildings etc. These are all key to the development of the high-tech style which soon developed through buildings that shared a common theme of the building as a system of standard sized, high quality components. The 1970s and 1980s brought a series of client-commissioned high-tech structures throughout the UK and Europe for factories, offices, exhibition halls, showrooms, homes and other building types (e.g. Renzo Piano's IBM Travelling Pavilion). From the earlier bespoke cladding systems, new proprietary and standard cladding products became available and the visual imagery of high tech spread through to speculative buildings. Despite the regard for the efficiencies and accuracy offered by precision assembly of off-site manufactured components, the best high-tech architectural precedents are still to be found in the bespoke examples, where production engineering was applied with care and consistency.

Endnote

In its original nature to make architecture precise, well-planned and perfectly assembled, high tech is still popular and is revered by architects with a 'technical' bias. Foster and Partners' new projects such as the Commerzbank in Frankfurt, Germany and the Swiss Re Tower in London are visibly high tech, but have a much keener eye on context, site and other issues such as environmental performance and sustainability. Another example of high tech 'moved on' is the bioclimatic architecture of Ken Yeang.

Further reading

Brookes, A. & Grech, C. (1996) *Building envelope & connections*, Butterworth-Heinemann, Oxford, UK.

Davies, C. (1988) *High tech architecture*, Thames & Hudson, London, UK.

Davies, C. & Lambot, I. (1997) *Commerzbank Frankfurt*, Watermark/Birkhäuser, Basle, Switzerland.

McKean, J. (1999) *Pioneering British high tech by Stirling & Gowan, Foster Associates and Richard Rogers Partnership*, Phaidon Press, London, UK.

Slessor, C. (2001) *Eco-Tech: sustainable architecture and high technology*, Thames & Hudson, London, UK.

JG

Hollow sections

See: STRUCTURAL STEEL

'Honesty'

A term used to describe an approach to design and specification that reflects the qualities inherent to, or associated with, construction materials and/or structural behaviour.

See also: AALTO, ALVAR; BRICKS AND BLOCKS; CLADDING; CONCRETE; CONNECTIONS; DESIGN LIFE; DURABILITY; KAHN, LOUIS; SCARPA, CARLO; SPECIFICATION; STRUCTURAL STEEL; SURFACE FINISHES; TIMBER – PRODUCTION AND FINISHES.

About 'honesty'

The idea of 'honesty' is based on the notion that architecture should embrace one of the essential precepts of Modernism, i.e. that materials specified for use in a building should be used in a manner befitting them. The key idea is that materials such as concrete, steel, brick or stone should be used in accordance to the properties and other characteristics inherent to, or associated with them.

These innate characteristics may be in their structural or aesthetic properties – for example, keeping the natural grain of timber exposed rather than painting the surface. Certainly it is an everyday experience for architects to resist painting (being representative as all that is anathema to Modernism) and support wholeheartedly leaving a concrete or timber element in its natural or as-struck state thereby letting the material 'be itself'. The other aspect to honesty is the way in which structural elements are treated (Modernism suggests that the same 'honest' approach should be applied to the structural form of a building). For structures, one might consider exposing the structure to the interior or perhaps developing beam/column profiles or connections to better express what is going on 'under the surface'. Hence the terms 'honesty' or 'structural honesty' are in common architectural parlance.

So, the 'honest' approach can be applied to the way structures are expressed in the form of a building, surface finishes are shown or articulated and to the way materials are combined/joined together. For the purposes of this book, the following basic definitions are suggested:

Aesthetic honesty – the general approach to building design that recognises and expresses the inherent qualities of materials and their 'natural' state and finishes. It may be appropriate to expose the natural grain of wood, to have an as-struck (direct) finish on concrete or to have a steel beam exposed (rather than having a sprayed on finish).

Constructional honesty – expressing clearly the inherent qualities and differences between materials, for example, through construction details, joints and juxtaposition. This could be done by maintaining a visual link between the material and the methods used to construct it such as expressed bolt-holes, fittings or making a conscious effort to incorporate a detail that shows a connection between one material to another.

Structural honesty – the way in which individual structural elements, aspects of structural behaviour or functions (hierarchy) undertaken by the structure present in a building are expressed through appropriate forms or materials. This could be shown by introducing a casting between individual structural elements or by isolating and showing normally unseen parts of a structure (rather than concealing them behind plasterboard etc.).

Built examples

Several well-known architects provide good examples of how 'honesty' can be used to create insightful and inspiring buildings.

Louis Kahn, Alvar Aalto and many other 20th century Modernist architects were well known for their determination to be 'honest' to the materials and construction techniques that they used. The seminal Louis Kahn lintel detail with its concave concrete compression element and steel bar tension element is a perfect example of how structural honesty can lead to an efficient and highly articulated architecture.

The principles of honesty to materials can be seen throughout the work of Carlo Scarpa who went to great lengths to ensure adjacent materials and structural elements were articulated very clearly. In the Castelvecchio project in Verona, Scarpa's intimate concern for materials extended to the careful detailing of handrails and door furniture in addition to the well-researched specification for the timber and natural stone elements.

In the work of Tadao Ando, in-situ concrete walls are often finished with bolt-holes and formwork fins left intact, these being a reference to the steel shuttering and/or plywood forms used to cast the concrete in the first place. In this way Ando is expressing how the concrete was formed in a way 'honest' to the material itself and the techniques used in its construction.

Attitudes towards 'honesty'

Honesty is clearly a Modernist principle that has had significant influence on the way materials are specified, designed and detailed in many key buildings. However it is true to say that not all architects share a respect for a long-term honesty to materials. Many architects actually fear and loathe the weathering patterns, patinas or staining that can naturally develop on buildings over time, and so the concept of honesty may break down as the pure and unblemished concept in the architect's mind's eye becomes a slightly grubbier version. Above all some may wish to retain the beautiful sight of the building on its opening day – in which case painting or sealing then seems to become valid. Indeed, the specification of finishes is often a matter for debate with the client, with the architects' intentions of being 'honest' needing to be balanced with long-term care of the building fabric.

JG

Hopkins, Sir Michael and Patty

One of the UK's most respected architectural teams, the Hopkins' portfolio is characterised by sturdy, environmentally responsible architecture that shows a variety of responses to technological innovation.

See also: ATRIUM; BRICKS AND BLOCKS; CONCRETE – STRUCTURES; FABRIC ENERGY STORAGE; FAÇADE ENGINEERING; HAPPOLD, SIR TED AND BURO HAPPOLD; HIGH-TECH; METALS; TEXTILE MEMBRANE ROOFS.

> *'The craft of architecture is very hard. Architects' lives are completely wrapped in their buildings. We never stop thinking about a design until everything is finished and long afterwards.'*

Sir Michael Hopkins

Michael and Patty Hopkins co-founded Hopkins and Partners (a London-based architectural practice) in 1976. Their remit is to design innovative, cost-effective and attractive beautiful buildings that enable their clients to make the most of their sites, programmes and budgets. The logical and clean designs created by the practice have been the result of the principle of 'truth to the materials and expression of structure' – from which stems the aesthetic quality, efficiency and popular appeal of their buildings. Since its creation, Hopkins and Partners have pioneered many aspects of architectural technology including fabric roofs, lightweight structures, energy efficient designs, the weaving of new structures into existing buildings, and the recycling of former industrial sites. The practice's contribution to architecture has been recognised in numerous awards including the RIBA Gold medal (1994). The practice believes in the close collaboration of all the parties involved in the building process. In addition, their interest in new structures and materials has created an approach to architecture that synthesises creative imagination with rational logic. This is perhaps best demonstrated in the technical relationships (a 'family' resemblance) between many of their key buildings.

Selected projects

Glyndebourne Opera House (East Sussex, 1988–94)

The new building is in the same location as an earlier structure, but turned through 180° on plan so it faces the south garden. From a distance the new fly-tower can be seen, although the natural slope in the site ensures that the height of the tower does not impose on the landscape. Within the building, there are architectural references to previous Hopkins' projects. For example the roof is similar to the circular lead roof of the David Mellor Cutlery factory (Derbyshire, 1989). Likewise, the fly-tower is somewhat reminiscent of the Schlumberger theatre (Cambridge) and the tented canopy similar to that used on top of the brick structure at the Mound Stand at Lord's Cricket Ground (London).

Bracken House (City of London, 1992)

The brief for this project required Hopkins to produce an 'intelligent' office block capable of accommodating the modern technology that is critical to the businesses within the City of London. Hopkins responded with a building that visually echoes its environment, clearly observes its modernity and accommodates IT provision as demanded. On the façade, glass and gunmetal oriel windows cantilever from rusticated stone bases. A steel and glass canopy hangs in tension marking the entrance to the building and a glass block atrium penetrates the central plan giving light to the many floors below.

Other works by Hopkins can be identified quite easily via the family of architectural and technological devices typically used by the practice. The stone and concrete post-tensioned column structures found around the perimeter of Portcullis House (the new Parliamentary building in Westminster) and the Queens Building at Emmanuel College, Cambridge (1993–1995) hark back to the earlier Inland Revenue headquarters in Nottingham. By the same token, the use of exposed concrete floor slabs in the Inland Revenue has been repeated in Portcullis House and elsewhere.

Further reading

Davies, C. (1993) *Hopkins: the work of Michael Hopkins & Partners*, Phaidon, London, UK.

Jenkins, D. (1991) *Mound Stand, Lords Cricket Ground* (Architecture in Detail), Architecture Design and Technology Press, London, UK.

Jenkins, D. (1993) *Schlumberger Cambridge Research Centre* (Architecture in Detail), Phaidon, London, UK.

Slessor, C. (1997) *Eco-Tech: sustainable architecture and high technology*, Thames and Hudson, London.

MT

'Hot desking'
See: ICT IN BUILDINGS

Hybrid construction
See: CONCRETE – STRUCTURES; COMPOSITE DECKING

ICT in buildings

Information and communication technology (ICT), now a widened definition from the previous IT, has had significant impact on building design in terms of the need to accommodate equipment and new working practices.

See also: BESPOKE; BUILDING MANAGEMENT SYSTEM; CORE (SERVICES); DESIGN LIFE; ENERGY EFFICIENCY; FABRIC ENERGY STORAGE; FIT-OUT; FLOORS; GRIDS FOR STRUCTURE AND LAYOUT; INTEGRATION; LIFE-CYCLE COSTING; MAINTENANCE; RISERS AND TRUNKING; SERVICES.

Introduction

The amount of servicing in modern buildings has increased, but it has also changed in nature. The demands on a modern office, school or industrial facility vary considerably from those of a few decades ago as we tend now to rely much more heavily on IT-based equipment to undertake tasks and on IT-based management of building services etc. Indeed, the development of information technology (IT) has had significant impact on people's working practices, communication technology and organisational strategies. The newly established term ICT (information and communication technology) covers this breadth of technologies and can be used to outline some of the aspects that need to be addressed in building design.

There is a particular set of building types that require a high, sometimes specialised level of ICT provision – this entry focuses mainly on the needs of such buildings, including:

- Offices;
- Call centres;
- Conference centres;
- Dealing rooms;
- Trading floors.

ICT in buildings

Aspects of the building that can be affected by decisions on ICT provision include:

- Basic layout of the building;
- Design of individual workspaces;

- Percentage of area given over to IT servicing;
- Amount of underfloor/ceiling space required for trunking;
- Daylighting amount and direction;
- Ventilation rates;
- Access floor design;
- Ergonomic furniture.

The key aspects of building design influenced by ICT are the layout, size and accessibility of the raised floors, trunking and risers (and thus floor–floor heights). ICT in buildings may physically include PCs, telephones, signage, document management and information management systems in addition to building management systems or automated production processes etc. However, the provision of these systems will be based on the overall ICT strategy for the business or client that occupies the space.

What's behind the changes?

In the case of many modern offices, there is a drive towards the '**paperless**' office, based totally on comprehensive ICT systems that replace 'mechanical' means of communication such as fax or photocopiers.

The second driver is towards a '**wireless**' office whereby the ICT provision is linked by infra-red devices or similar. This reduces the space needed for cabling and trunking etc., and thus may reduce the overall height of the building.

This however must be seen in parallel with changes in working practices to reduce space needs for both people and storage. 'Hot desking' involves workers dropping in and using a shared PC for example, without having their own desks. This is perfectly acceptable for organisations with a transient workforce, but much less appropriate for the more traditional nine-to-five operation. The option works well for say, airline staff, who are rarely on the ground but who require rapid access to information etc. when in the office. In other organisations, many people work from outside the main building, perhaps at home (sometimes called 'telecottaging') and do not need space of their own, they just dial-in via portable PCs. Document management systems that were previously organised mechanically can now be IT-based. They take up less room and are more powerful for the end-user. These different patterns of working will dramatically affect the form and layout of a building, but are much more fundamentally linked to adequate ICT provision.

The emergence of the call centre as an important new building type emphasises the ability of ICT to transform a business's core operations and the buildings that it requires. With call centres, the telephone queuing systems are actually less important than the ability of the operators to access customer's details on line. Customer information management provides the key component of a successful call centre, whatever its core business area.

For many years, stockbrokers, banks and other types of dealing rooms have relied on telephones and IT to provide a fast-moving working environment that enables them to trade on-the-spot with anywhere in the world. Current ICT technology is enabling these companies to operate in ever more compact buildings, where the space given over to cabling etc. is reducing continually.

Conclusion

The trend towards ICT-intense buildings is increasing and has transformed the working environments of many UK blue-chip companies. This is set to continue, but it is not clear when or to what extent the technology will start to 'travel' with the workers themselves rather than remain within a building. Perhaps the increasing incidence of 'server farms' (buildings hosting only IT equipment) is a useful indicator.

Further reading

British Council for Offices (2000) *Guide to best practice in specification for offices*, BCO, London, UK.

McGregor, W. & Shiem-Shen Then, D. (1999) *Facilities management and the business of space*, Butterworth-Heinemann, Oxford UK.

Worthington, J. (1997) *Reinventing the workplace*, Butterworth-Heinemann, Oxford, UK.

JG

Indoor air quality (IAQ)

See: AIRTIGHTNESS AND INDOOR AIR QUALITY (IAQ); NIGHT VENTILATION; SICK BUILDING SYNDROME (SBS); VENTILATION

Industrialised building

See: BUILDING SYSTEMS; MODULES AND MODULAR CONSTRUCTION

In-situ concrete

See: CONCRETE – STRUCTURES

Insulation

Most commonly associated with thermal performance and energy efficiency, these materials can also be used to prevent the transfer of sound, electricity and vibration. Their energy performance is measured in k values, or in a construction element, U values.

See also: ACOUSTICS; AIRTIGHTNESS AND IAQ; CARBON DIOXIDE; CLADDING; DYNAMIC THERMAL SIMULATION; ECOLOGICAL DESIGN; 'ECO-POINTS'; ENERGY EFFICIENCY; ENVIRONMENTAL DESIGN; FABRIC ENERGY STORAGE; FAÇADES AND FAÇADE ENGINEERING; FLOORS; HVAC; MAINTENANCE; MINERAL FIBRES; PERFORMANCE; PLASTICS – TYPES; ROOFS; SICK BUILDING SYNDROME; SPECIFICATION; SUSTAINABILITY; THERMAL BRIDGING; THERMAL COMFORT; THERMOLABYRINTHS; VENTILATION; WALLS; WINDOWS AND CURTAIN WALLING.

Introduction

Insulation products are produced in a wide range of shapes and sizes including loose fill, flexible rolls and mats, rigid boards and moulded shapes and sections. They are used in a variety of locations in a building to prevent the flow of thermal, sound or other types of energy. The term 'insulation' is most commonly associated with energy efficiency and the prevention of heat loss from a building via floors, walls, roof and openings. Although this entry focuses on thermal insulation, the full range of applications is:

- Thermal insulation for cavity wall, loft, internal and external wall, roof, underfloor and to prevent thermal bridging between the exterior and interior;
- Insulation of heating, chilling and pipework services, where heat loss can occur in either direction;
- Fire protection;
- Electrical protection;
- Acoustic applications to reduce noise transfer and vibration (although in the latter, mass material such as concrete or high resilience materials such as neoprene are often considered).

How is thermal performance measured?

The thermal performance of a building material can be measured in its own right, but it is more useful to calculate the overall insulation value of a construction element, as it will be constructed and function when in place. For example, a loadbearing cavity wall consists of two leaves of masonry, a layer of insulation, an air gap, vapour barrier, plaster, and several surfaces in between. These elements each have a thermal role to play – a U value is the sum of all the individual thermal performance levels in the wall; i.e. from all of the parts listed above. The U value therefore gives a good indication of the mean loss of heat from a structure – it is equal to the inverse of the sum of all the resistances.

Thermal transmittance (U value) is the unit measurement of the heat transferred through building components per unit of time per unit of area and is reciprocal of the total resistances.

The U value denotes the thermal transmittance of a structural element in W/m^2K; a lower value equates to better insulation.

NB: In the USA and some other countries, it is more common to see 'R value' used to describe thermal insulation values. This is simply the sum of all the resistances, i.e. the inverse of a U value.

Thermal conductivity (k value) is the heat transferred by conduction through a substance of a given thickness in a given time frame when a temperature differential is applied to a given area.

The k value denotes the thermal conductivity of a material in W/mK; again, a lower value equates to better insulation.

Standards and compliance

To give an indication of 'good' U values, UK standards have been $0.4-0.6$ W/m^2K in recent years, but this is now seen to be insufficient. For example, the government is demanding an improvement in domestic construction U values down to about $0.20-0.25$ W/m^2K, which will result in some new types of construction. Indeed, insulation standards vary between countries. According to the European Insulating Manufacturers Association (EURIMA), in a league table of 13 European countries, the UK is 11th for wall insulation and 7th for roof insulation. Sweden has the highest values currently for insulation thickness (450 mm for roofs and 240 mm for walls).

UK Building Regulations are reappraised on a regular basis, most recently to meet the growing need to reduce CO_2 emissions by improving energy efficiency. The new standard U values for dwellings and non-domestic buildings are much more demanding than previous versions, but the response from manufacturers has been rapid. An extremely high performance glazing system is now available with one pane of low emissivity glass in a sealed unit filled with argon gas between two panes. This gives a U value of 1.0 W/m²K, compared to 2.6–2.8 for standard double-glazing. Triple-glazed units can achieve a value of 0.6 W/m²K.

It is not just discrete building products that need to satisfy Building Regulations – there must be scope for innovations. There are actually three ways to demonstrate reasonable provision for limiting heat loss through the building fabric: the Elemental method, Target U-Value and Carbon index method. The Target U values and Carbon index methods provide greater flexibility than the Elemental approach by focusing on 'performance' rather than 'prescription'. Carbon index calculations are documented in the revised Building Regulations and will be incorporated from 2002. The carbon emission factors take account of all carbon dioxide emission sources; results need to be monitored and documented using the BREEAM method. In any case, it is prudent to seek advice from professional building services engineers with expertise of dynamic thermal simulation for buildings.

Environmental note

Many insulation materials use gases that are 'blown' into plastics to create foams. The gases used previously to perform this function were CFCs (chlorofluorocarbons). With the discovery that CFCs were detrimental to ozone (the layer in the Earth's atmosphere that protects against solar radiation) in the late 1980s, international agreements brought an end to their use as a 'foam blowing' agent for insulation products in 1995. Other chemically-based insulation materials known as HCFCs (hydrochlorofluorocarbons) have been developed, but are still classed as 'ozone depleting'. Alternative foam blowing gases such as carbon dioxide or the hydrocarbon pentane are widely available and economic to use. The abbreviation ZODC (zero ozone depleting chemicals) is used to denote compliant insulation materials.

The term 'embodied energy' is used to compare the energy notionally embodied in construction materials. It accounts for the total amount of energy used in the raw materials and manufacture of a given quantity of product and is part of ecological thinking. Although some insulation products have a high embodied energy value, their insulating properties may save a much higher amount of energy during their life-cycle than is consumed in their production. Embodied energy (EE) is measured in GJ/m³.

Insulation materials

The following list gives an overview of the typical materials used for insulation:

Plastic foam:

Petrochemical derivatives such as polystyrene, polyethylene and formaldehyde are the main products. These have high embodied energy content (4.05) from the raw materials of oil and gas, which in turn is significant in the creation of acid forming gases, and emission of toxic particulates. k values range from 0.024–0.039.

Foamed glass:

Made from pure glass with gas-filled bubbles (the addition of carbon to the glass melt forms carbon dioxide). It is available in slab form and is beneficial in flat roof construction (e.g. for grass roofs) where its zero vapour permeability and high dimensional stability is important for constructional long life. High embodied energy (2.70), it produces fluorides and chlorides during manufacture. k values range from 0.050–0.052.

Glass wool:

Basic raw materials are sand, limestone and refined borax. Soda ash, sodium carbonate along with phenol formaldehyde resins and other chemicals are added for blowing operations during production. There are some toxic emissions to the atmosphere during production, but the biggest risk is from inhalation in use. k values range from 0.032–0.040.

Mineral and rock wool:

Made in much the same way as glass wool, but instead of sand and limestone, volcanic ash, dolomite, silica sand and crushed coke are mixed as the fuel. Manufacturers are increasingly adding recycled materials (glass cullet and mineral wool waste). Mainly produced in slab forms, mineral wool insulation is a flame retardant and acoustic insulator. k values similar to glass wool. Embodied energy = 0.83.

Cellulose fibre:

Made from processed waste paper into a fluff that can be placed by hand or sprayed. Usually treated with sodium tetraborate, considered an environmentally accepted pesticide, for fire and insect resistance and is particularly useful for 'breathing wall' applications. Low on embodied energy (0.48). k values of about 0.037.

Wool:

A naturally biodegradable material, thought not to be toxic, although some concern has been expressed about the use of organophosphates in sheep dip. Suppliers of this extremely low embodied energy (0.11) material believe the thermal transmittance values to be as good as any chemically derived insulating material. It is cheap, effective and can be sourced locally in some areas of the UK.

Other insulating materials

- **Cork** which is a very sustainable product that can be grown and harvested;
- **Compressed straw slabs** another sustainable material that creates rural jobs and is excellent for thermal roof decking;
- **Wood-wool slabs** made from wood shavings bonded with cement and compressed.

Further reading

British Standards Institution (1999) *Thermal performance of buildings: transmission heat loss coefficient calculation method*, BS EN ISO 13789:1999.

Chartered Institute of Building Services Engineers, *CIBSE Guide* (Volume A), CIBSE, London, UK.

WH

Integration

A term used to describe an approach to architectural specification and design that considers the various components of a building integrally in terms of both function and form.

A good example of integration of structures and services: cellular steel beams in action in an industrial building. Photograph of the Frou Frou biscuit factory, Cyprus courtesy of Westok, Wakefield.

See also: ARUP, OVE; BESPOKE; BUILDABILITY; BUILDING SYSTEMS; CONCRETE – STRUCTURES; CONNECTIONS; DESIGN LIFE; ECOLOGICAL DESIGN; ENERGY EFFICIENCY; ENVIRONMENTAL DESIGN; FLOORS; FRAME; GRIDS FOR STRUCTURE AND LAYOUT; HIGH TECH; 'HONESTY'; KAHN, LOUIS; LE CORBUSIER; MODULES AND MODULAR CONSTRUCTION; PROCUREMENT; SCHINDLER, R.M; SERVICES; STRUCTURAL STEEL; TIMBER.

About integration

The increasing complexity of buildings has led to the desire to consider more effectively the ways in which structure, services and other components in a building are designed and actually function when in use. With the cost of servicing often amounting to 30% and more of the total construction costs, rationalisation of the layout and installation of structure and services can offer very significant cost savings, plus other benefits such as:

- Reduced materials cost;
- Time savings on site;
- Time savings in production;
- Reduced overall building height by reducing the floor void depths for servicing;
- Reduced need for re-work due to unplanned service routings;
- Reduced time on site for specialist contractors;
- Reduced snagging lists (last minute problems).

This approach demands early involvement of structures and services expertise in the design process and an explicit understanding that there are capital cost and buildability benefits to be gained from so doing. The types of building that can benefit most from an integrated approach to design, construction and operation are those which have a high services requirement, those which are being designed in a bespoke manner and those which employ some modularity in their design. For example:

- Offices;
- Dealing rooms;
- Hotels;
- Leisure facilities;
- Museums and galleries.

The degree of early stage design work involved in effective integration does rather work against small contractors or parties with little experience of sophisticated design and construction management protocols. However, it is not necessary to approach the whole building in an integrated way, smaller gestures may be equally useful in certain circumstances (e.g. in a simple shed building, having one integrated detail for steel roof beams and ducting).

Types of integration

Integration can be understood in a physical sense, i.e. buildings that are designed in such a way that structure and service runs are designed in tandem and are installed as closely-related elements. This approach can be seen clearly in the Lloyds building by Richard Rogers Partnership, in which the structure, services and other elements of the building work together in an architectural and aesthetic sense, but also in a functional way. For instance, the ceiling grids relate to the concrete frame, the lighting modules, the air handling modules, the flooring units, and so on. Thus there was a deliberate and considered attempt to integrate these various elements in a more streamlined, bespoke architecture than one might see in a more basic building. By designing and specifying in this way, the Lloyds Building is a particularly bespoke example of what design and construction integration can produce. However since that time, it has become more typical for architects to try to integrate structure and services, and there are examples from many different building types.

The role of procurement methods

It should be noted that traditional forms of procurement such as competitive tendering could work against good integrated design of structure and services etc. because the principal design work is carried out without input from specialists, and contracts are let in an iterative fashion. This prevents discussion between the parties and therefore reduces or removes the possibilities of cost and time savings. An 'integrated' approach to design and specification requires early discussion and agreement about how all the related parts of the building will work together when the building is complete, but also how (during construction) all the elements will be 'woven' together, i.e. buildability. Hence, good, integrated design is assisted by forms of procurement (such as partnering), where specialist trade contractors are involved early on in the process when strategic decisions are being made. They are then able to inform the design process, rationalise the planning in relation to both structure and services, rationalise buildability and advise on operational maintenance etc.

Historical note

In traditional buildings, there was little need to consider integration because few buildings contained any separately identifiable or even vaguely sophisticated environmental management equipment. Hence, design of the structure was simpler. However, there are exceptions to this rule – perhaps the best is the Roman hypocaust system (a fully integrated structure and underfloor heating system) whereby the floor structure was built up on pillars of tiles and warm air was allowed to circulate throughout. The trend towards integration can be identified in the work of several 20th century architects such as Gropius, Mies van der Rohe, Carlo Scarpa and Le Corbusier. However, it is the so-called 'high-tech' architects who have pushed forward a more integrated approach in more recent years, leading on from the real champion of integrated design and 'total' architecture, Ove Arup.

Further reading

Baird, G. (2001) *The architectural expression of environmental control systems*, E & FN Spon, London, UK.

Powell, K. (1994) *Lloyds building: Richard Rogers* (Architecture in Detail), Phaidon Press, London, UK.

JG

Intelligent façades and materials

A façade or material can be described as intelligent if it senses a change in its local environment and responds automatically.

Computer generated image of the intelligent façade for the '@Bristol' centre, in the west of England. Photograph courtesy of Ove Arup & Partners.

See also: ACOUSTICS; COMPOSITE MATERIALS; ECOLOGICAL DESIGN; ENERGY EFFICIENCY; ENVIRONMENTAL DESIGN; FAÇADES AND FAÇADE ENGINEERING; GLASS; GLASS – LAMINATED AND COATED; HIGH TECH; HVAC; INTUMESCENT PAINT; LIFE-CYCLE COSTING; LOUVRES AND BRISE SOLEIL; MAINTENANCE; NIGHT VENTILATION; NOUVEL, JEAN; PHASE CHANGE MATERIALS; PHOTOVOLTAICS; RITCHIE, IAN.

What is intelligence?

In the context of architectural technology, intelligence is about a material or device being able to respond to some change in conditions. This may occur as an inherent part of a façade or material, or may be created by sensible design to predict effects and program appropriate responses. In an environmental control context, an 'intelligent' building is one designed to operate in an energy efficient manner by balancing external environmental influences with internal environmental requirements. In this case, intelligence results as much from intelligent design as from any materials used. Examples of intelligent materials include:

- Intumescent paint which senses an increase in temperature, and responds by expanding to protect the underlying steelwork;
- Photochromic glazing, which senses a change in light conditions, and responds by going clear or opaque;
- Self-healing concretes, which respond to cracking by sealing the crack with resin.

There is a close relationship between 'intelligent' façades and 'adaptive' façades. In the case of the latter, there is scope not only for the materials and devices on the façade to act, but there may also be opportunity for human interaction i.e. occupant control. Hence, the phrase intelligent adaptive façade brings both approaches together.

Mechanisms of intelligence

Intelligent façades and materials vary in their degree of intelligence. Some (e.g. aluminium with its self-healing oxide film, lime mortar with its adaptive 'stretchiness' or a natural ventilation system) have intelligence as part of their basic material or system properties. Other materials require systems to process data, and combine separate components to increase the intelligence of the reaction. In this way, it is possible to create an intelligent or smart system by combining:

- A sensor, to sense a change in the local environment;
- An actuator, to respond to the change;
- A control system to effectively link the two devices.

The system of monitoring and feedback has been used effectively in automatic window openers, which sense changes in temperature and respond by opening or closing windows to control climate in a space (e.g. for night ventilation). It is also the basic principle behind active noise reduction where the waveform of noise in an enclosed space is monitored by a controller, which generates an equal and opposite signal. The signal is fed through a loudspeaker to create destructive interference with the original signal and effectively 'cancel out' the noise.

In a future scenario, it has been suggested that high performance glazing units could be linked to a building's Intranet and, over time, 'learn' their occupant's preferences. Tagging of each component would allow disassembly and later re-use elsewhere.

Discussion

The future of intelligent materials in construction remains uncertain, and the theoretical 'goal' of a totally automated façade or civil engineering structure may be some way from reality. Research into biomimetics shows that processes found in nature could have potential applications, but the discipline is at an early stage. In summary, intelligence can manipulate the building environment to maintaining comfortable conditions for the individual but it can also contribute to the broader aims of minimising energy use and reducing waste (i.e. meeting both short- and long-term sustainability goals). In order for this to happen, the client and the design team need to have a shared vision of what is expected, from the outset.

However, many questions arise regarding the mismatch of intelligent buildings with the expectations of users. One particular concern with intelligence is the psychological response of individuals to intelligent behaviour. In the same way that providing some occupant control over the thermal environment is said to improve perceptions of comfort, so people do not generally expect materials to compensate and act independently. For example, the drive towards photochromic glazing (which darkens automatically) has been displaced largely by research into electrochromic glazing (where the individual retains control) due to the increased comfort that results. Similarly, a fear of making the situation worse rather than better has led to increased use of passive rather than active solutions for high-risk earthquake protection solutions.

For these reasons, many designers are tending towards the goal of achieving simple, passive and integrated architecture, in which both the services and the envelope (skin) are intelligent. This is in the context where occupant needs and preferences are considered as paramount and that (intelligent) technology is simply a means to this end. For example the design of Renzo Piano's intelligent façade for the Aurora building in Sydney, Australia is based primarily on occupants' needs.

Further reading

Compagno, A. (1999) *Intelligent glass façades: materials, practice, design* (4th edition), Birkhäuser, Basle, Switzerland.

Harrison, A., Lee, E. & Read, J. (eds.) *Intelligent buildings in south east Asia*, E & FN Spon, London, UK.

Srinivasan, A.V. & McFarland, D.M. (2001) *Smart structures: analysis and design*, Cambridge University Press, Cambridge, UK.

Wigginton, M. & Harris, J. (2001) *Intelligent skins*, Butterworth-Heinemann, Oxford, UK.

OA

Interfaces
See: CONNECTIONS

Interstitial condensation
See: CONDENSATION

Intumescent paint

Intumescent paint is a fire protection system for steel which has the appearance of a normal painted surface until a fire occurs, at which time the heat causes it to form a thick insulating char around the steel.

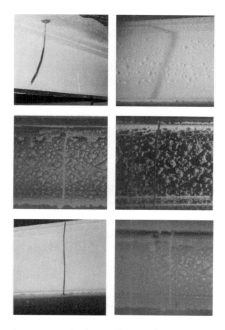

Intumescent paint during a fire test: the bubbling and creation of a protective skin can be seen clearly throughout this sequence. Photographs provided by Leigh's Paints Marketing Department/Ove Arup & Partners. Taken from a one-hour fire test of a loaded beam.

See also: BEAMS; COLUMNS; EPOXY; FIRE ENGINEERING; FIRE PROTECTION; FRAME; GLASS – LAMINATED AND COATED; STRUCTURAL STEEL; SURFACE FINISHES; TIMBER.

What is an intumescent paint?

Intumescent paints or coatings are defined as those that bubble and foam when subjected to flame temperatures to produce multicellular, insulative foams. They are one of a number of fire protection materials used to insulate steelwork, cast and wrought iron in the event of a fire and to give them structural integrity for periods of up to two hours. Clear intumescent varnish systems also exist which are used to improve the surface spread of flame on timber.

Intumescent paints have been used in construction for about 20 years. Early formulations were based on the epoxy ablatives used to protect spacecraft from the heat generated upon re-entry to the Earth's atmosphere. Thin film intumescents that were developed subsequently have a different binder and produce a more voluminous, less robust char than epoxy systems. Originally the solvent for an intumescent was an organic liquid, but more recently more environmentally acceptable water-based systems have been developed. Improving the water resistance of products has been an ongoing development goal. Initially the basecoat was extremely water-sensitive, but now systems exist which are suitable for exterior application and can withstand up to six months outdoor exposure without the application of a protective topcoat. The majority of coatings are formulated for internal use, however.

Two of the key benefits of current intumescent paint products are thinness and appearance. An intumescent can have a high quality painted finish, which enables architects to express the form of the steelwork, without the fire protection being obtrusive. This is in contrast to cementitious spray and board fire protection materials, which are typically 10–20 mm thick for one hour integrity. Both have rough surface finishes and are normally boxed in with plasterboard, metal cladding or hidden behind a suspended ceiling. Since intumescents are more costly than other fire protection types, they tend to be used most where the steelwork is visible, rather than hidden.

Using intumescent paints

An intumescent paint system generally comprises a primer, an intumescent basecoat and a decorative/protective topcoat. The primer ensures good adhesion to the steel, and may be part of the corrosion protection. The basecoat is the reactive part of the system and the topcoat protects the basecoat against mechanical damage and weathering. The basecoat is typically 1–2 mm thick for typical steel sections requiring 1 hour structural integrity. In the heat of a fire the basecoat breaks down and a chemical reaction takes place which produces a foam char about 50 times thicker than the unreacted coating which insulates the steel section. This char interlocks around sections with re-entrant (indented) profiles holding it in place. With hollow sections this cannot occur, so the intumescent coating needs to be thicker since it is more likely to crack and fall away during a fire.

The intumescent basecoat has four main components: an organic binder, a source of carbon, an acidic catalyst and a blowing agent. When the smoke and flame hits the paint film, the binder starts to soften and the catalyst decomposes to release phosphoric acid. A reaction then occurs between the phosphoric acid and the source of carbon. At the same time the blowing agent releases gases which cause large volumes of insulating carbonaceous char to form.

Traditionally, intumescent paints are applied to primed erected steelwork using airless spray, brush or roller after the building envelope has been completed. More recently off-site application has become more popular. The steel arrives on site already coated and once erected the fixings and any damage are made good. The benefits of this method are in the programming, more controllable application conditions, improved quality assurance, access and the removal of a wet trade from site. The disadvantages include damage to the coating during handling and the increased cost of welding. Off-site application may also be automated whereby the beam is blast cleaned, heated and passed through an automated spraying machine where the intumescent is applied. This enables the intumescent to be applied without a primer where it is to be used in internal heated, 'normal' environments.

Further reading

Association of Specialist Fire Protection Contractors and Manufacturers Ltd (1994) *Fire protection for structural steel in buildings, Supplement to 2nd edition (revised)*, 'Yellow Book', Association of Specialist Fire Protection Contractors and Manufacturers Ltd. (New volume due)

Yandzio, E., Dowling, J.J. & Newman, G.M. (1996) *Structural fire design: off-site applied thin film intumescent coatings, Part 1: Design guidance. Part 2: Model specification*, SCI Publication 160, Steel Construction Institute, Ascot, UK.

OA

Jiricna, Eva

Well known for her innovative high-tech design work, Eva Jiricna is perhaps best known for her spectacular staircases and interior designs for the fashion giant Joseph Ettedgui.

See also: BESPOKE; GLASS; GLASS – LAMINATED AND COATED; HIGH TECH; ROGERS, RICHARD; STAINLESS STEEL; STRUCTURAL STEEL.

'True freedom is to try with each successive project to do something different and better. To try to interpret an old principle in a new way, to do better tomorrow on what missed the target today'

Eva Jiricna.

Eva Jiricna graduated as an architect/engineer from the University of Prague in 1962. She was hired by the Greater London Council in 1968 and was still resident in the UK when the Russians invaded Czechoslovakia later the same year and she did not return there for twenty years. In 1969 she moved to the Louis de Soissons Partnership working on the Brighton Marina and by 1978, had formed her first practice (Jiricna Hodges). It was at this time that Jiricna began working on interior projects for Joseph Ettedgui. In 1984 she joined the Richard Rogers Partnership to design interior packages for the Lloyds of London Headquarters Building in London.

Eva Jiricna Associates was formed in 1985 and the practice went on to complete many retail, restaurant and commercial projects. She became known widely for her work in glass and steel and particularly for her spectacular staircases. In the retail store for Joan & David (Paris, 1994), Jiricna created a signature project. The shop is on two floors and a marvellous staircase linking the floors is a masterpiece of metal and glass. The 'box' surrounding it is clean and minimal with exquisite organisation, allowing the focus to fall upon the stair, which sweeps around glass and steel treads 'floating' amid elegant steel tension elements. The design is intended to have minimal impact on the space allowing transparency and thus giving users views through the shop.

In 1989 Jiricna was eventually able to return to the Czech Republic. She was appointed architectural consultant to President Vaclav Haval in 1995 and commissioned to rebuild an orangery on the site of the 15th century original at Prague Castle. In the same year she was appointed to design the interior of Anderson Consulting Czech HQ in a building designed by Frank Gehry. The modern glasshouse of the Prague orangery uses a criss-cross, steel and glass structure, spanning the orangery with few vertical supports. It provides a stark contrast with the ancient castle, but utilises a comparable method of using the ultimate in materials and structure available to the builders of the day.

In 1999 Jiricna designed the controversial Faith Zone within the Millennium Dome (Richard Rogers Partnership) in London. This was preceded by her design for what was then the Soul Zone (in fact, this had evolved from a great deal of research and would have been an incredible project in its own right). Unfortunately no sponsor could be found for this zone and the design had to be revised. In addition, the remit for the zone changed to become essential exhibition space for information about a selection of religions. The position within the dome was directly over the Blackwall tunnel and this meant that it was not able to take any substantial loading and a solid structure was thus ruled out. Jiricna's response was a lightweight construct of steel beams and textile membranes. There were nine 'life points', which represented the number of religions represented in the dome. At the core of the structure was a small central space for contemplation with a lighting installation that completed the serene effect.

Further reading

Boyarsky, A. et al. (1987) *Eva Jiricna Designs*, AA Publications, London, UK.
Jiricna, E. (2001) *Staircases*, Watson Guptill Publications, New York, USA.
Jiricna, E. (2001) *Staircases*, Laurence King Publishing, London, UK.

MT

Joints
See: CONNECTIONS

'Just-in-time' construction

The programming (almost like choreography) of construction elements to be delivered and installed on site at the most efficient point, i.e. 'just-in-time'.

See also: BUILDABILITY; BUILDING SYSTEMS; CONSTRUCTION PROGRAMME; CRITICAL PATH ANALYSIS; LEAD-TIME; 'LEAN' CONSTRUCTION; MODULES AND MODULAR CONSTRUCTION; OFF-SITE MANUFACTURE; PODS; PROCUREMENT; RISK MANAGEMENT.

The benefits of working off site

The number of construction elements and building components that are manufactured off site and delivered to site in a finished or almost finished state is increasing steadily. This is due to two main reasons: cost and quality.

The cost of time, rather than the cost of materials, often has more impact on a building project. The cost of time includes the cost of plant, labour and equipment hire on site. Items like tower crane hire can be so expensive that the whole construction programme needs to be shortened to reduce the impact of this cost component. For hotel clients in particular a fast build programme is vital: accommodation needs to be open earlier because rental returns per week are worth so much. To reduce the construction programme it may be fortuitous to spend a little more capital cost on producing elements off site than spending longer on site building them in situ. Factory production of building elements can facilitate a faster programme provided the scheduling of production, delivery and installation is well managed. The complexity of large projects such as office buildings is such that there may be thousands of items to be brought to the site and dozens of different sub-contractors to install them. In this eventuality, the key role for the main contractor/project manager/construction manager is to plan and oversee the construction programming. Hence the rise in off-site assembly as a means to shorten the programme.

The ability to achieve consistent quality is perceived as easier to obtain off site where work carries on in a controlled environment, rather than being at the mercy of the weather. It is also easier to keep on a regular, trained workforce in a factory production facility. Working in advance of progress on site also allows the project team to see samples or mock-ups at the factory to confirm their requirements. Thus off-site production is favoured by many project teams, provided they can supply sufficient information to the factory in time for their products to be manufactured. A factory runs on a production schedule and hence there is a 'lead-time' between order and delivery to site. This period must be accounted for in the procurement and construction programme. Nevertheless, being committed to the design and specification of a construction element from an early stage in the programme is beneficial.

About 'Just-in-time'

The regime of choreographing products (produced on- and off-site), personnel and equipment on site can be very difficult, but, provided deadlines are met, elements produced and installed correctly, then it is feasible to construct a building very quickly. It can be argued that the most efficient construction programme is one in which **all elements arrive on site exactly when they are needed**, thus avoiding double handling (i.e. taken off a truck, stored and then lifted again to final position) and possible damage or theft while in storage. This is 'just-in-time' construction – the careful and thoughtful planning of production, deliveries and installation to effect a faster construction programme. The potential of JIT to produce faster construction programmes was realised in Japan in the 1980s. The potential business benefits of approaching building construction with a mindset similar to that employed in car manufacture were identified as a means of:

- Overcoming limitations of constricted sites;
- Satisfying customer quality demands;
- Increasing construction starts;
- Reducing costs on site.

This approach is still being developed in Japan with a greater emphasis on automation on site, but their construction industry has since slowed down. The idea of JIT is used extensively on key UK projects but its full potential may not yet have been witnessed. Factors such as traffic delays, union action, legal or procurement loopholes may affect 'on the limit' JIT schedules. Hence, to guarantee a JIT schedule could be risky.

JIT example: precast concrete cladding

The following list shows key stages in the JIT procurement for cladding panels to an office building:

- Production slot in the factory is 'booked' in advance.
- Cladding units are designed, specified and detailed in collaboration with the specialist contractor.
- Connections to the frame are optimised for speed of installation.
- A sample panel is produced and may be installed in a mock-up to test connections.
- The production schedule is agreed and commences, while work has already started on site on the structure.
- Phased deliveries start some time later, overlapping with production of later panels.
- Deliveries continue to site on a regular basis until all cladding is installed.
- All panels are installed immediately, with no double handling.

Although elements such as steel beams and air-conditioning units have been brought to site in a similar way for many years, the trend towards off-site assembly has expanded to other items such as cladding panels and bathroom pods. The size of item to be delivered is restricted in size only by transportation (i.e. trucks and trailers). However, element size may not be an issue in all instances – the wheel for the London Eye at Westminster was floated in by barge down the Thames and then lifted into place. Whole room modules are now being assembled in steel, timber and concrete and brought to site with services, external and internal finishes all intact.

Further reading

Construction Industry Research and Information Association (1997) *Standardisation and pre-assembly*, CIRIA Report 176, CIRIA, London, UK.

Dear, A. (1988) *Working towards JIT*, Kogan Page, London, UK.

Department of Trade & Industry (1992) *Just in time: an executive guide to just in time*, London, UK.

Gibb, A.G.F. (1999) *Off-site fabrication: prefabrication, pre-assembly and modularisation*, Whittles Publishing, Caithness, UK.

Hay, E.J. (1988) *The JIT breakthrough: implementing the new manufacturing basics*, John Wiley & Sons, New York, USA.

O'Grady, P.J. (1988) *Putting the JIT philosophy into practice*, Kogan Page, London, UK.

Warszawski, A. (1999) *Industrialized and automated building systems* (2nd edition), E & FN Spon, London, UK.

JG

K-bracing
See: BRACING

'K' glass
See: GLASS – LAMINATED AND COATED GLASS

K value
See: INSULATION

Kahn, Louis

Kahn (1901–1974) was an American architect regarded widely for his use of clear expression and rigorous attention to architectural detailing.

See also: AALTO, ALVAR; BRICKS AND BLOCKS; CEILINGS; CONCRETE – STRUCTURES; CORE (SERVICES); ENVIRONMENTAL DESIGN; FLOORS; 'HONESTY'; INTEGRATION; LE CORBUSIER; SERVICES.

The Salk Institute, La Jolla, California: Louis Kahn used exposed concrete and Western Red Cedar cladding to excellent visual effect on this façade. Photograph by Author.

Any description of the architecture of Louis Kahn must start with an acknowledgement of its dual nature: simultaneously deeply rooted in the École des Beaux-Arts and Imperial Roman antiquity, and employing the most advanced techniques of structure and construction. He had studied under the Beaux-Arts trained Paul Cret at the University of Pennsylvania from 1920–24; from this he derived features of Beaux-Arts education such as *marche* (the rigorous analysis of spatial sequence) and *disposition* (combinations of forms), revealed typically through natural light. In his early private houses and wartime housing for the United States Housing Authority, however, he embodied the social and aesthetic ideals of the Modern Movement; his partner from 1942–47 was Oscar Stonorov who had edited volume 1 of Le Corbusier's *Œuvre Complète* (1929).

Kahn came to notice with the Yale University Art Gallery (1951–53) relatively late in his career. He intended specifically to challenge the limited spatial and material nature of International Modern architecture, which was gaining ascendancy among architects (incidentally, Kahn replaced Philip Goodwin, who had designed the Museum of Modern Art, New York in 1935, as architect of the Gallery). His intention followed a study of ancient ruins while a Fellow at the American Academy in Rome in 1950, in which the brick construction of public buildings (such as his favourite Baths of Caracalla), while not their intended appearance, had become apparent. The walls of the Gallery were made of exposed brick externally and exposed block internally, with floor slabs, not of the expected smooth construction, but of what was virtually an exposed space-frame of concrete tetrahedrons. The structure was stabilised by a massive concrete cylinder containing the staircase.

Kahn acknowledged the Trenton Jewish Community Centre (1954–59) as a turning point. He started to experiment with specifically classical forms of composition; the Bathhouse, an outdoor swimming pool, was planned as a group of five squares, of which the central one remained void. The Unitarian Church and School, Rochester, New York (1959–69) is a mature work from this period. The protracted design period and restricted budget meant that Kahn necessarily pared form down to what he considered its essentials: massive load-bearing masonry structures with clearly-expressed lintels and concrete floor and roof slabs. This theme was developed further in the Phillips Exeter Library and Dining Hall (1965–72).

Kahn experimented with other classical forms of construction in buildings which owe some allegiance to the French architect Henri Labrouste (1801–75) or the visionary Etienne-Louis Boullée (1728–99). These include the rectilinear frame and infill panels of the Yale Centre for British Art, New Haven (1969–74), or the vaults of the Kimbell Art Museum, Fort Worth (1966–72). These were rendered with an unprecedented attention to concrete detailing, which was also apparent in other, less classical, structures, such as:

- The post-tensioned Vierendeel frames of the Alfred Newton Richards Medical Research Buildings, Philadelphia, USA (1957–65);
- The post-tensioned concrete beams of the project for the Palazzo de Congressi, Venice, Italy (1968–74);
- The expanses of crisply detailed in-situ concrete at the Salk Institute for Biological Studies, La Jolla, San Diego, USA (1959–65).

Kahn's attention to constructional detailing may be seen as a parallel to the stereotomy of the École des Beaux-Arts, the cutting of stone into 3D structural forms. His interest in geometry was apparent in the floor slabs of the Yale University Art Gallery, projects for tetrahedron skyscrapers for Philadelphia (1957), and the cycloidal vaults of the Kimbell Art Museum. It derived as much from Rudolf Wittkower's *Architectural Principles in the Age of Humanism* as from recently-published books on organic geometry such as *On Growth and Form* by D'Arcy Wentworth Thompson, and as much from his experiences in Rome as from his friendship with Buckminster Fuller.

The massive construction, layered forms, large internal volumes and small openings meant that Kahn's buildings offered excellent environmental performance. He was, of course, able to take for granted the sophisticated heating, lighting and security systems prevalent in the USA. These services were always in concealed ducts, similar to hollow masonry 'poché', the opposite of contemporary architectural movements, such as Brutalism, with which he otherwise had much affinity. In the Richards Buildings, services were located in closed brick towers distinct from the more open office and lab areas, while in the Salk Institute services occupied entire, mezzanine-type mini-floors threaded through a Vierendeel structure. Kahn's approach to services was based on dividing spaces into one of two categories – 'served' spaces and 'servant' spaces.

The environmental and constructional approach of Kahn's architecture made his work suitable for less-developed regions without sophisticated services such as the Indian subcontinent, as may be seen in the Indian Institute of Management, Ahmedabad, India (1962–74) and Sher-e-Bangla Nagar, Dhaka, Bangladesh (1962–82). Although the third choice of architect after Le Corbusier and Alvar

Aalto, Kahn's buildings in Dhaka are arguably the most appropriate for the climate and conditions of construction there. Double skin walls of massive brick or concrete construction acted as thermal flywheels, with the outer walls shading the inner walls and providing a gradation of daylight while allowing ventilation.

Whilst Kahn has been taken as a mentor by many differing architectural factions, his most lasting legacy was to show that the classical aspects and tectonic language of architecture was rooted profoundly in experience, both spatial, spiritual and material. His work remains a clear and solid exemplar of an architecture that is as relevant and profound now as it has always been.

Further reading

Brawne, M. (1992) *Kimbell art museum: Louis Kahn* (Architecture in Detail), Phaidon Press, London, UK.

Brownlee, D.B. & De Long, D.G. (eds.) (1991) *Louis Kahn: in the realm of architecture*, Rizzoli, New York, USA.

Büttiker, U. (1993) *Louis I. Kahn: Licht und raum*, Birkhäuser, Basle, Switzerland.

Gast, K-P. (1998) *Louis Kahn: the idea of order*, Birkhäuser, Basle, Switzerland.

Komerdant, A.E. (1975) *18 years with architect Louis I. Kahn*, Aloray, Englewood, USA.

Larson, K. (2000) *Louis Kahn: unbuilt masterworks*, Monacelli Press, New York, USA.

Ronner, H. (1987) *Louis Kahn: complete works 1935–1974* (2nd edition), Birkhäuser, Basle, Switzerland.

Sharp, D. (1999) *20th century classics: Walter Gropius, Le Corbusier & Louis Kahn*, Phaidon Press, London, UK.

Steele, J. (1993) *Salk Institute: Louis Kahn* (Architecture in Detail), Phaidon Press, London, UK.

Wiggins, G.E. (1997) *Louis Kahn: the Library at Phillips Exeter Academy*, Van Nostrand Reinhold, New York, USA.

Williams Goldhagen, S. (2001) *Louis Kahn's situated modernism*, Yale University Press, USA.

TD

Kevlar™

See: COMPOSITE MATERIALS

Laminated glass
See: GLASS – LAMINATED AND COATED GLASS

Laminated plastics
See: PLASTICS – FABRICATION

Laminated timber
See: TIMBER – LAMINATED TIMBER

Lamps
See: LIGHTING – ARTIFICIAL LIGHTING

Lautner, John
Based in Los Angeles, John Lautner (1911–94) designed some of the most remarkable private houses throughout California and Mexico always testing the nature of construction and properties of materials.

See also: CONCRETE – FINISHES; CONCRETE – STRUCTURES; GLASS – LAMINATED AND COATED; GLASS – STRUCTURAL GLAZING; SURFACE FINISHES; TIMBER – LAMINATED TIMBER; WRIGHT, FRANK LLOYD.

John Lautner was born in 1911 in Marquette, Michigan, by the shores of Lake Superior, so he had been used to picturesque landscapes, pine forests and lakeside imagery. It was little wonder therefore, that in later life he often declared his hatred of Los Angeles and its ugliness. Lautner's mother was a painter and had designed their holiday cabin (constructed by Lautner, then aged 12 and his father).

Lautner learnt architecture through work experience. Rejecting conventional schools of architecture he heard about the Taliesin training programme and went to work with Frank Lloyd Wright in 1934 after graduating from Northern States Teachers college with a degree in English. He assisted in the Building of the Broadacre city model whilst on his apprenticeship. The School taught more than draughtsmanship; students became involved in masonry, carpentry as well as farm work and organising large dinner parties for their masters' guests!

Once he had set up his own practice in 1940 in Los Angeles, Lautner created his own interpretation of Wright's work. Perhaps because of his catalogue of hands-on experience he understood thoroughly the process, construction and materials of architecture. He followed the leaps forward that were being made in material and structural technology, experimenting and incorporating them into his designs. Lautner designed 188 projects in his 50 years of practice and 113 of these were built, many of them private houses. He used advanced technology to create fascinating and workable spaces for his clients. The designs are as stunning today as they were at the time of their construction; many are used in films and advertising.

The Carling house was constructed in Los Angeles in 1947 and although the overall appearance of the design is reminiscent of Frank Lloyd Wright the mechanics of the house are pure Lautner. Not only is a swimming pool sliced in two as a large glass door slides into place, but also one entire wall (with built-in sofa and clerestorey) swings out onto decking to create an outside seating area allowing flexibility between the inside and outside space. Many innovative factors in this house make it an architectural favourite. The Chemosphere or Malin House nestles into a steep hillside in Hollywood, California. Built in 1960, it used a single reinforced concrete column to support the building. Steel beams emerge from this central support and curved 'glulam' timber beams provide the main structure for the roof of the house. Construction was a problem on the steeply sloped site and a complicated set of guy ropes and winches had to be used. The client for the house was Leonard Malin, who was an aircraft engineer; he specified the use of an adhesive developed for aircraft joints to be used in the house. In 1963 Lautner built the Sheats/Goldstein house and he went back between 1980 and 1994 to carry out extensive remodelling. The triangular motif, which haunts the design, is repeated in so many ways: from the waffle in the concrete ceiling structure to the coffee table within. The juxtaposition of glass and concrete is explored in this design and combined with polished timber and stone. Glass walls, carried on steel cantilevers above the garden exploit the stunning view across the city. A glass sink is incorporated into one of the glass walls, combining the need for cleansing without detracting from the view (or meaning that one does not have to leave the view to wash).

To understand fully the extremities and genius of this architect it is vital to look at his complete oeuvre. His reluctance to settle with any single tried and tested construction method or material, ensure that his buildings continue to fascinate generations of architects and lay people alike. Lautner's work incorporates extraordinary technical achievements, concrete roofs, steel cantilevers, and double curves – it became representative of a new architecture of limitless possibilities.

Further reading

Campbell-Lange, B-A. with Gossel, P. (ed.) (1999) *John Lautner*, Benedikt Taschen, Koln, Germany.

Escher, F. (1998) *John Lautner Architect*, Birkhäuser, Basle, Switzerland.

Hess, A. (2000) *The architecture of John Lautner*, Thames & Hudson, London, UK.

MT

Le Corbusier

Le Corbusier (1887–1965), a Modernist with radical ideas to overhaul society, was extremely progressive. However, many of his innovations were let down by a lack of technical understanding.

See also: AIR-CONDITIONING; BUILDING SYSTEMS; COLUMN; CONCRETE – STRUCTURES; ENVIRONMENTAL DESIGN; FAÇADES AND FAÇADE ENGINEERING; HVAC; INTEGRATION; INTELLIGENT FAÇADES AND MATERIALS; LOUVRES AND BRISE SOLEIL; MODULES AND MODULAR CONSTRUCTION; NIEMEYER, OSCAR; PROUVÉ, JEAN; STRUCTURAL STEEL; TIMBER – PRODUCTION AND FINISHES; VENTILATION; WINDOWS AND CURTAIN WALLING.

Le Corbusier: Maison Jaoul, Paris (1952–54). In a rejection of his Puris-phase, Le Corbusier built these houses using loadbearing brickwork with structural 'Calalan' style vaults. Photograph by Thomas Deckker.

Le Corbusier (real name Edouard Jeanneret) was as unceasingly innovative with technology as he was in any other field of his endeavours, and with equally controversial results. He came to prominence in architecture in the 1920s in part by abstracting and promoting particular aspects of current architectural practice not as pragmatic constructional solutions, but as abstract and ideal forms of an industrial and technocratic society.

Le Corbusier's architectural forms were facilitated by both constructional and environmental innovations. The *plan libre* was dependent on a system of flat concrete slabs and cylindrical *pilotis*. This had been proposed initially in 1914 as the 'Domino' system and appeared in projects for the Citrohan House (1920–22), a pun on the car manufacturer Citroën, with whose director, André Citroën, Le Corbusier felt an entirely un-reciprocated affinity. The *mur neutralisant* (neutralising wall) and *respiration exact* (exact ventilation) was a form of air-conditioning by passing heated and cooled air inside a curtain wall, supplemented by internal ventilation. So convincing was Le Corbusier in promoting these that many came to believe that he had, in fact, invented air-conditioning.

Despite his ceaseless self-promotion, Le Corbusier did not pursue his own innovations as normative solutions but as a field for further invention, such as, for example, the 'four house types' which utilised the *plan libre* in different ways. It is apparent, however, that he had little grasp of basic engineering principles. In the Villa Savoye (1928–31), for example, the circular *pilotis* were compromised aesthetically by square columns and beams (such as at the main entrance), although these compromises served to enrich the architectural experience. In all the works of this period, Le Corbusier struggled with basic environmental control, as he reduced the construction to the point at which thermal and acoustic performance, and even weatherproofing, was completely inadequate. The *mur neutralisant*, which he promoted as appropriate for the North Pole and the tropics, met with firm rejection in Moscow in 1929 and Rio de Janeiro in 1936. It was flawed theoretically and discredited in tests carried out for the Centrosoyuz Building, Moscow (1929–33). He did use the simpler *pan-de-verre* (fixed curtain wall) in the Armée du Salut (1929–32) and the Pavillon Suisse (1930–32) in Paris, but with disastrous results.

Le Corbusier's trips to Spain and South America in 1929 marked a turning point in his work. Where exactly is not clear because a sketch of Catalan vaults (possibly derived from Gaudí), which was to be influential on his later work, is found in the sketchbooks made during his South American journey. In any case, the experience of flying in Argentina and the sensuousness of life in Brazil marked a change in direction. His trip to New York in 1935 – his first to the technically far superior United States – perhaps led him to reassess the reliance on mechanical services which his Ville Radieuse embodied.

In contrast to the initial Purist phase, Le Corbusier's few works in the 1930s mixed 'primitive' and industrial forms of construction. His first experiment with 'primitive' construction was for a project for the Errazuris House in Chile (1929) made of stone and unfinished timber, and stone walls appeared in the Pavillon Suisse and the apartment building in rue Nungesser-et-Coli, Paris (1933). His first complete house with exposed stone construction in cellular forms was La Tremblade, Mathes (1935), followed by the Petite Maison de Weekend, Paris (1934–35), in brick with concrete vaults.

After the Second World War, Le Corbusier abandoned the utopian and technological direction of his Purist phase almost entirely. In 1946 brise-soleil and a revised ventilation system were added to the Armée du Salut, and new glazing systems to Centrosoyuz and the Pavillon Suisse, which had been virtually uninhabitable. The Maisons Jaoul, Paris (1952–54) were built of brick with tiled vaults. Experiments in concrete construction became increasingly sophisticated; columns, walls, brise-soleil and *ondulatoires* (an infill system of fixed glazing and openable ventilators in concrete frames) were combined in lyrical compositions. In the Couvent de la Tourette, Lyons (1956–59), the repetitive structure of the cells was expressed physically and symbolically in precast façade units, while the public rooms were more freely articulated in situ; in the Unité d'Habitation, Marseilles (1946–52) the substructure in 'beton brut' is almost zoomorphic. The public buildings in Chandigarh (1950–64) were made entirely in situ with the least possible technology.

The more lyrical and expressive nature of his post-war work did not exclude practical problems, however. Wallace K. Harrison wrote of his incredulity at Le Corbusier's proposal to put brise-soleil on his project for the United Nations building, New York (1947) – they would have resulted in insuperable problems with snow. Criticisms have been voiced that the brise-soleil of the Chandigarh buildings are also unsuitable for the dusty North Indian plain; furthermore, the massive concrete construction acts as a heat store as it is a single layer. Although much of the imagery of the building was derived from technical sources (e.g. the Hall of the Legislative Assembly from a power station cooling tower) inadequate ventilation compounds the problems. On the other hand, the basic concrete construction of La Tourette has proved appropriate to the milder climate of the Rhône valley and the restrained life of its inhabitants.

In his last work, the little-known Heidi Weber Pavilion, Zurich (1962–66), Le Corbusier prefigured many aspects of the emerging 'high-tech' movement, with walls of interchangeable vitreous enamel panels and ready-made industrial fittings.

Despite his obvious technical shortcomings, the power of his imagery and the brilliance of his creativity, not least in the area of technology, mean that Le Corbusier is an architect to whom others will fruitfully return.

Further reading

Benton, T. (1987) *The villas of Le Corbusier*, Yale University Press, USA.

Boisiger, W. et al. (1929–1970) *Le Corbusier & P. Jeanneret Œuvre Complète* (8 volumes), Girsberger, Zurich, Switzerland (1929, 1934, 1938, 1946, 1952, 1957 and 1965) and Artemis, Zurich, Switzerland (1970).

Cohen, J-L. (1992) *Le Corbusier and the mystique of the USSR*, Princeton University Press, USA. (First edition: Mardaga, P. (ed.) 1987, Liège, France)

Le Corbusier (1960) *Précisions sur un état présent de l'architecture et de l'urbanisme*, Vincent Fréal, Paris, France. (First edition: Editions Crè, 1930 Paris, France)

Sharp, D. (1999) *20th century classics: Walter Gropius, Le Corbusier & Louis Kahn*, Phaidon Press, London, UK.

TD

Lead

A commonly used metal used typically in roofing, cladding and flashings.

See also: ALUMINIUM; CEMENT; CLADDING; CONCRETE; COPPER; CORROSION; DESIGN LIFE; DURABILITY; GLASS; METALS; MORTARS, CEMENT AND LIME; ROOFS; SERVICES; STAINLESS STEEL; STRUCTURAL STEEL; SURFACE FINISHES; TIMBER – PRODUCTION AND FINISHES; WATER MANAGEMENT AND DRAINAGE; WEATHERING.

What is lead?

Lead is a soft metal that is used as a roofing material (mainly for flashings on roof-wall junctions) for buildings primarily in the refurbishment market, rather than for new buildings. It is utilised in the soldering of pipework and has been used in the manufacture of glass for thousands of years. It is also associated with other applications, because it can be added to steel as a coating to protect against rust (i.e. terne-coated stainless steel).

On a historical note, many churches from the Middle Ages used lead roofing and its use in plumbing dates back to Roman times (the Latin word for lead is *plumbum*, hence the term plumbing). The ductility and durability of the metal made it useful for moulding, installing and joining plumbing, water distribution and rainwater pipes – this practice continued until recent times. After it was established some years ago that ingestion of lead, and most of its compounds, is harmful to humans its use became very restricted for these purposes. Its use in paints is also now governed very strictly.

Lead is based on a natural ore called galena. It is processed and refined (which removes impurities), and then formed using either milling or continuous-casting on a drum. In both instances, a sheet product is made that can be used for roofing, cladding or flashings. The sheets come in lengths of up to six metres and are coded by thickness from 1.32–3.55 mm (nominal), and often known only by their colour codes from 'green' (the thinnest, code 3) to 'orange' (the thickest, code 8). The only exception is sand-cast lead, which is specified in conservation work e.g. for churches. This is hand-made using traditional techniques: it typically uses lead recovered from existing buildings.

Design and construction considerations

Lead has a blue-grey patina (film of tarnish), which forms readily on contact with air. A patination oil can be applied when installation is completed to prevent further changes. Lead can last in place for hundreds of years, but consideration must be given to the weight of the material. It is heavy and will 'creep' under its own weight. The sheets need freedom to extend, but the overall extension can be limited by using a lead alloy containing a small amount of copper. On site, lead can be worked easily at room temperature (i.e. it is very malleable), which makes it particularly useful for details with complex geometries such as flashings where waterproofing, durability and ductility are vital. In use, lead is very resistant to corrosion, but can be corroded undetected by trapped moisture between the lead and roof decking, thus ventilation is important.

Lead can be used on roofs with a range of pitches from flat roofs to 80° pitches, however the fixing and lapping details will alter as the roof pitch increases. Cladding applications use sheets, strips or pre-formed clip-on panels. Lead can be reclaimed and recycled.

Compatible materials and safety

In accordance with strict safety laws governing the use of lead and the galvanic series, designers should exercise caution when using lead in combination with a number of materials. If in doubt, British Standards, Building Regulations or relevant manufacturers should be consulted.

Lead can corrode the following materials:

- Aluminium (especially in marine environments);
- Copper;
- Steel.
  (Fixings should be copper or stainless steel).

The following materials can corrode lead:

- Acid soils: peat and ash residues;
- Damp oak, teak and western red cedar;
- Mosses (acidic rainwater run-off);
- Wet Portland cement, lime and concrete.

It is recommended that designers check the constituents of any timber, underlay, sealants, adhesives, concrete, mortars or metals that might come into contact with lead.

Built examples

The David Mellor Cutlery factory in Hathersage, Derbyshire uses traditional lead roofing techniques in the delightfully detailed circular building by Michael Hopkins & Partners.

Further reading

British Standards Institution BS EN 12588:1999 and BS 6915:2000

JG

Lead-time

The period of time that elapses between ordering a component or package of works, and it being delivered to site (mobilised).

See also: BESPOKE; BUILDABILITY; CONSTRUCTION PROGRAMME; CRITICAL PATH ANALYSIS; 'JUST-IN-TIME' CONSTRUCTION; 'LEAN' CONSTRUCTION; OFF-SITE MANUFACTURE; ON-SITE PRODUCTION; PROCUREMENT; RISK MANAGEMENT.

About construction programming

Producing building elements such as steelwork, cladding panels and mechanical ventilation units in a factory is commonplace in construction. Off-site construction can offer cost and quality benefits and can allow efficient scheduling of components arriving and being installed on site. However, this must be integrated with those activities already underway on site and it is in this programming that 'lead-time' becomes important, whether or not an item is made in the factory. All construction products or packages of work need to be timetabled when a building is under construction. Thus, there is a need to plan ahead in terms of:

- Design and detailing;
- Production period;
- Delivery schedule;
- Installation time;
- Contingency plans.

Following the design and specification stage of a project, the onset of project planning for the construction period (on site) means that products with either a lengthy production period or that are in heavy demand must be considered at an earlier stage than one might think necessary. This is to address what is called 'lead-time' i.e. the period of time that elapses from the point at which a component is ordered to the point at which it arrives on site ready to be installed. It is sometimes called 'lead-in time'.

How long might this be?

Individual companies may quote slightly different lead-times (according to their own circumstances), but all will include the time taken to complete the following tasks:

1. Working drawings;
2. Approve working drawings;
3. Procure materials;
4. Manufacture;
5. Provide/agree samples;
6. Mobilisation.

The lead-time for a product can vary from a few days to several months depending on:

- Availability of raw materials;
- Availability of labour;
- How standard or bespoke the product is;
- Summer holidays/factory shutdown;
- Market demand for that product;
- Factory workload: number and size of jobs.

Lead-times are actually a good indicator of the health of the construction market; lengthy lead-times can indicate a busy industry with manufacturers and contractors working at full capacity. Some typical figures for a range of construction products in the UK are shown in the table below. In a stable market, these times fluctuate by about 1–2 weeks, but the appearance of a few large public sector works packages on the market can change the situation overnight.

UK lead-times are tracked on a quarterly basis in *Building* magazine; see example below.

Item	Lead-time (weeks) Figures from mid-2001
Air-conditioning	9–10
Bespoke cladding	41–42
Brickwork	4–5
Curtain walling	20–21
Escalators	20
Furniture	9–10
Concrete works	9–10
Joinery	16
Lifts (special order)	39–40
Light fittings	7–8
Metal roofing	11–12
Structural steelwork	11

How should lead-times be addressed?

Ideally, if products with a long lead-time are being specified then this should be flagged up early in the scheme design stage so that advice can be sought from specialist contractors or suppliers. This is absolutely critical if expensive bespoke work is to be undertaken. If contracts for the supply of such products are to be let, then this should be done as early as possible to allow suppliers to earmark a production slot where necessary. When a sub-contract has been let, then agreement on the specification should be reached as early as possible to reduce the possibility of delays to the programme. All too often projects are delayed because of late, unnecessary changes, which may not be easy to accommodate.

JG

'Lean' construction

This is an approach to eliminating waste from the construction process by focussing on what the customer (client) regards as 'value-adding'.

See also: BESPOKE; BUILDABILITY; CONSTRUCTION PROGRAMME; CRITICAL PATH ANALYSIS; 'JUST-IN-TIME' CONSTRUCTION; LEAD-TIME; OFF-SITE MANUFACTURE; ON-SITE PRODUCTION; PROCUREMENT; RISK MANAGEMENT; VALUE ENGINEERING.

Lean thinking (LT) is an approach to managing and improving the construction process, based on ideas from the car manufacturing industry in Japan (lean manufacture) where it has been adopted widely and recorded significant improvements in productivity. Hence, LT has spread from the manufacturing sector into other industries such as construction. The principles of lean thinking are to:

- Eliminate waste;
- Specify value from the point of view of the client;
- Identify processes that deliver this value;
- Eliminate processes that do not add to this value;
- Let the client drive the process;
- Strive for continuous improvement.

Lean construction

The ideas of lean manufacture can be applied to the construction industry. This focuses on eliminating waste in the form of time, effort and materials, i.e. activities that require resources, but result in no added value. This could include delays, inactive time and mistakes in orders. The aim is to achieve 'right first time' by ensuring things can't go wrong. 'Lean' in this case means streamlined and efficient. It is not a set of rules; rather it is a way of looking at the construction process to see if it can be undertaken more efficiently. It is not supposed to be used as a method of cost cutting – it should be employed to achieve buildings with zero defects, completed on time and on budget. The goal is to examine the entire supply chain, and thereby develop a seamless, integrated process (value stream) from design to construction and completion. Lean construction as a concept is of great interest to clients as it focuses on the needs of the customer first. It then works back through construction and design – identifying waste time, effort and materials and removing them. The discipline of supply chain management (SCM) has evolved from the LT philosophy and the Latham and Egan reports (see *Procurement*), in that it seeks to streamline the supply of goods and services.

How is LT applied to construction?

It is clear that lean thinking should happen early on in a project to maximise the opportunities for success, ideally at the briefing stage before any architectural design is commissioned. However, the philosophy of lean thinking can be applied throughout a project as part of continuous improvement during the following stages:

Design: design discussion and negotiation can be facilitated by the use of 3D visualisation techniques and client-oriented communication techniques (e.g. CAD walk-through images of a design or dynamic thermal simulation programs). Detail design and construction can be made much more efficient by the use of such tools.

Procurement: use of supply chain management, partnering and non-competitive forms of contract should all contribute towards a lean approach. This type of enhanced understanding of business processes makes faster and higher quality buildings possible.

Production planning: allied to the previous point, benchmarking, clear construction programming and risk management are all key aspects of streamlining the stages immediately prior to and during construction.

Logistics: one of the most effective methods of working is 'Just-in-time' construction, which facilitates rapid delivery and installation of products from off-site manufacturing facilities. This should increase speed and reduce double-handling and is usually combined with streamlined approaches to any in-situ (on site) working practices.

Construction: during the construction phase, clear reporting and monitoring of progress will enable incremental and major improvements to construction productivity. Hand-held PCs using programs such as CALIBRE (BRE's productivity tool) can be used on even the largest sites. This also enables information to be used and fed back to the next project or subsequent stages within the same project.

Further reading

McCabe, S. (2001) *Benchmarking in construction*, Blackwell Science, Oxford, UK.
Womack, J. et al. (1990) *The machine that changed the world*, Simon & Schuster, New York, USA.
Womack, J. & Jones, D. (1996) *Lean thinking*, Simon & Schuster, New York, USA.

JG

Life-cycle analysis (LCA)

A range of environmental accounting techniques that enable the design team to establish the life-cycle impacts of a product, process or entire building.

See also: ECOLOGICAL DESIGN; 'ECO-POINTS'; LIFE-CYCLE COSTING; SUSTAINABILITY.

What is LCA?

Life-cycle analysis is a method of assessing the various environmental impacts of a product, process or entire building over its projected lifetime. This is becoming increasingly important because building specifications are under pressure from government, clients and designers to become 'greener'. Life-cycle analysis can be considered as a part of the wider scope of 'Environmental Impact Assessment' (EIA), which places greater emphasis on the building within its context (arising from a planning perspective).

LCA allows the design team to compare the impacts of bulk materials (e.g. steel, timber, concrete), finished products (e.g. lintels, bricks, windows) or entire buildings against agreed environmental parameters through all or some stages of their life-cycle, which can include impacts associated with the following stages.

- Raw materials extraction;
- Materials production and processing;
- Design;
- Component production;
- Transportation of bulk materials or finished goods;
- Construction;
- Use of the product/building (inc. refurbishment);
- Recycling and/or re-use;
- Demolition.

When considering LCA, it is typical to group the stages above into two key phases:

1. **'Behind factory gate'** (which includes all those stages from winning raw materials to completion of a product in the factory).
2. **'Beyond factory gate'** (which includes all those stages from transport of finished goods to end of useful life/recycling).

What exactly does LCA measure?

Life-cycle analysis in its own right is simply an approach to measuring environmental impacts. It is up to the design team/specifier to select **which impacts** they wish to measure in their LCA and **how important** these are (i.e. in terms of relative ranking). There are quite literally hundreds of environmental (and other sustainability) parameters or indicators that can be selected from a wide range of economic, social, and environmental perspectives.

However, not all of these indicators will be suitable for the purposes of comparing construction materials and products in a life-cycle analysis. By way of example, some that would be appropriate are shown in the table below. These are based on indicators for measuring environmental performance in the cement and concrete industry.

The Building Research Establishment has undertaken a major project to attempt to gather as much accurate life-cycle information as possible, aided by the various construction materials and products industries. This 'Environmental profiles' database is a useful source, but accounting methods are becoming more sophisticated and accurate on an almost daily basis. In general the LCA data available to the UK construction industry is limited in scope, but this is likely to change as R&D in this area continues apace.

A degree of skill is required to understand and interpret the figures currently available. While it may be useful to look at life-cycle data from other countries, users must be aware that the accounting methods, not to mention the manufacturing methods and scoring criteria, may be very different to those applicable to the UK.

Indicator	Units
Carbon dioxide	Tonnes (t)
Carbon monoxide	Tonnes (t)
Electrical energy	Giga-Joules (GJ)
Extracted minerals	Kilo-Tonnes (Kt)
Fossil fuel energy	Giga-Joules (GJ)
Heavy metal to air	Kilograms (Kg)
Nitrogen dioxides	Tonnes (t)
Particulates to air	Kilograms (Kg)
Sulphur dioxide	Tonnes (t)
Transport	Kilo-tonne kilometre (Ktkm)
Waste to landfill	Tonnes (t)
Water consumption	Cubic metres (m^3)

The scope of LCA is such that many designers have come to rely on environmental rules of thumb as a guide, rather than entering the rather more complex realms of full LCA studies (see Howard & Shiers reference below). These rules of thumb are likely to become more accurate as detailed research filters through to the mainstream of practice.

Further reading

Building Research Establishment, *Environmental profiles*, BRE, Watford, UK (NB: this is a subscriber-only database).

Howard, N. & Shiers, D. (1996) *The green guide to specification*, Post Office Property Holdings, UK.

JG

Life-cycle costing

A method for accounting systematically for the capital and operational costs of a building from design through use to demolition.

See also: DESIGN LIFE; DURABILITY; ECOLOGICAL DESIGN; 'ECO-POINTS'; LIFE-CYCLE ANALYSIS; MAINTENANCE; PERFORMANCE; SPECIFICATION; SUSTAINABILITY.

What is life-cycle costing?

In an approach not dissimilar to life-cycle analysis, rather than accounting for environmental impacts, life-cycle costing (LCC, sometimes called whole-life costing, WLC) is usually applied to establish both medium- and long-term capital and operational costs for a building. This approach can be used for a part-life or whole-life scenario, but it is most typical for the calculations to be based on an expected design/service life. So, for example, an expected design life of 60 years might be used for an office, school or hospital. This amount of time is deemed reasonable as one would expect to carry out routine maintenance, changes to the servicing in the building, undertake refurbishment works, perhaps some structural alterations and several internal paintwork renewals in that period. Perhaps most importantly, the long-term costs of operational energy use are included in any LCC. There may be very useful trade-offs between an initial cost increase in installing more wall insulation, say, and the amount of energy costs recouped over time as a result.

The basic principles

Based on the number and projected costs of carrying out normal works and the long-term needs of the building (i.e. energy use) the LCC can be assessed (and manipulated) on a spreadsheet. For example, the spreadsheet could incrementally calculate the following tasks on the basis that costs might increase by 5% year on year:

- Re-paint interiors every 5 years @ current cost of £15,000;
- Replace air-conditioning every 25 years @ current cost of £450,000;
- Service lifts and escalators every year @ current cost of £3,500;
- Change the flooring in heavy circulation areas every 2 years @ current cost of £8,000;
- Renew seating in café every 3 years @ current cost of £6,500.

The data used for the LCC may also include projected rentals, incomes and changes of ownership, particularly for offices. The results will give trends and totals of expenditure, which can be manipulated as appropriate. One very useful feature of LCC is that it allows clients to weigh up the relative advantages and disadvantages of choosing either outright purchasing or service agreements for items such as mechanical ventilation, furniture, telephone systems and carpets.

Using life-cycle costing

This is a highly predictive tool, which is more akin to preparing a business case than the traditional methods of accounting for capital costs used in quantity surveying, although there are some similarities with discounted cash flow analyses. Hence, relatively few quantity surveyors and cost planners are in a position to undertake such works. Moreover, speculative developers will have little interest as they have no long-term interest in the completed building; likewise funders are not yet accustomed to dealing with LCC information. The most likely customers for a LCC analysis is a small, but growing number of conscious owner-occupiers that take a more cost and environmentally responsible approach to building development as they will also have the responsibility of running the building through its life. Nonetheless, there is increasing interest in LCC as a tool for more sustainable construction and use of buildings. As techniques become simpler and computer software is now available to aid calculations, the pressure on clients and developers to engage with this type of approach is increasing and will continue to increase.

Further reading

Ashworth, A. (1999) *Cost studies of buildings* (3rd edition), Longman, Harlow, UK.

Ashworth, A. & Hogg, K. (2000) *Added value in design and construction*, Longman, Harlow, UK.

Ferry, D.J., Brandon, P.S. & Ferry, J. (1999) *Cost planning of buildings* (7th edition), Blackwell Science, Oxford, UK.

Morton, R. & Jaggar, D. (1995) *Design and the economics of building*, E & FN Spon, London, UK.

Seeley, I. (1996) *Building economics* (4th edition), Macmillan, Basingstoke, UK.

JG

Light steel frame

Light steel frames use cold formed steel sections (50–300 mm deep) for the structural frame in whole building systems, modular buildings, and rapid dry envelope walls.

See also: BUILDING SYSTEMS; CORROSION; FIRE PROTECTION; FRAMES; GALVANISING; METALS; MODULES AND MODULAR CONSTRUCTION; OFF-SITE MANUFACTURE; PLASTERBOARD; STRUCTURAL STEEL.

Introduction

When produced in thicknesses from around 3.5 mm down to 0.9 mm (or even 0.55 mm in the case of dry lining studs), steel can be 'cold formed', usually by pressing or roll forming, giving the potential to make complex, structurally efficient sections in volume. A range of sections between 50–300 mm deep are used for anything from internal walls and small enclosures to buildings of six storeys. The use of such light steel frames (LSF) for building structures has developed as a result of there being a wide range of individual components (notably lintels, purlins and rails, and dry lining studs) and coating technology to assure acceptable levels of durability. The technique was exploited originally in Australia and the USA, where light steel frame building systems were developed and well established by the 1970s. European manufacturers followed five to ten years later, encouraged by similar market forces (particularly the demand for a high quality, fast track output from a labour market that was losing its skill-base).

Applications for LSF

Light steel frame uses fast, dry construction methods on site and there is sufficient flexibility in the system to incorporate a variety of internal and external finishes. Rapid enclosure to structural frames and a short time to a dry envelope can be achieved, thereby moving finishing trades off the critical path. Complex lightweight sections can be used for medium span roofs, whilst purlin structures create larger open roof areas. Refurbishment systems using LSF to convert roofs from 'flat to pitch' are now available. LSF is appropriate for a number of major construction industry sectors including:

- **Commercial and education** – the use of enhanced elements such as lattice beams and composite decking provides for floor loadings of 3–5 kN/m^2 over acceptable spans for schools, hotels, and office buildings;
- **Industrial** – with portal frames, spans of up to 14 m can be achieved with ribbed enhanced sections joined by moment connections;
- **Modular buildings** – volumetric units for sectors such as education, health, hotel and leisure, and residential buildings can be manufactured off site;
- **Residential developments** from individual homes to low/medium rise residential and apartment buildings.

Materials and manufacture

Galvanised strip steel is used to produce the cold formed sections for light steel frames. The steel is pre-galvanised with a minimum 275 grammes/m^2 coating, which has excellent durability for internal applications (light steel is designed to be enclosed within the fabric of the building).

The commonest method of manufacture is roll forming, where sections are formed by feeding steel sheet, or strip from a coil, through a series of roll formers. As it passes through the rolls, the steel is gradually formed into the finished section and can at this point have holes punched for connections and services. Individual members are cut to length at the end of the process, and the ends may be specially formed to create a connection detail. The LSF elements can be factory assembled into frames on jigs, or site assembled, using conventional connection methods (i.e. welding, rivets, self-drill screws, bolts and clinches).

Typical sections are channels, lipped channels, and zeds. Structural efficiency is sometimes enhanced by the addition of ribs, swages, or more complex shapes, to the basic sections. Depending on prospective floor loads and point loads, hot rolled steel sections or light steel/concrete composites are sometimes incorporated within the frames.

Design considerations

Structural performance: Dead and imposed loads are specified in BS 6399: Parts 1 & 3. The structural performance of loadbearing walls and floor joists comprising cold formed steel sections should satisfy BS 5950: Part 5 (and Eurocode 3) in terms of bending and shear resistance. Floor joists are generally designed on serviceability criteria.

Durability: Attention to detailed design and the use of galvanised steel, ensure that acceptable durability is achieved by eliminating the possibility of corrosion. LSF is designed to be enclosed within the building envelope.

Energy efficiency: Light steel frame uses conventional insulation products applied to the cavity face of the studs (as 'thermal sheathing'), between the studs, or a combination of the two. Major considerations such as dew point position, vapour control, cold bridging, and airtightness, all demand careful detailing, and warm frame principles should be followed (i.e. keeping the frame element within the insulation envelope).

Fire protection: structural elements in floors and walls are usually protected by firecheck plasterboard in single or multiple layers according to recommendations of the board manufacturers.

Acoustic insulation: Acoustic separation is achieved generally by the lining, absorbent quilt in the stud cavity and discontinuity of structural elements.

Further reading

Clough, R.H. & Ogden, R.G. (1993) *Building design using cold formed steel sections: acoustic insulation*, SCI Publication 128, The Steel Construction Institute, Ascot, UK.

Grubb, P. J. & Lawson, R. M. (1997) *Building design using cold formed steel sections: construction detailing and practice*, The Steel Construction Institute, Ascot, UK.

Jackson, N. (1996) *The modern steel house*, E & FN Spon/Van Nostrand Reinhold, New York, USA.

Rhodes, J. & Lawson, R.M. (1992) *Design of structures using cold formed steel sections*, SCI Publication 089, The Steel Construction Institute, Ascot, UK.

Trebilcock, P. J. (1994) *Building design using cold formed steel sections: an architect's guide*, SCI Publication 130, The Steel Construction Institute, Ascot, UK.

Webb, G. P. (2000) *A guide for inspectors: light steel framing for housing*, Corus UK Ltd.

GW

Lighting – daylighting

The luminous environment is composed of daylight illumination, glare, visual contrast, view, occupational needs and lighting.

See also: AALTO, ALVAR; ATRIUM; ENERGY EFFICIENCY; ENVIRONMENTAL DESIGN; FAÇADES AND FAÇADE ENGINEERING; GLASS; GLASS – LAMINATED AND COATED; INTEGRATION; INTELLIGENT FAÇADES AND MATERIALS; LIGHTING – ARTIFICIAL LIGHTING; LOUVRES AND BRISE SOLEIL; WINDOWS AND CURTAIN WALLING.

Introduction

> *Lighting is an art and a science. It can provide both a visual experience for the observer of a scene and conditions to enable a task to be performed, although the relative importance of these aspects will vary with application. Given the differences in visual tasks, building form and surface finish that occur, and the different light sources, from daylight that enters through windows and other apertures, luminaires, and control systems that are available, there is plenty of opportunity for variety in design.*

Chartered Institute of Building Services Engineers (1994) *Code for Interior Lighting*, CIBSE, UK.

This extract suggests that the 'art of lighting' is about more than just the numerical fulfilment of task-oriented lighting design requirements, rather it should be about the purpose of expressing architectural form, creating a mood or providing emphasis. This is perfectly compatible with the need to improve energy efficiency in buildings by balancing the efficient use of artificial lighting and natural daylighting. Hence this entry is the first of two on lighting, which should be read as two parts of a whole.

In architectural terms, it is more common to talk of 'quality of light' than adequate illumination, but the aesthetic effect and the numerical standards must work side by side to achieve well-lit and inspirational buildings. Most lighting guides will use the term 'daylight factor' as a means of predicting the adequacy of daylight penetration to a space as designed (a figure in the range of 1–5% based on the proportion of glazed area to depth and height of the space). In the context of the statement above, daylight factors should be used only as a simple benchmark that the basic requirements have been met; they are not the ultimate goal of good lighting design.

About daylight

Daylight sources can be either '**direct**' (i.e. direct sunlight and diffused skylight) or '**indirect**' (i.e. light from reflective or translucent diffusers that were illuminated originally by primary or other secondary sources). For example, a light shelf allows direct low winter sunlight to penetrate the space but prevents the ingress of direct hot summer sunlight, allowing only indirect daylighting. Daylight can be admitted into a building via windows, doors, atria or rooflights to perform any of a number of basic functions:

- Allow the entrance of sunlight (passive solar energy) to contribute to thermal comfort;
- Increase the general brightness of the space;
- Provide a view (perhaps the most important for building occupants);
- Provide illumination for a task or activity.

These functions should be studied independently and then integrated within the building design. Integration is important because potential glare problems may be overlooked if the main emphasis is only on views for example. A good example of bringing together location, maximum sunlight hours, daylighting and acoustics can be found in the ING Bank HQ building in Amsterdam, the Netherlands (1987). The ten specially oriented tower elements were designed to maximise daylight, while limiting glare. An internal 'street' atria connecting the towers provides additional daylight to the deep interior spaces to minimise the use of artificial lighting.

Designing for good daylighting

Planning the building layout to maximise daylighting can be undertaken at an early stage. US architect Fuller Moore suggests a 'safeguarding approach' to ensure daylight is available where it is wanted – present on, and between, the façades of buildings (in order to provide good interior and exterior illumination) as well as being maintained in any adjacent buildings and land developments. Building design strategies should include a 'daylight obstruction survey' as part of the normal array of location surveys that are carried out (i.e. sun, wind, rain, shadow, noise, external pollution) etc. Alternative daylighting design solutions should also be investigated such as the use of atria, light shelves and daylight 'tubes' that typically direct light into the heart of a building. Modelling and manipulating the effect of these options is now easier with dedicated daylight design computer software.

Further reading

Baker, N. & Steemers, K. (2001) *Daylight design of buildings: a handbook for architects and engineers*, James & James, London, UK.
Berger, H. (1996) *Light structures, structures of light*, Birkhäuser, Basle, Switzerland.
Chartered Institute of Building Services Engineers (1994) *Code for interior lighting*, CIBSE, London, UK.
Phillips, D. (2000) *Lighting modern buildings*, Butterworth-Heinemann, Oxford, UK.
Pritchard, D.C. (1995) *Lighting* (5th edition), Longman, Harlow, UK.
Riley, T. (1995) *Light construction*, MoMA, New York, USA.

WH

Lighting – artificial lighting

Electric 'artificial' lighting is used to supplement daylight provision and for night-time use.

See also: BESPOKE; ENERGY EFFICIENCY; ENVIRONMENTAL DESIGN; FAÇADES AND FAÇADE ENGINEERING; FIT-OUT; GLASS; GLASS – LAMINATED AND COATED; INTEGRATION; INTELLIGENT FAÇADES AND MATERIALS; LIFE-CYCLE COSTING; LIGHTING – DAYLIGHTING; LOUVRES AND BRISE SOLEIL; WINDOWS AND CURTAIN WALLING.

In this example, careful uplighting is combined with daylighting to create a stimulating, but well-distributed quality of light (Nicholas Grimshaw's Paddington Station redevelopment). Photograph courtesy of The Concrete Society.

Introduction

Daylight is not always sufficient to provide enough light to carry out a task or fully emphasise an architectural feature. Electric lighting can be used as a broad, background source to supplement daylighting or it can provide emphasis or mood lighting and is used commonly on emergency escape routes. It is important that designers understand the various terms used in lighting design. Even if a specialist is to undertake the work, the architectural intention regarding 'quality of light' needs to be clearly communicable. Common terms used in lighting parlance include:

Lux – the SI unit of illuminance, equal to one lumen per square metre (lm/m^2).

Luminance (cd/m^2) – where cd is the Candela, the SI unit of luminous intensity, equal to one lumen per steradian (sr), which is the unit of solid angle. This is the physical measure of the stimulus, which produces the sensation of brightness as measured by the luminous intensity of the light emitted or reflected in a given direction from a surface element, divided by the projected area of the element in the same direction.

Luminous area – the area of a lamp or luminaire, which emits light. Luminous efficacy is the ratio of the luminous flux (flicker) emitted by a lamp to the power consumed by the lamp. When the power consumed by control gear is taken into account this is known as lamp circuit luminous efficacy (lumens per circuit watt).

Artificial lighting design and specification should always be part and parcel of energy efficiency discussions. In the UK, the heating cooling and lighting of buildings accounts for about 50% of total UK carbon dioxide emissions, i.e. energy use. There is now more pressure on designers to reduce this energy use, which can be seen in changes to the UK Building Regulations. Recent revisions to the Building Regulations include standards for lighting. Compliance criteria are to be introduced. These can be satisfied with lighting with an initial efficacy, averaged over the whole building, of not less than 40 luminaire-lumens/circuit watt.

About lamps

Lamp bulbs vary in intensity, longevity and colour; the fittings (luminaires) in which they are placed can modify their overall effect. Lamps are specified by wattage, luminous efficacy, colour properties, shape and cost. The principal types are described in the table below.

About luminaires

Luminaires control the distribution of light and include all the components necessary for fixing and protecting the lamps, in addition to connecting them to the power supply. A wide range of lamps and luminaires is available to satisfy most design requirements, but in some instances it may be desirable to create bespoke luminaires (e.g. to incorporate an array of lamps or include some acoustic absorbency). Luminaires can take many different forms, but all have to provide support, protection and electrical connection to the lamp. In addition, luminaires have to be safe during installation and operation and be able to withstand the conditions of the operating environments. The standard that covers most luminaires in the UK is BS 4533, which in turn is based on IEC 598. These apply to luminaires containing tungsten filament, fluorescent and other discharge lamps running on supply voltages not exceeding 1kV and cover the electrical, mechanical and thermal aspects.

Lamp type	Properties
Filament lamps	An incandescent filament sealed in a glass bulb, usually containing an inert gas filling. The most common filament lamps are General Lighting Service (GLS), decorative, candle lamps and reflector PAR lamps.
Fluorescent lamps	The light output comes from phosphors, which convert energy from a low-pressure mercury discharge. There are a wide range including 'white' (daylight-mimicking) lamps and special colours. Main advantages are long life and relatively low cost. The 'flickering' of some can cause stroboscopic effects that induce headaches and nausea. The use of induction lamps can overcome these effects.
Sodium, Mercury and Metal halide lamps	Long life and low maintenance, these lamps are used for road lighting as well as high space areas, e.g. exhibition centres, sports halls, shopping centres, warehouses and swimming pools.

According to research undertaken at the Bartlett School of Architecture, the best outcome is provided by a combination of visual 'lightness' and visual 'interest'. An average luminance of 40 cd/m^2 with contrast areas having 10 cd/m^2 difference offers stimulation and satisfaction to the viewer.

Further reading

Baker, N. & Steemers, K. (2001) *Daylight design of buildings: a handbook for architects and engineers*, James & James, London, UK.

Berger, H. (1996) *Light structures, structures of light*, Birkhäuser, Basle, Switzerland.

Brandi, U. & Geissmar-Brandi, C. (2001) *Lightbook: the practice of lighting design*, Birkhäuser, Basle, Switzerland.

Chartered Institute of Building Services Engineers (1994) *Code for interior lighting*, CIBSE, London, UK.

Phillips, D. (2000) *Lighting modern buildings*, Butterworth-Heinemann, Oxford, UK.

Pritchard, D.C. (1995) *Lighting* (5th edition), Longman, Harlow, UK.

WH

Lime

See: MORTARS, CEMENT AND LIME

Lintel

See: RETAINING WALLS

Loadbearing

See: WALLS; FRAME

Louvres and brise-soleil

Internal or external devices used to provide a variety of functions such as shading, improved ventilation and quality of lighting.

What are louvres and brise-soleil?

Louvres is the term usually given to arrays of slim metal, glass or plastic elements that are placed alongside windows, façades or over atria to enhance their performance by providing shading or bouncing light into the building. Alternatively louvres can be bespoke glazed units within the façade assembly with openable glass fins, typically used for ventilation purposes. This entry focuses on the former definition and the concept of using louvres as 'climate modifiers'. Brise soleil (the French term meaning a sunbreak) is the term usually associated with horizontal and vertical louvres used for shading purposes.

Louvres are used in both hot and temperate climatic zones to provide shading, in addition to countries close to the Polar Regions, where high sun glare occurs. Other architectural forms such as overhanging roofs and verandahs perform a similar function, providing buffer zones with shading and reducing solar gain incident on the building. In the hottest locations, comfort conditions are helped by a combination of louvres in horizontal and vertical screening. In the cooler northerly latitudes it may be useful to provide a combination of shading and 'light shelves', which can improve daylight levels within the building. US environmental architect G.Z. 'Charlie' Brown was an early supporter of light shelves, noting their usefulness to shade glazing, evenly distribute daylight, increase light levels away from windows and reduce glare, which in turn all have a positive effect on daylighting and cooling.

Brise-soleil provide shading to the entrance of the train station in Monte Carlo, Monaco. Photo by Author.

Design

In any climate, louvres and other shading devices must relate to a building's shape, size, orientation and construction, which in turn affect the building's behaviour in terms of heating and cooling. The key issue is care and attention to understanding climate as a context and making full use of information on solar gains, wind, rain, sunpath and orientation. However, in areas subject to hurricanes, cyclones or typhoons the design of external louvres may need particular attention. Louvres can be external or internal; they can be fixed, movable by hand or mechanical means or completely removable (an economic option for small buildings). Shading devices can vary in size without changing their shading characteristics, provided the ratio between the depth and the spacing of the elements remains constant.

Insulated louvres with the use of self-inflating curtains and other retrofitted environmental controls are part of a new generation of adaptive environmental solutions. In Europe research into ways in which a building can control its own interior environment has produced a series of louvred devices. This includes a series of solar-induced thermosiphon systems and a 'solar environmental wall' for the south west façade of an apartment building in Dedemdvaartsweg in The Hague developed by Battle McCarthy and local architects Neutelings Riedijk.

Built examples

Exterior shading devices whether horizontal, vertical, slated or egg-crate have been used by architects to achieve a comfort environment within a building space, such as:

- Louis Kahn (Radbill Building, Philadelphia);
- Frank Lloyd Wright (The Price Tower, Bartlesville, Oklahoma);
- Le Corbusier (La Tourette monastery in France and the Millowers Building, Ahmedabad, India).

More recently, the Commerzbank tower in Frankfurt by Foster and Partners used a dual louvre and light shelf element as part of the façade design for office spaces. Their business promotion centre at the Microelectronics Park at Duisberg in Germany uses a twin-skin glass façade with an integral louvre system between the internal and external glass leaves. The building revered by most architects in terms of louvres is the Menil Gallery in Houston by Renzo Piano with its long arrays of elongated S-shaped GRC louvres that shade the gallery spaces below. The patterns of light from the shades provide constant interest within the interior. In a useful combination of photovoltaics and brise-soleil, a ground breaking product called 'Shadovoltaic' was installed on 500 new homes in the Netherlands (to generate 1 MW of electricity). The brise-soleil arrays look conventional, but actually feature PV cells on their upper surfaces.

Further reading

Brown, G.Z. (1985) *Sun, wind, and light: architectural design strategies*, John Wiley & Sons, New York, USA.

Cofaigh, E.O., Olley, J.A. & Lewis, O. (1996) *The climatic dwelling*, James & James, London, UK.

Davies, C. & Lambot, I. (1997) *Commerzbank Frankfurt*, Watermark/ Birkhäuser, Basle, Switzerland.

WH

Lubetkin, Berthold

A name associated with Modernism in the UK, Berthold Lubetkin (1901–90) is revered by many for his simple brilliance, particularly seen in the Penguin Pool at London Zoo.

See also: ARUP, OVE; CONCRETE; CONCRETE – STRUCTURES.

One of the pioneers of Modernist architecture, Lubetkin brought radical ideas from Russia and France to the UK and designed some of the country's best and most influential 20th century buildings.

Lubetkin was born in Tblisi, Georgia and he picked up on the socialist idealism of the Bolshevik revolution but, as Modernist architecture fell out of favour in the inter-war years, he emigrated to Paris. There he studied at the Atelier Perret where he learnt the principles of reinforced concrete construction from the acknowledged master and pioneer of the technique. In Paris he built a fine apartment block on the Avenue Versailles (1927) with Jean Ginsburg. He came to England in 1930 and two years later he set up a grouping of architects calling themselves Tecton. In a reactionary architectural climate Lubetkin's first major works were for animals rather than people.

The Penguin Pool for London Zoo (designed with Ove Arup) was a *tour de force* of sculptural design which took its cue from Constructivist sculpture and which highlighted the tectonic possibilities of reinforced concrete in its sinuously curving ramps. Other buildings at London, Whipsnade and Dudley zoos (1932–37) introduced the dramatic forms of Russian Constructivism and the sculptural potential of reinforced concrete to England's artificially pastoral landscapes.

Highpoint I (1935), a fine apartment block in north London introduced London's Bohemian upper-middle classes to the thrill of the collectivist worker-housing aesthetic. One of inter-war Britain's most influential buildings, it also brought the aesthetics, and the reinforced concrete construction, of Le Corbusier to London. Its successor, Highpoint II (1937–38) introduced a diluted, more playful version of Modernism, which led the way for developments after the war. The Finsbury Health Centre (1938) was a building more in keeping with Lubetkin's socialist ideals. Composed of a pair of arms metaphorically reaching out to embrace the community it was intended as a model of community health care. After the war Lubetkin finally constructed some social housing with the Spa Green and Priory Green Estates (both 1951) near the Finsbury Health Centre in London. Lubetkin's plans for the new town at Peterlee however (1955) were not adopted and he went into virtual retirement for the remainder of his life. Lubetkin's brilliant contributions to British architecture continue to inspire and fascinate.

Further reading

Allan, J. (1992) *Berthold Lubetkin: architecture and the tradition of progress*, RIBA Publications, London, UK.

Coe, P. & Reading, M. (1981) *Lubetkin and Tecton: architecture and social commitment*, Triangle Books, London, UK.

EH

Maintenance

The function of keeping a building in good working order throughout its life.

See also: AIR-CONDITIONING; BUILDING MANAGEMENT SYSTEM; DESIGN LIFE; DURABILITY; ENVIRONMENTAL DESIGN; FIT-OUT; HVAC; INTELLIGENT FAÇADES AND MATERIALS; LIFE-CYCLE COSTING; PERFORMANCE; SICK BUILDING SYNDROME; SPECIFICATION; SUSTAINABILITY; WEATHERING.

Introduction

Once completed and handed over to the client for occupation, a building should be 'looked after' to maintain its appearance and performance. This may involve routine activities such as cleaning windows and façades, regular cycles of checking the integrity of roofing and replacing carpeting. On a rather larger scale, maintenance is about repairing and even replacing components such as servicing, lighting, roofing or interior fittings and furnishings. Hence, the term 'building care*' is now used, which covers the activities and the programme that is devised at the outset to manage them.

A building needs care throughout its life-cycle and it is common practice now for the design team to produce a building maintenance handbook, which is handed over to the client on occupation of the building. The costs of activities associated with building care are usually considered separately from the operational energy costs required to run the building (i.e. heating, cooling and lighting), rather they cover the maintenance activities to sustain these systems, including parts and labour. However these two aspects of life-cycle cost are related very closely, as discussed here.

The role of responsible specification

Decisions made at design stage can have a 'ripple effect' throughout the life of a building. To demonstrate this, consider that the costs to run and maintain a building are typically in the order of five to ten times greater than the capital costs to build it in the first place. It is clear therefore that there are benefits to be had by investing in good quality materials, plant and equipment in the first place in order to try and reduce the operational costs as well as improving energy efficiency. In the same way anticipating maintenance at the design stage can reduce long-term costs. However, the 'first-cost' culture, which pervades the UK construction industry prevents such a sensible and sustainable approach to building care. Designers and clients should

---

* With due acknowledgement to Brian Wood (Oxford Brookes University) for use of this term.

therefore develop a shared responsibility to work with building services engineers to achieve more sustainable maintenance programmes.

Critical to all design specifications are the detailed regulations and daily, weekly and monthly checks of all installed equipment. The importance of ensuring that every item of equipment is in full working order on the day of hand-over cannot be over emphasised, because it is all too often overlooked.

The costs of building care

Maintenance costs are incurred by keeping any plant in an operational condition (e.g. repairs, cleaning and monitoring by staff). Costs are incurred in two categories: direct costs from labour and materials and indirect costs (on-costs) from staffing, supervision, support services such as workshops, sick leave, etc. The retention of in-house skilled maintenance fitters, with workshop provision for on-site repair, can lead to savings in replacement costs. A good example can be seen in the Royal Festival Hall in London, where after 50 years the same equipment is still in use, achieving the same efficiency, with another 20–30 years life left. However, the availability of skilled operatives to repair plant and equipment and costs to retain them may not be an expense that a building client/occupier is willing to cover. In this case, the use of modular plant packages will reduce staffing costs, but may have a more frequent maintenance and replacement cycle than conventional equipment. These alternatives can be evaluated at the design stage on the basis of the client's expectations of how the building will be used.

Further reading

Chanter, B. & Swallow, P. (2000) *Building maintenance management*, Blackwell Science, Oxford, UK.
Markus, T.A. & Morris, E.N. (1980) *Buildings, climate and energy*, Pitman, UK.

WH/JG

Masonry
See: BRICKS AND BLOCKS

MDF: medium density fibreboard
See: TIMBER – MANUFACTURED BOARDS

Metals

A major group of materials that provide a wealth of components for construction from structural elements such as beams to detailed components such as glazing connections.

See also: ALUMINIUM; CASTINGS; CEILINGS; CLADDING; COMPOSITE DECKING; COPPER; CORROSION; COR-TEN STEEL; DESIGN LIFE; DURABILITY; FRAMES; GLASS – STRUCTURAL GLAZING; LEAD; LIGHT STEEL FRAME; LOUVRES AND BRISE SOLEIL; OFF-SITE MANUFACTURE; ROOFS; STAINLESS STEEL; STANDING SEAM ROOF; STRUCTURAL STEEL; SURFACE FINISHES; WEATHERING; WINDOWS AND CURTAIN WALLING; ZINC.

Introduction

Most buildings contain metal products in some form or other. People have been using smelting and other working techniques to create metal artefacts such as cutting tools for thousands of years. Metals (in the form of ores) can be found throughout the world and are a strategic resource for many countries. Current data suggests that the natural resource is dwindling rapidly, so recycling needs to increase and designers need to act more responsibly in their use of metals. The processes used to create most metals results in high embodied energy, but this is offset somewhat by their longevity and durability. Metals offer a marvellous architectural opportunity for a wide range of applications, including:

- Façade systems and shading;
- Furniture and fittings;
- Ironmongery (for doors and windows);
- Lighting;
- Roofing;
- Services;
- Stairs, lifts and escalators;
- Structural frames (beams, columns, floors etc.);
- Windows and curtain walling profiles.

Discussion

The range of ferrous (containing iron) and non-ferrous (not containing iron) metals available for use in buildings is broad and constantly developing. It is underpinned by the basic 'building blocks' of the common building metals of steel, aluminium, copper, zinc and lead together with a range of durable alloys such as bronze (copper and tin). In contrast to other high-tech industries (e.g. aerospace), the development of specialised metals and alloys for building construction has not been extensive because normal conditions simply do not require very high strength or other exceptional properties.

However, the trend towards multi-storey structural glass façades has led to some refinement of metals used in glazing connectors, which may have to cope with complex and occasionally severe loads in service. Without doubt the largest single market for metals in buildings is steel structural frames, which dominate the medium to high-rise buildings market in the UK. Other major uses include roofing, walling and cladding components, used in industrial and commercial applications.

Benefits of using metals

Structural efficiency: for example, structural steel uses slim members with a relatively high tensile strength, which are connected together (assembled) easily and are lightweight, thus requiring lower capacity foundations. In most buildings, steel is combined with concrete to provide shear strength to the steel 'stick' structure.

Simple procurement: fabrication is virtually a 'one-stop shop' using off-site production, in which much of the detail design is negotiated with and undertaken by the fabricator. Despite needing to plan for lengthy lead-times for non-standard fabrication, delivery is direct to site and on a 'just in time' basis.

Versatility: there is a vast range of options available in terms of sizes, shapes, structural and performance properties as well as surface finishes. Fabricators usually offer bespoke options in addition to standard ranges. Specialist techniques such as casting offer high quality structural connectors.

Recyclability: most metals can be recycled entirely at end of useful life, but they have to be recovered, which can be difficult unless the design team has allowed for this option. Steel in particular is marketed as being 'on loan from the Earth', which is perhaps overstating the case somewhat.

Disadvantages of using metals

Most metals tend to exhibit two major disadvantages in relation to their use in buildings, and in particular for structural applications. These are:

Fire: many metals have a low melting point and if exposed to fire will soften, deform and eventually fail. This needs to be addressed in design and is covered by UK Building Regulations. Several methods of fire protection are available including sprayed coatings, concrete encasement, intumescent paints or plasterboard casings, but are not usually needed in non-structural applications.

Corrosion: this is of concern for particular metals such as steel in instances where the material is exposed to air and water (e.g. rain). Again, protection systems include cladding, paints, galvanising or COR-TEN® (otherwise known as weathering steel). Corrosion is a well-understood difficulty, which is addressed best by using recommendations from the fabricator/manufacturer.

Endnote: combining different metals

Included in each individual entry on metals in this book (i.e. aluminium, copper, lead, stainless steel, and zinc) is a note about the practical combination of different metals in a design. This is important because metals behave differently in the presence of one another, in accordance with a list called the 'galvanic series'. A particular metal's position on this list will determine how it behaves in the presence of the others: some combinations will corrode badly, whereas others will not. This is called 'bimetallic' or 'galvanic' corrosion, because one metal acts as a cathode deteriorating the other. For example, both copper and lead will corrode aluminium; lead will corrode both copper and mild steel. For this reason, it is common to see either stainless steel or epoxy resin components in many metal fixings because these tend not to be affected (see *Corrosion*).

JG

Mineral fibres

Man-made mineral fibres (MMMF) are synthetic fibres made from a variety of inorganic materials, used in thermal insulation, GRC, GRP and roofing felt products.

See also: CEMENT; CLADDING; COMPOSITE MATERIALS; CONNECTIONS; DURABILITY; ECOLOGICAL DESIGN; FIRE PROTECTION; GRC; INSULATION; PLASTICS; SERVICES.

What are MMMFs?

This is a term for a group of materials called man-made mineral fibres. These have been produced commercially in the UK since the early 1950s. MMMF may broadly be categorised according to their composition and properties into the following groups, which are described in turn.

- Mineral wools;
- Ceramic fibres;
- Special purpose fibres;
- Continuous filament fibres.

Mineral wools, which are the most widely used type of MMMF products, are manufactured from molten glass, rock or slag. These produce MMMF of a 'woolly' consistency and each type can be known by the material from which it is manufactured, that is to say, glasswool, rockwool and slagwool. Mineral wool products are used mainly for fire protection and insulation work. The materials may be preformed to a particular shape to pipework or process vessels. Many people will have encountered mineral wools as they are used as insulation, either as loose fill fibres that are blown into lofts or cavity walls, or using hand laid blanket insulation in attics.

Ceramic fibres are generally of a smaller diameter than mineral wools, with a mean of 2–3 μm (compared to a range of 4–9 μm). In addition ceramic MMMF products do not tend to have an organic binder holding together the fibres; unlike mineral wool products, which incorporate a resin binder to some degree. As such, ceramic MMMF products can be used for refractory applications, such as in furnaces or in fire seals, as they can withstand temperatures greater than 1,000 °C without appreciable distortion or softening occurring. The products are formed mainly into insulation boards, blankets and ropes.

Special purpose fibres have a mean diameter less than 3 μm and have been described as 'superfines'. Special purpose MMMF products may use ceramic materials or glasses, such as alumina or silica, depending on the application. These products may be found in the aircraft industry or as industrial filter media. Glass fibres are manufactured from silica sand, boron, limestone and sodium carbonate, all of which are non-renewable, but plentiful.

Continuous filament fibres are usually made from glass, with mean diameters from 8–10 μm that are woven into cloth for reinforcing plastics and cement products. The flame resistant properties of the fibres were exploited commercially, which resulted in an increase in the development of glass fibre fabrics.

Uses and applications

The range of mineral wool products available reflects the variety of benefits that the material has to offer. Mineral wools are used primarily for their fire performance. They are largely non-combustible and do not 'flashover', that is to say that the products of combustion do not ignite suddenly. As such, building services use many tonnes of mineral wool material for fire protection, especially in confined and inaccessible areas. As well as mineral wool being used to insulate hot pipes, it can be used to insulate refrigeration. Excellent thermal performance is due to the entrapment of air within the mineral wool. Unlike other thermal insulants that are produced with blowing agents, which escape gradually with time, mineral wool is stable and maintains its structure.

In addition, mineral wool exhibits good acoustic properties because the sound waves are able to penetrate into the porous material and the energy is absorbed due to the air molecules experiencing frictional forces in the material. As mineral wools provide this additional benefit of reducing noise levels, their usage is preferred as an insulating material over the more rigid materials. Mineral wools are chosen in preference to the foam plastic insulants as they offer better fire protection and for pipe lagging in damp conditions. Less concern is raised when mineral wool is used compared to phenolic foam (the least combustible foam plastic insulant) because the leachate produced is neutral or slightly alkaline, rather than acidic. An acidic leachate produced from phenolic foam could corrode steel and copper pipework and fixings.

Health and safety

The use of MMMF products has increased considerably since the 1970s. This coincided with the discovery of the carcinogenic properties of asbestos fibres and subsequent phasing out of asbestos materials in buildings. Comparisons are made between the health effects of MMMF and asbestos materials because both are essentially fibrous. There are numerous published sources of information relating to the effects of fibre inhalation for both MMMF and asbestos, and these references should be consulted for further information. In particular, guidance from the HSE deals with exposure limits of man-made mineral fibres stemming from both manufacture and use. Dust arising from processes can cause throat and chest complaints. Other health effects of MMMF include irritation to the skin and eyes, but this can be avoided by wearing suitable eye protection and protective clothing. Specialist advice should be sought for more information. Finally, during removal and disposal of MMMF materials, it is good practice to minimise fibre release. Up-to-date guidance and practices should be employed in MMMF disposal.

Ecological alternatives

Ecologically conscious designers may choose natural materials, such as sisal as an alternative to mineral fibres. Organic alternatives for insulation etc. may be derived from natural vegetation or sheep wool. Other materials include; cork, expanded rubber, wood wool, wood fibre, cellulose and natural wools which are renewable and reclaimable on demolition.

Further reading

Clough, R. & Martin, R. (1995) *Environmental impacts of building and construction materials*, (Vol. B – Mineral Products), CIRIA, London, UK.

Health & Safety Executive (1990) *HSE Guidance Note EH46: Man-made mineral fibres*, HMSO, London, UK.

HM Inspectorate of Pollution (1992) *Glass fibres & non-asbestos mineral fibres*, IPR 3/4, HMSO, London, UK.

OA

Mixed mode ventilation

See: VENTILATION

Modules and modular construction

The systematised approach to design, construction and installation of a variety of building components which have a rigour in their dimensions and connections or other aspects.

View inside a factory in Germany that makes precast concrete room modules including structure, windows, services and finishes. The working environment is clean and very efficient. Photograph courtesy of Veit Dennert KG.

See also: BESPOKE; BUILDING SYSTEMS; CONCRETE; CONSTRUCTION PROGRAMME; CRITICAL PATH ANALYSIS; GRIDS FOR STRUCTURE AND LAYOUT; INTEGRATION; 'JUST-IN-TIME' CONSTRUCTION; LE CORBUSIER; LEAD-TIME; LIGHT STEEL FRAME; OFF-SITE MANUFACTURE; SERVICES; STRUCTURAL STEEL; TIMBER – STRUCTURES; TOLERANCE.

Introduction

The terms module, modular construction and modularity are used in building to describe an approach to design and construction that has an overarching system-based approach to the design, production and installation of building components or elements. To be considered as 'modular', elements need to be designed to a rational system of dimensions and connections perhaps to be inter-linked. They may be designed to fit the structural grid, allowing dimensional co-ordination with other elements.

The idea of modules in buildings can be applied to a wide variety of elements at different scales from walls, floors and roofs to services, windows and furniture. In each case it means that these items are designed and manufactured to be connected together with other like objects (somewhat like a systems approach). Modularity means considering these components as a system, considering their dimensions in a systematic way such that ordered arrangements can be made and connected in a rational manner. In simple terms, 'modules' might have a plug-in quality i.e. they are designed and connected straightforwardly. Despite this breadth of meaning, the term 'module' and 'modular' have come to be associated primarily with factory-produced components or elements, i.e. highly accurate items that connect together in a systematic way.

Modules in design

Designers tend to understand modules as large-scale building components such as whole rooms or cladding units that are designed and connected together in a systematised way. They also interpret modular layout as a means by which a building can be set out such that all these modules can be installed on a pre-determined grid. Hence, the general association is that modular construction uses components or elements produced off site connected in an assembly-type process on site.

Using a modular approach to buildings can facilitate faster, more accurate and better co-ordinated architecture with high overall quality and high client satisfaction. However, such an approach needs to be considered from an early stage; it may require bespoke manufacture of components, a lengthy lead time and could restrict future adaptations in the building. Cost may also be an issue.

For these reasons, although the modular approach can be used to produce many elements in a building (e.g. furniture modules that relate to a standard grid), there are only limited examples of wholly modular buildings. These tend to be either small scale (e.g. temporary site buildings) or building types with rigorous, standardised planning modules such as:

- Fast food restaurants;
- Hotels and motels;
- Prisons;
- Residential accommodation – student halls.

However, whole room-size modules are gaining popularity with social housing providers amongst others. These usually include bedroom, bathroom or kitchen accommodation modules. Services modules of mechanical ventilation/air-conditioning are also a common feature in offices and other commercial buildings, sometimes called 'packaged plant'. Larger, structural modules can be produced in steel, timber and concrete.

Built examples

Steel modules were used for the Peabody Trust housing scheme at Murray Grove, Hackney in London (1999). This five storey modular apartment building attracted significant interest because it was constructed very quickly and was architecturally appealing with its terracotta cladding and cylindrical corner tower. The Lloyds Building in the City of London by Richard Rogers Partnership (1986) illustrates several aspects of modular design in its bathroom modules, floor and services grids and external lifts. This building became known for its innovative approach to component design.

Historical note

Proportional systems (a form of modular building) can be seen in architecture over the centuries from Europe, the Arabic countries and elsewhere. Such dimensioning systems can be found in Japanese vernacular architecture, European church buildings and many other cultures. In many instances, the proportioning systems were related to the dimensions of the human body or had some cosmic or religious significance. The so-called golden section was used widely in European Renaissance architecture. A modern version by Le Corbusier called 'Le Modulor' was also based on human dimensions. Such systems are related to a modular approach to design, but not really to construction. Modular construction techniques are a more contemporary response to integrating both design and construction. An important precedent is Moshe Safdie's 1966 modular accommodation (Habitat, Montreal) built with 80 ton precast concrete room modules to a design that expressed very clearly the nature of the construction method.

Further reading

Construction Industry Research and Information Association (1997) *Standardisation and pre-assembly*, CIRIA Report 176, CIRIA, London, UK.

Gausa, M. (1999) *Housing: new alternatives, new systems*, Birkhäuser, Basle, Switzerland.

Gibb, A.G.F. (1999) *Off-site fabrication: prefabrication, pre-assembly and modularisation*, Whittles Publishing, Caithness, Scotland.

Warszawski, A. (1999) *Industrialized and automated building systems* (2nd edition), E & FN Spon, London, UK.

JG

Moment frames

See: BRACING

Monopitch roof

See: ROOFS

Mortars, cement and lime

Brickwork construction needs mortar to keep it together. Architects may consider the use of lime (for added flexibility) or coloured mortars for decorative purposes.

See also: BRICKS AND BLOCKS; BRICKS AND BLOCKS – FINISHES; CEMENT; CONCRETE; CONCRETE – FINISHES; CONNECTIONS; INTELLIGENT FAÇADES AND MATERIALS; SURFACE FINISHES; WALLS.

About mortar

Mortars are blends of the following ingredients:

- Binder material (such as cement and/or lime);
- Fine aggregates (sand);
- Other additives (such as plasticisers);
- Water.

Mortar is a vital part of brick and blockwork construction as it forms both a bearing layer and a 'sealant' between adjacent and subsequent layers of masonry units. It also helps weatherproofing and is important for airtightness of the building envelope. Mortar is applied in a wet, but cohesive form and will settle under the weight of masonry. Most settlement happens in the first few weeks of construction, but designers should allow for this to continue in the form of appropriate shrinkage detailing. In many ways the traditional methods of masonry construction are useful because they allow for slight dimensional inaccuracies. To account for both shrinkage and any other movements in a masonry wall, mortar should allow some movement between the masonry units. This is achieved by specifying a compressive strength somewhat lower than that of bricks/blocks, but not too low or the durability of the wall will be compromised. Higher strength mortars are useful in exposed locations and structural brickwork.

As it is a blend of individual materials, mortar can be made up as appropriate, by volume or 'parts', shown below. Bagged products make this task even easier: simply add water. Some typical designated mixes:

- Cement/lime/sand;
- Cement/sand + plasticiser;
- Masonry cement/sand.

It is usual to specify ready-mixed mortar, which, if needed in significant quantities, can be delivered to site in large silos and used as required. For projects with extensive ranges of masonry and stonework walling these can be very convenient and economical. Although cement is useful in mortar because it provides high strength, in some instances this strength is less desirable as it can lead to cracking in adjacent brickwork. In this case, the strong mortar resists movement unnaturally restraining the weaker bricks, which may then crack in response. Lime-rich mortars retain some moisture and are not as strong as cement mortar, but they do allow movement (see below). Some cement mortars are now available with additional ingredients, which allow a degree of movement similar to lime mortars. Restoration work with mortars also requires careful matching of the sand used.

About lime

Before OPC was developed, lime was used in all mortars and renders – it is a softer, more porous material than cement. However, just like cement, lime for building construction is manufactured from limestone. Having burnt the material at 950 °C, water is added to create a white powder (slaked lime). This can be used in mortars or other building products. The benefit of using lime is that it retains moisture, helping workability. It is also more cohesive to poor surfaces like old brickwork. In a way, lime is an intelligent material. It is self-healing – 'unconverted' lime absorbs rainwater and heals any microcracking caused by movement. However, lime mortars are not suitable for tall buildings as hardening will take too long. Hydraulic limes have a higher clay content than slaked lime, which makes them particularly suitable for restoration work as they will give an initial set after a few hours and are less likely to crack in the long term.

Coloured mortar

In non-critical applications like everyday construction work, there is no need to be overly prescriptive about mortars. It is only sensible to consider basic mixes and locally available materials. However, for masonry with specific architectural or aesthetic requirements, coloured mortar offers the designer a further option in terms of the appearance that is produced. One can then specify both the brick/block and the mortar colour to achieve a particular look. The issues to consider for coloured mortars are similar to those discussed in *Concrete–finishes*.

Further reading

Roberts, J.J., Tovey, A., & Fried, A. (2001) *Concrete masonry designers handbook*, E & FN Spon, London, UK.

JG

Mosaic
See: CERAMICS

Movement joint
See: CONNECTIONS

Mullion
See: WINDOWS AND CURTAIN WALLING

Nervi, Pier Luigi

Pier Luigi Nervi (1891–1979) is credited as one of the most important innovators in structural concrete in the 20th century. He is best known for the enormous long span concrete shells and domes for public buildings, constructed in Italy in the 1950s.

See also: BEAM; CANTILEVER; CONCRETE; CONCRETE – STRUCTURES; ROOFS.

The most brilliant manipulator of reinforced concrete of the modern age, Nervi was just as impressive an architect as he was an engineer.

Realising the limitations of poured concrete early in his career, Nervi developed a series of precast elements, which could be used together with concrete poured in situ. Among his innovations was a technique, which he termed 'ferro-cemento'. This was essentially layers of steel mesh which were sprayed with cement, a system which could be strengthened by the addition of reinforcing rods between mesh and mortar. This system allowed great flexibility, both aesthetically and structurally and he showed its effectiveness in the building of Florence's Municipal Stadium (1930–32). Seating 35,000 people, the stadium was a cantilevered structure about 20 m deep with a series of sculptural concrete spiral stairs cantilevered from the rim of the stadium structure. He followed this with a series of aircraft hangars for the Italian Air Force (including examples at Orvieto 1936 and Orbetello 1939–41) each a refinement of his essential structure of a vault of a network of diagonally intersecting concrete beams. The hangars show Nervi's development from his early attempts using in-situ concrete for roof beams to later efforts for which he used lightweight precast lattice ribs. Formed in sections and assembled on site, these elements were held in place in the curving roofs using in-situ poured concrete ribs held up by buttress-like supports (at first solid, later branching into two elements as they flared out towards the ground) at the open end of the structure.

In a pair of enormous exhibition halls (Halls B & C) in Turin (1948–49 and 1949–50), Nervi used his ferro-cemento technique to demonstrate the scale and delicacy of what could be done in concrete. Hall B was covered by a corrugated roof of pre-cast ferro-cemento units with windows, while in Hall C Nervi used the diagonally intersecting system of beams familiar from the hangars – light is admitted through a kind of clerestory at the base of the roof. The Palazzetto dello Sport, Rome (1956–57) was created from the basic form of Turin Hall C and is a magnificent domed sports hall in which the diamond-patterned roof seems to float above the space due to the band of glazing directly above the stadium seating. The larger Palazzo dello Sport (designed with Marcello Piacentini), also Rome (1959–60), seated 16,000 and was covered by a domed roof spanning over 100 m which was an extension of the corrugated principles developed in Turin's Hall B.

Nervi also collaborated with other architects on a number of seminal buildings. He was the engineer for the structure of the UNESCO Building in Paris (1953–56), designed by Marcel Breuer, a Y-shaped block supported on massive inclined concrete piers. Nervi was responsible for the remarkable external spiral stairs, which rise through the full height of the elevation and the cantilevered concrete canopy above the entrance. Nervi was also responsible for the structure, which allowed Gio Ponti's Pirelli skyscraper, Milan (1955–58) to remain so effortlessly sleek. Other influential structures included a tobacco factory in Bologna (1951–52), Festival building in Chianciano (1952), Stadio Flaminio, Rome (1958–59), the Palace of Labour, Turin (1960–61), another, even bigger exhibition hall in Turin (1961) and a huge audience hall for the Vatican (1970).

Further reading

Huxtable, A.L. (1960) *Pier Luigi Nervi*, Mayflower, London, UK.

EH

Neoprene

See: CONNECTIONS; PLASTICS – TYPES

Neutra, Richard

Richard Neutra (1892–1970) was one of the early Modernist architects on the US West Coast. He tended to use steel frames combined with natural ventilation and extensive areas of glazing in a move towards 'healthier living'.

See also: CEMENT; CLADDING; CONCRETE – FINISHES; CONCRETE – STRUCTURES; ECOLOGICAL DESIGN; ENVIRONMENTAL DESIGN; LE CORBUSIER; LOUVRES AND BRISE SOLEIL; SCHINDLER, R.M.; STRUCTURAL STEEL; VENTILATION; WINDOWS AND CURTAIN WALLING; WRIGHT, FRANK LLOYD.

Richard Neutra emigrated to California from his native Vienna in 1923, and brought with him a commitment to the European Modernism, which he developed gradually into a style dubbed 'California Modern' by the Museum of Modern Art, New York for an exhibition in 1982. He worked briefly for Frank Lloyd Wright in 1924, but little direct influence can be seen in Neutra's work.

The Lovell House, Los Angeles (1927–29) was his first masterpiece in the European Modern style (dubbed the International Style by the Museum of Modern Art, New York for an exhibition in 1932 in which the house featured). While the final appearance was apparently of concrete floor levels with steel ribbon windows, the structure consisted of a steel frame (as well-known contemporary photographs show) covered in stucco (a form of render). Its owner, Dr. Philip Lovell, an early and progressive promoter of physical culture, promoted it consciously as the Lovell Health House. Such an association must have been of interest to Neutra as well.

After the Lovell House, Neutra relinquished stucco in favour of materials more suitable for the California building industry:

- *Plywood*, as in his own house in Los Angeles (1932), known as the VDL Research House (after the Dutch industrialist Cornelius van der Leuw who financed it);
- *Horizontal timber boards*, as in the McIntosh House, Los Angeles (1939);
- *Sheet steel sidings*, often painted to look like aluminium.

In the Beard House, Altadena (1934) and the von Sternberg House, San Fernando Valley (1935) he experimented with loadbearing metal wall panels, which did not prove successful.

It is apparent that Neutra was beginning to feel that the dialectic opposition of pure building form and virgin landscape of the International Style (so striking in Lovell House) was not really appropriate for the 'indoor-outdoor' living of southern California. He mutated the constructional methods gradually to allow more varied internal spaces, to be more responsive to the climate and to allow greater integration with the landscape. The Miller House, Palm Springs (1937) was a precursor of this approach, which reached fruition in the more prosperous post-war period. This approach was more influential on later developments in southern California, both through the Bailey House, Los Angeles (1947–48), part of the Case Study House programme promoted by John Entenza for the magazine *California Arts and Architecture*, and through his pupils Gregory Ain and Raphael Soriano.

This change in direction in his architecture was mirrored in two highly regarded publications:

- *Wie Baut Amerika* (How America Builds), 1927.
- *Amerika: Die Stilbildung des neuen Bauen in den Vereinigten Staten* (America: The Style of New Building in the United States), 1930.

In these books, Neutra moved away from an uncritical admiration for the United States, doubtless because of his increased familiarity with its conservative architectural climate. His own thoughts were articulated more fully in *Survival through Design* (1954), in which he wrote of the necessity of a relationship between architecture and landscape as well as the emotional and material nature of architecture. In his projects for 'Rush City Reformed', he proposed ameliorating the developing suburbia through better house design.

The Kaufmann House, Palm Springs (1946) and the Tremaine House, Santa Barbara (1947) were two houses that characterised the mixed constructional methods of the California Modern style. The Kaufmann House had masonry walls, which extended the plan into the landscape and a very delicate steel-framed structure. The Tremaine House featured a lower floor of heavy masonry with concrete-framed upper floors. Both had extensive opening windows protected by roof overhangs and swimming pools integrated into the plans, which linked the houses to their sites.

It cannot be doubted that it was Neutra's little-known involvement with countries in Latin America that provoked the greater range of his work. Unlike many Modern architects, Neutra undertook genuine research into practical and cost-effective construction methods for poor countries, principally in Puerto Rico, as part of Federal policy during the Second World War. Technologies included through-ventilation, horizontal pivoting brise-soleil big enough to form entire walls and deeply overhanging roofs. This research was condensed into a book *Arquitetura Social* (Architecture of Social Concern) intended to counter the influence of Le Corbusier and European Modernism in Brazil. He was also concerned with low-cost housing in the United States under the Federal Housing Administration, but later projects for Los Angeles were not in keeping with the post-war political direction in the United States, and it is his single-family houses which remain his most successful and well-known works.

Further reading

Boesiger, W. (ed.) (1950, 1956 & 1959) *Richard Neutra: buildings and projects* (Three volumes), Artemis, Zurich, Switzerland/Thames & Hudson, London, UK.

Drexler, A. & Hines, T.S. (eds.) (1982) *Richard Neutra: from international style to California modern*, MoMA, New York, USA.

Hines, T. (1982) *Richard Neutra and the search for modern architecture*, OUP, New York, USA.

McCoy, E. (1975) *Five California architects*, Praeger, New York, USA.

Neutra, R. (c.1944) *Architecture of social concern*, Gerth Todtmann, São Paolo, Brazil.

Neutra, R. (1954) *Survival through design*, Oxford University Press, New York, USA.

Neutra, R. (1962) *World and dwelling*, Universe Books, New York, USA.

TD

Niemeyer, Oscar

Oscar Niemeyer (b. 1907), the acclaimed Brazilian architect can be credited with bringing Modernism to fame in South America. Most well known for his buildings in the capital Brasília, he has continued to explore the use of concrete.

See also: CONCRETE; CONCRETE – STRUCTURES; LE CORBUSIER; LOUVRES AND BRISE SOLEIL; PROUVÉ, JEAN.

Oscar Niemeyer: Tribunal Superior de Justiça, Brasília (1963). Roof overhangs shelter the large glazed area from the tropical sun. Photograph by Thomas Deckker/Zilah Quezado Deckker.

Oscar Niemeyer was born in Rio de Janeiro, Brazil, and grew up at a time when Brazil was determined to 'modernise' and throw off its rural and agrarian past. Niemeyer was fortunate to be part of a brilliant circle of 'Modern' architects, engineers, and not least, clients. Gustavo Capanema, the Minister, who commissioned the Ministry of Education building in 1935, and Juscelino Kubitschek, who commissioned Pampulha in 1940 as Mayor of Belo Horizonte and went on to commission Brasília in 1957 as President of Brazil, were deeply cultured and genuinely passionate about architecture.

Two factors made European Modernism fruitful in Brazil: the advanced state of concrete construction and the otherwise primitive state of the building industry. There were no steel mills in Brazil before 1943: structural steel, and the technical supervision of the construction, had to be imported from the USA. Reinforced concrete had the advantages of being prepared on site and of not requiring specialised labour. As workers were illiterate, no working drawings need be prepared; the use of a good engineer, however, was vital to design an appropriate concrete frame, and very simple detailing was essential as the integration of components could not be anticipated. Virtually all fittings and finishing materials had to be imported from the USA, which not only resulted in high initial costs, but also made maintenance an almost insuperable problem.

A protégé of Lucio Costa (1902–1998), Niemeyer did not initially show any evidence of his extraordinary abilities. He learnt all he needed to know about the Modern architectural language in a few weeks in August 1936 during Le Corbusier's brief visit to Brazil as adviser on the Ministry of Education building. It was Niemeyer however, who must take the credit for turning Costa's rather naive initial proposal and Le Corbusier's clumsy sketches into the final building. It was the first tall Modern

Movement building, and utilised pilotis of several sizes and spacings to give a dynamic rhythm to the form. Horizontally pivoting brise-soleils in bright blue asbestos cement were used for the first time. The engineer was Emilio Baumgart (1888–1942), who had set the world record height for concrete construction with the 'A Noite' building, Rio de Janeiro (1928).

Niemeyer did not feel he had achieved maturity until the more free-form buildings in Pampulha (1940–43) such as the Casino, the Casa de Baile, the Yacht Club and the Church of São Francisco, which was his first use of shell vaults. Niemeyer continued to build extensively in Belo Horizonte and the state of Minas Gerais under the patronage of Kubitschek, and began to acquire an international reputation, being a consultant on the United Nations building, New York (1947) and building an apartment block at the Interbau exhibition, Berlin (1957). Some projects of this period, such as the Museum in Caracas (1954), an inverted pyramid, were extraordinarily powerful, but after 1957 all his energy was concentrated on Brasília.

The main Government buildings in Brasília all employ some form of deep-plan concrete construction with light perimeter columns. He was fortunate to collaborate with another brilliant concrete engineer, Joaquim Cardoso (1897–1978); the twin-domed Congresso Nacional (1957–60) was virtually a monolithic concrete shell. The rectilinear Ministries, however, were steel-framed and clad in heat-absorbing glass, which did not function well and led to the hasty installation of wall-mounted air-conditioning units. Perhaps surprisingly, however, Niemeyer's Palaces in Brasília are comfortable. The high ratio of heavy roof construction to building volume (necessitated by the long spans and deep plans), the wide overhangs, the provision for cross-ventilation in the glazed walls and the landscaping mean that internal temperatures are moderate. In the Alvorado Palace (1957), for instance, only the library is air-conditioned. In his apartment blocks in the residential quarters, the use of 'cambogo' (pierced masonry screens), 'bandeiras' (louvred timber screens) and brise-soleil mean that environmental conditions in these shallow-plan and poorly built apartments are actually reasonable.

Despite the programme of modernisation in Brazil, a considerable amount of the structural steel and finishing materials in Brasília had to be imported from the United States. This, and the cost of developing the city, led to the cessation of building activity in 1960 when only the main Government buildings and about 10% of the apartment buildings had been built. The military coup in 1964 led quickly to Niemeyer's exile. Niemeyer was fortunate to extend his career in France – the Communist Party Headquarters, Paris (1967–80), the Cultural Centre in Le Havre (1972–83), Italy – the Mondadori Headquarters, Milan (1968–75), and Algeria – the University of Constantine (1969–72). He collaborated with Jean Prouvé on the Communist Party Headquarters, which doubtless made the curtain wall more acceptable in the more rigorous climate of Paris. Although this building sensuously exploits its corner site in the 19th century Parisian *streetscape*, later buildings became more formal exercises in concrete construction.

After his return to Brazil following the fall of the military dictatorship in 1984, Niemeyer modified many of his buildings to solve outstanding environmental problems. The addition of brise-soleil to the Palaces and Ministries in Brasília has not reduced their architectural power. In his latest works, such as the Latin America Centre, São Paulo (1987) and the Museum of Contemporary Art, Niterói (1997) Niemeyer has continued to exploit the plastic nature of concrete.

Further reading

Niemeyer, O. (2000) *The curves of time: the memoirs of Oscar Niemeyer*, Phaidon Press, London, UK.
Papadaki, S. (ed.) (1950) *The works of Oscar Niemeyer*, Reinhold, New York, USA.

Quezado Deckker, Z. (2001) *Brazil built: the architecture of the Modern Movement in Brazil*, E& FN Spon, London, UK.

TD

Night ventilation

Methods to utilise the thermal storage capacity of buildings to provide cooling as well as purging (flushing) the daily build up of contaminants.

See also: AIRTIGHTNESS AND IAQ; DYNAMIC THERMAL SIMULATION; ENERGY EFFICIENCY; ENVIRONMENTAL DESIGN; FABRIC ENERGY STORAGE; FAÇADES AND FAÇADE ENGINEERING; GLASS – LAMINATED AND COATED; HEAT RECOVERY; HVAC; INSULATION; INTELLIGENT FAÇADES AND MATERIALS; STACK EFFECT; THERMAL COMFORT; THERMOLABYRINTHS; TROMBE WALLS; VENTILATION RATE.

Introduction

Night ventilation is used for two basic reasons; to cool or re-charge thermal mass and to purge the indoor air of normal building 'pathogens' or contaminants that have built up during the day. For more details of the latter function, see *Airtightness and IAQ* and *Ventilation*.

How does night cooling work?

Fabric energy storage utilises the thermal mass in heavyweight construction materials, such as masonry, concrete and stone to reduce peak internal temperatures and delay their onset. The drop in outdoor temperatures at night means that external air, when introduced into the building, can contribute to cooling. Night ventilation flushes or purges the building fabric of heat absorbed during the day. To be effective, it is important that the ventilating airflow is in direct contact with the thermal mass. This can be effected by induced ventilation via the stack effect or wind towers, or activated by opening louvres at soffit height and 'thrust' fans to accelerate air movement. The use of fans to ensure the required air flow may also be advisable due to lower wind speeds at night (due to the absence of solar radiation and consequent convection).

Night flushing is particularly useful in buildings that are in use throughout the day, allowing the mass to be discharged effectively using night air temperatures well below the accepted comfort zone. However, the higher standards now required for insulation in walls and façades have created a situation in which the building heats up disproportionately during the day. In this instance, night ventilation and fabric energy storage may need to be combined with solar control glass to control heat gain and daytime ventilation via wind towers or the stack effect.

Case study

The Emerald People's Utility District HQ in Eugene, Oregon (USA) built in 1988 provides a useful example of night ventilation issues. The 2,230 m^2 office was designed to use daylighting, passive solar heating and night cooling to achieve annual energy savings of 27%, in a climate similar to the UK. To maximise the potential for night cooling, the design team chose to increase the mass surface by using precast hollowcore concrete slabs. Although the building was predicted to use 90 $kW/m^2/yr$, in the first year of operation it used $126\,\text{kW/m}^2/\text{yr}$, which led to an investigation of the way the building was being used. In subsequent years, changes in occupancy activities and patterns of use improved the overall performance of the building. This demonstrates that such strategies for cooling can be compromised in use. Nevertheless, the US Department of Energy now recommends natural ventilation and night flushing together with shading and insulation in its strategies for the design of commercial buildings.

Further reading

Allard, F. (ed.) with Santamouris, M. (1998) *Natural ventilation in buildings: a design handbook*, James & James, London, UK

Chartered Institute of Building Services Engineers (2000) *Mixed mode ventilation: CIBSE Applications Manual 13*, CIBSE, London, UK.

Moore, F. (1993) *Environmental control systems: heating, cooling and lighting* (International Edition), McGraw Hill, New York, USA.

Santamouris, M. & Asimakapolous, D. (eds.) (1996) *Passive cooling of buildings*, James & James, London, UK.

WH

Nouvel, Jean

Inspirational and heroic buildings characterise the portfolio of French architect Jean Nouvel (b.1945). His supreme intellect combined with a love of expression and innate understanding of the sensory quality of materials have made him one of Europe's finest architects.

See also: CONCRETE; COR-TEN®; STEEL; FAÇADE ENGINEERING; INTELLIGENT FAÇADES AND MATERIALS; LIGHTING – DAYLIGHTING.

> 'He remembers the seasoned professionals he worked with during his sink-or-swim period with genuine gratitude and respect. No doubt they are the people who imparted to him the taste for sending absolute beginners out to face the realities of construction work, literally putting them up against the wall.'
>
> Olivier Boissière, writing about Nouvel.

Jean Nouvel entered the Ecole des Beaux-Arts in Paris in 1966. His initial desire to become a painter soon gave way to his interest in architecture and he went on to gain his degree in 1971. He opened his first office with François Seigneur in 1970. In 1976 he was a co-founder of the MARS movement of French architects and was soon to receive many awards for his endeavours in innovative and ground breaking architecture. The firm 'Jean Nouvel, Emmanuel Cattani et Associes' was opened in 1988 and continued to be the source of many exciting projects through to 1994 when Nouvel began to operate independently. He continues to win significant awards and to be a mentor to many practising architects. Perhaps his first real outing on the international stage was with the Institute du Monde Arab, Paris (1981–87). This showcase for the Arab world culture had to explore several diametrically opposite positions. It needed to link but differentiate between the Arab and Western cultures; it needed to deal with the history and modernity; it is on a site which borders a dense urban area and the more open Universitée de Jussieu region. In response, the building follows the curve of the roadway, but opens up to the University. The building uses modern construction methods, but also reflects the history of the Arab tradition with a treatment of light that revolves around grids, frames and filters. The construction palette is a concrete structure with glazed façade and aluminium trim. The south-facing façade uses layering of light to the optimum via a grid of geometric elements commonly used in Arab culture, but consisting of mobile diaphragms that are adjusted according to light intensity. This play of light is one of the special effects that gives the building a magical quality.

Since the Institute was completed, Nouvel's oeuvre has been watched keenly by the architectural world to see just what innovative technology he will utilise next. In the same way that fashions in clothing are determined on the Paris catwalks, so does Parisian Nouvel set future 'fashions' in architectural technology. The Hotel Saint James (Bordeaux-Bouliac, France, 1988–89) was built for a talented emerging chef in the shadow of the spire of a village church. This small hotel plays on the rustic village look using simple house-like shapes, which are actually rusty metal grids laid over grey cladding. The grids are also laid across the glazing but in these areas they can be opened to vary the light on the interior. Once again Nouvel used materials and light to create the desired effect.

The 'Tour Sans Fins' (infinite tower) was a winning competition design that unfortunately was not built. Again experimenting with building technology, Nouvel's tower would have been dark at its base as it rose from the earth (with granite cladding), becoming lighter in colour and structure (with mirror glass), as it neared the sky, thereby increasing the optical illusion given by its tall structure. At 430 metres in height, but only 43 metres in diameter it would have been one of the most slender buildings in the world.

Further reading

Anon (1997) *Masters Vol.2: Arata Isozaki, Jean Nouvel, Legorreta Arquitectos, Steven Holl*, St. Martin's Press, London, UK.

Boissière, O. (1996) *Jean Nouvel*, Birkhäuser, Basle, Switzerland.

Boissière, O. (1992) *Jean Nouvel, Emmanuel Cattani et Associés*, Ellipsis, London, UK.

Goulet, P. (1987) *Jean Nouvel*, Electa France, Paris, France.

Morgan, C.L. (1998) *Jean Nouvel: the Elements of Architecture*, Thames & Hudson, London.

MT

Nylon

See: PLASTICS – TYPES

Oak

See: TIMBER – HARDWOODS AND SOFTWOODS;
TIMBER – PRODUCTION AND FINISHES

Off-site manufacture

Off-site manufacture is about undertaking manufacturing, construction, or finishing operations in locations other than the construction site.

See also: CONSTRUCTION PROGRAMME; CRITICAL PATH ANALYSIS; DRY CONSTRUCTION AND WET CONSTRUCTION; 'JUST-IN-TIME' CONSTRUCTION; LEAD-TIME; 'LEAN' CONSTRUCTION; LIGHT STEEL FRAME; MODULES AND MODULAR CONSTRUCTION; PODS; TIMBER – STRUCTURES.

What is off-site manufacture?

Precast concrete floor unit being lowered into position, having been cast and finished off site in a factory. The unit is designed for lifting by crane off the truck and into its final place in the structure. Photograph by Barry Bulley, courtesy of Trent Precast Concrete Ltd.

Construction activities can take place either on site or in other locations such as factories and workshops elsewhere. Each method has its advantages and disadvantages, but it is becoming more common to see a significant amount of 'work' being carried out off site, in the protected environment of a factory. The two principal reasons for this are to remove building elements from the 'critical path' and to achieve a cost, quality or performance gain by using factory production and assembly techniques. Shorter construction programmes, skills shortages, and demands for improvements in quality, have supported the increasing use of off-site manufacture for many items from small sub-assemblies to full scale elements of structure and modules. The application of 'Lean Thinking' to the building process has created a formalised framework within which manufacturers can work.

Advantages of working off site

The supply of major packages can usually be on a 'just-in-time' basis having been manufactured off site often independently of the critical path, then delivered to site only when needed. The speed advantage of assembly-style construction is enhanced by simple standard connections for these pre-finished elements, which can shorten the construction programme. Production in factory conditions can deliver higher standards of compliance and finish. Waste is eliminated as far as possible with centralised materials control compared to disparate control methods. Key skills and expertise can be retained at manufacturing centres, avoiding the difficulties of recruitment and retention of key staff on site. All these factors mean that compliance to design and specification is easier to achieve.

Disadvantages

Despite all the potential benefits, not all suppliers are able or willing to supply to a tight programme, particularly because of the risk arising from trying to get the design team in a position to finalise design and specification at an early stage. Manufacturing capacities vary – this can limit the availability and release of finished packages ready for site. Two delivery costs are involved; first, taking the materials to the supplier, then taking the finished package to site, with specialist transport required sometimes. There may also be a cost implication from structural duplication for major elements (cladding panels, modular toilets), and some 'doubling up' is likely. The costs to retain a permanent workforce and run a factory facility must also be passed on to the customer.

What elements can be made off site?

- Floor cassettes;
- Lift assemblies and enclosures;
- Modular bathrooms and toilets (for offices, hotels, housing);
- Modular rooms (for hotels, leisure/catering);
- Pre-finished cladding panels;
- Services modules (e.g. hot and cold water packages, air-conditioning units);
- Small elements – pre-cut, pre-finished joinery packages, pre-hung, pre-finished door sets;
- Staircase flights, landings, and enclosures;
- Structures and modules.

Most parts of the building process can take advantage of off-site manufacture, from pre-finished components and sub-assemblies to whole structural elements and modular units. Specialist contractors or industries in associated fields usually provide the manufacturing capacity for off-site sourcing. For example, the market dominance of bathroom modules in the 1980s commercial building boom was supplied mostly by spare capacity in the offshore oil industry, where the norm of working to tight deadlines and specifications was appropriate. On a smaller scale, however, existing suppliers are able to re-focus their approach, often partnering with customers. The joinery industry is typical of this, where first and second fix joinery for housing is supplied in prepared 'packs', with much of the second fix pre-painted.

Further reading

Construction Industry Research and Information Association (1997) *Standardisation and pre-assembly*, CIRIA Report 176, CIRIA, London, UK.

Gibb, A.G.F. (1999) *Off-site fabrication: prefabrication, pre-assembly and modularisation*, Whittles Publishing, Caithness, UK.

Warszawski, A. (1999) *Industrialized and automated building systems* (2nd edition), E & FN Spon, London, UK.

Womack, J. & Jones, D. (1996) *Lean thinking*, Simon & Schuster, New York, USA.

GW

On-site production

On-site production is manufacturing, construction, or finishing operations on site.

General view of construction under way on site at the Toyota GB headquarters building in Surrey. Activities under way include groundworks and frame construction. Precast concrete elements can also be seen being off loaded. Photograph by Barry Bulley, courtesy of Trent Precast Concrete Ltd.

See also: BRICKS AND BLOCKS; CONCRETE; CONSTRUCTION PROGRAMME; CRITICAL PATH ANALYSIS; DRY CONSTRUCTION AND WET CONSTRUCTION; 'JUST-IN-TIME' CONSTRUCTION; LEAD-TIME; 'LEAN' CONSTRUCTION.

Introduction

On-site construction (sometimes called in-situ construction) is usually associated with the use of traditional building materials and techniques such as masonry, stone and other 'wet trades', but it also encompasses the installation of any components made off site. It includes any operation that is carried out in the place where the building will be founded including the following activities:

- Groundworks;
- Foundation (substructure);
- Services;
- Superstructure;
- First fix;
- Second fix;
- Other finishing activities;
- Fit-out.

(any of which could be made wholly or partly off site).

Issues

There are several aspects to on-site production of buildings that are worth exploring, particularly in relation to the debate about on-site versus off-site activities.

Weather – different countries have different preferences for on- or off-site working. Clearly, in countries with very cold climates one tends to prefer factory working and shorter times on site, ideally scheduled for the milder spring and summer months. In very hot climates, on-site work may be restricted to the cooler hours of the day or night time (in Middle Eastern countries for example concrete is mixed with crushed ice to keep it cool). Countries with a very wet climate may confine work to the dry season. The key operation on site in the UK, for example, is to complete the roof and envelope as soon as possible.

Quality control – this is a difficult issue. Most people presume that quality control is less easy to manage on site than in controlled factory conditions. However this may not always be the case, despite the weather and other unpredictable aspects of working on site. The same specification and expectations can be applied to on-site production, bearing in mind the differences in construction techniques employed and what standards one can reasonably expect to achieve. What can be said for certain is that quality control of both on-site and off-site production is very important, and this is particularly so when both types of construction come together on the same project.

Labour and employment – this is a massive issue that is affecting all parts of the UK construction industry. The debate centres on the demand for the ever-dwindling resource of skilled workers, such as bricklayers. This reliance was of course not a problem when traditional methods of construction were commonplace, but several factors have conspired to drastically reduce the number of skilled workers available to the industry including:

- Greater proportion of off-site manufactured goods;
- Lack of continuous employment opportunities;
- Problems with inadequate site provision and issues with the management of site safety.

The industry reaction to this has been to reduce the risk by selecting semi-skilled methods of construction and/or moving production off site.

Programme – in another entry (*Construction programme*) this is discussed in greater detail. Suffice to say that the programme required by the client's operations (e.g. hotels etc.), the site conditions and the dovetailing of trades will all play a part in deciding what and how much of the activities will take place on or off site. The key issue is that on-site construction need not take longer to complete than off-site manufacture (the lead-time must also be taken into account). Indeed, in studies conducted jointly by the commercial developer Stanhope and the University of Reading, tough weekly progress benchmarks on a floor-by-floor basis were achieved by combining techniques of on- and off-site construction. Planning on paper was vital to achieving the most benefit on site. This becomes critical to developers with tight programmes; the 'cost' of being on site too long results directly in a loss of revenue or rental from the completed building.

JG

OPC: Ordinary Portland Cement
See: CEMENT

Operational energy
See: CARBON DIOXIDE (CO_2); 'ECO-POINTS'; INSULATION

OSB: oriented strand board
See: TIMBER – MANUFACTURED BOARDS

Otto, Frei

Frei Otto (b.1925) is best known for the cable net roof over the Munich Olympic stadium, but he was a structural innovator whose work still influences roof design.

See also: BEAM; CABLE NETS; FRAME; TEXTILE MEMBRANE ROOFS; ROOFS.

Solely responsible for the adoption of tensile and cable net structures into the language of modern architecture, Otto's achievement bridges architecture, engineering and a visionary and unique exploration of the structures and forces of nature and world.

Otto's early experiments with tent structures were made during the 1950s and employed cotton canvases of only modest spans. He later began to use roofs of steel-web suspended freely on cable nets, themselves stretched between heavy-gauge steel cables and suspended from masts anchored in the ground. Influential structures like the Interbau Pavilion (Berlin 1957); a series of undulating multi-purpose star pavilions in Hamburg (1963); the Snow and Rocks Restaurant Pavilion at the Swiss National

Exhibition in Lausanne (1964) caused much interest and seemed to provide an organic alternative to the monotony and repetitiveness of much modern architecture. However it was with the remarkable and ambitious buildings for the German Pavilion for Expo 67 in Montreal (his first major cable net roof) and the structures for the Munich Olympics (1972) that Otto gained visionary status.

He was much influenced in his adoption at this time of asymmetrical, picturesque forms by the architect Rolf Gutbrod. Otto in turn exerted a huge influence on Gunter Behnisch who worked with him on the design of the Munich Olympic buildings and employed similar cable-net techniques to great effect in his own buildings. Otto later developed the convertible roof, where the membrane covering can be retracted to create a wholly alfresco space, a device used to best effect at the Open Air Theatre at Bad Hersfeld (1968). Otto founded the Development Centre for Lightweight Construction in Berlin in 1957 and the activities of the Centre were later moved to the Institute for Lightweight Structures in Stuttgart. Since the early 1970s, Otto has been concentrating his research on biological forms and structures and the development of grid shells.

Despite the organicism and seemingly free-flowing nature of Otto's structures, it would be a mistake to see him as anything other than a rationalist in the tradition of Modernist architecture. His structures expend minimal energy, using pure compression or tension-stressed shapes. Despite their radical appearance these are highly efficient forms constructed in harmony with the laws of physics rather than battling against them. Consequently Otto's structures display empathy for nature and the landscape, which is rare in modern architecture.

Further reading

Drew, P. (1976) *Frei Otto: form and structure*, Crosby Lockwood Staples, London, UK.

Glaeser, L. (1972) *The work of Frei Otto (Exhibition catalogue)*, MoMA, New York, USA.

Rasch, B. (1995) *Frei Otto: finding form, towards an architecture of the minima*, Editions Axel Meyer, Germany.

EH

Overcladding

Overcladding is the retro-fitting of a new 'skin' to an existing building to improve the performance of its walls, façade or roof.

See also: BRICKS AND BLOCKS; CLADDING; CLADDING COMPONENTS; CONCRETE; CONDENSATION; DESIGN LIFE; DURABILITY; FAÇADES AND FAÇADE ENGINEERING; FIRE PROTECTION; INSULATION; LIGHT STEEL FRAME; PERFORMANCE; THERMAL BRIDGING; WEATHERING; WINDOWS AND CURTAIN WALLING.

Introduction

In the event that weathering or durability problems deteriorate a building to such an extent that it requires retrofitting (refurbishment) works to be carried out, then overcladding may be used. This is the application of a new external façade to a building, usually retaining the original fabric as a substrate (lower layer). The technique is also applied successfully to the refurbishment of both walls and roofs. Overcladding is usually carried out in order to extend building life by upgrading the façade, whilst also improving thermal performance, weathertightness, and condensation/dew point control. Upgrades to other façade elements can be carried out at the same time (e.g. windows, balconies). For roofs, a 'flat to pitch' conversion can be achieved, or extra accommodation can be added.

Why use overcladding?

An otherwise sound and serviceable building may suffer from defects that compromise its usefulness and shorten its lifespan, such as:

- Condensation;
- Deterioration of the fabric and façade;
- Fire performance;
- Ponding and leakage (on roofs);
- Poor insulation;
- Thermal bridging;
- Weather ingress.

As a more sustainable alternative to major works or even demolition, overcladding can be specified to address all of these problems, while substantially extending the life of a building. In some instances, the appearance or architectural style of a building may need to be simply 'smartened up' or changed. For walls, new cladding, insulation and a spacer/support system is added. For roofs, new cladding is often used to effect a conversion and a cure for inadequate falls. Proprietary spacer systems or conventional trusses are used to achieve the pitch. As with walls, this is an opportunity to install additional insulation.

Generic systems

Two generic types of system are in use, distinguished by their approach to weathertightness.

Face sealed – this represents a broadly conventional cladding system fixed to the existing substrate instead of the more usual structural frame. The façade is designed and detailed to be impervious, effectively airtight and weathertight.

Rainscreen – the functions of rain shedding (outer layer) and air tightness (inner layer) are separated by a cavity, which allows water penetrating the outer layer to drain out. The inner layer normally incorporates insulation. Rain screen systems can be detailed in two ways, firstly as drained and ventilated systems, where water penetrating the open joints is drained out as part of the design. Secondly, a further development, 'pressure equalised rainscreen' (PER) systems, in which penetration of wind-driven rain is reduced by careful design of open joint and cavity, allowing wind pressure to enter the cavity, reducing its pressure difference from the outer face.

Design considerations

Cladding materials can be selected from:

- Brick slip/insulation systems;
- Cassettes (coated steel, aluminium);
- Coated, profiled metal sheet (steel, aluminium);
- Flat sheet (self-coloured fibre cement, aluminium/plastic composites);

- Insulated composite panels;
- Insulating render systems.

The cladding is supported by a conventional grid of supports and spacers using metal angle, top hat or purpose designed sections. Support systems must allow for differential movement between cladding and existing fabric. This can be achieved with slip joints, slotted fixing brackets, etc. Attachment is made either to the existing cladding face, or direct to the main structure. All fixings must be designed for load transfer between the overcladding and the existing fabric. Fixings to the existing structure will depend on the type and condition of the existing fabric; resin anchors, expanding anchors, and self-tapping masonry anchors are used.

Behaviour in fire must take account of the need to prevent spread of fire in the cavity behind the cladding face. Cavity barriers in prescribed locations are normally required.

Insulation as an inner layer must be part of an impermeable system, either with integral facings (e.g. foil-faced foam boards), or as open materials such as mineral wool, protected by a separate breather membrane. U values can be improved from worst case figures around $1.5 \text{W/m}^2{}^\circ\text{C}$ down to $0.42 \text{W/m}^2{}^\circ\text{C}$ (or even lower with high efficiency insulation) to approach compliance with current standards. It is advisable to ensure that the inner layer can breathe as part of the overall condensation control strategy using, for example, breather membrane or vapour permeable joints between boards.

Further reading

Centre for Window and Cladding Technology (1996) *Standard and guide to good practice in rain screen walls*, University of Bath, Bath, UK.
Construction Industry Research and Information Association (1988) *Rain screen cladding: a guide to principles and practice*, CIRIA, London, UK.
Lawson, R.M. (1999) *Over-cladding of existing buildings using light steel*, The Steel Construction Institute, Ascot, UK.
Lawson, R.M. & Gorgolewski, M. (1998) *Over roofing of existing buildings using light steel*, The Steel Construction Institute, Ascot, UK.

GW

Oversizing

The conscious decision to make a building element larger than one would normally expect, for a variety of reasons.

See also: BESPOKE; BEAM; CONNECTIONS; COLUMN; CONCRETE; DESIGN LIFE; FIRE PROTECTION; 'HONESTY'; SPECIFICATION; TIMBER – PRODUCTION AND FINISHES; TIMBER – LAMINATED TIMBER.

Introduction

The word oversize simply means 'of more than the usual size', but in architectural technology it has other more specific interpretations. The decision to deliberately oversize a building element, usually a structural one, is discussed here.

Why use oversizing?

For aesthetic reasons, an architect may wish to make a statement with the structural elements in a building. This may be to emphasise certain parts visually, or to reflect the character of a natural building material. This intention is similar to the desire behind 'honesty', expressing connections clearly etc., but it goes a step further in attempting to really emphasise particular elements.

The specification of natural timbers with large sectional sizes (e.g. green oak) is often done for aesthetic reasons, to expose the beauty of the wood and its grain. Such timber elements in a structure may well be oversized to emphasise the architectural intention in this regard. The decision to oversize timber may also be based on the need to provide sufficient sectional thickness to allow for a 'sacrificial layer' that chars and protects the inner core of the element in a fire. This is a natural attribute of large section timbers. In addition to providing sufficient thickness for fire protection purposes, the design discussion may also be steered towards oversizing because timber does not behave uniformly in all directions in terms of its structural performance. Hence, a tendency towards higher factors of safety in structural members will also favour oversizing.

The issues

In addition to the impacts on tolerances, standards and dimensional accuracy, the decision to use oversized elements may have further implications in terms of:

Structural efficiency – by oversizing an element its structural behaviour will be different in terms of loadbearing capacity, flexural strength and it may require connection details to be designed differently.

Weight – an oversized element weighs more and so this will have an impact on the connection details, adjacent loadbearing elements and ultimately also on the foundations.

Cost – this is particularly an issue for large section timbers, for which an increasing sectional thickness incurs a disproportionately increasing cost. In this instance, an architectural intention to oversize timber for example might result in the decision to use laminated timber rather than solid timber as the laminated timber would usually be more economical.

Practical note

It should be noted that in construction, an oversize item might not always be thought of as desirable. If a product such as a brick is larger than the nominal size and if a dimensional tolerance is specified, this may deviate from the specified dimensional limits. Hence, the product could be rejected on the grounds of a British or European Standard or the actual specification for the building.

Unexpected variations to nominal sizes will also affect arrangements for dimensional tolerances and setting out tolerances in a building. For these reasons, if the decision is taken to oversize any elements, this must be discussed at the design stage, agreed with the structural engineer and stated explicitly in the specification.

In structural engineering, design codes discuss 'factors of safety'. For example a beam might be designed to a British Standard, which stipulates a six-fold factor of safety. This is a separate discussion from oversizing. Any queries on how oversizing relates to factors of safety should be referred to the structural engineer for clarification.

JG

Paints

See: SURFACE FINISHES

Panels

See: CLADDING; FAÇADES AND FAÇADE ENGINEERING

Passive design

See: ENERGY EFFICIENCY; ENVIRONMENTAL DESIGN; SOLAR PANELS; STACK EFFECT; WIND TOWERS

Patina

See: COPPER; LEAD; METALS; WEATHERING; ZINC

Performance

The level to which a building, or part of a building, satisfies a variety of criteria in its specification or relevant standards.

See also: ACOUSTICS; CORROSION; DESIGN LIFE; DURABILITY; ECOLOGICAL DESIGN; 'ECO-POINTS'; ENERGY EFFICIENCY; ENVIRONMENTAL DESIGN; INSULATION; SPECIFICATION; SUSTAINABILITY; THERMAL COMFORT; WEATHERING.

Introduction

For buildings, the term 'performance' describes the degree to which a building or component of a building satisfies goals laid down in relation to a very broad range of criteria such as:

- Acoustics;
- Design life;
- Ecological design;
- Environmental design;
- Indoor air quality;
- Structural attributes (e.g. durability, serviceability);
- Thermal comfort.

Although these can be measured over any length of time, in most instances, performance is considered as a long-term attribute that relates to the qualities of a building during its predicted life. Performance is a broad term that can be applied to the structure, envelope or other parts of a building. The measurement of a building's performance has to be made against criteria such as those listed above, which can usually be quantified or measured accurately. In the case of performance criteria that cannot be measured scientifically it may be appropriate to use the phrase '**performance indicators**' that demarcate a trend rather than absolute data, for example performance attributes relating to social behaviour.

Working with standards

Design life (predicted service life) will affect the performance specification for a building in that it will determine the level of durability, serviceability and longevity required. In some building specifications, one may see very particular standards laid down against some of performance criteria, or reference to relevant British or European Standards. Many aspects of building performance (such as thermal insulation values and structural integrity) will be predetermined by such standards, however variations and interpretations to these absolute values very often appear in building specifications.

In many countries there is a trend towards '**performance specification**', which specifies the result to be achieved, rather than to state exactly what materials and methods should be used to achieve that result. Hence, it offers much more scope than the traditional, prescriptive approach. This is an important step forward in facilitating innovative approaches to architectural technology as it allows new techniques and materials to be compared with tried and tested methods on a more equal footing. The USA, Australia and Canada are particularly forward looking in this regard, with the USA pioneering performance specifications in the early 1960s.

Performance measurement

Different types of performance will be measured or tested in different ways during the life of a building. During the design stage, they will also be predicted and modelled in different ways. It is common at the design stage to have to make changes and compromise as a result of trying to find the best ways to satisfy a whole range of performance requirements. Solutions that are appropriate to satisfy one criterion may not suit another, which is what architectural technology is all about, i.e. striking a balance.

The in-use performance of a building can be measured by various techniques such as non-destructive testing (NDT) methods for structures and Post Occupancy Evaluation (POE) surveys for thermal, environmental and architectural aspects.

JG

Permanent formwork
See: COMPOSITE DECKING; CONCRETE – STRUCTURES

Permeability

Permeability is described here in the context of solid/fluid interaction behaviour in building structure and materials.

See also: AIRTIGHTNESS AND IAQ; BRICKS AND BLOCKS; CONCRETE; DESIGN LIFE; DURABILITY; PERFORMANCE; STONE; VENTILATION; WEATHERING.

What is permeability?

Permeability has a specific scientific definition and use in relation to magnetic flux behaviour, but is also used in a wider, colloquial sense. The permeability of materials can be generally thought of as being to do with the ease with which fluids can pass into or through a porous solid. In buildings, this property, termed 'permeability' has a number of important implications. In regards to the fabric the permeability (sometimes referred to as the breathability) will have an important impact on moisture vapour control, comfort and condensation. In other situations the permeability of the fabric may influence air leakage and the ingress of pollutants into sensitive spaces such as galleries and museums.

For porous, externally exposed construction materials (e.g. bricks, blocks, concrete and stone) there are a number of durability hazards related to permeability, including:

- Freeze thaw behaviour of stone, brick and concrete (any of which may suffer damage if a sufficient degree of saturation is reached when the material is undergoing extreme temperature change);
- Salt crystallisation, which derives from salt solutions in water, evaporating near the solid surface forming residual, physically disruptive salt crystals;
- Carbonation-induced corrosion of reinforcement in concrete following the ingress of carbon dioxide gas and water vapour;
- Chloride ion-induced corrosion of reinforcement in concrete after the migration of chloride ions in water solution.

Understanding the mechanisms

The concept of permeability follows from its scientific definition, which is 'the property of a porous medium, which characterises the ease with which a fluid will pass through it under a pressure difference'. The permeability measured or quoted may be for a specific solid/fluid combination e.g. the water permeability of concrete, or may be expressed as a property of the porous solid alone – its intrinsic permeability. Permeability differs from the related property of **diffusivity** (from diffusion) in that diffusivity is concerned with the flow or movement under a concentration gradient. The third linked, and to some extent interchanged concept, is of **absorptivity** (from absorption) which is the property where a porous solid takes in a fluid to fill spaces within the material. All of the properties described here should ideally be described under a steady state condition and can be described and manipulated mathematically.

While this is rather a scientific subject area, designers should appreciate the basic differences between permeability, and diffusivity properties essentially describing flow and porosity, as these might be inadvertently used interchangeably leading to confusion. For example, a solid with high voidage but where the voidage is not interconnected will have a high porosity but low permeability. Conversely a continuously connected network of capillaries may have low porosity but high permeability.

The fluids concerned with permeation, diffusion or absorption can be liquids (most often water) or gases e.g. oxygen, carbon dioxide or water vapour. There are many test methods for measuring or quantifying permeability characteristics and a bewildering array of units! (see below) Some of the test methods do not measure permeability directly but some aspect of performance, which is related to permeability. These are sometimes termed '**permeability indices**'. It is implicit in the scientific definitions of permeability or diffusivity that the fluid and the solid do not interact chemically i.e. that the system is inert. For some materials, this is not always true, e.g. water permeability of cement and concrete.

Typical parameters and units
- Coefficient of permeability m/s;
- Intrinsic permeability m^2;
- Diffusion coefficient m^2/s;
- Water vapour permeability g/m^2/day;
- Water vapour permeance g/MNs.

Further reading
The Concrete Society (1987) *Permeability testing of site concrete*, Concrete Society Technical Report TR31, The Concrete Society, Crowthorne, UK.

OA

Phase change materials
These are materials that store and release heat by changing their state (phase), usually from a solid to liquid and back.

See also: ENERGY EFFICIENCY; FABRIC ENERGY STORAGE; HEAT RECOVERY; INTELLIGENT FAÇADES AND MATERIALS; SOLAR PANELS; THERMOLABYRINTHS.

Introduction
The better management of energy storage in buildings in order to reduce heating and cooling needs is a current concern for designers. Phase change materials (PCMs) offer a highly efficient solution to the problem of sensible heat storage. When a material changes state or phase (e.g. liquid to gas) a large amount of heat must be absorbed, or released, in order to make that transition. Phase change materials exploit this phenomenon to the benefit of energy efficiency. In an architectural context, the applications and reasons for use are similar to those for fabric energy storage, but clearly in that instance the heavyweight masonry does not fundamentally change its composition to perform the 'thermal flywheel' function.

Examples of PCMs
PCMs can be included in the category of 'smart' or intelligent materials. New types of wallboards for internal use are being developed that have enhanced thermal performance owing to the use of PCMs. One particularly good example is **aerogels** (transparent insulating materials). Silica aerogels are a highly porous and lightweight glass, with molecular arrangements that have been stretched as far as possible, giving an appearance of frozen smoke. The hazy, transparent structures can be used as thermally insulating raw material and sandwiched between two panels of glass to create a highly efficient double glazing system, or used to construct more efficient solar panels for buildings. Their conductivity value is 0.017W/mK, which gives twice the insulation performance of normal foam plastic insulation. Aerogels were discovered more than 60 years ago, but their widespread use has been limited by their extreme fragility (they have to be transported in special bags to prevent any undue pressure, which could cause the glass to shatter). However, the use of aerogels in construction is now looking more favourable as prices are beginning to decrease.

Domestic heat pump applications for inter-seasonal storage were seen as a major development for the use of crystalline phase change materials, especially in the early 1980s when heat pumps were to be linked to solar panels in the development of low energy housing in the UK. One example was the 'cascade' heat pump, in which energy stored in the summer period could be augmented to higher outputs for winter use. In the 1980s, the UK's Building Research Establishment also investigated the use of 'heat of fusion' storage media, such as Glauber's Salts for enhanced heat storage purposes. These materials offer a greater heat storage capacity per unit volume than those using conventional materials or even water. However, the potential was not capitalised upon in the UK and the technology was adopted instead in other countries such as Germany, the Netherlands and Scandinavia (countries with a better track record of implementing the new generations of heat pumps, solar panels and phase change material systems).

WH/JG

Photochromic glass

See: GLASS; GLASS – LAMINATED AND COATED GLASS; INTELLIGENT FAÇADES AND MATERIALS

Photovoltaics (PV)

Photovoltaic cells generate electricity from daylight, most productively in bright sunlight. They are usually located on roofs, façades or free-standing arrays.

See also: CARBON DIOXIDE; CLADDING; ECOLOGICAL DESIGN; 'ECO-POINTS'; ENERGY EFFICIENCY; ENVIRONMENTAL DESIGN; FAÇADES AND FAÇADE ENGINEERING; ROOFS; SOLAR PANELS; WINDOWS AND CURTAIN WALLING.

Introduction – energy generation

With the realisation that the environmental costs of producing and distributing energy may cause grave problems for future societies, means of generating energy in cleaner and more localised ways needs to be developed. As society has progressed, the use of energy has become increasingly important to that development. In early times this was limited – for example, the sun was used to bake bricks and fire was used to cook food and provide light in the hours of darkness.

As industrialisation proceeded however, various aspects of nature were used, such as fire to generate steam or water (or animals) to turn a shaft. In general this rotation was used to drive, through belts, various machines. As this method of driving machinery was superseded by the introduction of electrically powered apparatus, the electric motor became the standard method of powering industry. This however required the development of electricity generation and delivery systems and these largely used fossil fuels as the power source. Those fuels are generally oil, gas and coal, but also include hydro and nuclear, each having their own ecological problems. Transport is still based largely on oil derived fuels.

The renewable energy systems – biomass, wind, solar, geothermal, wave and tidal power – generally use non-fossil based methods, but most still have to be linked to generators to produce electricity. Photovoltaics (PV) are a system that generates electricity directly from the sun and is now widely available.

How do photovoltaics work?

Photovoltaic systems convert light directly into electricity, but only when there is daylight, unless the energy generated can be stored in some way. Most solar panels currently on the market are made from thin wafers of crystalline silicon metal to convert sunlight to electricity. The wafers are about 150 mm square and 0.3 mm thick. 24 of these, assembled into panels or modules 1000 mm x 700 mm, are capable of generating 100 watts of electricity at full capacity. Photovoltaic systems have no moving parts, require no consumables and need little servicing. However they do generate heat in use, with temperatures reaching 30 °C behind the active panels, which will affect detail design.

The technology is now available. Availability of space should not be a problem – a PV generating complex with an area of 100 miles radius could provide all of the USA's electrical energy needs. However, the delivery of energy over long distances is a problem; the system is more viable when generated close to the user. Commercial use of these systems, though slow initially, grew to 280 MW generating capacity at the turn of the millennium and is forecast to reach 2,400 MW by 2010. Improvements in technology and volume production continue to bring down the cost. This reduction will continue whereas fossil fuel costs will continue to rise.

In some countries such as Japan, Germany and The Netherlands, governments have introduced programmes where grants or subsidies are available for consumers to install PV systems on roofs, selling electricity generated during the day to the supplying utility, and buying it back at night. Systems can either be added to the existing building (on walls or roof) or can be incorporated in the design of new developments (thus, building integrated photovoltaics or BIPV). In the year 2000 alone, Japan spent £300 million in support of PVs (for 70,000 rooftop installations by 2004) and Germany is planning 100,000 by the year 2003. In the UK however, take-up has been limited, but an account of one architect's experience of using PV in her own energy-efficient home, the Oxford Eco-House, will be of interest to readers (Roaf et al. 2001).

Other examples of photovoltaics in the UK include the BRE's Environmental building in Watford (designed by Feilden Clegg Bradley) and Studio E's PV-powered offices at Doxford in Sunderland. The latter features a massive curtain wall with 400,000 photovoltaic cells, which can generate over 55,000 kWh per annum. A new canopy by Feilden Clegg Bradley at the Earth Centre, near Doncaster will be one of the largest single arrays in the UK. It comprises 1,000 m² of PV modules supported by a timber space grid structure.

The real problem facing all renewable energy systems is that the move from traditional power sources to the new ones needs the active support of governments and industry to make progress against current commercial vested interests. Even though the system has great potential, it and other methods have not made great inroads against more traditional generating systems. As the change from carbon to silicon based methods of energy generation proceeds, photovoltaics may play a major part in the forthcoming 'hydrogen' economy. They may aid the conversion by electrolysis of water into hydrogen to be used either in special internal combustion engines or converted into electricity using fuel cells – the only emission being clean water.

Further reading

Bottger, W.O.J. & Schoes, A.J.N. (1995) *Building with photovoltaics*, Den Hagen, The Hague, The Netherlands.

Humm, O. & Toggweiler, P. (1993) *Photovoltaics in architecture*, Birkhäuser, Basle, Switzerland.

Roaf, S., Fuentes, M. & Thomas, S. (2001) *EcoHouse: a design guide*, Butterworth-Heinemann, Oxford, UK.

Sick, F. & Erge, T. (1996) *Photovoltaics in buildings*, James & James, London, UK.
Thomas, R. & Fordham, M. (2001) *Photovoltaics and architecture*, E & FN Spon, London, UK.

CS/JG

Piano, Renzo

Renzo Piano (b. 1937) has a most impressive portfolio of buildings to his name, all of which share a common theme in their delightful architectural detailing.

See also: CASTINGS; CLADDING; COMPOSITE MATERIALS; CONNECTIONS; FAÇADES AND FAÇADE ENGINEERING; FLOORS; GRC; HAPPOLD, SIR TED AND BURO HAPPOLD; HIGH TECH; INTEGRATION; KAHN, LOUIS; LOUVRES AND BRISE SOLEIL; PLASTICS; RICE, PETER; ROGERS, RICHARD; SERVICES; STRUCTURAL STEEL; TIMBER – LAMINATED TIMBER; WIND TOWERS; WINDOWS AND CURTAIN WALLING.

Piano & Rogers: Centre Georges Pompidou, Paris (1971–77). Escalators snake upwards in a delicate and transparent structure (by Peter Rice), which complements the building's sensitivity to urban place. Photograph by Thomas Deckker.

Renzo Piano was born in Genoa; he graduated from the School of Architecture of Milan Polytechnic in 1964. In 1965 he worked briefly for Louis Kahn in Philadelphia, and his influence may be seen strongly in Piano's early projects for geometrical structures such as the reinforced-polyester (GRP) pyramids of the vaulted Mobile Sulphur Extraction Factory, Pomezia (1966). He also lived in London: between 1971 and 1977, he was a partner with Richard Rogers in Piano & Rogers, and from 1977 to 1979 with the engineer Peter Rice (as Piano & Rice). Piano now practices as the Renzo Piano Building Workshop in Genoa, Paris, and Berlin. Piano is often thought of, with good reason, as a 'high-tech' architect, although his approach is rather distinct from this movement, with an interest in a wide range of constructional and social issues.

Piano and Rogers were the architects, with the engineer Peter Rice, of one of the most brilliant and controversial buildings of the 1970s: the Centre Georges Pompidou, Paris (1971–77). Apparently rooted in the pop architecture of 1960s London, with giant kinetic displays towards the 'place'. It also reflected the work of Kahn, for example in the separation of servant and served spaces; circulation towards the 'place', mechanical services towards the rue de Renard, with the open gallery spaces in between and the provision of what is in effect an entire service floor between the trusses. These 3 m deep trusses give an uninterrupted floor span of 50m; they end on the line of the exterior wall, where they are supported by cast steel cantilever beams known as 'gerberettes', which in turn rest on steel columns stabilised by steel tension rods. All the mechanical services were exposed both inside and out, most spectacularly the air-handling plant on the roof and extract ducts in the 'place'.

The Centre Pompidou initiated the use of several new technologies in architecture such as cast steel and fabricated trusses, as well as the fashion for brightly-coloured ducts. All the technologies were either new or untried at this scale and much research was conducted, not least into fire protection, such as the water-filled columns. Piano, however, denied that his motivation was technological innovation, but rather urban and expressive. The Centre Pompidou has, in fact, been extraordinarily popular and acted as the driver for the renovation of the Marais district in Paris.

As might be expected, the Centre Pompidou has been subject to much popular criticism for its novelty. On the other hand, it has been overwhelmed by its success as a public space. The colossal visitor numbers, combined with a reduced specification for finishes towards the end of its construction period, resulted in an extensive refurbishment programme led by Piano between 1996–2000. At a professional level, there have been criticisms that it is not suitable as a repository for works of art, which are displayed in a rather conservative exhibition space built as a virtually separate building. These have been countered by citing the flexibility and adaptability of the structure as suitable for contemporary conceptions of design for example at the opening, with an entire range of tractors and earth-moving equipment on the ground floor.

As might be expected, Piano was not able to undertake much other work during the construction of the Centre Pompidou. In 1979, he devised a programme for the restoration of historic towns in Italy for UNESCO. This followed a consultancy, with Peter Rice, for FIAT in which they proposed to replace the monocoque construction of cars with a tubular frame with replaceable infill panels; this introduced Piano to technologies such as polycarbonate, ductile iron and adhesives. In 1981, Piano started the restructuring of the Schlumberger Headquarters in Paris, which led to the commission for the Menil Collection, Houston in 1982, again with Peter Rice as engineer. The Menil Collection is scarcely less brilliant than the Centre Pompidou, although at the scale of an American suburban house rather than a Parisian *hôtel*. It consisted generally of single-storey galleries clad in cedar boards over a steel frame, but with the astonishing device of brise-soleil in the roof made of ferro-cement lamina held in a ductile steel frame. It is a theme continued in his recent work at the Beyeler Foundation Museum, Basle (1991–97).

Piano's work is not restricted to 'high-tech' materials, however; he initiated the interest in terracotta rainscreen cladding, which had the advantage of removing site labour from the construction of brick walls. It was first used on the Rue de Meaux Housing (1987–91) and the IRCAM Extension (1988–90) in Paris, and subsequently at the Cité Internationale in Lyon.

Timber and lightweight construction had been constant preoccupations with Piano since his early days; these may be seen in the IBM travelling pavilion (1983) which consisted of a series of polycarbonate shells forming a space frame with timber struts. As recognition of the craft element that played a large part in 'high-tech' architecture, the timber struts were laminated into cast steel nodes. In the travelling Musical Space for the Opera *Prometeo*, Venice and Milan (1983–84), a separate performance space was built from laminated timber ribs to house the stage and 400 spectators. Timber construction reached its extreme in scale in the Jean Marie Tjibaou Cultural Center, Nouméa, New Caledonia (1993–1998) in which enormous laminated timber columns act as screens (i.e. wind-catchers) to ventilate the buildings.

Piano is now engaged in several very large-scale works such as the reconstruction of a section of Potsdamer Platz, Berlin (1996–2000) and Kansai International Airport Terminal, Osaka (1990–94), which at 1.7 km long, is one of the biggest buildings in the world. It has curvaceous steel trusses, which also act as laminar ducts for the air-conditioning. These projects have pushed Piano's ability to organise to the extreme and it is to his credit that he has completed them successfully without sacrificing the attention to detail, which characterises his more modest projects.

Further reading

Buchanan, P. (ed.) (1993, 1994, 1997 and 2000) *Renzo Piano building workshop: complete works* (Volumes 1–4), Phaidon Press, London, UK.

Piano, R. (1989) *Renzo Piano Building Workshop: buildings and projects 1971–1989*, Rizzoli International Publications, New York, USA.

Piano, R. (with Lampungnani, V.L.) (1995) *Renzo Piano 1987–1994*, Birkhäuser, Basle, Switzerland.

Piano, R. (with Brignolo, R.) (1997) *The Renzo Piano logbook*, Thames & Hudson, London, UK.

TD

Pilotis

See: COLUMNS; LE CORBUSIER; NIEMEYER, OSCAR

Pisé

See: EARTH CONSTRUCTION

Planning grid

See: GRIDS FOR STRUCTURE AND LAYOUT

Plasterboard

A gypsum-based board material with heavy-duty paper facings; used as a lining in timber and light steel frame construction methods.

See also: ACOUSTICS; BRICKS AND BLOCKS; CONDENSATION; DRY CONSTRUCTION AND WET CONSTRUCTION; FIRE PROTECTION; FIT-OUT; LIGHT STEEL FRAME; TIMBER; WALLS.

What is plasterboard?

Plasterboard comprises heavy-duty paper facings, bonded either side of a gypsum core. It is used generally as a lining to walls and ceilings, and occasionally as an interlayer in floors. Different board specifications and developed systems enable it to be tailored to particular applications, supported by extensive testing and assessment by the manufacturers. Continuous, market focussed development provides a considerably extended range of applications e.g. acoustic and fire resisting applications with multiple layers of plasterboard, or plasterboard in conjunction with other board materials, coatings and insulation.

About the material

Gypsum plasterboard, or wallboard, has developed from common usage as a lining board for timber stud walls, as an alternative to wet plastering on masonry walls, and an integral part of the performance and specification of light steel frame elements. Consistent product and manufacturing standards have generated a market for recommended specifications of a wide variety of fire, acoustic and thermal requirements giving assured performance levels when applied correctly. The gypsum plaster core materials are sourced either from pure mined gypsum, or from chemically recovered gypsum. Core density can be defined during manufacture by entrapment of air in the gypsum slurry; properties can be modified further by use of additives such as glass fibre or vermiculite. Paper facings are generally supplied one side for decoration direct (in jointed finishes), and one side for plastering (in skimmed finishes). Alternative facings (e.g. with foil) are applied for specific functions such as moisture or vapour resistance.

Boards are usually made in widths of 400, 600, 900, or 1200 mm, and once fixed can be finished by jointing with special compounds, or by a wet plaster skim coat over the whole wall. Commonly available thicknesses are 6, 9.5, 12.5, 15 and 19 mm. Board weights therefore vary accordingly and by manufacturer, but typically fall within 5.5–15.5 kg/m². The use of plasterboard is covered by British Standards: BS 1230, BS 8212, and BS 5234. The basic types of plasterboard include:

- **Standard wallboard** (Type 1) – general application for wall and ceiling linings;
- **Moisture resistant boards** (Types 3 and 4) – greater resistance to moisture, but vapour permeable;
- **Firecheck boards** (Type 5) – improved fire protection properties;
- **Baseboard** (Type 6) – lining board for wet plastering;
- **Vapour check** – impermeable face for vapour control situations;
- **Impact resistant boards** – robust specification for partitions vulnerable to impact damage;
- **Acoustic boards** – specially formulated for use in acoustic built up systems;
- **Thermal laminates** – boards bonded to insulation for improved thermal performance.

Plasterboard can be direct fixed by the use of nails (to timber), adhesive bonding (to masonry or other substrates), or self drill screws (to light steel stud or frame sections). Proprietary fixing systems are available for application of boards to substrates that are not level, plumb, or in sufficiently sound condition for direct fix methods. It is normal for manufacturers to offer a range of stud systems, bead trims, decorative panels and accessories for use with their boards. A number of manufacturers also produce paperless, fibre reinforced gypsum boards that offer increased fire resistance and enhanced structural performance.

Information from manufacturers is the best source of data for plasterboard specification.

GW

Plastics

A wide range of synthetic materials created by chemistry rather than nature that are found in many aspects of building construction.

See also: AIR SUPPORTED STRUCTURES; CLADDING; COMPOSITE MATERIALS; EPOXY; ETFE; GRC; INSULATION; MINERAL FIBRES; PLASTICS – FABRICATION; PLASTICS – TYPES; PLASTICS FOR ADHESIVES AND FINISHES; SEALANTS; SICK BUILDING SYNDROME; SINGLE PLY MEMBRANES; TEXTILE MEMBRANE ROOFS.

Introduction

Plastic materials were developed during the 20th century and are the creation of chemists; they are not found in nature. It was once considered that they might become the 'wonder' materials of the future for all applications, but the areas of use are now well defined, based on where the specific properties are most appropriate. The next four entries are devoted to plastics: their types, fabrication and uses. This first entry provides a general introduction to what is now a very broad subject area.

Historical overview

The 20th century saw many technological developments, but one of the most important advances was in the field of materials technology. There are a few materials in nature that have some of the properties of plasticity, including bitumen, shellac, casein, cellulose, rosin and of course natural rubber from trees. However, it was industrial chemists who invented and developed materials that did not exist in any natural state and which were made from basic chemicals. Progress has been so great that the very term 'plastics' describes an enormous range of materials that differ very widely from one another both in properties and applications.

Modern plastics are derived chemically from crude oil (and sometimes from natural gas) and are mostly carbon based. In the oil refining process the oil is split into different types, the difference being their range of boiling points. Many of these are used as fuels, but the materials generally used to make plastic materials are Naptha based. This is 'cracked' or broken down into large hydrocarbon molecules that result in a gas or liquid that has polymerised to form long chain molecules. From this liquid the specific raw material needed is made in the form of a fluid, powder or granule.

Initially, man-made plastics developed slowly. In the 1860s cellulose nitrate was processed, known as 'Celluloid' (a thermoplastic), casein derived from milk was used as mouldings and as an adhesive (a thermoset). Cellulose acetate superseded 'Celluloid' and in 1907 phenol-formaldehyde, known as 'Bakelite' (a thermoset) came into use. Much development took place in the 1920s and 1930s, but the greatest strides were made in the 1940s and 1950s, especially post 1945 when the basic plastics were developed. Plastics chemistry and production technology then saw the development of most of the engineering and specialist plastics; in fact it is now technically possible to have a plastics material 'tailored' to the required end use.

Basic chemistry

The chemistry of plastics is quite complex, but a simple explanation will suffice. Atoms are very small particles, but they form together to make molecules and are joined by 'bonds' or 'valencies'. The carbon atom will link with hydrogen in various ways and numbers. 'Paraffins' will give methane, ethane, propane and butane, while 'olefins' give ethelene and propelene. When making plastics, the chemist will induce a chemical change to the paraffinic chain, which is called polymerisation; the result is a polymer. Thermoplastics are generally formed by 'addition polymerisation' where the compounds called monomers are triggered by a catalyst. Thermoset and some thermoplastics are formed by 'condensation polymerisation' where the reaction caused by a catalyst will give off water or another simple substance to form the plastic material.

Thermoplastics and thermosetting plastics

Thermoplastic materials, when subjected to heat, will turn from a solid into a fluid, which can then be manipulated or formed, and when the heat source is removed and the material cools, will again become solid. This change therefore is a physical change only since it is reversible. The raw material is generally available in powder or granule form. It can be moulded directly into its final shape or made into a suitable form such as sheet for further processing.

Thermosetting materials however undergo a chemical change when a catalyst is added and/or when heat is applied – the long chain molecules cross-link and cannot be reformed. The raw material is generally a powder when pressed in a mould or a liquid when 'laid-up' (see *Plastics – fabrication*).

Uses

Plastics have so many applications that almost every person regularly comes into contact with them, often unknowingly. Plastics are used in buildings mainly for non-structural elements (except for certain GRP mouldings). Plastics have superseded many natural materials and can now be found in applications such as:

- Insulation – much use is made of foamed polystyrene and polyurethane;
- Pipework – PVC and ABS, and fittings of all kinds;
- Windows – UPVC is now very widely used.

Plastics mouldings feature in everyday products, from computers to kitchen bowls to packaging etc. However other products and systems use plastics often in an unrecognised form; many fabrics are now either wholly or partially made from plastics materials from clothing to furnishing, and most currently used finishes and adhesives are plastics based. Its use in building structures is quite limited. In the early days of plastics development, prototypes of complete plastic houses were constructed, but were never developed into large-scale use. There have been examples of special roof structures, but most applications have been for non-structural applications, such as cladding panels. Remember however that plastics applications include fabrics and membranes; plastics can be seen in air supported and textile membrane roof structures. However mouldings on a large scale can be seen; in some European budget hotels the bathrooms are complete GRP mouldings.

Responsible specification

When specifying plastics products, the type of plastic used should be appropriate for that application, but when faced with a choice (i.e. different finishes), advice should be taken. When plastics were first developed there was concern over environmental impacts of raw materials, factors in use and disposal. Raw materials are carbon based, so in the future there may be the need to investigate alternatives. In use it has been found that plastics do degrade, and concern has also been expressed about chemical emissions. Plastics do not last forever, and the need for recycling is well understood.

Further reading

Birley, A.W. (1988) *Plastics materials, properties and applications*, Blackie & Sons, UK.

Brydson, J.A. (1999) *Plastics materials*, Butterworth-Heinemann, Oxford, UK.

Dietz, A.G.H. (1969) *Plastics for architects and builders*, MIT Press, Massachusetts, USA.

CS

Plastics – fabrication

Since plastics are produced in a fluid or granular form they have to be processed into a useable state to suit the intended application. The fabrication of thermoplastics and thermosetting plastics are described.

See also: AIR SUPPORTED STRUCTURES; CLADDING; COMPOSITE MATERIALS; EPOXY; ETFE; GRC; INSULATION; MINERAL FIBRES; PLASTICS; PLASTICS–TYPES; PLASTICS FOR ADHESIVES AND FINISHES; SEALANTS; SINGLE-PLY MEMBRANES; TEXTILE MEMBRANE ROOFS.

Introduction

Different production systems are necessary partially because of the differences in processing thermoplastics and thermosetting materials, and also the scale and nature of the required end product. The systems described below are used to produce final products, or to process the material into a form so that further working may take place. Different systems are needed when using plastics as finishes or adhesives. The choice of plastic material and the fabrication system to be used is also affected by production economics. For instance an injection-moulded container that takes only a minute to form can be totally complete when it is ejected from the machine. However, when the cost of the mould and the capital outlay on the machine are taken into account, high volumes are necessary to justify the investment. A GRP lay-up uses comparatively simple moulds, but quality pattern-making skills are needed. The equipment is basic, but the process is labour intensive and tends to be used to make low volume, high value products.

Thermoplastics

The raw material is normally in granular form, so most systems are designed for this. However some processes use the plastic in film or sheet form, which has to be pre-made.

Vacuum forming – In vacuum forming a sheet of plastic is formed over a simple shape or mould. Although once a popular method for forming larger items such as baths and skylights and for packaging applications, the benefits of injection moulding in smaller sized items and the need to use already processed plastic in sheet form lessens the attractiveness of the process. In this basic method a container or box is made from which air can be extracted. The mould is placed in the container and a sheet of plastic is clamped above the open face of the container, held in a frame, which is airtight. The plastic sheet is heated and when at the correct flexibility the air in the container is removed and atmospheric pressure presses the plastic sheet over the mould. When the sheet has cooled the plastic item can be removed from the frame and the part that is required, i.e. the area formed over the mould, can be trimmed. However, since this simple arrangement makes the plastic sheet quite thin, advanced machinery has been developed where the sheet is heated on both sides, and the mould moves hydraulically up into the sheet.

Extrusion – The basic principle is that of a toothpaste tube. A fluid is forced through a shaped opening (or die) and a length of material is extruded. The actual machinery, of course, is much more complicated. The plastic granules are fed through a hopper into a barrel. The plastic is moved by an Archimedian screw along the barrel, which is heated so that the plastic is fluid and under pressure. At the end of the barrel is a die that will give the extruded plastic the desired section. As the plastic is pushed through the die the extruded shape is supported and cooled. Many different dies can be used and almost any shape, including tubes and sheets, is possible. Most thermoplastic materials can be formed by this process.

Injection moulding – The basic principle is that of a hypodermic syringe. The fluid material is heated as in the extruder, but the plastic will be injected into a closed mould where the void is the required final shape. The injection machine has a plunger that delivers a measured amount of plastic into the mould. The mould is cooled, the plastic solidifies, the mould opens and the moulding is ejected. Very complex shapes can be made but the cost of moulds and machines is very high, although labour costs are low.

Blow moulding – This method is based on either the extrusion or the injection machines. With the extrusion method special dies are made to enable the extruded section to be blown into the required shape, while a similar method is used when injection moulding. Most plastic bottles are made from this method.

Rotary moulding – It would be too expensive to make an injection mould tool to make a container as large as a car, but if large volume containers are needed the rotary moulding method can be used. A large but simple sheet metal mould that can be heated is made. The plastic powder is introduced into the heated mould while it revolves in all directions. The plastic initially flows to form a skin on the inside face of the mould and as the heat is reduced, solidifies on the mould surface.

Thermosetting plastics

Since these cure when exposed to heat, different techniques and approaches to the above are needed.

Compression moulding – The principle used is that of a two part closed mould into which a measured amount of plastic is inserted. The mould is then closed and heated so that the plastic cures and hardens under pressure. Because of advances in both machinery and plastic materials technology, this moulding method is used less, since advanced thermoplastics can be used instead of thermosetting plastics and some machinery has been adapted to inject thermoplastic materials.

GRP lay-up – At its basic, this is a very simple technique (sometimes referred to as 'bucket and brush') and is suitable for large-scale work at low volumes. The materials concerned consist of a liquid thermosetting plastic and specific reinforcing membranes. An example of use has been in making complex and sculptural architectural forms. The general approach is to:

1. Make a timber/plastic/resin 'plug' of the item that is required;
2. From this, make a mould (generally in GRP) that is sectioned so that it may be dismantled when the item is complete;
3. Apply release agent to the surface of the mould;
4. When dry, apply a gel coat of resin; this will duplicate the surface of the mould, whether it be smooth or textured;
5. Lay up with resin, any reinforcing mats, with as many layers as required;
6. When cured, trim the edges, dismantle the mould and polish the surface of the item. In certain applications internal ribs may be laid up on the interior surface to strengthen the moulding.

This method is in general use, but for large mouldings the resin and glass strand mat can be sprayed into position. If the item is small, but injection moulding is not economically feasible, GRP items can be compression moulded using low pressure matched moulds.

Resins and reinforcing

The common resins and reinforcings used are polyester resins of various viscosities and glass fibres in the form of chopped strand mat or woven fabric. However, for special work the resin may be epoxy or any other hard wearing thermosetting plastic and the reinforcing, in addition to glass, can include carbon fibre or similar high strength plastics.

Foamed plastics

The above sections refer to plastics as a solid, but they can be manufactured in other forms (such as fabric). A common use is as foams; most plastics can be formulated in this way. The most commonly available foamed thermoplastic is polystyrene and is well known as insulation tiles or sheets. This is formed in closed moulds by introducing steam into the mould, which causes the styrene to foam.

The most common thermoset when used structurally is polyurethane (PU) – polyethers and polyesters are used in furniture upholstery foam. PU is a very economic method of producing mouldings and uses fairly cheap low pressure moulds. A blowing agent is incorporated with the plastic when the foam is pumped into the cavity causing the PU to foam and expand to fill the space. It has the advantage of being able to be formulated to make a skin when the material comes in contact with the mould surface.

As well as being moulded, PU can also be formulated as a spray which is sprayed on to a surface where the fluid will adhere to that surface but expand and then cure. This is often used for insulation purposes. Many plastics can also be used as sealants and are simply extruded into position from a simple 'gun' applicator.

Rapid prototyping

A problem with many of the above systems was that it could be very difficult to make products with undercut shapes or re-entrant curves that made removal from the mould very difficult. However, a method of producing three-dimensional items directly from a computer programme has been developed for rapid prototyping. Stereo lithography is one of these systems whereby a fluid resin is placed in a container and a three-dimensional laser is directed through the volume of the fluid. Where the laser points meet, the fluid solidifies and thus a very complex moulding with threads and all manner of 3D shapes can be produced. Even though this is often used for a pre-production prototype, it will be possible to manufacture very special items directly for use.

Further reading

Birley, A.W. (1988) *Plastics materials, properties and applications*, Blackie & Sons, UK.

Brydson, J.A. (1999) *Plastics materials*, Butterworth-Heinemann, Oxford, UK.

Leggatt, A. (1984) *GRP and buildings; a design guide for architects and engineers*, Butterworth-Heinemann, Oxford, UK.

CS

Plastics – types

The full range of plastics would be a very long list: the following are those typically used in construction and building products.

See also: AIR-SUPPORTED STRUCTURES; CLADDING;
COMPOSITE MATERIALS; EPOXY; ETFE; GRC; INSULATION;
MINERAL FIBRES; PLASTICS – FABRICATION; PLASTICS FOR
ADHESIVES AND FINISHES; SEALANTS; SINGLE-PLY MEMBRANES;
TEXTILE MEMBRANE ROOFS.

The following plastics have been given a code to indicate their method of manufacture:

- **Tp** Thermoplastics;
- **Ts** Thermosetting plastics.

ABS Acrylonitrile Butadiene Styrene (Tp)

This has better chemical resistance and surface gloss than Polystyrene (Ps) or Polypropylene (Pp) and is strong and tough. Generally injection moulded, but can be used for vacuum forming. Used for all automotive parts and domestic products. Sometimes available in sheet form but generally as granules for precision mouldings. In buildings it is used in paint coatings for concrete and in formliners (plastic sheets that produce patterns on the surface).

Acrylic (PMMA) Polymethyl Methacrylate (Tp)

A clear sheet with good optical properties and weathering resistance, but can be brittle. Used as an interlayer in laminated glass. Can be moulded but often available in sheet form. Originally used as a plastic equivalent of glass and in the early days of aviation for aircraft. It has the interesting property of transmitting light from edge to edge in strip or sheet form. Can be machined, vacuum formed or moulded, but due to acrylic's brittleness, polycarbonate is now preferred for glazing applications.

Glass fibre (GRP) (Ts)

The two constituent parts are resin and a reinforcing material. The resin has to have a catalyst added to it in order to start the chemical reaction and often an accelerator is added to control the rate of curing. The common resin used is polyester (see below), but higher performance resins such as epoxy may be used.

Nylon PolyAmide (Tp)

Has excellent mechanical properties, is rigid, has good dimensional stability and fair heat resistance. Can be moulded by normal processing methods and is used for a range of industrial components such as gear wheels etc. Also used widely as fibres and filaments for clothing and is generally available in its end use form.

Polycarbonate (Tp)

In addition to being transparent it has good mechanical and electrical properties. It is very tough and has a hard, gloss surface. It has properties such as low water absorption, high heat resistance and is self-extinguishing. It can be processed by both injection and extrusion methods and is used for engineering and technical applications. Presently preferred in glazing applications to acrylics. Polycarbonate was specified by Herzog & De Meuron for their Ricola factory in France. Coloured polycarbonate cladding is also available.

Polyester (Ts or Tp)

Although certain formulations can be thermoplastic it is generally found as a thermoset. Most commonly used as a laminating resin (see GRP above). It is also used as a fibre (terylene) or as a film (melinex) and is often used as a surface coating.

Polypropylene (Tp)

It has a fair resistance to heat and chemicals, has good resilience, resistance to creep, does not stress crack and can be moulded by the usual methods. It has one very interesting property; unlike other plastics when a thin section is flexed it does not break, but becomes stronger. This has caused it to be used as a hinge and in products such as chair shells and other applications where this feature is advantageous. It is very versatile, can be moulded, blown into containers, made into ropes and nets, fibres for clothing and many other applications.

Polystyrene – Ps (Tp)

Solid Ps is a very common moulding material, since it moulds well, replicates detailed surface textures from the mould surface and is relatively inexpensive. However, for quality applications ABS or polypropylene may be preferred. Toughened Ps gives the material better properties but also increases price. However it has been used for vacuum forming applications. Expanded Ps is available in moulded or sheet form. It has very good insulation properties and is often used in packaging applications.

Polyurethane – PU (Ts)

This is available in many different forms such as foams, surface coatings, moulded components and fibres and is generally of two types either flexible or rigid. Rigid foams compete with Ps foam, but as well as being moulded they can be sprayed or poured. PU finishes are tough and chemically resistant. Mouldings have a high abrasion and impact resistance while fibres are made into many different types of fabric. Flexible foams are used widely in upholstery.

PTFE PolyTetraFluoroEthelene – Teflon™ (Tp)

This has many advantages. It has good resistance to chemicals and weathering, high temperature resistance and its main feature its low friction and non-stick properties. The disadvantage is that it can be difficult to mould using the normal processes, rather it has to be sintered into blocks and fabricated or sintered onto metal surfaces. Most of its uses are for industrial applications and bearing lubrications and of course for its non-stick properties in kitchenware. Also used for coatings on canopy roofs.

PVC PolyVinylChloride (Tp)

Available in many forms, it is a good general purpose plastic. In its rigid formulation it has been used in many products including rainware, soil pipes and windows. In its plasticised form it has been used as clothing and upholstery fabrics. It can be moulded in all the different processes. However, with the development of plastic materials tailored to specific end uses some of its applications have devolved to newer materials.

UPVC Unplasticised PolyVinylChloride (Tp)

PVC as described above is normally flexible, and has to be modified in order to be used as a rigid material, and therefore the unplasticised formulation is used in the most common applications. This makes the plastic suitably rigid and easily joined by using solvent jointing/welding. It has good thermal stability and is used above ground for rainwater goods and windows, where its properties of rigidity, low cost, UV stability, chemical resistance and ease of jointing are well recognised. Below ground it is used for drainage, but for some complex injection moulded products an alternative such as ABS is substituted. The issue of longevity is important however. PVC, amongst other plastics, have been found to be effective in the short to medium term, but time is needed to confirm the amount of degradation in very long term for above ground use.

Further reading

Birley, A.W. (1988) *Plastics materials, properties and applications*, Blackie & Sons, UK.

Brydson, J.A. (1999) *Plastics materials*, Butterworth-Heinemann, Oxford, UK.

Leggatt, A. (1984) *GRP and buildings; a design guide for architects and engineers*, Butterworth-Heinemann, Oxford, UK.

CS

Plastics for adhesives and finishes

Even though plastics are recognisable as products, it must be remembered that they are also used in other common, but less obvious applications.

See also: AIR-SUPPORTED STRUCTURES; CLADDING; COMPOSITE MATERIALS; CONNECTIONS; EPOXY; ETFE; GRC; INSULATION; MINERAL FIBRES; PLASTICS – FABRICATION; PLASTICS – TYPES; SEALANTS; SINGLE-PLY MEMBRANES; SURFACE FINISHES; TEXTILE MEMBRANE ROOFS; TIMBER – LAMINATED TIMBER.

Adhesives

Until the early 20th century, adhesives were based on natural materials, but the plastics industry has developed to the extent that plastics-based adhesives are now much stronger and used more widely. In joining timber, naturally based materials would often suffer in damp conditions and because of this, laminating and pre-forming of timber did not become practical until the development of synthetic resins. Initially based on Urea Formaldehyde and then latterly using phenol or resorcinol chemicals the resulting adhesive bonds were much stronger than the timber itself and are entirely waterproof. Modern PVA adhesives have also vastly improved, and special adhesive systems can be tailored to suit the material and its end use.

The joining of metals is more of a problem, but epoxy resins were developed as were 'super glues' based on isocyanates. In some industries, however, such as aircraft manufacturing, adhesives have been developed that are as strong as traditional welding especially when using advanced metal alloys.

Finishes

Similar to adhesives, finishes were based on natural materials. Various 'paints' were available and generally based on natural powders (e.g. lime), oils and lead. In timber finishing, linseed oil, shellac-based fluids and natural waxes were used.

As plastics were developed for moulding materials, chemistry was used to make surface coatings that were much stronger and durable than their natural alternatives. Due, however, to ecological concerns, many manufacturers are now supplying water-, not solvent-, based finishes and the use of these materials has become quite common in the timber finishing industries.

For finishing of metals, a major method has been based not on surface application, but by forms of electrical deposition of another metal that is less susceptible to corrosion; various types of plating are in common use, the widest known are chromium plating and galvanising for steel and anodising for aluminium. Most of the paint systems, however, are now plastics based; the type used is dependent on the end use of the product.

Plastics can be applied using powders rather than a paint system on to metals. If using thermoplastics, powder coating provides a method of encapsulating the metal parts. The component is heated, dipped into a 'fluidised bed' where the powder is suspended by air jets, the plastic melts and adheres to the component and after removal is normalised to an even film thickness in a lower temperature oven. It is possible, however, that since in this case plastic does not form a strong bond with the substrate, cuts in the film can allow moisture penetration and allow corrosion underneath the plastic. This can be largely alleviated by using a thermoset material. The method is similar but the powder adheres to the metal and, on further heating, crosslinks to form a hard surface, which is fused to the substrate.

In timber finishing, paints and lacquers based on various plastic materials are used. In the early days these were based on phenol urea or melamine formaldehyde, but more recently, finishes have been based on polyurethane, polyester or epoxy resins.

Further reading

Birley, A.W. (1988) *Plastics materials, properties and applications*, Blackie & Sons, UK.
Brydson, J.A. (1999) *Plastics materials*, Butterworth-Heinemann, Oxford, UK.
Leggatt, A. (1984) *GRP and buildings; a design guide for architects and engineers*, Butterworth-Heinemann, Oxford, UK.

CS

Plywood

See: TIMBER – MANUFACTURED BOARDS

Pods

Modular fully finished room units made off site, often for bathrooms or other highly serviced facilities.

See also: BUILDING SYSTEMS; CONCRETE; CONSTRUCTION PROGRAMME; CRITICAL PATH ANALYSIS; 'JUST-IN-TIME' CONSTRUCTION; 'LEAN' CONSTRUCTION; LIGHT STEEL FRAMING; MODULES AND MODULAR CONSTRUCTION; OFF-SITE MANUFACTURE; PROCUREMENT; SERVICES; TIMBER; TECHNOLOGY TRANSFER.

What is a pod?

The use of modular construction methods for fully finished units enables the production of complex, highly serviced rooms off site, with the same general benefits as for other off-site manufacture. This enables the building, commissioning, and testing to be completed prior to installation. The word 'pod' is generally given to a self-contained module that requires only minimal work to connect when it arrives on site. The term was used in the offshore oil industry for many years before 'technology transfer' brought it to buildings. The main advantage of pods is to take wet trades in particular off the list of critical path activities being undertaken on site. Serviced pods are used to apply the benefits of off-site manufacture to bathrooms, toilets and kitchens, ICT, lifts, plant rooms (HVAC, M&E, etc.), switchgear, telecommunications and radio equipment.

Advantages of pods

The major benefit from using pods is the match with the principles of 'Lean thinking'; offering customer-focused deliverables and value.

- **Critical path** – the supply of pods can be on a JIT basis ('Just-in-time'), manufactured off site at a different point in the programme, then delivered when needed;
- **Speed** – the installation of pre-finished units dramatically reduces construction times at all levels;
- **Quality** – production in factory conditions usually delivers higher standards of compliance and finish, in particular allowing pre-installation testing and certification;
- **Elimination of waste** – centralised manufacture improves materials control when compared to piecemeal methods;
- **Skills** – key skills can be retained at centres of manufacture. The effects of lower skill levels on site are avoided;
- **Design** – compliance to design and specification is easier to achieve and check;
- **Adaptability** – roof level service modules are removed easily for refurbishment or replacement.

Design notes

Most of the considerations in the design of pods are the same for any modular type of construction. Currently the dominant structural material for pods is light steel frame, although hot rolled steel, timber frame, or other methods are sometimes used such as precast concrete (useful for durability e.g. in prison cells). The size of pods is usually limited by road transport constraints. In the UK the normal maximum size is 2.9 m wide and 4.5 m high (although localised restrictions might reduce these figures). Greater widths are possible, subject to police escort. For inclusion in shipping containers a maximum height and length of 2.3 × 12.2 m usually applies. If the overall size exceeds sensible transport arrangements, the pod can be designed to comprise several modular units. Units are designed to retain rigidity during lifting and transport in order to eliminate damage to finishes, but when the framework alone is insufficient for this, diaphragm rigidity is achieved with rigid board linings such as plywood, gypsum fibreboard, or profiled steel sheet. Perhaps the most important consideration is that both the pod and the main structure for which it is destined must be designed to be compatible:

- Access for installation must be considered as part of the design concept; pods may be craned in from above or fed in from a loading bay;
- The main structure must be designed to support the load imposed by the pod;
- Service connections must be pre-determined early and ready for installation;
- Depth of the pod floor deck must be allowed for if a level access/egress is required.

Further reading

Building Services Research & Information Association (1999) *Prefabrication and pre-assembly – applying the techniques to building engineering services*, BSRIA, Bracknell, UK.

Construction Industry Research and Information Association (1997) *Standardisation and pre-assembly*, CIRIA Report 176, CIRIA, London, UK.

Gibb, A.G.F. (1999) *Off-site fabrication: prefabrication, pre-assembly and modularisation*, Whittles Publishing, Caithness, UK.

Warszawski, A. (1999) *Industrialized and automated building systems* (2nd edition), E & FN Spon, London, UK.

Womack, J. P. & Jones, D. T. (1996) *Lean thinking*, Simon & Schuster, New York, USA.

GW

Polycarbonate
See: PLASTICS – TYPES

Polyester
See: PLASTICS – TYPES

Polypropylene
See: PLASTICS – TYPES

Polystyrene
See: PLASTICS; PLASTICS – FABRICATION; PLASTICS – TYPES

Polyurethane
See: PLASTICS; PLASTICS – FABRICATION; PLASTICS – TYPES

Porosity
See: PERMEABILITY

Post-occupancy evaluation
See: PERFORMANCE

Precast concrete
See: CONCRETE – STRUCTURES

Prefabrication
See: OFF-SITE MANUFACTURE

Pre-patination
See: COPPER; METALS; ZINC

Pressure-equalised rainscreen
See: OVERCLADDING

Procurement

The framework within which a project is delivered, which often includes contractual arrangements.

See also: CONSTRUCTION PROGRAMME; CRITICAL PATH ANALYSIS; 'JUST-IN-TIME' CONSTRUCTION; LEAD-TIME; 'LEAN' CONSTRUCTION; OFF-SITE MANUFACTURE; ON-SITE PRODUCTION; RISK MANAGEMENT; VALUE ENGINEERING.

Introduction

The term procurement describes the general circumstances under which a building is delivered (i.e. conceived, designed and constructed). Three basic scenarios for the UK context are presented here (for more detailed accounts of the various routes, please refer to the books listed at the end of this entry). The term 'procurement route' has come to mean the framework for the legal, contractual and operational conditions that influence or control the way a project progresses. Thus, procurement can include more than just contractual terms; it may also include protocols for the strategic long-term working relationships between clients, designers and contractors (suppliers). The choice of procurement route will depend upon several factors including:

- Advice from the client's agents (e.g. architects, letting agents, surveyors);
- Any special characteristics in the brief;
- Building type under consideration;
- Client priorities e.g. speed, economy or high quality;
- Client's previous experience;
- Financing arrangements;
- Market conditions.

Traditional routes

The so-called 'traditional' routes are based on the premise that obtaining the lowest cost is the prime consideration in the decision-making process. Hence, competitive tendering requires an architect to work up a design to such a level of detail that individual contractors can price the job and submit a tender for consideration. This route may appeal to clients who are sure of what they require, perhaps with a small project using a tried-and-tested design, or are confident that their architects will design the scheme 'right first time'. However competitive tendering ignores the possibility that input from contractors, and specialist sub-contractors, may inform the quality of the design as a whole. Thus the tender prices may be artificially high to accommodate what may be an 'unbuildable' design. Indeed, following the 'letting of the contract' on a successful tender, contractors would be appointed at quite a late stage, when their advice may be difficult to incorporate in the design. Traditional routes favour small projects with 'normal' construction methods that can be managed by a main contractor, but these are fast becoming outdated for government and other large building clients, who are now looking to alternative procurement routes to satisfy their needs (i.e. 'Best Value' – the public sector procurement protocol). If a client continues to let discrete tenders on every project, then there is also little potential to develop long-term relationships that could help continuous improvement.

D&B and construction management

Perhaps the next logical step on from traditional procurement methods is to enlist the involvement of contractors earlier on in the process by having them undertake some of the design aspects as well. 'Design and build' contracts were the first step towards handing detail design responsibility over to the practitioners rather than architects, but there is no doubt that this route is best suited to simple buildings without any particularly important aesthetic requirements. A further development of the design-build idea extends the contract further into the operation of the building. This is design-build-finance-operate (DBFO) and is offered by some of the larger contracting organisations that also have facilities management expertise.

A more general development is 'construction management' whereby a construction management firm is in direct contact with the client early on in the design process to provide expertise before detailed design is undertaken and before specialist contracts are let. This much reduces the risks associated with competitive tendering. The construction manager provides input throughout the process, takes on single-point responsibility for the construction of the building and acts as translator between client and specialists. As some building types and client requirements have become more and more complex, the role of the construction manager has increased in importance. This is now a very popular procurement route and there are now several highly rated construction management firms in London alone, many of which have a multi-disciplinary approach, which reaps dividends on complex projects.

Partnering

Perhaps the next obvious step on from construction management is partnering. This is a procurement route that is suited to large, experienced clients that wish to establish better working relationships with their suppliers (architects, contractors and manufacturers) by negotiating, not on a project basis, but on a long-term relationship basis. In recent years, major UK construction clients (including government – public spending accounts for 40% of new build) have become dissatisfied with competitive tendering as a means of delivering good quality design and good quality buildings (see Latham (1994) and Egan (1998) reports). Partnering allows clients to establish stronger relationships with their suppliers and contractors, recruiting in accordance with their own value criteria. Thus the partners are able to work much more closely with the client organisation, discussions can be more wide ranging and focus on continuous improvement and learning that can be fed into more than just one project at a time. The client body can determine the criteria it uses to recruit its partners and can set targets (key performance indicators) to monitor progress on specific projects. The promise of ongoing work for large clients is a considerable lure for contractors and suppliers, but they have to fully support the notion of partnering and be prepared to engage in long-term improvements that benefit the client and the team as a whole. Critics of partnering suggest these can be 'cosy cartels' that discriminate against small, 'unfavoured' suppliers.

Further reading

Baden Hellard, R. (1995) *Project partnering: principle and practice*, Thomas Telford, London, UK

Bennett, J. (2000) *Construction: the third way*, Butterworth-Heinemann, Oxford, UK.

Bennett, J & Jayes, S. (1995) *Trusting the team*, Thomas Telford, London, UK.

Bennett, J. & Jayes, S. (1998) *The seven pillars of partnering*, Thomas Telford, London, UK

Egan, J. (1998) *Rethinking construction: the report of the Construction Task Force*, HMSO, London, UK.

Franks, J. (1998) *Building procurement systems: a client's guide*, (3rd edition), Longman, Harlow, UK.

Latham, M. Sir (1994) *Constructing the team: joint review of procurement and contractual arrangements in the UK construction industry*, HMSO, London, UK.

JG

Profiled metal decking

Steel strips formed in a 'corrugated' shape to add stiffness; typically used in floor and roof construction.

See also: ACOUSTICS; ALUMINIUM; BRACING; CEILINGS; CLADDING; CLADDING COMPONENTS; COMPOSITE DECKING; CONCRETE; FLOORS; GALVANISING; METALS; ROOFS; SURFACE FINISHES; ZINC.

What is profiled metal decking?

Adding strength to metal sheet by forming it into a corrugated profile has its origins in the 19th century with corrugated iron. In forming the profile, the effect of a series of linked webs and flanges is created, to give an economical structural support to other materials. The contemporary application is for floor, cladding and roof construction. Generically, these products are similar to profiled metal cladding, often in identical profiles, but with protective and decorative paint systems applied. Decking sections are either supplied in plain galvanised finish, painted to give a fair faced soffit, or aluminium.

Manufacture

Early profiles were curved or sinusoidal in section, but by the mid-20th century trapezoidal or box profiles broadened the range and capabilities of metal decking. Most profiles now follow this format, and some are further stiffened with ribs, or have re-entrant sections to suit services hangers. Sections are formed by feeding metal sheet (or 'strip') from a coil, through a series of roll formers. As it passes through the rolls the metal is gradually formed into the finished section and is then cut to length as it emerges. Some specialist shallow profiles are press formed. A range of profiles, in depths from 19 mm up to 225 mm (and 0.7, 0.9, 1.2 mm thickness), makes these products suitable for a wide variety of applications, typically supporting finishes or interlayers between main structural members, without the need for intermediate support. The concept has been developed further for permanent formwork and composite decking, used with in-situ concrete.

Applications and uses

These lightweight, but fairly stiff, steel and aluminium sheets have proved useful in a number of applications, mostly in the construction of floors and roofs for a wide variety of building types such as offices, warehouses, sports facilities, industrial buildings and retail.

Flat roofs – the decking spans between purlins or roof beams to support insulation, moisture control membranes, and the weathering layer. Typical specifications for large industrial or retail buildings use single ply membranes. Some manufacturers now offer bonded composites of decking, insulation, and weathering layer.

Pitched roofs – the decking spans between purlins as a sarking layer to support battens and tiles, along with membranes and insulation where specified.

Mezzanine floors – the decking spans over steel joists (often cold rolled sections), and supports either a boarded finish (e.g. chipboard, cement particle board), or lightweight concrete (as permanent formwork).

Composite decks/permanent formwork – used in conjunction with concrete, decking can act as permanent formwork for a lightweight in-situ slab, or as a composite deck.

Floor and wall panels – the structural characteristics of metal decking sections make them suitable for floor or wall diaphragm panels, either alone or screwed to board products. The composite action increases stiffness significantly.

Acoustic soffits and linings – acoustically perforated decking is manufactured by perforating the sheet before roll forming. A typical design features 4.5 mm holes in the web of the profile, behind which is sound absorbent material (e.g. mineral wool). Perforating reduces spanning capability by only about 10%.

Design notes

Decking sections are usually specified from the manufacturer's load span tables, based on a deflection limit of length/250 and calculated to BS 5950 (the structural code for steelwork). For roofing, a typical dead and superimposed load of 1.5 kN/m^2 is taken, but tables indicate a maximum load for a given span condition. Manufacturers can advise on extended load or span requirements. Spans vary from around 1.8 m for shallow aluminium decks, up to around 9.0 m for the deepest steel sections. Applications can be designed to take advantage of diaphragm action of a fixed profiled deck. This can provide wind bracing panels in roofs, or shear panels in walls.

Further reading

Couchman, G. et al. (2000) *Composite slabs and beams using steel decking*, SCI Publication 300, The Steel Construction Institute, Ascot, UK.

Lawson, R.M. (1989) *Design of composite slabs and beams with steel decking*, SCI Publication 055, The Steel Construction Institute, Ascot, UK.

Mullett, D.L. (1992) *Slim floor design and construction*, SCI Publication 110, The Steel Construction Institute, Ascot, UK.

Mullett, D.L. (1998) *Composite floor systems*, Blackwell Science, Oxford, UK.

Mullett, D.L. & Lawson, R.M. (1993) *Slim floor construction using deep decking*, SCI publication 127, The Steel Construction Institute, Ascot, UK.

GW

Proprietary goods and standardisation

Products that are made to a standard, branded and sold as such. Proprietary goods range in size from fixings to columns.

Bricks, windows, doors and balconies – standard goods are in use throughout buildings. This Dutch housing development gives an indication of the scope available. Photograph courtesy of Belton/Bevlon, Netherlands and the British Precast Concrete Federation.

See also: BESPOKE; OFF-SITE MANUFACTURE; SPECIFICATION.

Introduction

This entry considers the case for mass production of building elements from nails, screws etc. to doors and even up to whole building services modules. As a whole, this subject covers an approach to the production of buildings and their various component parts based on the rigour, efficiencies and economies of scale of a Fordist manufacturing industry. This is tempered by the need to meet the needs of users in providing either bespoke items or the capacity to 'customise'.

Proprietary and standard goods

In building construction the term proprietary is usually given to mean a standard product, available from manufacturer's stock, rather than a bespoke (tailor made) item. In legal terms, it may also be applied to any product that is protected by a registered trade name e.g. 'Slimdek' – steel floor beams (Corus plc) or 'Roofmate' – thermal insulation (DOW plc). Such stock items range from nuts and bolts to joinery and air-conditioning units. The benefits arising from proprietary products are:

- Choice from a 'normal' range;
- Simple, easy ordering;
- Rapid availability;
- Economic prices;
- Standard details to accompany;
- Proven tested products (often certified by the British Board of Agrément).

Standardisation

Clearly there are benefits to be gained from producing items on a large scale. For example, ordering is simple, there is consistency of operations in the factory, stock is easy to monitor and raw materials can be purchased in bulk quantities. Where products or building elements can be standardised (i.e. made to a consistent standard or model) all the benefits of mass production become available.

However, where buildings are designed by architects, the drive to satisfy end-user needs is often considered more important than forcing a building to be made to the logical manufacturing regime. This results in either designing the building to include some bespoke items or providing the capacity/opportunity for occupiers to personalise that building. In either case, it is the architect who would usually make the decision to provide such options.

There is a consistent historical trend that, despite many architects seeking the goal of a standardised building, more often than not this does not work on the whole building scale. Not only do architects find it difficult to conform to the regime of standardisation but their clients also find it very difficult to occupy such buildings. Suffice to say there are only a few exceptions to this rule including the UK post-war 'prefabs', erected as temporary housing, many of which still exist today and are Listed Buildings.

Striking a balance

The compromise in today's construction industry is that some elements of a building will appear as standardised with proprietary goods or repetitive elements within a standard specification. But almost without exception, these will be accompanied by a significant amount of other items made to customer-specification. The situation now is that suppliers of building products and components offer standard ranges, but many are equally willing to manufacture bespoke items. This affects a wide range of available products including:

- Building services;
- Cladding;
- Doors;
- Drainage;
- Flooring;
- ICT services;
- Kitchens;
- Lifts and escalators;
- Lighting;
- Roofing;
- Staircases;
- Structure: beams, columns, rafters;
- Windows.

The conclusion is that, where possible, building elements are standardised, but this is limited to those that are used on a very regular basis. In all other cases, items are produced on a less formal basis (customer specification) or completely tailor-made (bespoke).

JG

Prouvé, Jean

Jean Prouvé (1901–84) is perhaps best known for his contributions to the development of metal cladding and adaptive façade design.

See also: ALUMINIUM; CASTINGS; CLADDING; FAÇADES AND FAÇADE ENGINEERING; INTELLIGENT FAÇADES AND MATERIALS; LE CORBUSIER; METALS; MODULES AND MODULAR CONSTRUCTION; NIEMEYER, OSCAR; OFF-SITE MANUFACTURE; RITCHIE, IAN; WINDOWS AND CURTAIN WALLING.

Trained as a blacksmith and ironmonger in Nancy, France, Prouvé became perhaps the key 20th century figure in the application of industrial processes to modern construction. Whereas other modernist architects attempted to apply a degree of machine-made aesthetic to their buildings, Prouvé was the first to conceive and achieve the production of entire buildings as pure industrially designed and manufactured structures.

The Roland Garros Flying Club, Buc, France (1936, destroyed 1940) was probably the first fully industrialised building with mass produced pressed metal being used for its walls, roof, ramps and other components. Working with architects Beaudouin and Lods (Prouvé was not himself an architect), Prouvé went on to design highly adaptable buildings, the best of which was the Maison du Peuple in the Clichy district of Paris. This building was characterised by slender structural components, which gave high transparency to a building intended as an extension of the public realm, which housed a market hall, auditorium and social facilities. The floor, walls and roof of the 2,000 seat auditorium could be moved mechanically to allow enlargement or conversion to open air space. The structure was clad in a pioneering curtain wall system composed of stressed-skin panels separated from each other by coil springs. The building's hard, industrialised, 'nuts-and-bolts' construction became the architectural aesthetic in an expression of the working-class nature of the area. The architectural systems which Prouvé developed, from a movable wall system called 'mur rideau' (c. 1930), the first workable, movable wall system to metal cladding systems, were adopted and used by many of the great Modernist architects including Le Corbusier and Oscar Niemeyer. It is perceived by many as an early, mechanical example of an 'intelligent, adaptive façade'.

His next period of great creativity and influence came in the Post War era when he designed a great many single-storey buildings in pressed aluminium, which became his trademark, including his prefabricated Sahara-type houses (1958). Among his best buildings were:

- Housing estate of small dwellings made of aluminium at Meudon (1949);
- Spa building in Evian (1958);
- Temporary school in Villejeuf (1953);
- Free University in Berlin (1967–69);
- Congress hall in Grenoble (1967);
- Office tower at La Defense, Paris (1967);
- Service stations for Total (1968).

Jean Prouvé demonstrated that architecture could become an industrialised process without losing its soul and, furthermore, that costs could be kept down to allow the masses access to well-designed structures from considered and affordable components. Unfortunately, few that followed him were competent enough to have learnt the lessons he gave.

Further reading

Sulzer, P. (1999) *Jean Prouvé Complete Works (Volume 1: 1917–1933)*, Birkhäuser, Basle, Switzerland.
Sulzer, P. & Sulzer-Kleinemeier, E. (2000) *Jean Prouvé Complete Works (Volume 2: 1934–1944)*, Birkhäuser, Basle, Switzerland.

EH

PTFE: Teflon™
See: PLASTICS – TYPES; ETFE

PU: polyurethane
See: PLASTICS; PLASTICS – FABRICATION; PLASTICS – TYPES

Pultrusion
See: PLASTICS – FABRICATION; CASTINGS

Purging
See: NIGHT VENTILATION; VENTILATION

PVC: polyvinylchloride
See: PLASTICS – TYPES

Rainscreen
See: OVERCLADDING; WINDOWS AND CURTAIN WALLING

Raised access floor
See: FLOORS

Rammed earth
See: EARTH CONSTRUCTION

Ready-mixed concrete
See: CONCRETE

Reconstituted stone
See: CONCRETE – FINISHES

Refurbishment
See: DESIGN LIFE; FIT-OUT; LIFE-CYCLE COSTING; OVERCLADDING

Recycling
A process to recover useful materials such as metals and plastics and re-use or re-form them for another purpose/use.

See also: ALUMINIUM; CONCRETE; CONCRETE – STRUCTURES; EARTH CONSTRUCTION; ECOLOGICAL DESIGN; 'ECO-POINTS'; ENVIRONMENTAL DESIGN; INSULATION; LEAD; METALS; PLASTERBOARD; PLASTICS; STRUCTURAL STEEL; SUSTAINABILITY.

Introduction: the historical context
In the 1930s Picasso made old objects into art with what were called 'ready-mades', where a manufactured item could either possess artistic merits in its own right or

be reused in the creation of a composite sculpture as a 'found object'. During the Second World War, 21,000 salvage companies were created for the collection of metals including gum, chocolate and cigarette aluminium wrappers for aircraft fuselages as well as cooking fat for explosives. Such ideas of thrift, though necessary at that time, were soon replaced in the 1950s with the notions of disposability; the throwaway consumer society. In recent years, something in the order of about 80% of products are thrown away within six to eight weeks of purchase, which means that within two months of being produced, 98% of materials go to waste. **This is not sustainable**.

In the UK and Europe, there now exists specific legislation that requires the construction industry to recycle. Reclaiming old building materials is part of a protocol accepted by both the UK government as well as the European Parliament, which can be applied to building materials in the following ways. If a building can be re-used, then this is the best option. However, if it is to be wholly or partially demolished, then whole components such as doors, windows, bricks and tiles should be reclaimed. Individual materials such as brick rubble etc. should be recycled into aggregates or fill, and plastics reformed into new products.

About recycling

Recycling, i.e. the recovery and re-use of unwanted materials or products is an important way of reducing waste. It is a key part of sustainable design and construction, and reduces the environmental impacts associated with these activities. Recycling may take a variety of forms, depending on what is being recovered and for what purpose. For the purposes of this book, the following terms are used. Whole, intact products such as bricks can be **reclaimed**, rubble can be **recovered** and metals can be retrieved to be **recycled**. Commonly sought after products within the construction industry include:

- **Aluminium** (can be recycled at a fraction of the energy used in its production);
- **Bricks** (older sizes are valuable; ten old bricks notionally contain the energy equivalent of one gallon of petrol);
- **Concrete** (can be used for aggregate or fill);
- **Lead** (can be reclaimed and re-used);
- **Materials for aggregates** (e.g. stone, concrete and brick rubble);
- **Plasterboard** (off-cuts can be recycled);
- **Scrap steel for reinforcement** (UK produced reinforcement is made from 100% steel scrap);
- **Structural steel** (can be reclaimed or recycled).

Recycling and recycled products can actually prove to be useful building products for architects. In addition, they can create new sustainable industries, jobs and investment opportunities. There is a cash value in recycled products as well as an environmental value, hence the growth in architectural salvage companies.

Case study

In 1990, the Dutch government produced a 200-point comprehensive National Environment Plan with a 20-year aim to redirect their economy. Within the first ten years, several specific targets have been met; 55% of total waste is re-used and 10% prevented. All new houses are fully fitted with separate waste bins for food and garden products, wastepaper, electrical batteries, bottles, old clothes and shoes. Special days are set aside for the collection of other household items including metals, heavy wood and a 'chemo-car' for poisons, paints, etc. In addition, all districts have central collection bases and patrols of 'environmental police' to enforce the codes of practice. Recycling within a street or district area between neighbours is also encouraged and provisions are made within urban and architectural design. The plan also ensures that dangerous and toxic elements that might be included in the manufacture of cars, electrical goods (refrigerators, television sets, etc.) and other products are safely recovered. Consumers are simply required to pay a small 'recycling tax' on the cost of products.

Endnote: built examples

If one purchases a new BMW car, around 70% of it comes from recycled materials. On the other hand, if one procures a new building typically less than 1% comes from reclaimed materials or goods. This is changing, but slowly. The BRE's Environmental building was a test-bed for all devices environmental, including:

- 80,000 reclaimed bricks;
- 96% of the building it replaced was re-used;
- 90% of the in-situ concrete used recycled aggregate;
- Reclaimed wood parquet flooring was used.

The Wessex Water HQ near Bath by Bennetts Associates Architects and Buro Happold used concrete from recycled railway sleepers in an award-winning sustainable design. The Earth Centre near Doncaster used recovered concrete from an old colliery to form loose-fill, gabion style walls for its conference centre. In addition, all UK-produced steel reinforcement is a 100% recycled product, using only steel scrap in its manufacture.

Further reading

Hawken, P. (1993) *The ecology of commerce*, Harper Collins, London, UK.
The Institution of Structural Engineers (1999) *Building for a sustainable future: construction without depletion*, ISE/SETO, London, UK.

WH/JG

Reinforcement
See: CONCRETE – STRUCTURES; METALS; STAINLESS STEEL

Render
See: CEMENT; CONCRETE – FINISHES

Resin
See: EPOXY; PLASTICS; SEALANTS

Retaining walls

A retaining wall is used to hold back soil or other material. Retaining walls are built from all the common construction materials and can take a number of different forms.

See also: BRICKS AND BLOCKS; CANTILEVERS; CONCRETE; CONCRETE – STRUCTURES; DESIGN LIFE; DURABILITY; PERMEABILITY; STONE; STRUCTURAL STEEL; WALLS.

What is a retaining wall?

Retaining walls can be external walls, sometimes constructed with a decorative facing and used in landscaping, part of civil engineering works, or a basement construction – either as permanent or temporary works. A retaining wall is used to 'retain' or hold back soil or other material behind it. The retained material exerts a horizontal, or lateral, pressure on the wall that the wall must resist. The value of the earth pressure is a function of the material retained, its height, the level of the water in the ground and the extent to which the wall bends or moves under the action of the material behind it. The presence of water in the ground greatly increases the lateral forces and therefore has a profound effect on wall stability. Retained ground may slope up behind the wall. Retaining walls are found in a number of different locations including:

- Basements, either as temporary and/or as permanent retaining structures;
- Boundary walls, for example to parks or cemeteries;
- Bridge abutments;
- Landscaping – either as free-standing walls or as a facing to an embankment or slope;
- Other civil engineering works to river and canal banks, roads and railway lines.

There are two broad categories of retaining wall: gravity walls and embedded walls, which are described in turn.

Gravity walls

Here, the stability is provided by the weight of the wall, which resists both the sliding and overturning forces exerted by the retained material. Gravity walls are built of precast or in-situ concrete, or may be of brick, block or stone. They may be of quite massive construction in order to provide the necessary resistance to earth pressure. Flexible walls, in which the stem is designed as a cantilever, or less often as a beam where the top of the wall is propped, may be seen as a specific type of gravity wall. These are often of reinforced concrete, commonly used in basement construction. Brick or block walls of this type will generally be reinforced, using hollow units with grouted reinforcement, pocket reinforcement or buttresses.

Embedded walls

These are used for deep excavations or for less deep construction where the groundwater level is high and a cut-off is required. They are often used where movements of the ground outside the excavation need to be limited to protect structures or buried services. These may be of sheet pile construction, diaphragm walls constructed under bentonite, or various forms of bored pile construction.

Sheet piles are heavy corrugated steel sections, which interlock by means of a clutch at each side of the pile. They are installed using special driving equipment; historically this has been a noisy process causing considerable vibration, although more recently the piles have been pushed into the ground rather than driven in, with a corresponding reduction in the disruption caused.

Diaphragm walls are constructed using special equipment, which excavates the wall in panels. The sides of each panel are supported using bentonite, a suspension of clay, which exerts sufficient lateral pressure on the ground to keep the excavation open temporarily. A reinforcement cage is lowered into each panel and the wall is then concreted using a tremie pipe, which displaces the bentonite. The latter is collected and should be disposed of in a way that avoids polluting the environment. Adjacent panels interlock as the grab excavates the end of the previous panel.

For the rather different **pile walls** the piles will either be contiguous, in which there is a small space between adjacent piles, or of secant form where the piles overlap. King post walls are a particular form where planks of timber, precast concrete, or corrugated steel span between piles (the 'king posts') which are usually steel or precast concrete.

Design notes

These walls will be supported in different ways. Cantilever walls, which have no support, may be used up to a certain height, perhaps around three metres. Where supports are required these may be props down to an excavation base or a system of waling beams and struts across an excavation. The wall may also be tied back at one or more levels using ground anchors; these are generally only used in the temporary condition, with permanent support being provided by the new construction.

The embedded wall types described will usually not be seen as the finished wall in the permanent condition. They do not themselves have good resistance to water penetration and the exposed face will be irregular. More commonly, particularly for buildings, an internal facing wall of in-situ reinforced concrete will be constructed, or an inner skin of blockwork with a drained cavity between the inner and outer walls connected to the permanent drainage system. This allows any water that does enter to be collected and disposed of behind a more aesthetically acceptable surface. The details will depend on the use of the space inside the wall and the required environmental conditions within it.

Further reading

Construction Industry Research and Information Association (2000) *Modular gravity retaining walls: design guidance*, Report C516, CIRIA, London, UK.

OA

Retrofitting

See: OVERCLADDING; MAINTENANCE; DESIGN LIFE

Rectangular hollow section

See: STRUCTURAL STEEL

Rice, Peter

Peter Ronan Rice (1935–92) is regarded as one of the most outstanding engineers of the late 20th century. His work is characterised by the pioneering use of unusual construction technologies and rigorous, innovative concepts of structural design and analysis. He worked unusually closely with several architects (most notably Renzo Piano) to the point that the structural concept was inseparable from the architecture.

See also: ARUP, OVE; CASTINGS; CONCRETE – STRUCTURES; FRAMES; GLASS – STRUCTURAL GLAZING; HAPPOLD, SIR TED AND BURO HAPPOLD; INTEGRATION; LOUVRES AND BRISE-SOLEIL; NERVI, PIER LUIGI; PIANO, RENZO; RITCHIE, IAN; ROGERS, RICHARD; STRUCTURAL STEEL.

Peter Rice: Nuage. A pioneering use of suspended fabric structures to make a wind deflector underneath the Grande Arche, Paris (Otto Spreckleson 1986). Photograph by Thomas Deckker.

Rice was born in Dublin in 1935; he graduated in Civil Engineering from Queen's University, Belfast in 1956 and then moved to London where he undertook post-graduate studies at Imperial College. He subsequently joined the Structures 3 Group at Ove Arup & Partners under Ted Happold. Rice's first work at Ove Arup & Partners was on the Sydney Opera House (Jorn Utzon; 1957–73). The Structures 3 Group was charged with converting Utzon's sketches into a buildable 3D form. After three years of structural analysis, this was finally achieved by defining each segment of the shell vaults as part of a sphere, which allowed them to be built of prefabricated concrete units. Rice became Resident Engineer at the Opera House in 1963. Before his return to London in 1968 he spent a year as a visiting scholar at Cornell University.

Rice regarded the work on the Pompidou Centre, Paris (Piano + Rogers; 1971–77) as his first individual work. The unusual demands of the architectural concept (totally flexible and clear-span interior space flanked by service and circulation zones) were resolved by Rice with a combination of long-span trusses in the interior space and cast steel cantilever brackets known as *gerberettes* in the service and circulation zones. These reduced the main spans to a minimum. The technology of cast steel was unknown at that time in architectural circles and was derived from the nuclear and North Sea oil industries; the final manufacturer was Krupp, who apparently used their expertise in armaments manufacture. The delicacy and transparency of the structure of the Pompidou Centre, which offset the massive scale of the building, were facilitated by the structural language of compression tubes, tension rods and trusses. This language was used subsequently on other buildings by Rice and became commonplace among 'high-tech' architects.

Following the Pompidou Centre, Rice developed new methods of structural analysis to stretch existing technologies and develop new technologies of glass and fabric structures. Between 1977 and 1979 Rice entered a short-lived partnership with Renzo Piano as Piano Rice, based in Genoa, to promote joint architectural and engineering designs. Although this partnership was unsuccessful (as they could not find appropriate commissions), there was one interesting project for FIAT. Rice proposed to replace the conventional monocoque construction of cars with a tubular 'space-frame' with replaceable infill panels which would result in stiffer and quieter bodies: several derivatives have subsequently been developed by FIAT and other manufacturers.

Rice continued to collaborate extensively with Piano, at that time practising as the Renzo Piano Building Workshop. In the travelling IBM Pavilion (1981), he developed a composite structure of polycarbonate pyramidal units stabilised by laminated timber struts to provide a light, translucent, and easily transportable structure. The Stadium, Bari (1986–90) used a concrete cantilevered structure with a fabric roof, and Kansai International Airport Terminal, Japan (1988–94) incorporated a glazed roof formed by a vault of asymmetrical steel trusses.

The Menil Gallery, Houston (1981–6) is considered a masterpiece of their collaboration. The roof was designed in conjunction with Tom Barker (of Ove Arup & Partners) and Paul Winkler (Director of the Gallery). The aim was to control illumination; its final form was a three-layer composite of glass weatherproofing, structure and light diffuser, which Rice resolved using composite units of ferro-cement laminas and ductile iron trusses, which form a structural brise-soleil. Ferro-cement had initially been used by Pier-Luigi Nervi in the 1930s and had subsequently been used for boat construction. The laminas were manufactured in England rather than the USA because the process was highly labour-intensive.

Rice became a Director of the Ove Arup Partnership in 1983, and founded RFR in 1984, based in Paris, with Martin Francis (b. 1942) and Ian Ritchie (b. 1947). For the Lloyds of London Building (Richard Rogers & Partners; 1978–86), Rice developed an in-situ concrete frame to a sophistication and elegance equivalent to the steel frame of the Pompidou Centre. In the stair towers of the Museum of Science and Industry, Paris

(Adrian Fainsilber; 1981), he pioneered the use of glass as a structural material, with entirely self-supporting walls of glass, braced only by tension wires. The courtyard glazing at the Louvre, Paris (I M Pei; 1985) inaugurated the use of lightweight glass roofs on historic buildings. The Nuage, a wind deflector (1986) suspended beneath the Grande Arche, Paris (Otto Spreckleson; 1986) is a Teflon™-coated PVC membrane in a tensile steel net; the name derives from its resemblance to a cloud. In the Pabellon del Futuro, Seville (Martorell Bohigas MacKay; 1992), Rice designed a structure of stone held with tensile steel cables instead of mortar joints which was an extension of his work with structural glass. The Moon Theatre, Gourgoubes, Provence (Humbert Camerlo; begun 1992) used lightweight mirrors to provide an open-air theatre lit entirely by moonlight.

His untimely death in 1992 left numerous projects unfinished at both Ove Arup & Partners and RFR, including Terminal 3 at the Aéroport Charles de Gaulle, Paris and stations for the Ligne Météor, Paris.

Rice received numerous awards. In France, he was awarded the Medaille d'Argent from the Societé d'Encouragement pour l'Industrie Nationale in 1987 and from the Academie d'Architecture in 1989. In Britain he was elected an honorary member of the RIBA in 1988 and received the RIBA Gold Medal in 1992. In Ireland he was elected an honorary member of the RIAI in 1990.

Further reading

Anon (1992) *Exploring materials: the work of Peter Rice* (exhibition catalogue), RIBA, London, UK.

Rice, P. & Dutton, H. (1997) *Structural glass* (2nd edition), E & FN Spon, London, UK.

Rice, P. (1996) *An engineer imagines* (2nd edition), Ellipsis, London, UK.

ZD

Ring beam
See: BEAMS

Risers and trunking

Risers (wet and dry) are enclosed areas where gas, water, electrical and fire precaution systems are brought into a building. Service systems in buildings also use enclosed metal and plastic routeways known as 'trunking'.

See also: AIR CONDITIONING; BRACING; CEILINGS; CORE (SERVICES); CORE (STRUCTURAL); FIRE PROTECTION; FLOORS; HVAC; ICT IN BUILDINGS; SERVICES; WATER MANAGEMENT AND DRAINAGE.

Introduction

Riser is the term given to all essential incoming services to a building, i.e. gas, water and electrical main supplies, but the term is also used in other contexts. **Wet risers**, are risers in which water is transported through the building for fire purposes. The pipes are attached to fire hydrants for immediate flow of water through hoses in the case of fire, or via a sprinkler system. **Dry risers** are installed in high-rise buildings allowing fire crews to direct water into the building from the outside (i.e. for safety reasons). The risk of fire is a major consideration in the design of service risers. It is very important that gas, water and oil supply risers are constructed from masonry or concrete to keep them separate from any other electrical and other cabling services because of the risk from cross-circuiting and fire. At an early stage, the design team should discuss even the initial concepts with fire officers and other environmental and safety officers to ensure co-ordinated and proper planning, which meets all relevant legislation.

Types of risers

Gas services – these need magnetic as well as fuseable link safety valves fitted at the point of entry to a building for immediate shut down in case of fire. The gas pipework services should be fabricated from high quality heavy-duty PVC pipe, in accordance with current standards and any local byelaws.

Water services – these normally consist of a metered supply (the meter being installed in a special cupboard in the basement or ground floor area) that goes direct to header storage tanks adequate for 24 hour supply or more in the case of special buildings, such as hospitals. Unmetered water supplies serve fire hydrants and sprinkler systems.

Water services (for fire) – these are contained in concrete or masonry enclosures with access at each floor. At the base of the main service duct there should be a drain of adequate size to take away any spillage, rupture of a pipe or failure of the water system.

Electrical risers – these must be placed in their own brick/masonry encased service duct with appropriate bunding around each system. Electrical bus bars and mains transmission cables should be encased in heavy metal or specially reinforced plastic trunking or casings. Individual switch and fuse boards should be mounted at each floor inside the cupboard with a solid door, special locks and a plate fixed to the door warning any personnel of high voltage electricity cabling and equipment.

Oil pipes – such as risers to roof top boiler houses. These are a fire hazard and must be enclosed, with means to close down supply before a fire can rise up the whole shaft. Oil pipes were common in 1960s and 1970s medium- to high-rise buildings.

Trunking

This is a generic term for all metal or plastic rectangular, oval, or circular ductwork systems for the conveyance of air for air conditioning and ventilation systems. It is also used to describe the point at which electrical cables are inserted to change the supply from high to lower voltage systems. In colloquial terms, trunking is often used to describe electrical services distribution such as the plastic dado level fittings that feature in many modern offices, hospitals and schools. In the case of the latter, the trunking may also be part of the ICT strategy for the building. For healthcare facilities such as residential nursing homes and 'lifetime' homes for elderly people, trunking at dado level has proved very successful. It replaces skirting level electrical fittings, which are often difficult to reach for the less mobile.

Trunking for heating, ventilating and air conditioning is discussed in detail elsewhere. However, it is worth noting that there has been a tendency for higher velocities and therefore smaller duct or trunking systems (favoured by architects concerned about the spatial needs of building services). However, all ducting systems must be accessible and cleanable, with adequate access doors and room to work. These requirements should be accommodated in the overall design as early as possible.

Further reading

Chadderton, D.V. (2000) *Building services engineering* (3rd edition), E & FN Spon, London, UK.

Greeno, R. (1997) *Building services, technology and design*, Longman, Harlow, UK.

Greeno, R. & Hall, F.E. (2001) *Building services handbook*, Butterworth-Heinemann, Oxford, UK.

WH

Risk management

The systematic analysis of unexpected events, that could pose a threat to the project.

See also: CONSTRUCTION PROGRAMME; CRITICAL PATH ANALYSIS; 'JUST-IN-TIME' CONSTRUCTION; LEAD-TIME; 'LEAN' CONSTRUCTION; PROCUREMENT; VALUE ENGINEERING.

Introduction

There are a broad variety of things that could 'go wrong' in the design, manufacture, construction and use of buildings and so 'risk management' describes an approach used by teams to manage their response to such hazards. This approach is seen to be of growing importance for larger, complex projects where delays, errors or simple misunderstandings can sometimes end in lengthy and costly litigation.

Before risk is discussed in more detail, there are two basic premises to be addressed. First, the word 'risk' can be understood in two ways, negative risk (consisting of hazards) or positive risk (consisting of opportunities). It is more typical for people to assume that all 'risk' is negative, but this is not necessarily the case. This brings us to the second premise, that people's perceptions of risk are different. Some people can be described as '**risk averse**' i.e. they perceive risks as negative and wish to avoid them at all costs. Other people are '**risk hungry**' in that they seek challenges as potential openings for innovation and advancements. Others are not particularly concerned either way ('**risk neutral**'). Most companies actually contain a mixture of all types, but it is common to find that only risk hungry characters will rise to the high echelons of senior executives. This means that the majority of senior managers and project managers are probably going to be risk averse. This may fly in the face of innovation and change, so risk management protocols offer a chance to redress the balance in a systematic manner.

Examples of risk

The list below suggests some aspects of a project with associated risks. By identifying these possibilities early on, in the safety of the office, the design team can seek to manage, mitigate or deflect the risk (perhaps even adapting the design or construction process to remove the risk altogether).

- Bad weather delays progress;
- Client is not satisfied on completion;

Reducing risks on site by planning tasks properly – in this case using harnesses and other safety equipment as part of normal practice in placing concrete floor units. Photograph courtesy of Birchwood Concrete Products Ltd and the British Precast Concrete Federation.

- Components are delivered in error or too late;
- Components are not available or have a longer lead-time than expected;
- Designers change their minds during construction;
- Discovery of archaeological remains disrupts progress;
- Elements do not fit or do not meet the specification;
- Environmental protestors blockade the site;
- New conditions come to light, which require testing;
- Road works cause traffic disruption;
- Skilled labour is not available when construction is due to start;
- Union action temporarily halts all work.

The list illustrates the breadth of potential areas that can be considered in risk management, but it is now fairly common to begin assessing, prioritising and assigning them using risk management protocols.

Using risk management (RM)

Risk management is really another project planning tool, but one with significant potential rewards. By setting project risk objectives, identifying risks, assessing them and assigning responses to the various members of the team, risk management enables the team to establish an agreed action plan. This improves the chances of innovating, minimises uncertainty and clarifies ownership of the various risks, thus reducing the possibility of legal recourse should the worst happen. Risks can be owned, shared or passed outside of the team. They can be assigned to different levels of management as appropriate, for example:

- Strategic risks – Senior Management/Executives;
- Project risks – Project/Contracts Manager;
- Task risks – Line manager.

In the UK, it is quite common to find that the real expertise in risk management lies within construction management companies, quantity surveyors or cost planners. Facilities managers may also be involved in the process to help deal with ongoing (residual) risks. Some of the larger contractors use risk management as a matter of course, but it is unlikely that architects will be leading the process. Indeed, the negative risks associated with construction are such that the onus is most often on the main contractor or construction manager. Hence, these organisations tend to take risk management more seriously.

Computer software packages for risk management of construction projects are available, such as RiskCom from CIRIA.

Further reading

Blockley, D.I. & Godfrey, P.S. (2000) *Doing it differently: systems for rethinking construction*, Thomas Telford, London, UK.

Flanagan, R. & Norman, G. (1993) *Risk management and construction*, Blackwell Science, Oxford, UK.

Grey, S. (1995) *Practical risk assessment for project management*, John Wiley & Sons, Chichester, UK.

The Institution of Civil Engineers and The Faculty and Institute of Actuaries (1998) *RAMP: Risk analysis and management for projects*, Thomas Telford, London, UK.

JG

An early use of suspended glass assemblies at the Centro de Arte Reina Sofia, Madrid, Spain. 1987 (engineered by Peter Rice). Photograph by Thomas Deckker.

Ritchie, Ian

Ian Ritchie is one of the most sophisticated of the 'high-tech' architects and his work shows a dazzling use of materials combined with an intelligent manipulation of space. His more recent work shows his ability to apply a 'technical' approach to architecture through a broad range of materials.

See also: FAÇADE ENGINEERING; FOSTER, SIR NORMAN; GLASS; GLASS – STRUCTURAL GLAZING; HIGH TECH; PROUVÉ, JEAN; RICE, PETER; STRUCTURAL STEEL.

He is one of the first architects of a new English house who is enthusiastic enough to show how it can be done, arrogant enough to keep arguing and talented enough to make a house with that elusive image – quality – of which we should not be frightened.

Peter Cook, writing about Ian Ritchie (from *Architects Journal*, October 26th 1983, p. 73)

Ian Ritchie studied at Liverpool University, where he spent much of his time with poets. He worked in Germany and then in Japan and, although he states that he wasn't particularly interested in architecture, he was struck by the work of Arata Isozaki. Having attained his architecture degree in 1972, he went on to work for the firm of Norman Foster and Michael Hopkins where he collaborated on the famous Willis Faber Dumas building in Ipswich. From this early stage he worked closely with other disciplines, particularly with engineers such as Anthony Hunt and Martin Francis, but also with Jean Prouvé.

In 1981 he formed the technical design studio RFR (Rice Francis Ritchie) with Peter Rice and Martin Francis when he was just 34. The firm continues to keep the name, although Peter Rice sadly died in 1992. Ritchie surrounds himself with collaborators from a wide variety of professions to continue constant debate and cross-fertilisation, keeping his practice lively, challenging and informed. The *modus operandi* of RFR is to discover technologies which, although they might not be utilised immediately, are kept as a store of innovations for use when the opportunity arises.

Ritchie's continuous quest for new technologies and his desire to make a new architectural statement came together in an important commission in the Sussex countryside – the Eagle Rock House (1981–82). An imposing steel canopy stretches across the site (like the outstretched wings of an eagle), with the main living quarters in a central corridor and the two wings leading out on either side. A central structural frame positioned above the central section is the prime aesthetic focus. This modest house demonstrated the talent and yearning for knowledge of new technology that have become the signatures of Ritchie's high-tech design.

For his Ecology gallery for the Natural History Museum (1989–91), Ritchie studied the work of the building's architect (Alfred Waterhouse). He decided to ensure that the installation could be removable at the end of its projected life (10 years) without damage to the original structure. The installation consists of two long sandblasted glass walls lit with coloured lamps and four bridges that enable visitors to weave their way through the gallery. The bridges, which are formed from mild steel sheets and post-tensioned steel cables, bow in shape across the gallery. At the end of these is a 'quadrisphere', a large bank of screens that project 360° images of bodies of water.

More recent projects include the staggering suspended glass façade at the Reina Sofia gallery in Madrid and the London Rowing Club in London's Docklands, which features expanses of exposed in-situ concrete and a stone-filled gabion entrance wall.

Further reading

Rocca, A. & Ritchie, I. (1999) *Ian Ritchie: Technoecology*, Watson-Guptill Publications, New York, USA.

MT

Rogers, Richard (Lord Rogers of Riverside)

Richard Rogers (b.1933)

See also: ATRIUM; BRICKS AND BLOCKS; CASTINGS; HAPPOLD, SIR TED AND BURO HAPPOLD; HIGH TECH; 'HONESTY'; INTEGRATION; JIRICNA, EVA; MODULES AND MODULAR CONSTRUCTION; PIANO, RENZO; RICE, PETER; SERVICES; STAINLESS STEEL; STRUCTURAL STEEL; TEXTILE MEMBRANE ROOFS.

Richard Rogers is the most high tech of high-tech architects. His work is defined by an obsession with the aesthetics of technology. His career began in partnership with the other British high tech pioneer Norman Foster in Team 4. He later formed a partnership with Renzo Piano and it was with the Italian architect that he designed what remains his most impressive building, the Centre Pompidou in Paris (1971–77). While Rogers built on the imagery of Prouvé and Chareau he also blended in the pop ideas of Cedric Price, Archigram and the Japanese Metabolists to create a stunning, sci-fi aesthetic which aimed to treat a building as a mechanism of interchangeable parts. In order to create a flexible interior Rogers placed the services and structure on the outside, so that they could be accessible without interfering with the internal functions, while leaving the interior uncluttered and free. Grids of cross-braced steel elements with powerfully-detailed junctions, deep trusses and a spaghetti of ducts and services created elevations resembling an oil refinery which were both shocking in traditional Parisian context, yet appropriate to the hard urban grain of the area. Finally the escalators were placed on the outside to bring the movement of the building to the streets and bring the experience of the city into the building.

A number of industrial and laboratory buildings followed including the Fleetguard Building, Quimper, France (1979–81), PA Technology Laboratories and Offices, Princeton, NJ (1982–83) and the Inmos Microprocessor Factory, Newport, Wales (1982), all of which displayed Rogers' use of external structures and servicing with loads suspended from central mast elements. These buildings successfully brought overtly industrial articulation to his oeuvre, which had hitherto been dominated by dull expanses of conventional structure and they remain exemplars of the use of the expression of structure to create an architectural aesthetic.

Rogers' next major breakthrough came with the Lloyd's of London HQ, London (1978–1986). More complex than the Centre Pompidou, the Lloyd's building was based around a central atrium. In its structure an expressed reinforced concrete frame and the elevational composition was made dramatic by the addition of sculptural elements including a metal-encased escape stair, expressed glazed atrium, cranes at roof level and the usual barrage of services and ducts. It is useful to compare the building with Norman Foster's contemporary Hong Kong and Shanghai Bank as these two structures form the apex of British high-tech architecture. Another major building in London came with the Channel 4 Television HQ in Victoria (1990–94) and others followed including offices at 88 Wood Street (1999–2000).

In more recent buildings Rogers has attempted to address environmental issues with innovative approaches to ventilation and services for buildings including the European Court of Human Rights at Strasbourg (1989–95) and a building for the Ministry of Justice in Bordeaux (1992–98). His best known building is probably the New Millennium Experience, colloquially known as the 'Millennium Dome'. Rogers' design for the dome itself was impressive and on an ambitious scale not seen in England since the construction of the Crystal Palace in 1851. The world's largest textile membrane roof, the dome is supported by twelve 100m high lattice steel masts from which a tensioned net of steel cables is suspended. At the centre, a 30-metre diameter cable ring restrains the forces while a compression ring beam running around the perimeter and huge reinforced concrete ground anchors keep the cables in tension. The dome is covered in 80,000 m^2 of Teflon^{TM} coated glass fibre. The dome's engineer was Buro Happold.

Recent buildings including the Montevetro development on the River Thames in London with its precise terracotta cladding. Rogers is also known for his large-scale urban planning including an intelligent plan for the centre of London and a major re-planning of Shanghai, neither of which have yet come to fruition. However his work as Chair of the Urban Task Force is bringing him closer to the UK urban design fraternity than before.

Further reading

Appleyard, A. (1986) *Richard Rogers: a biography*, Faber & Faber, London, UK.

Campbell Cole B. & Eli, R. (1985) *Richard Rogers + architects*, Architectural Monographs, Academy Editions, John Wiley & Sons, London, UK.

Powell, K. (1994) *Richard Rogers*, Artemis, London, UK.

Powell, K. (1999) *Richard Rogers; Team 4, Richard and Su Rogers, Piano & Rogers* (volume 1), Phaidon Press, London, UK.

Powell, K. (2001) *Richard Rogers: Complete Works* (Volume 2), Phaidon Press, London, UK.

EH

Roofs

The roof is a vital building element that forms a structural and environmental protective barrier between the internal areas of a building and the outside. While there is a wide range of regional variations, a few generic forms tend to dominate design.

See also: AIR SUPPORTED STRUCTURES; ALUMINIUM; CABLE NETS; CERAMICS; COMPOSITE DECKING; CONCRETE; COPPER; DESIGN LIFE; DURABILITY; ETFE; GLASS; GRASS ('GREEN') ROOFS; INSULATION; LEAD; LOUVRES AND BRISE-SOLEIL; MAINTENANCE; METALS; NERVI, PIER LUIGI; OTTO, FREI; OVERCLADDING; PLASTICS; PROFILED METAL DECKING; PHOTOVOLTAICS; ROGERS, RICHARD; SINGLE-PLY MEMBRANE; STANDING SEAM ROOF; STRUCTURAL STEEL; TEXTILE MEMBRANE ROOFS; TIMBER – LAMINATED TIMBER; TIMBER – MANUFACTURED BOARDS; VON GERKAN & MARG; WATER MANAGEMENT AND DRAINAGE; ZINC.

The Great Glasshouse of the National Botanical Garden of Wales with its massive glazed roof structure. Photograph by Trevor Jones, courtesy of The Concrete Society.

Introduction

Roofs can be designed to many different shapes and sizes and using a range of materials in different combinations. Roofs are generally termed as 'pitched' or 'flat', where 'flat' roofs are usually built with a minimal pitch of about 4° (to encourage drainage). There are many different designs in existence, some of which are associated with local vernacular traditions. In essence, a roof may perform any or all of the following basic functions:

Structure – the main structural elements and other components may play a key role within the structure of the building as a whole. This can be as a means of transferring loads between frame elements or sometimes the roof element acts as a diaphragm to provide lateral stability to a structure.

Insulation – although this is not always the case, in the UK most roofs include an insulation layer to prevent heat escaping from the building during the lengthy heating season. This insulation may be placed above or below the main roof structure depending on the design.

Weatherproofer – the most important function of any roof is to prevent rain and snow etc. from entering the building. This may be achieved with a damp proof membrane (DPM) and can be further enhanced depending on the type of material used on the surface of the roof. In any case detailing and workmanship of the joints is critical.

Other factors – in addition to these basic functions, a roof will also usually be designed to act as a moderator in terms of moisture and air movement. In other words, it has to cope with air change rates and provide sufficient ventilation to prevent interstitial condensation. This may occur between materials which are at different temperatures or have different rates of thermal conductivity. Roof design should take account of potential imposed loads such as snow loads and access for maintenance work.

Generic roof design

In providing structural, environmental and performance integrity to a building, the roof plays a key role in any building. These functions are performed regardless of shape and style. However, in architectural terms the design of a roof may impact on the way in which the roof will ultimately perform. The plethora of designs means that it is only possible to give a brief overview of the basic principles of roof design. Interested readers may also wish to make reference to specialist books on the many roof types that exist such as canopy roofs, cable nets and grass roofs. The following sections provide an overview of roof design in terms of: a) structural performance and; b) thermal performance.

Generic roof designs for structural performance

The two broad categories described below encompass the majority of roof structures, excepting specialist solutions such as grass roofs and canopies, etc.

Flat roofs – The first thing to say here is that flat roofs are not flat! This may come as a surprise and there are many critics of the use of this term, but to the naked eye when one sees a flat roof, it does appear to be perfectly flat. In fact, 'flat' roofs are typically slightly pitched (successful flat roofs have slopes in the range 4–15°). Although low pitches with leadwork have been used in the UK for hundreds of years, the modern use of flat roofs originates in hot, dry countries and was really introduced by Modernist architects seeking a particular 'cubular' design aesthetic. However, flat roofs have proved rather difficult to maintain in the cool, wet UK climate. The practical application of the technology has not been very successful, so the flat roof has not proved particularly popular with lay people. Nevertheless, technology for flat roof construction has moved on apace with improvements to materials and application methods. Concrete slabs, timber decking or structural steel can form the structure to a flat roof, but the crux is the waterproofing. The five principal options for the waterproofing of flat roofs are:

- Built-up roofing – typically where layers of high strength fabric reinforced bituminous sheeting, are laid and bonded in hot bitumen;
- Mastic asphalt in which two or more coats of a natural or manufactured asphalt coating are applied to the roof;
- Sheet metal roofs – e.g. lead, copper and zinc;
- Single-ply membranes – fabricated sheets of synthetic polymer or elastomer, fixed, overlapped and sealed to form a continuous membrane;
- Thin liquid applied elastomeric coatings in which thin layers (typically 2 mm) of a liquid elastomer, often polyurethane, are applied and bonded to the roof substrate.

Pitched roofs – The pitched roof category includes simple pitched roofs, hipped, gable, mansard and monopitch roofs. These roofs tend to be pitched (i.e. angled or inclined) at greater than 15°. In countries with high degrees of rainfall roof pitch tends to be quite steep. Historically, many UK buildings had steeper pitched roofs than is typical today – some researchers believe these ventilated themselves more effectively than shallower examples. Some roofing materials such as slate need to be installed at a steeper pitch than say tiles or metal sheeting. This is related to the permeability, draughtproofing and run-off qualities of the material. In cold areas, pitched roofs are designed to support and withhold a covering of snow through the winter months (partly as extra insulation). Contemporary designs for pitched roofs to Building Regulations requirements are highly efficient, with many of the components, if not all, producible off site. Hinged timber roofs from the Netherlands can be procured with insulation and detailing intact; only tiling and rainwater fittings need to be attached on site. In this case, solid gables provide the structural stability and so the full roof space is available for use by the occupants. In fact, in many instances a pitched roof also gives the option of having habitable space in the roof itself by way of rooflights or dormer windows. If this is envisaged, they should be constructed in such a way that the number of trusses crossing the space is minimised. Ideally, the shear stability should be provided in the plane of the roof itself, thus leaving the entire roof space free. This can be accommodated, but is best discussed at an early stage. To have no lateral structural elements in the roof is more feasible in smaller buildings such as housing and domestic scale construction (see *Timber – manufactured boards)*.

Generic roof designs for thermal performance

There are three basic arrangements, which are categorised according to the position of the insulation relative to the waterproofing layer and the main structural elements.

Cold roof – in this example the structure is 'outside' of the insulation (and therefore 'cold'), but is still inside the waterproof DPM. This roof design depends on adequate ventilation between the insulation and the structure/roof deck to prevent condensation occurring on the external (cool) side of the insulation.

Warm roof – here, the structure is 'inside' the insulation and therefore described as being 'warm'. The DPM sits outside the insulation. Ventilation is not necessary but care should be taken where this roof design is used because the surface of the roof is effectively weak (the insulation sits just below the DPM and direct access would damage the roof surface).

Warm (inverted) roof – the insulation is outside the structure, but it is also outside the DPM. The structure is within the interior and sometimes exposed. This solution is most often used in flat roofs where rigid insulation is covered with concrete paving slabs to keep it in place and prevent surface damage. Access to the insulation is simple and the integrity of the DPM can easily be checked.

Materials

Even in a simple roof, it is common to see a combination of different materials, each playing a different role. The main structural elements in smaller or domestic scale construction tend to be timber, but concrete or light steel framing are also used. Primary steel or reinforced concrete elements are seen more often in larger buildings such as offices and warehouses. Bespoke structural roofing elements such as shell structures, barrel vaults and portal frames are common for larger spans or more architectural applications. 'Glulam' timber beams can span long distances and are very aesthetically pleasing. There is often an architectural preference to expose roof structures (and sometimes the services weaving in amongst them) as a form of aesthetic expression. This tendency has also led to increased use of structural steel castellated beams or cellular beams (these having holes for the services to pass through).

Surface coatings or roof coverings forming a waterproof or weatherproof layer include coated steel sheeting and panels, standing seam rolled metal such as copper or aluminium, single-ply membranes, textile membrane and other plastics in addition to built-up roofing systems. Clay or concrete tiles, cedar shingles or slates are often found in domestic pitched roof construction. Modern materials such as single-ply membranes reduce the overall weight of the roof but rely on good workmanship to achieve well-sealed joints. A roof can be made to incorporate photovoltaic panels to generate electricity for the building users. In a similar way, grass ('green') roofs are popular for ecological and aesthetic reasons.

Further reading

British Flat Roofing Council/CIRIA (1993) *Flat roofing: design and good practice*, BFRC/CIRIA,London, UK.

British Standards Institution (1982) *BS 6229: Code of practice for roofs with continuously supported coverings*, BSI, London, UK.

Building Research Establishment (1986) *Flat roof design: the technical options*, BRE Digest 312, BRE, Watford, UK.

Mindham, C.N. (1999) *Roof construction and loft conversion*, Blackwell Science, Oxford, UK.

Wilkinson, C. (1996) *Supersheds* (2nd edition), Butterworth-Heinemann,Oxford, UK.

JG/GW

Sacrificial layer

See: OVERSIZING; TIMBER – PRODUCTION AND FINISHES

Scarpa, Carlo

Carlo Scarpa (1906–78) was an Italian architect whose designs became renowned for their invention, drama, fine detailing and inspired use of materials. He was a devotee of rationalism as well as the Modern Movement. Scarpa's designs are characterised by a mastery of volumetric juxtapositions; 'floating' staircases, daring gantries and sometimes surprising combinations of materials which showed his skill and understanding.

See also: CONCRETE; CONCRETE – FINISHES; CONCRETE – STRUCTURES; 'HONESTY'; GLASS; INTEGRATION; METALS; STONE.

Carlo Scarpa won much praise from those who worked for him. Not only did he encourage them to contribute to the creation of his buildings, but he also demonstrated a mastery that they did not expect in an architect. Born in Venice in 1906, Scarpa studied there at the Accademia di Belle Arti. In 1927 he began work as an independent practitioner, quickly becoming known for his elegant interiors and serene exhibition installations. The first major recognition for Scarpa's work came with the renovation of the Galleria Nazionale della Sicilia in the Palazzo Abbatellis in Palermo. Like his exhibition designs, this utilised his well observed sense of scale, delicate decoration and knowledge of materials. He spent his last six years from 1972 to 1978 as the Director of the Universitario di Architettura.

Two projects in particular stand out as demonstrating most clearly the Scarpa approach to architecture and its detailing; the Museo di Castelvecchio, Verona (1956–73) and the Fondazione de Querini Stampalia, Venice (1961–63), both of which are featured heavily in any publication about his work.

Scarpa's work at the Castelvecchio took place over almost two decades. In 1959 he renovated the castle's west wing residence, building a gallery, bridge and staircase to enhance the space. The most important transformation of this incredible project took place when Scarpa re-installed the sculpture gallery on the ground floor and moved the museum entrance to the north east corner of the courtyard. From then on, he continued to develop the project in stages. Each transformation afforded the castle challenging and yet sympathetic elements to the original structure. One key feature is the execution of windows, in which timber and iron components vary in shape and size according to their location. In all cases, the windows are positioned to make the most of natural light within the room to highlight exhibits and demonstrate the possibilities for openings not available to the original Gothic builders of the Castelvecchio. The various handrails, door furniture and sconce-like small shelves for religious artefacts all show supreme intellect in architectural detailing.

With Querini Stampalia, Scarpa's work to renovate the ground floor and courtyard was opened in June 1963. He reclaimed the ground floor (which was prone to flooding) by elevating a floor section and allowing water movement in restricted areas via a water gate. The walls were covered with plaster and travertine panels detached from the wall to enhance air circulation and drying out in damp periods. A new entrance bridge was constructed from timber and steel, the combination of materials and the innovative fixings expressing an understanding of modern materials as well as an acute historic awareness. The courtyard mirrors the delicacy of the interior with its use of flowing water within controlled, serene rills.

Other works of interest by Scarpa include:

Olivetti Showroom, Venice (1957–58). This small, but exquisite shop by St Marks Square in Venice demonstrates one of Scarpa's great delights: the 'floating' staircase. Made from Aurisina marble, the stair blocks sit upon one other, but shadow gaps give the impression that they are hovering.

Brion family tomb, San Vito d'Altivole, Italy (1969–78). In what is perhaps Scarpa's best example of the use of concrete, this is a truly inspirational scheme. The chapel and shelters for the family sarcophagi were executed with grace and presence. Scarpa used stepped, profiled concrete details and seeing the project now after many years shows also how well he considered the effects of weathering.

Further reading

Dal Co, F. & Mazzariol, G. (1986) *Carlo Scarpa, The complete works*, Architectural Press, Oxford, UK.

Friedman, M. (ed.) & Lambert, P. (1999) *Carlo Scarpa – Architect*, Monacelli Press, New York, USA.

Los, S. (1994) *Carlo Scarpa*, Benedikt Taschen, Köln, Germany.

Murphy, R. (1990) *Carlo Scarpa and the Castelvecchio*, Architectural Press, Oxford, UK.

MT

Schindler, R M

Rudolf (RM as he preferred) Schindler (1887–1953) was an Austrian émigré who was an architectural and technical pioneer of West Coast Modernism in the USA.

See also: CONCRETE; CONCRETE – STRUCTURES; FRAME; INTEGRATION; NEUTRA, RICHARD; STRUCTURAL STEEL; WRIGHT, FRANK LLOYD.

The seminal King's Road House in West Hollywood (1922), which set a trend for Californian Modernism – a humane, yet radical approach to design. Photograph by Author.

Born in Vienna and trained under Otto Wagner, Schindler emigrated to the USA in 1913 where he became almost the sole link between the nascent functionalist tradition in Europe and the pioneering, but individualistic oeuvre of Frank Lloyd Wright, with whom he worked later. Hence, Schindler is the missing link in the development of 20th-century architecture.

Until quite recently, Schindler's achievements were overlooked by architectural historians because, living in the US, he worked outside the Modernist mainstream. He is now recognised, however, as one of the pioneers of Modernism, his Lovell Beach House designed in 1922 and built 1925–26 compares very favourably with the work of his European contemporaries.

Schindler worked on his own in Chicago first then, in 1918, he worked for a while in the offices of Frank Lloyd Wright. Finding Wright overbearing he started up his own practice in Los Angeles. His work was a thoughtful blend of Constructivism and De Stijl tempered with the free-flowing space and love of Japanese domestic design, which he had learnt well from Wright. He began to work with his friend, the engineer Clyde Chase. The twin dwelling he designed for himself and Chase (1921) is the perfect example of his rich blend of influences and his quest to resolve the dwelling archetypes of the cave and the tent. He lived in the Kings Road house in West Hollywood until his death. It is an important building as it represented a very pure functionalism, its form based solely on its pattern of use rather than on aesthetic or sculptural principles. Schindler used a concrete tilt-up system on the house with slabs being cast on the ground and then lifted into place, as Irving Gill had also used in his early West Coast houses.

The Lovell Beach House was technically far more complex and demonstrated Schindler's grasp of concrete technology. The building is supported on five deep concrete piers from which the other walls and floors are suspended. This allowed him to utilise the sea views fully but also to allow the suspended floors and roof to move independently of the main structure in case of an earthquake while the deep spaces between the piers at ground level served as boat sheds. Apart from the El Pueblo Ribera Courts in La Jolla (1923–25) almost all of Schindler's best works were expensive private houses for the California rich. His wealthy clientele also served to separate him from the mainstream of European modernism with its predilection for social housing and minimal living. His finest houses include the Howe House (1923), the Wolfe House (1928), the Sachs Apartments (1929), the Oliver House (1933), Buck House (1934), McAlmon House (1935), Fitzpatrick House (1937) and the Falk Apartments (1939).

From 1925 Schindler worked in partnership with another great Austrian émigré architect and former pupil of Wagner, Richard Neutra (1892–1970). Together, these two Central Europeans formulated the look of modern Californian living. Not only did they experiment with alternative construction methods but they were also intent on integrating philosophy, living style, climate and architecture. Hence, their work is still critically revered today.

Further reading

McCoy, E. (1975) *Five California architects*, Praeger, New York, USA.

March, L. & Sheine, J. (eds.) (1993) *RM Schindler*, Academy Editions, John Wiley & Sons, London, UK.

Steele, J (1999) *RM Schindler*, Bendikt Taschen, Koln, Germany.

EH

Sealants

Sealants are materials that are applied to joints in buildings to typically protect against the elements.

See also: CLADDING; CONCRETE; CONNECTIONS; DESIGN LIFE; DURABILITY; FAÇADES AND FAÇADE ENGINEERING; FIRE PROTECTION; GLASS; GLASS – STRUCTURAL GLAZING; STONE; WINDOWS AND CURTAIN WALLING.

The purpose of a sealant

Connections between materials or components usually require protection at their edges to prevent failure via ingress of water, air, dirt or even fire. The jointing materials to 'fill' these gaps can be chosen from three basic options:

- **Grouts/mastics**: only appropriate for zero/low movement joints;
- **Gaskets**: preformed polymer materials, compressed into a joint to effect a seal;
- **Sealants**: wet-applied materials, formulated to solidify in situ and adhere to the joint surfaces.

The technology of grouts and mastics is covered sufficiently in most construction textbooks. Gasket design and composition is usually highly-specific to particular glazing or cladding assemblies for example, so these are best investigated via manufacturers' literature. This entry will focus on sealants, which are now being used increasingly. Today's sealant systems comprise either wet applied sealants (such as silicone, polysulphide and polyurethane) or acrylic. These offer varying levels of performance as shown below.

Sealant	Typical movement (as % of joint width)	Life expectancy (years)
Acrylic	15	15
Polysulphide	25	20
Polyurethane	30	20
Silicone	50	25

Silicone is used widely as it offers the greatest movement capability and expected life. It has become a commonly specified sealant for high performance façades and for structural systems, where careful design, application and maintenance of the silicone sealant enable it to act structurally in supporting glass. Special grades of silicone are available to create translucency, to permit maximum movement and for structural glazing. Special products are also available to minimise staining of adjacent substrates (particularly stone).

Practical matters

Sealants are typically gun-applied into a prepared joint, and the subsequent performance of the sealed joint depends on a number of factors. These include:

- Correct design assessment of maximum movements versus flexibility of the sealant;
- Installation of the sealant into a clean, sound, dry joint;
- Use of appropriate primers (as recommended by manufacturers) to promote bond on certain substrates and/or to prevent reaction with incompatible materials;

- Effective use of backing strips, both to act as a support when the sealant is tooled (pushing the sealant against the joint sides) and to enable free movement at the base of the joint. The backing strip helps to develop an appropriate sealant geometry in order to permit the levels of movement accommodation outlined above;
- Achievement of an appropriate width to depth ratio and maximum sealant depth as recommended by manufacturers to achieve optimal performance. The ratio is typically 2 : 1 width : depth ratio and 20 mm maximum sealant depth for silicone sealants;
- Careful consideration of compatibility between sealant and adjacent materials. Long term durability can be compromised if incompatibility exists, and can be a particular problem with sealant staining of stone substrates and bitumen attacking sealant materials.

Given the increasing design life of buildings compared to the expected life of sealants, it is becoming increasingly important to consider the maintenance and resealing of joints. Joints need to be accessible for repair and/or replacement, and the initial sealant specified to minimise any leaching that may inhibit subsequent resealing.

Further reading

Amstock, J.S. (2001) *Handbook of adhesives and sealants in construction*, McGraw Hill, New York, USA.

British Standards Institution (1993) BS ISO 11600, *Building construction – sealants – classification and requirements*, BSI, London, UK.

British Standards Institution (2000) BS 6213: 2000: *Selection of construction sealants – guide*, BSI, London, UK.

Ledbetter, S.R., Hurley, S. & Sheehan, A. (1998) *Sealant joints in the external envelope of buildings: a guide on design, specification and construction*, CIRIA Report 178, CIRIA, London, UK.

Woolman, R. & Hutchinson, A. (ed.) (1994) *Resealing of buildings: a guide to good practice*, Butterworth-Heinemann, Oxford, UK.

OA

Self-compacting concrete

See: CONCRETE

Serviceability

See: DESIGN LIFE; DURABILITY; SPECIFICATION

Services

'Building services' constitute a number of systems designed to maintain a controlled, comfortable interior environment.

See also: AIR-CONDITIONING; AIRTIGHTNESS AND IAQ; CEILINGS; DYNAMIC THERMAL SIMULATION; ENVIRONMENTAL DESIGN; ECOLOGICAL DESIGN; FLOORS; HVAC; LIGHTING – ARTIFICIAL LIGHTING; MAINTENANCE; NIGHT VENTILATION; RISERS AND TRUNKING; VENTILATION; WATER MANAGEMENT AND DRAINAGE.

The term 'building services' encompasses:

- Air conditioning;
- Ancillary services (e.g. gas, water supply, fire precaution systems, sprinklers, wet and dry risers);
- Drainage and soil systems;
- Electrical power;
- Hazard management (e.g. from noise, vibration or chemical spills);
- Heating;
- Hot and cold water;
- Lifts, escalators and other systems of transportation;
- Lighting;
- Vacuum systems;
- Ventilation;
- Waste disposal.

The internal environment of a building can be manipulated to mitigate the effects of the external microclimate. This can be achieved either with simple architectural devices that are part of the built fabric, such as wind towers and louvres etc., or via mechanical means such as HVAC. These systems should not be considered in isolation and may well need to be considered as part of the environmental design strategy for a building, in both passive and active approaches to say energy efficiency and indoor air quality. Thus, the interaction between all these may become complicated, due also to the mathematical function of the physical laws underpinning such building physics. The design of services is undertaken principally by the building services engineering company in the design team. This firm will have expertise in both passive and active approaches to servicing a building. It should be able to prepare and demonstrate the overall strategy (and its constituent parts) to the client/design team clearly, perhaps using dynamic thermal simulation to model heat flows for example.

In many buildings, the active and passive means to manipulate the internal environment may be designed around a simple system of 'flows', with incoming flows being gas, water and electricity and outgoing being drainage and waste. However, in process industries, laboratories or manufacturing facilities, building service design may comprise a much more complex set of 'flows' – for example they may include chemical distribution and a number of separate air handling systems. In both instances, the services must accommodate both internal and external conditions. Indeed, the microclimate has a two-way exchange with the internally controlled environment of the fabric of the building. The ways in which services and passive environmental controls are designed and operated will clearly affect the comfort of human occupants in a building and in recent years there has been significantly more attention paid to thermal comfort and indoor air quality issues within the remit of building services design.

Space for services

The equipment, pipework, cabling or ventilation ducts which are used in building services may be seen as constraints to good architectural design. Concealment in suspended ceiling, raised floors, service cores, etc. has become common and these elements are usually accepted as 'necessary evils' in architecture. However, this attitude towards services is not helpful – the installations require room for access, maintenance and repair. The location and size of plant rooms, service ducts and core systems should be part of an early discussion between services engineers and the design team. For example, low velocity, large sized ducts may take up more space, but the use of slow speed centrifugal fans requires less electrical energy – the system is quieter and less sound attenuation is required. On the other hand, high velocity ductwork systems need specialist dampers and increased noise control. A compromise in many instances is ductwork systems that use many small fans, to individual ductwork systems, which can be interlinked. With ICT provision now heavily utilised in many building types, this must also be an integral part of building services design.

Built examples

A radical approach can be seen in the Pompidou Centre in Paris, France (1973) which like its successor the Lloyds Building in London (1986) 'wears its insides out'. The services run on the façades in a series of multi-coloured tubes, ducts and pipes, releasing a vast amount of uninterrupted floor and ceiling space inside for exhibition and leisure use. In a very different scenario, which illustrates the possible intensity with which services can now be installed in a building, there is the example of a new 'server farm' in London (a building to house ICT network hardware). Reported to require the same amount of electricity as a small city, this ten storey building will require the equivalent of the following to service 100,000 powerful computers:

- Chilling power of 1.8 million fridges;
- Fuel storage capacity of 400 buses;
- Electricity to power 80,000 houses;
- Diesel generators equal to 726 cars.

... in addition to 250 security cameras, high-pressure fire protection and enough data cables to transport 15,000 times all the current data traffic in Europe. This is a rather extreme example and has some clear implications in terms of the energy use associated with the growth in the ICT industry. It is no surprise then, that the building services industry and ICT providers are now aligning their businesses to offer integrated solutions.

Further reading

Baird, G. (2001) *The architectural expression of environmental control systems*, E & FN Spon, London, UK.
Chadderton, D.V. (2000) *Building services engineering* (3rd edition), E & FN Spon, London, UK.
Greeno, R. (1997) *Building services, technology and design*, Longman, Harlow, UK.
Greeno, R. & Hall, F.E. (2001) *Building services handbook*, Butterworth-Heinemann, Oxford, UK.
Nelson, G. (1995) *The architecture of building services*, Batsford, London, UK.

WH

Service cores
See: CORE (SERVICES)

Service life
See: DESIGN LIFE

Shear walls
See: BRACING

Shrinkage
See: DRY CONSTRUCTION AND WET CONSTRUCTION;
MORTARS, CEMENT AND LIME

Sick building syndrome (SBS)

The designation of a range of illnesses brought on by a 'cocktail effect' of indoor pollutants, outdoor pollutants and poor air quality.

See also: AIRTIGHTNESS AND IAQ; ENVIRONMENTAL DESIGN; ECOLOGICAL DESIGN; 'ECO-POINTS'; NIGHT VENTILATION; SUSTAINABILITY; VENTILATION.

> ... *a disease that we managed to create for ourselves when trying to design and construct systems for internal comfort. Such systems must be properly monitored and maintained.*
>
> (Source: UK Health & Safety Executive, 1989)

The designation 'sick building syndrome' (SBS) was introduced in the 1980s when the link between tightly sealed interiors, outgassing of chemicals from synthetic materials and a range of health problems was established. But 'unhealthy buildings' are not a new phenomenon: poor ventilation, dampness and condensation have been causing chest infections and breathing difficulties since Victorian times. The case of poor living conditions in tower blocks is well documented, but this was also due to the mismatch between 'social engineering' and inappropriately specified heating systems.

Sick building syndrome is diagnosed by the incidence of health complaints, the presence of synthetic furnishings, carpets etc and an envelope with a very low ventilation (air change) rate with, perhaps, even a faulty or poorly maintained, mechanical ventilation system. Local conditions such as traffic pollution may also have a contributory effect. The cost to UK businesses from lost productivity due to the symptoms of SBS is said to be in the region of £500–750 million per annum.

The medical symptoms and illness associated with unhealthy buildings and SBS are:

- Allergic symptoms, such as watery eyes or runny nose;
- Asthmatic symptoms, such as chest tightness;
- Dryness, of the skin, eyes, nose and/or throat;
- General feelings, such as lethargy, headache or malaise.

Note that 'humidifier fever' and occupational asthma are illnesses related to buildings, but they are usually considered separate from the less specific SBS because their causes can usually be identified. Another example is Legionnaires' disease arising from *Legionella pneumophila*, a small bacterium that thrives in warm, non-sterile water such as water-based cooling towers.

Prevention of SBS is based on better design and specification of HVAC equipment, the use of night ventilation to clear any indoor pollutants that have built up during the day, natural ventilation where possible and allowance for good maintenance. Wherever possible, designers should also aim to minimise the amount of finishing and furnishing materials that are likely to outgas VOCs etc. in use (see below).

Air quality issues

In both urban and rural areas, the term 'fresh air' is increasingly difficult to evaluate. Since the Industrial Revolution, carbon dioxide concentrations in the atmosphere have continued to rise. According to the UK Institute of Terrestrial Ecology there is an enormous complexity and uncertainty about the magnitude and interaction of such pollutants, including electromagnetic forces and a range of chemical and volatile compounds.

Many items and materials in a building give out gases, in addition to chemicals for cleaning and synthetic building materials 'outgassing' other toxic components. A simple checklist includes:

Ammonia; Asbestos; Benzene; Biocides; Carbon monoxide; Detergent dust; Ethanol; Fibreglass; Formaldehyde; Hydrocarbons; Methanol; Motor vehicle particulates; Nitrogen oxide; Ozone; Paints; PCBs (although banned in the UK are still found in electrical appliances); Pesticides; Radon; Solvents; Tobacco smoke; Vinyl chloride.

There is increasing evidence of illnesses caused by exposure to electromagnetic fields from normal household devices such as microwave ovens, televisions and computer VDUs. Researchers at the US Environmental Protection Agency have detected up to 300 volatile organic compounds in a single building and dozens of separate compounds in just one office. The study of indoor air pollutants is developing rapidly with major industry input from the construction materials manufacturers in North America and Europe. For example, tests on building materials indicate that hard, inert natural materials such as ceramics, concrete and stone offer good health credentials for surface finishes. Measurements for indoor pollutants have been established (the OLF and the DECIPOL), the latter being a correlation between the mix of pollutants and the dilution caused by ventilation.

Addressing the problem

Dr Sherry Rogers of the North East Centre for Environmental Medicine, Syracuse, New York, USA has, over a period of 20 years, proved that many of the rules of medicine are becoming obsolete when it comes to understanding hypersensitivity to chemicals. The symptoms that people complain about are predictable and variable. Over 2,000 patients participated in a 'blind' testing programme on building health. In addition to physical symptoms, some suffered personality changes. The trigger was found to be high concentrations of volatile chemicals in home furnishings, floors and the use of paints. Once the source material was removed and ventilation and air quality improved, the patients became healthy once again.

Further reading

Curwell, S., March, C. & Venables, R. (1990) *Buildings and health: the Rosehaugh guide*, RIBA Publications, London, UK.

Hansen, D.L. (1999) *Indoor air quality issues*, Taylor & Francis, New York, USA.

Holdsworth, B. & Sealey, A.F. (1992) *Healthy buildings: a design primer for a living environment*, Longman, Harlow, UK.

London Hazards Centre (1990) *Sick building syndrome: causes, effects and control*, London Hazards Centre, UK.

Rogers, S. (1986) *The E.I. (Environmental Illness) syndrome*, Prestige Publishing, USA.

Rogers, S. (1990) *Tired or toxic*, Prestige, USA.

Rostron, J. (ed.) (1997) *Sick building syndrome: concepts, issues and practice*, E & FN Spon, London, UK.

WH/JG

Silicone

See: SEALANTS

Single-ply membranes

Single-ply membranes are used in waterproofing, usually for flat roofs, but also for basements and linings.

See also: ALUMINIUM; COMPOSITE DECKING; COPPER; GRASS ('GREEN') ROOFS; LEAD; PLASTICS; PROFILED METAL DECKING; ROOFS; STANDING SEAM ROOFS; ZINC.

What are single-ply membranes?

Flat roofs in particular have proved rather difficult to use in the cool, wet, UK climate. While there is clear sense in using the flat roof as part of an overall architectural schema, to produce a particular aesthetic of form, the practical application of the technology has not been very successful. Hence, the flat roof has not proved popular with lay people. However, technology has moved on; single-ply membranes have shown a good track record as an alternative to built-up roofing, sheet metals, mastic asphalt and elastomeric coatings. The design and selection of the membrane itself will be influenced by previous experience, particular project needs, availability of products and commercial opportunity. Membrane sheets can be manufactured from a wide range of polymers or elastomers; some of the more common are:

- Chlorosulphonated polyethylene;
- EPDM;
- Olefin co-polymers;
- Plasticised PVC.

Proprietary systems may be unreinforced or reinforced with a fabric core, often of a woven polyester fibre.

Practical matters

Single-ply waterproofing membranes are essentially a system comprising fabricated sheets of a synthetic polymer or elastomer, which is fixed, overlapped and sealed to form a continuous membrane over the whole roof. Fixing is required primarily to resist wind uplift but also to stop traffic creating tears or damage, or on sloping roofs to locate the membrane. Fixing is most commonly achieved by mechanical means into the substrate but can also be by adhesives or ballasting. Mechanical fixings penetrations are protected against leakage by the overlap seal with the adjacent sheet. All of these fixings systems can be appropriate depending upon other project needs. Mechanical fastening can allow very rapid waterproofing with large areas 'rolled out' and sealed. The principal drawback with these isolated fixings is the potential water leakage route beneath the membrane should it become damaged. Adhesive fixing (if full bonded) is a much slower installation process, but can give some protection against water tracking beneath the membrane. Ballasted roofs can be simple to install with no fixing penetrations through the membrane. Should damage or leakage occur, tracing leaks beneath the ballasting can be very time-consuming. An associated concern is sometimes raised regarding the use of single-ply membranes in the inverted warm roof construction approach.

Performance

Whether mechanically or adhesively fixed, the membranes are usually fully exposed and hence subject to full weathering with exposure to UV, water leaching and possibly to aggressive chemicals in the local environment. With the relatively thin sheets, the inherent durability of the polymer or elastomer sheet formulation is central to long-term performance. Even within a particular polymer type (e.g. PVC) the specific formulation and ingredients specific to particular proprietary products may give differing in-service performance. Standard assessment methods used by European Agrément bodies, together with assessment of existing installations can be helpful in deciding potential suitability.

Sealing of edge laps and ends of sheets are made by adhesive or by heat welding, often using automated welding machines. Some systems use off-site welding fabrication to produce large area sheets, which are lifted onto the roof. Many of the single-ply membrane products have an accessory range of preformed detail pieces, which can facilitate waterproofing of service penetration and edge details. Simplicity of joining together with specialist trained installers are essential to achieving successful waterproofing in a system which requires perfection at all laps and joints.

Environmental considerations

Assessing the environmental impact and health and safety implications of single-ply membranes is as complicated as for any proprietary product. The membranes utilise relatively low volumes of material, which serve to reduce the impact and some may be recyclable at the end of service life. For solvent-based adhesive systems there are impacts on health and on safety implications through solvent release, and recycling is more difficult.

Further reading

British Flat Roofing Council/CIRIA (1993) *Flat roofing: design and good practice*, BFRC/CIRIA, London, UK.

British Standards Institution (1982) BS 6229: *Code of practice for roofs with continuously supported coverings*, BSI, London, UK.

Building Research Establishment (1986) *Flat roof design: the technical options*, BRE Digest 312, BRE, Watford, UK.

OA

Siphonic drainage

See: WATER MANAGEMENT AND DRAINAGE

Siza, Alvaro

Alvaro Joaquim de Meio Siza Vieira is a Portuguese architect with a penchant for exposed concrete.

See also: BRICKS AND BLOCKS; CONCRETE; CONCRETE – STRUCTURES; ECOLOGICAL DESIGN; ENVIRONMENTAL DESIGN; FABRIC ENERGY STORAGE; SURFACE FINISHES; VENTILATION.

Alvaro Siza: the Setubal College of Education (1986–93). The simple concrete construction allows a great variety within the internal spaces and openings. Photograph by Thomas Deckker.

The work of Alvaro Siza has come to epitomise the approach of some, mainly European, architects who have rejected technological display in their work in favour of more sophisticated architectonic developments in areas such as use of daylight and relation to the site. They have developed a broad attitude of political and social responsibility to the construction and utilisation of their work, an approach that has been called 'critical regionalism'. Architectural critic Kenneth Frampton emphasises the experiential nature within such work over the graphic (aesthetic).

Portugal is one of the poorest countries in Europe with a very undeveloped building industry. Siza uses local materials and works closely with local craftspeople to achieve an extremely high quality of detailing. As in many countries in Southern Europe, this means rendered concrete frames and terracotta block infill. This flexible and adaptable technology allows not only varied relationships of solid to void (e.g. window to wall), but also sheltered openings and high thermal mass appropriate to the climate.

There are reasons beyond the material nature of the construction, however, which explain why Siza is regarded so highly. The sensitivity to the handling of building volumes, internal spaces, staircases, natural light, and views through windows is a deliberate counterpoint to their generalised treatment in much contemporary architecture. The building is treated as an extension of its context, but in no sense historicist. It is not its appearance, but the movement around the site and into the building and the disposition of building volumes, which relate to the context.

Siza was born in Matosinhos in the North of Portugal in 1933. He studied at the School of Architecture at the University of Oporto from 1949 to 1955, and began to build even before he graduated. He came to notice with works such as the Boa Nova Restaurant, Matosinhos (1958–63), the Swimming Pool at Leça de Palmeira (1961–62), and the Pinto e Soto Maior Bank, Oliveira de Azemeis (1971–74). The response to context was noticeable. In the Pool at Leça de Palmeira, the walls that form sheltered swimming pools are a direct response to sea levels and the rock formation. In the Pinto e Soto Maior Bank the site is a modest urban square and the volumes of the building, the openings and the pattern of movement form an extension to it.

Siza's first public buildings after the Revolution in 1974 were for the construction of public housing and the renovation of urban districts in Oporto, Bouça (1973–77) and São Victor (1974–77) for SAAL ('Serviço de apoio ambulatorio local', the local support service). These were extremely low-cost projects in which great attention was necessarily paid to the urban spaces. They led to the commission for the Quinta da Malagueira housing (1977, under construction) in Évora. This was an entire urban quarter outside the walls of the old town, one of Portugal's most beautiful cities, which had been preserved relatively intact. The building form was of rows of two storey terraces back-to-back with access roads for cars and pedestrians between the rows, organised around an aqueduct reminiscent of the 16th century 'Aguas da Prata' aqueduct in Évora, disused and now incorporated into the urban fabric. The construction of concrete and blockwork intentionally left room for degree of adaptability in plan form during and after construction to meet the differing circumstances of the inhabitants.

The Quinta da Malagueira housing led to commissions for housing at the Schlesische Tor, Berlin (1980–84) and a series of urban plans and housing: 'De Punkt en de Komma' (1983–88) and the Doedijnstraat estate (1989–to date), Schilderswijk, The Hague. This increased Siza's international reputation and he now has commissions throughout Europe.

Siza's recent works include the Faculty of Architecture at the University of Oporto (1987–93), the Setubal College of Education (1986–93) and the Galicia Museum of Modern Art, Santiago de Compostela (1988–93). At the Faculty of Architecture the public spaces form a route along the contours of the site, leaving a podium facing the river for the studios. The Setubal College of Education has an 'H' shape plan reminiscent of the nearby monastery at Cape Espichel; the classrooms open to a courtyard with deeply overhanging roofs. The Galicia Museum of Modern Art lies on a narrow street on a steep hill in an historic town. It consists of three interlinked blocks: an entrance block aligned to the street, a small lecture theatre protruding into the street and a long sequence of galleries along the contours behind.

Due to simple and generally massive construction, highly varied window sizes and provision of shading devices, the internal environments in Siza's buildings are usually excellent. The brilliance and economy with which he achieves these for many architects, calls into question the necessity of overt displays of technology.

Further reading

Barata, P.M. (1997) *Alvaro Siza 1954–1976*, Editorial Blau, Lisbon, Portugal.
Dubois, M. (1998) *Alvaro Siza – inside the city*, Whitney Library of Design, New York, USA.
Frampton, K. (2000) *Alvaro Siza: complete works*, Phaidon Press, London, UK.
Testa, P. (1996) *Alvaro Siza*, Birkhäuser, Switzerland.

TD

Slate

See: STONE

Slim floors

See: COMPOSITE DECKING

'Smart' glazing

See: GLASS – LAMINATED AND COATED GLASS

'Smart' materials

See: INTELLIGENT FAÇADES AND MATERIALS

'Smart' skin

See: INTELLIGENT FAÇADES AND MATERIALS

Softwoods

See: TIMBER – HARDWOODS AND SOFTWOODS

Solar control glass

See: GLASS – LAMINATED AND COATED GLASS

Solar panels

An active method of transmitting solar energy into a circulating medium of air or water, to be used for heating and hot water services.

See also: ECOLOGICAL DESIGN; ENVIRONMENTAL DESIGN; FAÇADES AND FAÇADE ENGINEERING; LOUVRES AND BRISE-SOLEIL; PHOTOVOLTAICS; PHASE CHANGE MATERIALS; ROOFS; SERVICES; THERMAL COMFORT.

What is a solar panel?

The heat from sunlight can be utilised passively in buildings to warm interior spaces simply by passive solar design and orientation of the building. It can also be used more specifically in active systems to heat a medium such as water, which can be pumped around a building for both heating and as a hot water supply. The 'solar panel' is a device on the roof or façade of a building through which pipes containing water are designed to run. Here they are exposed to the sun's warmth, and in its flow through the panel, the medium is heated and is recirculated. It is a simple device that is very effective in warm climates, but still quite useful in cooler zones.

Product development

Solar panels have been produced commercially since the 1880s, when they were featured in the mail order catalogue from US store Sears & Roebucks. The panels were shipped out to the Pioneer towns of western America in their thousands. The technology of the 'collectors' developed throughout the early part of the 20th century, with use peaking during the 1970s. Since then, liquid-type, flat-plate collectors have been used alongside air-type, flat collectors and parabolic collectors.

In the Netherlands today, all renewable technologies are developing apace, supported actively by government initiatives to generate new industry, investment and employment. In particular, a new generation of the traditional flat plate collector has been developed. In a study of 44 projects, which involved individual homes, social housing, offices, large apartment blocks and small factory units, 85% of the heating and hot water for 22 buildings was provided by solar panels coupled to solar, low water content, high efficiency boilers.

New developments in solar energy collection tend to look at combining this technology with others such as PV, heat recovery, louvres and shading in addition to fabric energy storage or combined heat and power schemes. For example, Battle McCarthy and local architects Neutelings Riedijk developed a series of solar-induced thermosiphon systems and a 'solar environmental wall' for the south west façade of an apartment building in Dedemdvaartsweg in The Hague.

Solar power in the UK

The success of solar panels in the UK has been rather limited. Previous government strategies on energy generation were oriented towards fossil fuels and nuclear power, with alternative, renewable energies such as solar power and wind power lower on the agenda. This is changing, however, with new targets being set for the UK to achieve 10% of its energy generation via renewable sources in the next few years. For solar panels (and photovoltaics), the lengthy payback time in terms of cost and resultant energy savings has prevented widespread adoption of the technology. This is particularly problematic because other energy costs are very economic. However, until significant changes are made to energy billing and resource depletion is 'chargeable', then the current situation is unlikely to change.

Further reading

Anderson, B. & Wells, M. (1981) *Passive solar energy*, Brick House Publishing, Massachusetts, USA.

Hastings, S.R. (1999) *Solar sir systems: built examples*, James & James, London, UK.

Hastings, S.R. & Mørck, O. (2000) *Solar air systems: a design handbook*, James & James, London, UK.

Steven Winter Associates & Crosbie, M.J. (ed.) (1998) *The passive solar design and construction handbook*, John Wiley & Sons, New York, USA.

WH/JG

Specification

To describe in exact detail the characteristics, performance and application of materials, products or systems, in addition to commissioning and maintenance procedures.

See also: BESPOKE; CONSTRUCTION PROGRAMME; CRITICAL PATH ANALYSIS; DESIGN LIFE; DURABILITY; LIFE-CYCLE COSTING; MAINTENANCE; PERFORMANCE; PROPRIETARY GOODS AND STANDARDISATION; SUSTAINABILITY.

Introduction

It goes without saying that there is a wealth of choice in the materials, products, technologies and offerings from individual manufacturers and suppliers in the construction industry (there are thought to be about 20,000 such businesses). There is also a wealth of codes and standards that govern their use. This information is so vast that for an individual project, a clear means of communicating is needed stating exactly what is required for a building. This is achieved within a package of information, such as drawings, construction plans, cost information and maintenance manuals, but these must be accompanied by a document that sets out the precise nature of the materials and products needed.

This is called a '**specification**'. Within this document, the design team specifies (i.e. is precise, specific) about what it requires in terms of landscaping, façades, furniture, in fact everything that the client needs for its building. Hence, the specification is a key element in making simple and understandable all the specifics of process and performance to the rest of the design team, contractors, specialist contractors, client and building users. The 'spec' is devised on the basis of what is required by the client and of course standards (see below). A three-tier system based on quality levels has been suggested as a way of clarifying specifications, i.e. budget, standard and premium. But designers should be wary of 'over-specification', in which, erring on the side of caution in terms of performance for example, can result in a disproportionately greater cost. For example the cost of timber increases almost exponentially with larger section sizes.

What's in a specification?

In most instances, the specification is unique to the project in hand, written to best serve that particular building. It will include descriptions relating to all aspects of:

- Groundworks;
- External works;
- Foundation (sub-structure);
- Services and M&E;
- Superstructure (frame etc);
- Fit-out.

Thus, it will be a 'bespoke' document, tailored to the business, operational, economic and environmental requirements of the client and locality. For example, a specification may account for sustainable design. This has necessarily increased the coverage and complexity of the specification document, with its holistic approach to ecology, energy and economy.

In cases where multiples of a building type (e.g. houses, factories or fast-food restaurants), are being built, then a 'standard specification' can be developed. There are also sector standards for specifications such as those for structural steel and concrete structures; these documents are very helpful for these commonly used materials and are used on a daily basis by many design teams. European integration is also beginning to affect the UK construction industry with the introduction of EC codes, regulations and technical specifications. Clear and concise guidance on the use of these codes and regulations for construction quality and quality standards needs particular attention and constant upgrading.

It is interesting that many new codes are oriented towards **performance specification**. This is a different use of the term specification, but it is relevant because it is about moving away from prescriptive standards towards specifying only the result or outcome to be achieved. While this is an excellent opportunity for innovation, it does mean that design specifications are set to become even more bespoke than they are now. Specification management is therefore becoming an onerous, but critical task in the design office. This can be aided by the use of IT applications, and the better integration now of CAD drawing packages and specification information tools. These also facilitate better working relationships with construction programming and critical path analysis methods.

Further reading

Atkinson, G.A. (1995) *Construction quality & quality standards*, E & FN Spon, London, UK.

Cox, P.J. (1994) *Writing specifications for construction*, McGraw Hill, London, UK.

Emmitt, S. & Yeomans, D. (2001) *Specifying buildings: a design management perspective*, Butterworth-Heinemann, Oxford, UK.

Howard, N. & Shiers, D. (1996) *The green guide to specification*, Post Office Property Holdings, UK.

Rosen, H. (1998) *Construction specification writing: principles and procedures*, 4th edition, John Wiley & Sons, New York, USA.

Willis, C.J. & Willis, J.A. (1997) *Specification writing for architects and surveyors* (11th edition), Blackwell Science, Oxford, UK.

WH/JG

Spider connector

See: GLASS – STRUCTURAL GLAZING

Stack effect

The 'stack effect' is the result of air density decreasing as temperature increases. The greater the temperature difference, the greater the buoyancy effect and hence the more effective the air circulation in the stack.

See also: ATRIUM; BUILDING MANAGEMENT SYSTEMS; DYNAMIC THERMAL SIMULATION; ENERGY EFFICIENCY; ENVIRONMENTAL DESIGN; FABRIC ENERGY STORAGE; FAÇADES AND FAÇADE ENGINEERING; HVAC; VENTILATION; WIND TOWERS.

Introduction

This entry discusses the energy efficiency potential of managing air flows in a building via a natural mechanism called the 'stack effect'.

Air density varies approximately as the inverse of temperature. The weight of two vertical columns of air at different temperatures, separated by a vertical surface, will differ and a pressure difference will be created across the interlayer. Where openings exist in the surface, the pressure difference will cause a flow of air to occur. Passive cooling systems are now being designed based on the fact that warm air rises through the phenomenon of convection, and is replaced by colder air. It is possible to enhance this '**stack effect**' by using the sun to create a 'chimney', thereby increasing the convective flow by increasing the temperature (and pressure) difference.

The rate of airflow through a building depends upon the areas and resistances of the various apertures and the pressure differential across the building. Air will move from low-level outlets to high-level outlets in a heated building, or in an opposite direction if the building is cooler than outside. Other influencing factors of pressure distribution are the presence of atria, stairwells, lift shafts, ventilators and mechanical ventilation and exhaust systems.

(Source: CIBSE Guide, Section A4)

Using the stack effect

The stack effect is best managed by designing a form of 'chimney or flue' within a building. This could be a double-skin façade, a wind tower or an atrium. The performance and overall effectiveness of these features is dependent on solar orientation, wind patterns and the perceptions of building users as to their thermal comfort. In most examples, one sees a wind-activated ventilator cap (e.g. mechanically activated ridge vents at the top of an atrium) to ensure airflow is always positive. Sometimes these take the forms of 'cowls' that swivel to take advantage of the pressure difference caused by the prevailing wind. Indeed, the development of passive cooling in buildings is starting to create exciting new and modified architectural forms as designers experiment with the potential of this energy efficient approach. For example, passive downdraught cooling (e.g. in wind towers) requires four major architectural elements to be considered:

- **Supply tower** designed to 'catch' the wind or use buoyancy forces to drive the airflow;
- **Transitional space** (chimney or buffer) that can be open or closed, providing vertical distribution of the air;
- **Internal occupied space** ventilated from the transitional space, with cooled air moving towards the perimeter of the building;
- **Openings** or exhaust shafts to release air to the exterior.

The design team and building services engineer can use dynamic thermal simulation to model air flows and evaluate different options, based on local variations in temperature, relative humidity and air velocity. The geometry and disposition of openings at different levels in a building typically provide the major influence on performance, with M&E services providing the fine-tuning. In some instances, extra cooling can be induced (i.e. in passive downdraught evaporative cooling) by having water present in the system.

Built examples

Devices based on the stack effect such as double skin façades (using glazed thermal buffers) have been shown to save energy, reduce mechanical heating, cooling and air conditioning costs and allow generous amounts of daylight into a building. Two examples of buildings using the stack effect via twin-skin façades are: The Dutch Ministry of Housing & Environment (VROM) in The Hague (designed in 1992 by architect Jan Hoogstad) which used a second glass, acoustic skin; and a cargo building at Schipol Airport, near Amsterdam (designed by Neutelings Riedijk Architects) which uses a double skin with external vents to allow natural ventilation. These close whenever aircraft noise rises above a certain level, as well as at night and in the winter to help retain the heat in the building.

Further reading

Battle McCarthy (1999) *Wind towers*, Academy Editions, John Wiley & Sons, London, UK.

Chartered Institute of Building Services Engineers, *CIBSE Guide Volume A*, CIBSE, London, UK.

Moore, F. (1993) *Environmental control systems: heating, cooling and lighting* (International Edition), McGraw Hill, New York, USA.

WH/JG

Stainless steel

A commonly used metal found in roofing, cladding and other building elements.

See also: ALUMINIUM; CASTINGS; CLADDING; CONCRETE – STRUCTURES; CONNECTIONS; COPPER; CORROSION; COR-TEN®; DESIGN LIFE; DURABILITY; GLASS – STRUCTURAL GLAZING; METALS; ROGERS, RICHARD; ROOFS; SERVICES; STANDING SEAM ROOF; STRUCTURAL STEEL; SURFACE FINISHES; WALLS; WEATHERING; WINDOWS AND CURTAIN WALLING; ZINC.

What is stainless steel?

Stainless steel is a term that actually describes quite a wide range of steel alloys that have in common the addition of chromium. General properties are good resistance to corrosion, abrasion, heat and damage. Chromium is an 'intelligent' material – on contact with air it forms a protective oxide layer, which will self-repair if scratched or cut. This property can be enhanced further by the addition of nickel and molybdenum in the alloy. Hence, bright shiny stainless steels are used in many applications where high quality and durability are valued performance attributes. Although stainless steel is about five times the cost of 'normal' steel, it has the benefits of better weathering and corrosion resistance, which reduce inspection and maintenance costs. This metal is also recyclable and has a very high value as a scrap metal.

Production is in three main stages: steel scrap is melted, refined and alloyed (as set out below), then cast into ingots for forming into sheets, plates or bars. Casting, machining and folding of the metal are all feasible, in addition to spinning (suitable for pipes etc). Components can be connected together by welding.

Design considerations

All grades of stainless steel contain at least 10–12% chromium and varying amounts of other metals, as outlined in the table below.

Uses in architecture

Specific stainless steel products for buildings include:

- Bespoke castings;
- Decorative architectural profiles;

Compositions (types and alloy metals)	Applications
Austenitic 17–18% chromium 8–11% nickel	Rural to moderate urban, industrial and marine settings.
Ferritic 17% chromium	Suitable for light interior uses only.
Duplex 22–23% chromium 4–5% nickel 3% molybdenum + nitrogen	Severe industrial or marine applications. Addition of molybdenum helps in more aggressive conditions.

- Extruded profiles for façades;
- Fixings and fasteners;
- Plumbing components;
- Reinforcement bar, fabric, rod and wire;
- Roof cladding;
- Structural connectors;
- Structural glazing connectors;
- Tension structure components;
- Wall cladding panels;
- Wall ties for masonry.

The art of imparting surface finishes on stainless steel is such that there are no reference specifications, rather the design team should discuss requirements with a specialist finisher. Pattern printing, mirror finishing and polishing are often specified. Acid-etching and silk screen techniques can be used for bespoke patterns, logos etc. Although the 'natural' finish can also be coloured by cathodic treatment or chemical stains it is more common to see stainless steel left 'as is' (it is the only form of steel that can withstand weathering and remain so). Regular washing or careful design for run-off of rain can extend the life of the material. Note that non-continuous support gives a 'ripple' effect' to the stainless steel that can be seen clearly.

Compatible materials

Designers should exercise caution when using stainless steel in terms of long-term robustness. If in doubt, the British Standard BS EN 10088 or relevant manufacturer's literature should be consulted. Corrosion can be caused via a few key mechanisms:

- Crevices that retain moisture;
- Galvanic (bimetallic) contact with copper;
- Localised attack from salts, humidity or corrosive agents;
- Pitting of the surface;
- Stress corrosion cracking.

Stainless steel may itself cause some surface damage to zinc and aluminium due to bimetallic corrosion. Contact should therefore be avoided by using isolating connections.

Built examples

Perhaps the foremost precedent is the stainless steel cladding on the Empire State building, built in 1939 in New York. Recent case studies include:

- European Court of Human Rights, Strasbourg (Richard Rogers); built 1994, uses 5,000 m² of stainless steel cladding in the form of rainscreen panels;
- Highly reflective stainless steel cladding designed by Peter Rice covers the curved surfaces of the spherical La Geode in the Parc Villette, Paris, France;
- Canary Wharf, London: One Canada Square, a 245 m tall tower clad in stainless steel by US architect Cesar Pelli;
- One of the world's tallest buildings, the Petronas Towers, Kuala Lumpur, Malaysia (1996). Cesar Pelli designed the stainless steel-clad, twin 88 storey towers with landmark walkways at 41st floor level;
- Waterloo International terminal in London (Grimshaw, 1992) features profiled roofing, cast glazing connectors, interior screens, counters etc in the broadest UK portfolio for this metal;
- Renzo Piano's Kansai airport in Osaka, Japan (1994) uses stainless steel 'tiles' for cladding to the roof, which mimics the metallic-glazed 'kawara' tiles of Japanese traditional architecture;
- The use of punched stainless steel cladding to a Prada store in San Francisco, USA has been proposed by OMA. The 25 mm thick sheets will be pierced with thousands of circular holes to give daylight to the interior.

Further reading

Baddoo, N., Burgan, R. & Ogden, R.G. (1997) *Architects' guide to stainless steel*, SCI Publication 179, Steel Construction Institute, Ascot, UK.

Burgan, B.A. (1993) *Concise guide to the structural design of stainless steel* (2nd Edition), Steel Construction Institute, Ascot, UK.

Pelli, C. & Crosbie, M.J. (2001) *Petronas Towers*, John Wiley & Sons, New York, USA.

JG

Standardisation

See: PROPRIETARY GOODS AND STANDARDISATION

Standing seam roof

A very common form of roofing in architecture, this is a method for fixing metal roof finishes.

See also: ALUMINIUM; CLADDING; CLADDING – COMPONENTS; CONNECTIONS; COPPER; CORROSION; INSULATION; LEAD; METALS; OVERCLADDING; PROFILED METAL DECKING; ROOFS; STAINLESS STEEL; SURFACE FINISHES; WEATHERING; ZINC.

Introduction

In metal roofing and cladding, 'standing seam roof' denotes a generic class of systems that feature the ability to fix to structure, and join adjacent sheets, without penetrating the outer sheet with fasteners. This is achieved by concealing the fasteners, the use of 'clip fix' assembly and, usually, locating the actual sidelap well above the trough or pan of the sheet. This is of great architectural benefit because the roofline can thus be kept clean, clear and elegant; the finish and quality of the metal roofing is paramount, giving the best first overall impression to the viewer.

The standing seam concept is a development of two traditional methods. Most current systems follow one or the other approach.

Concealed fix – In lead roofing, the relatively narrow width of the roll necessitates the making of joints under a timber batten, over which the lead of the next sheet is dressed. This is the commonly seen detail on church roofs. Modern equivalents, with profiled metal sheet, achieve this concealed joint by a clip fix detail on the side lap. The side of each sheet is fixed down to the structure (purlin or rail) either directly or by means of a clip. The next sheet is then clipped over the side lap upstand of the first sheet, and so on across the roof. Concealed fix systems are used primarily for very low pitch roofs (different manufacturers recommend minimum pitch between $1\frac{1}{2}°$ and $4°$), and for long ridge/eaves lengths. At the lower end of this range, tolerances in level of the main structure can effectively reduce the design pitch. Some systems can be curved in the horizontal plane and/or tapered on plan (e.g. for circular or domed roofs).

Welted joints – Early metal sheet roof cladding formed the joint by turning up the edge of the sheet, then folding it over with that from the adjacent sheet, and often took the form of 'tiles'. This can still be seen on some older railway buildings. Current practice uses special site tools to run along the joint between two sheets, welting or turning over the edges. Welted joint systems are usually specified for special finishes to non-vertical elements such as mansards, or for complex, feature roof forms. These are available as ridge to eaves systems, or as smaller panels.

Design notes

Materials for standing seam roofs include steel, typically given a surface coating such as galvanising (with zinc/aluminium), colour-coated paint finishes, lead or copper on galvanised steel or stainless steel. Aluminium is used plain or with an embossed mill finish, surface plated finish or colour-coated paint finish.

The ability to roll and fix long lengths enables standing seam systems to run from ridge to eaves without an end lap. The ultimate restriction on sheet length is transport limitations, but some manufacturers have site-rolling facilities that transport the metal to site as coil, then cold roll it to almost any required length. Curved and tapered sheets, backed up by manufacturers' CAD support, make complex roof forms possible. Openings for rooflights, ventilators, and the like, are detailed specially and remain either between ribs, or run across several ribs with an arrangement for draining the upslope side.

Standing seam systems, like other metal cladding systems, need to fulfil a number of functional criteria:

- **Structure** – Wind loads and other live loads are transferred to the supporting structure; dead loads from the cladding itself are supported. Movement control is an integral part of maintaining appearance and weathertightness. Specification is based on span characteristics and deflection under load. No diaphragm action is achieved, but systems with metal liners gain some purlin restraint.
- **Weathertightness** – this is generally achieved by the side lap detail (effectively the joint is well above the pan of the sheet), although some systems incorporate a mastic bead in the overlap.
- **Airtightness** – standing seam systems are generally permeable, permitting the interlayer to breathe. However, requirements for reducing air permeability may be fulfilled by careful vapour barrier detailing.
- **Durability** – facing materials are specified with a design life, or period to first maintenance, in mind. Coated steels might require maintenance at 40 years or less (depending on specification and location), and aluminium may last beyond 40 years. By comparison, fairfaced brickwork, for example, can last 100 years or more before maintenance (re: pointing), whilst site painted timber requires

attention at around five years. The durability of the substrate may also be a factor, especially on exposed sites.

GW

Steel

See: STRUCTURAL STEEL; STAINLESS STEEL;
COR-TEN® (WEATHERING STEEL)

Stone

Natural stone materials have been used in architecture for thousands of years. Although their use in contemporary architecture tends to be limited to traditional styles and refurbishment work, there are some notable exceptions.

See also: BESPOKE; BRICKS AND BLOCKS; CEMENT; CLADDING; COLUMN; CONCRETE; DESIGN LIFE; FABRIC ENERGY STORAGE; FAÇADES AND FAÇADE ENGINEERING; FOUNDATIONS; 'HONESTY'; KAHN, LOUIS; LIFE-CYCLE ANALYSIS; MORTARS, CEMENT AND LIME; SCARPA, CARLO; SURFACE FINISHES; VAN DER ROHE, MIES; WALLS; WEATHERING.

Introduction

Rock can be extracted from the Earth as small particles (rubble or aggregates for concrete) or as cut stone for use as a building material. Stone is the term given to rocks that are quarried, shaped and have a purposeful function. The Pyramids in Egypt, Greek temples or Stonehenge in Wiltshire would probably be most people's initial thoughts about the most ancient use of stone in architecture, but of course numerous stone antiquities were constructed all over the world, many dating from several thousand years ago. As a locally available material that could be quarried at surface, stone provided many communities with a basic building material – its loadbearing qualities meant that walls and columns could be erected. Hence, stone is still thought of as the basic building block for civilisation. Modern developments in transport enabled stone to be quarried in one location and then carried to site elsewhere, in which case we see stones such as Carrara marble (from Italy) used in say North America and Brazilian granites used in the UK. However, stone is a limited natural resource and so designers must appreciate that not only is there a cost implication associated with transporting stone over great distances, but also an environmental impact. For example, the best quality slates can represent just 1% of a quarry's output – the other 99% may be discarded.

The rest of this entry provides an overview of contemporary uses for stone in architecture, with greater emphasis placed on modern technology rather than stone's use in Classical or Classical Revival architecture and related forms of traditional masonry detailing. While the latter is important in refurbishment, conservation and some new build projects, it is described in detail in other publications.

Basic categories

Stone for architecture is hewn from rock, which can be classified into three broad types:

- **Igneous** – these crystalline rocks have been formed by cooling magma and dominate the Earth's crust. Deep under the Earth's surface, the cooling process is slow, so grains tend to be coarse (e.g. granite), but nearer the surface, cooling is quicker, so fine grains result (e.g. porphyry and basalt). Igneous rocks are typically hard, dense and durable and are often simply called 'granites'. The incidence and distribution of mineral particles, such as feldspar (white, pink or red), quartz (white or greyish) and hornblende (dark grey to black) determine the colour and texture of the various rocks. Dramatic patterns can be found in samples where later igneous intrusions disrupt a previously even particle distribution. Decorative work may incorporate the rarer porphyrys (shades of red, purple or green). Granites are quarried in Scotland or imported from Brazil and Scandinavia.
- **Sedimentary** – these are layered rocks, with particles laid down over time by wind or water. They share a common appearance of clearly defined horizontal bands (strata). Properties will vary according to the source and nature of the deposition. Examples include conglomerate, sandstone, shale, limestone-marble, dolomite, travertine and onyx-marble. Appearance of sedimentary rocks depends on the angularity (or roundness) and concentration of mineral particles, the thickness and variability of the layers (bedding) and any irregularities. Limestones in particular come in a great variety of forms; UK sources produce colours from white and cream to pink, grey and brown.
- **Metamorphic** – this third group is composed of either igneous or sedimentary rocks that have been changed by pressure or temperature. Mineral compositions or concentrations may change, but there will be a 'family' resemblance to the original (parent) rock. Examples include gneiss, schist, crystalline-marble, serpentine and slate. The colours of these rocks are much 'cooler' than the warmer sedimentary limestone marbles. Serpentine is known for its deep green colour. Slates tend to be greyish in colour and are split easily into thin (4–10 mm) sections, making them useful for roofing and flooring. Slates can be sourced in red, blue-green and even purple hues from around the world. The UK imports its marble from several Mediterranean countries including Italy and Sicily.

The high degree of variation between the three types of rock and the range of stones within these categories, and in individual locations, means that stone properties are very varied indeed. This should be regarded as a natural quality, rather than an inherent fault. Textbooks explain the basic properties in adequate detail; the supplier and specialist architectural stonemason will provide good advice on applications. The basic properties of the common building stones such as limestone, marble and slate are well understood, but some testing may need to be carried out for unusual applications. Discussions at the design stage should cover both the stone's design characteristics (listed below) and its likely life-cycle characteristics. Some typical properties that differentiate stones are:

- Hardness;
- Light transmission;
- Modulus of rupture/elasticity;
- Porosity;
- Strength (tensile and compressive);
- Thermal expansion;
- Water sorption.

Over its lifetime, the inherent properties of a stone will determine how it wears and weathers, for example some stones will erode slowly (e.g. suitable for steps) and some are more suitable for cutting very thinly (e.g. suitable for brise-soleil). Performance in terms of deformation, seismic response together with the effects of UV light, sunlight, atmospheric gases, rainwater, frost and wind should be discussed. Organic material such as bacteria and mosses etc. may also be considered. It would be prudent to also map out an appropriate maintenance/cleaning programme. On an aesthetic note, the colour stability of the various minerals may not be consistent over time – this should also form part of the design discussion.

Uses and applications in buildings

Stone is a naturally occurring, non-renewable resource, but its durability does mean that in many instances in can be recovered and reused. Nonetheless, the prohibitive financial cost associated with stone quarrying, transportation and installation, in addition to the environmental impacts caused by extraction, means that the use of stone in architecture is often focussed on a few specific applications such as 'highlight' applications that use a minimum of material to the maximum aesthetic effect or in conservation areas and Listed Buildings. The latter often requires that refurbishment work, or even new build, conforms with the appearance of existing and adjacent buildings. Local planning authorities may demand a particular type of stone, or even stone from a specific quarry. In cities such as Cambridge, Edinburgh and York the prevalence of a particular stone has defined the architectural quality of the townscape for centuries. The warm, buff coloured oölitic limestones used in Oxford and Bath form a key component of the imagery associated with these cities.

For buildings, stone is a tremendously versatile material used in masonry, cladding, floors, facings, carvings, mullions, lintels, cills, piles, façades, columns, roofs, paving and cut stone (ashlar). However, its image as an old-fashioned building material means that its potential can be overlooked. For truly excellent specification and detailing of stonework with a Modern and 'honest' bias, Louis Kahn and Carlo Scarpa provide some splendid examples. A more extravagant precedent is Mies van der Rohe's Barcelona Pavilion of 1928–29: the highly figured onyx wall is its highlight set amid chrome columns and on a travertine floor.

On an everyday level, the use of stone facing layers on concrete cladding panels transforms the appearance of a façade without needing to use fully loadbearing construction methods. Thinly cut stone sections from onyx or marble can be used as delicate, attractive screens or windows, providing a very soft quality of light (e.g. onyx windows in Hagia Sofia mosque in Istanbul, Turkey and brise-soleil at Monte Carlo's railway station). Flints need not be used just in vernacular architecture – they also offer a dramatic silvery, grey facing material to concrete blocks and cladding panels. Slate roofs are a key part of UK historic architecture but are so versatile that their dark grey colour is still fashionable today. Perhaps the most outstanding example of the use of stone in Modern architecture is the Great Library at Alexandria in Egypt by Norwegian architects Snøhetta. This recently completed megastructure is wrapped from ground level with dark granite walls, carved intricately with inscriptions using all the world's languages.

Further reading

Shadmon, A. (1996) *Stone – an introduction* (2nd edition), Intermediate Technology Publications, London.

Winkler, E.M. (1997) *Stone in architecture – properties, durability* (3rd edition), Springer, Berlin, Germany.

JG

Stressed skin

See: TEXTILE MEMBRANE ROOFS

Structural grid

See: GRIDS FOR STRUCTURE AND LAYOUT

Structural cores

See: CORE (STRUCTURAL)

Structural glazing

See: GLASS – STRUCTURAL GLAZING

Structural steel

Steel is a term used to describe a group of metals; structural steel is the name given to particular grades of steel that are used in building frames and other structures.

See also: BEAM; BRACING; BUILDING SYSTEMS; CALATRAVA, SANTIAGO; CASTINGS; COLUMN; COMPOSITE DECKING; CORROSION; COR-TEN®; DURABILITY; FIRE PROTECTION; FLOORS; FRAMES; GALVANISING; GROPIUS, WALTER; INTUMESCENT PAINT; LE CORBUSIER; LIGHT STEEL FRAME; METALS; NEUTRA, RICHARD; PIANO, RENZO; PROFILED METAL DECKING; PROUVÉ, JEAN; RECYCLING; ROGERS, RICHARD; ROOFS; SCHINDLER, R.M.; STAINLESS STEEL; VAN DER ROHE, MIES; VON GERKAN & MARG; WEATHERING.

Steel erection underway for office buildings; such structures can be erected quickly and easily. Photograph of Cambourne Business Park courtesy of Frank H. Dale Ltd, Leominster.

What is structural steel?

Steels are a family of metal alloys formed by the basic process of purifying pig iron, which is then combined with carbon, to a controlled percentage. This percentage addition of carbon, together with other elements (e.g. chromium), creates a variety of physical and chemical properties tailored to particular applications (the properties can be altered further by heating, cooling or quenching).

Structural steel sections are made by passing a white hot cast ingot of steel through a hot rolling mill, perhaps via a series of rollers, to form the finished section. Columns and beams are the main products used for structural frames in buildings, but the production process can also draw off strip steel for use in cladding and other products. In the UK alone, many millions of tonnes of structural steel are used every year in the construction industry for frames, floors and roofs. This includes structural frame elements for medium to high-rise buildings: offices, residential, retail and many other building types. In addition, steel has complete command of the low-rise 'shed' market, with portal frames and trusses used for industrial, commercial and retail structures. The advances in production and the availability of guaranteed delivery times have influenced specifiers so that steel is very often the preferred choice for speed and economy. However, as with most off-site manufacturing activities, ordering well in advance is necessary, particularly for bespoke items.

Steel production

The modification of iron by purification, controlled addition of other elements, and by processing methods, produces a wide variety of grades of steel. In the basic process the extraction of iron involves heating the ore, with coke and limestone, to remove oxygen by combining it with carbon. The resultant iron still contains around 10% carbon and other impurities, and its re-processing in the furnace, in the presence of oxygen, enables the close control of carbon content. The controlled presence of carbon and other elements affects the microstructure of the metal and thus its properties. The most commonly used types of steel are shown in the table below. Within each category, there is a range of specific grades and alloys. For example:

Low carbon steels are used typically for pressed and cold rolled sections, where the properties of the steel are enhanced by 'work hardening' as it is formed, adding to the strength gained from the finished shape.

Medium carbon steels are termed structural steels, and are used for the hot rolled beams, columns, and other sections that make up structural steelwork.

Type of steel	Carbon (%)	Other elements*	Typical uses
Low carbon mild steel	<0.3	Mn	Low stress (constructional)
Medium carbon steel	<0.7	Mn	Medium stress (structural)
High carbon steel	<1.7	Mn	High stress (e.g. springs, tools)
Low alloy steel	<0.2	Mn, Cr, Ni	Petrochemical and aerospace
High alloy steel	<0.1	Mn, Cr, Ni	Stainless steel
Cast iron	<4.0	Mn, Si	Casting

*Other elements are:
Cr   Chromium
Mn   Manganese
Ni   Nickel
Si   Silicon

Structural steel sections

A range of sections (shapes) is produced, with a very broad variety available as standard items, in addition to the option of bespoke fabricated items.

Universal beams – I beams, for which the web is deeper than the flange width (normally up to 914 × 419 mm).

Universal columns – H sections with a square (or almost square) aspect (normally up to 356 × 406 m).

Joists – I sections in smaller sizes from 254 × 203 mm down to 76 × 76 mm;
Channels – U sections normally up to 432 × 102 mm;
Equal angles – 90° angles up to 250 × 250 mm;
Unequal angles – 90° angles up to 200 × 150 mm;
Structural tees – split from universal beams or columns.

Further sections are produced by fabrication, such as 'slim floor' beams with a plated bottom flange and cellular or castellated beams cut and re-welded to create special service holes. A further range of steel products is hollow sections. Correctly termed 'hot finished structural hollow sections' (HFSHS), these are manufactured in square, rectangular, and circular sections in a very wide range of sizes. A special range of seamless circular sections is also made.

- **Square** – 40 × 40 mm up to 400 × 400 mm;
- **Rectangular** – 50 × 30 mm up to 500 × 300 mm;
- **Circular** – 21.3 mm–503 mm diameter;
- **Circular (seamless)** – 193.7–660 mm diameter.

Hollow sections have benefitted from CAD/CAM techniques enabling complex welded junctions to be executed neatly for exposed steelwork. This group of structural steel elements is of particular architectural interest. The circular sections have been used extensively as columns and as chords to roof trusses where the structure is to be exposed for aesthetic purposes. For example, CHS sections were fabricated into steel 'trees' to support the roof canopy over Stansted Airport Terminal building in Essex (Foster and Partners).

Practical matters

Structural members are joined by welding, or bolting, and are the subject of specialist design details. Special self-tapping techniques have been developed for hollow sections. Lightweight components may be fixed to hot rolled steel with self-drill and tap fasteners. In a bid to prevent corrosion, structural sections are usually either primed or galvanised on fabrication. Additional, decorative coatings may be applied at the fabricator or on site.

Structural steelwork normally requires protection from the effects of fire. The commonest methods are cladding with plasterboard products, concrete encasement, sprayed insulation, and intumescent coatings. Design methods such as 'slim floor' make economical use of the floor slab concrete by incorporating the steelwork within its depth, usually as part of a composite decking design, and thereby achieving the required encasement as well. Further information is available from the Steel Construction Institute.

Further reading

Blanc, A., McEvoy, M. & Plank, R. (1993) *Architecture and construction in steel*, E&FN Spon, London, UK.

British Constructional Steelwork Association (1989) *National structural steelwork specification for building construction*, Steel Construction Institute, Ascot, UK.

British Constructional Steelwork Association (1996) *Commentary on the 3rd edition of the National structural steelwork specification*, Steel Construction Institute, Ascot, UK.

Eggen, A.P. & Sandaker, B.N. (1995) *Steel, structure, and architecture*, Whitney Library of Design, New York, USA.

Hayward, A., Weare, F. & Oakhill, A.C. (2001) *Steel detailer's manual*, (2nd edition), Blackwell Science, Oxford, UK.

Jackson, N. (1996) *The modern steel house*, E & FN Spon/Van Nostrand Reinhold, New York.

Ogden, R.G. et al. (1996) *Architectural teaching resource: studio guide*, SCI Publication 167, The Steel Construction Institute, Ascot, UK.

Wilkinson, C. (1996) *Supersheds* (2nd edition), Butterworth-Heinemann, Oxford, UK.

GW

Supply chain management
See: 'LEAN' CONSTRUCTION

Surface finishes

There are a number of basic issues that need to be considered when designing and specifying surface finishes. These include the type of finish, how it will be attained and its performance characteristics.

See also: ALUMINIUM; BESPOKE; CEILINGS; CEMENT; CONCRETE – FINISHES; CERAMICS; COPPER; CORROSION; COR-TEN®; DESIGN LIFE; FAÇADES AND FAÇADE ENGINEERING; FIT-OUT; FLOORS; GLASS – LAMINATED AND COATED; GRC; 'HONESTY'; LIGHTING – DAYLIGHTING; LIGHTING – ARTIFICIAL LIGHTING; METALS; PLASTICS FOR ADHESIVES AND FINISHES; SEALANTS; STAINLESS STEEL; STONE; STRUCTURAL STEEL; TIMBER – HARDWOODS AND SOFTWOODS; TIMBER – PRODUCTION AND FINISHES; WALLS; WEATHERING; ZINC.

Precast concrete façade with elegant glazed units form the striking, high quality surface finishes to offices at 10 Crown Place, London. Photograph by Trevor Jones, courtesy of The Concrete Society.

Introduction

Part of the design team's role is to decide on surface finishes throughout the building. These can range from simple painted finishes to mosaics, but there are many issues to be taken into account, not least of which may be the overarching architectural intention for the building. This may include the concept of 'honesty' – the desire to express the purity of construction materials – which can impact considerably on the choice of surface finishes. In this case, paint or other coatings may be highly inappropriate.

In some instances, the architect may make all the decisions regarding finishes, whereas, for example, in large corporate buildings the client may have a significant influence on the choice of materials, colours and textures used (it may even have its own colour way or logo that must be used). From time to time the design team may include an interior designer or stylist, particularly for buildings with a large fit-out budget such as shops, theatres, health clubs or executive offices. Finishes are specified for most internal and external building elements including walls, floors, ceilings, structural elements and other fittings (such as partitions, counters etc). The design team will make decisions based on numerous aspects, some of which are described below.

Colours

These may be selected from a palette for the whole building, based on corporate identity or selected on a room-by-room basis. Designers can choose from exposed construction materials, plaster, paint, stains, render, lime wash, ceramics, wallpaper, fabric or even metal sheeting to achieve the colour ways required. Materials for exterior finishes also include cladding with metal, plastic, timber or concrete, the colours of which may be restricted to manufacturers' standard palettes or based on recommendations for the project under consideration. In both interior and exterior work, it may be necessary to consider the impact of fading, depending where the finish is located (some strong hues will fade on continued exposure to direct sunlight). Practical aspects such as degree of wear and tear will also affect colour choice as will daylighting and artificial lighting, which can both affect the overall effect of the interior architectural design. The Natural Colour Dimensioning System (NCS) is a means of accurately mapping a colour and replicating it for precise colour matching of finishes and products. An interesting example is a chameleon-like paint, which dates from the 19th century, which is being used on new buildings. Owing to powdered mica in the paint, the colour of the building appears to change from blue to green depending on the angle at which it is seen.

Textures

These can be pre-determined by the decision to expose the construction material in use (e.g. timber or concrete) or can be chosen more specifically via applied finishes such as render, wallpaper or paints. In applications where the surface will be exposed to considerable wear and tear a smooth, easily cleaned finish is useful. High build or delicate textures are best kept out of reach. For some materials such as copper, the colour and surface texture may change over time as a surface 'patina' develops. People's hands touching exposed concrete cause it to darken over time unless it has been sealed. In addition, the choice of texture will have an effect on the overall colour impression of the finish in the same way that lighting will also change its appearance. Note that surface flatness is of particular importance for industrial ground floors, on which high bay storage systems may be installed. Hence, accuracy of the ground slab is vital; the term 'superflat floors' describes this aspect of the specification for floors.

Other issues

The choice of materials specified and methods used to achieve the desired colour and texture specification can also be affected by a range of other factors including capital cost, design life, operational costs (maintenance, repair and renewal), weathering, environmental concerns, likelihood of vandalism and of course general wear and tear. An indication of the growing interest in environmentally friendly paint products can be found in Germany where these products now account for at least 3% of the total market.

Built examples

The colour palette for much contemporary UK architecture seems to be based on the Modernist range of pale colours (white, cream, light grey etc), with 'honest' exposed materials becoming increasingly popular. This type of subtle, restrained colour way is characteristic of the Modern movement and can be found in the buildings of Foster and Partners and David Chipperfield. Exposed concrete, natural stone, natural timber, metals like aluminium and zinc, and pale coloured painted or rendered walls feature heavily.

On a more colourful note, 'heritage' colours such as terracotta and deep greens abound in retrospective architecture, refurbishment projects and traditional rural styles. Bright Mediterranean hues of yellow and red also feature in some buildings as vivid highlight areas. In the UK, architects John Outram and Piers Gough of CZWG have demonstrated their fascination with colour and its symbolism throughout their works. John Outram's Judge Institute of Management Studies in Cambridge is highly decorated and colourful. CZWG's China Wharf in London is an early example of their use of bright colours with its vivid red façade overlooking the River Thames.

Further reading

Dean, Y. (1996) *Mitchell's Building Series: Finishes* (4th edition), Longman, Harlow, UK.

JG

Suspended ceiling

See: CEILINGS

Suspended glazing

See: GLASS – STRUCTURAL GLAZING

Computer generated image of a section through the BedZed development in Surrey (Bill Dunster Architects). This sustainable 'zero energy development' features 100 homes and 20 businesses. Image courtesy of the Peabody Trust.

Computer-generated image of the main entrance to the Princess Margaret Hospital in Swindon, a zero waste project that will consume 30% less energy in use than a typical hospital. Image courtesy of the Movement for Innovation & Carillion plc.

Sustainability

Sustainability is about addressing the requirements of future generations while fulfilling the immediate needs of current generations. In particular, sustainable development, design and construction are key aspects of achieving a more sustainable built environment.

See also: AIRTIGHTNESS AND IAQ; BUILDING MANAGEMENT SYSTEMS; CARBON DIOXIDE; DESIGN LIFE; DURABILITY; ECOLOGICAL DESIGN; 'ECO-POINTS'; ENVIRONMENTAL DESIGN; ENERGY EFFICIENCY; FABRIC ENERGY STORAGE; INSULATION; INTEGRATION; INTELLIGENT FAÇADES AND MATERIALS; 'LEAN' CONSTRUCTION; LIFE-CYCLE ANALYSIS; RECYCLING; SICK BUILDING SYNDROME; SPECIFICATION; WATER MANAGEMENT AND DRAINAGE.

Sustainability

This term can be defined in many ways, but the general understanding is based on the definition from the Brundtland Report of 1987:

> *The need to ensure that development meets the needs of the present without compromising the ability of future generations to meet their own needs.*

This description has been used as the basic explanation of sustainability ever since. The notion of living more sustainably can be applied to all aspects of human activity from industry to housing, from transport to the cultural and political parts of global society. A more sustainable society can only be achieved by addressing together the '**triple bottom line**', i.e. economic, environmental and social issues. To exist sustainably requires society to achieve a balance between environmental protection, social progress and economic growth, while working in harmony with Earth's ecosystems. Clearly this is a global issue, but relevant action can also be taken at national, regional and local levels. UK government is addressing sustainability in the broadest terms by implementing policy, strategies and appropriate targets and indicators. An indicator is an assessment tool; a means by which a trend can be identified and tracked – for example, the number of bus routes is an indicator of local transport provision.

There are three specific areas that are of particular relevance to architectural technology, i.e. sustainable development, sustainable design and sustainable construction.

Sustainable development

This term encompasses all aspects of the built environment from economic planning, urban design and construction activities in addition to the life-cycle performance of individual buildings. This is a broad category, which is important because it deals with the built environment at many different scales. Sustainable development is often best dealt with within appropriate policy at international, national and regional levels through which the far-reaching actions necessary to effect sustainable development can be realised. In essence, four key objectives need to be addressed by any such policy:

- Effective protection of the environment;
- Maintenance of high and stable levels of economic growth and employment;
- Prudent use of natural resources;
- Social progress which recognises the needs of everyone.

Sustainable design

Sustainable design in its broadest terms covers architecture, urban design, town planning and infrastructure design, but in this instance we will focus particularly on buildings. One way in which building designs can be considered is according to their relative contribution to detrimental effects such as global warming, ozone depletion and resource depletion. Although building materials and construction techniques do make an impact, it is important to put this into context. The list below is in order of increasing magnitude of impacts:

1. Construction of buildings;
2. In-use impacts from buildings (operational energy consumption etc.);
3. Development – of towns, cities and infrastructure;
4. Refurbishment of buildings and structures;
5. Society – how we use our built environment, in particular transport impacts.

Sustainable design is less critical to achieving overall social sustainability than other issues which affect the quality of the built environment such as, for example, the energy use and air quality problems associated with car travel. Indeed, the impacts from buildings are mainly from their use (i.e. heating, cooling and lighting), rather than the energy 'embodied' within building materials. Nevertheless, responsible design has its part to play in sustainability and buildings are a very good 'advert' for what can actually be achieved. It is also important that designers address these issues in the order of the magnitude of their overall impact rather than the relative ease with which they can be tackled.

Sustainable construction

This describes a framework through which investment, growth, environmental protection and development can happen more sustainably. The construction industry has a very important role to play because it is responsible for constructing and maintaining buildings, which are currently responsible for half of the UK's carbon dioxide emissions. The industry also produces several million tonnes of waste per annum. Sustainable construction is about reducing waste, reducing emissions, reducing the use of natural resources and providing a better quality built environment for the future. As a case study of good practice in sustainable construction, the Princess Margaret Hospital relocation in Swindon used a portfolio of materials and methods to achieve a 50% reduction in waste (compared to the construction of a typical hospital). Built on remediated brownfield land, the project employed a consultant to oversee sustainability issues. Actions undertaken included recycling unused plasterboard fragments, using thermal mass in the concrete frame and cladding to reduce energy use and utilising wood-soap based paint on internal surfaces to lessen VOC emissions.

What action can be taken?

The UK government has developed a strategy for sustainable construction, in which there are ten themes for action:

1. Re-use existing built assets;
2. Design for minimum waste;
3. Aim for lean construction;
4. Minimise energy in construction;
5. Minimise energy in use;
6. Do not pollute;
7. Preserve and enhance biodiversity;
8. Conserve water resources;
9. Respect people and their local environment;
10. Set targets.

These priorities affect the ways in which buildings are designed, constructed and maintained. Various tools are available to help designers evaluate the impacts associated with construction materials, construction methods, M&E and interior fittings. Arup's 'SPEAR', BRE's 'Eco-points' and other similar tools are being developed to offer sustainability assessments that incorporate both quantitative and non-tangible aspects/indicators. The following titles should be consulted for further information.

Further reading

Edwards, B. (1998) *Sustainable architecture* (2nd edition), Butterworth-Heinemann, Oxford, UK.

Edwards, B. & Hyett, P. (2001) *Rough guide to sustainability*, RIBA Publications, London, UK.

Edwards, B. & Turrent, D. (eds.) (2000) *Sustainable housing: principles and practice*, E & FN Spon, London, UK.

Institution of Structural Engineers (1999) *Building for a sustainable future: construction without depletion*, Institution of Structural Engineers, London, UK.

Langston, C A. & Ding, G.K.C. (2001) *Sustainable practices in the built environment* (2nd edition), Butterworth-Heinemann, Oxford, UK.

Melet, E. (1999) *Sustainable architecture: towards a diverse built environment*, NAI Publishers, The Netherlands.

Slessor, C. (2001) *Eco-Tech: sustainable architecture and high technology*, Thames & Hudson, London, UK.

Smith, P. (2001) *Architecture in a climate of change*, Butterworth-Heinemann, Oxford, UK.

Williams, K., Burton, E., & Jenks, M. (2000) *Achieving sustainable urban form*, E & FN Spon, London, UK.

JG

System building

See: BUILDING SYSTEMS

Technology transfer

The concept of importing ideas, techniques or products from other industries into architecture.

See also: BESPOKE; CASTINGS; CERAMICS; COMPOSITE MATERIALS; CONCRETE; ETFE; FOSTER, NORMAN; FRAME; GLASS – LAMINATED AND COATED; GRIMSHAW, NICHOLAS; 'HONESTY'; MINERAL FIBRES; PHOTOVOLTAICS; PLASTICS – TYPES; PROUVÉ, JEAN; TEXTILE MEMBRANE ROOFS; STRUCTURAL STEEL; TIMBER; TOLERANCE.

Introduction

'Technology transfer' is the term used to describe instances where designers look at other industries or sectors for inspiration and then use, or manipulate, the production techniques or products from these industries in their own building designs. Hence, a transfer of technology (from the Greek 'techne', meaning way of doing) from one industry or activity to another.

On a historical note, architects have experimented with imagery of cars, ships and planes for many years as representative of speed and thrilling excitement. Many buildings from the 1920s and 1930s demonstrate their designers' interest in these dynamic forms, which are streamlined and seemingly aerodynamic. For instance, the French engineer Jean Prouvé became increasingly dissatisfied with the traditional nature of the building industry compared to the manufacturing industries, which appeared to be advancing quickly under better quality and investment regimes. Therefore, he looked to the car industry for inspiration for his early, yet seminal external metal cladding systems. Clearly the space walks and 'man on the moon' cultural revolutions in the 1960s influenced contemporary art and architecture at that time and further encouraged the desire to transfer technology from the exciting aerospace industry.

Applications

In recent decades, interest has developed more fully into a transfer of technology, rather than just a transfer of imagery or aesthetics and is now much more commonplace. Examples of technology transfer into architecture come from a range of sources, many of which are predominantly manufacturing activities, such as:

- Aviation engineering;
- Boats and marine engineering;
- Cars and automotive;

- Computing and IT;
- Fashion, photography and the arts;
- Plastics manufacture;
- Space craft;
- Other production processes.

Technology transfer describes the use of design or production techniques used in these industries, or even the use of actual products or elements within architecture, perhaps as structural elements, cladding or fittings. In some cases, the products are used directly with no fundamental changes (such as yacht sail rigging accessories for balustrades, balconies or handrails). Alternatively, the technology transfer may involve some manipulation of the original to meet the required architectural purpose. For example, the high performance ceramics and photovoltaic cells first used on the exterior of space shuttles to generate energy have now been developed to suit domestic and commercial buildings.

To many designers, the ability to transfer such technologies can be highly beneficial and some believe that it is vital to rejuvenate construction in this way, because it might otherwise remain trapped in the past.

The different demands or pressures on the more advanced manufacturing industries tend to push their R&D efforts into highly innovative areas. On a more domestic level, the non-stick coating used in saucepans (PTFE – Teflon™) has proved remarkably effective as a waterproofer for textile membrane roofs. The need for lightweight but strong metals in aircraft led to development of titanium alloys and the need for more fuel-efficient engines led to the use of composite materials for the jet engine blades. Composite materials in particular are proving to have significant structural and performance advantages for roofing, connections, retrofitting and strengthening.

Built examples

Examples are many and varied throughout the works of Norman Foster, Renzo Piano and Nicholas Grimshaw, but perhaps one of the practices that have most considered technology transfer comprehensively is Future Systems. Jan Kaplicky and Amanda Levete have investigated a variety of sources for their architecture from monocoque structures to 3D composite cladding panels.

Further reading

Brookes, A. (1998) *Cladding of buildings* (3rd edition), E & FN Spon, London, UK.

Brookes, A. & Grech, C. (1996) *Building envelope & connections*, Butterworth-Heinemann, Oxford, UK.

Field, M. (1999) *Future Systems*, Phaidon Press, London UK.

Future Systems (1996) *For inspiration only*, Academy Editions, John Wiley & Sons, London, UK.

Future Systems (1999) *More for inspiration only*, Academy Editions, John Wiley & Sons, London, UK.

JG

Tension structures

See: TEXTILE MEMBRANE ROOFS

Terracotta

See: BRICKS AND BLOCKS; CERAMICS

Terne coating

See: LEAD; METALS; STAINLESS STEEL

Textile membrane roofs

Textile membrane roofs are a category of surface structure having similarities with 'cable net' constructions.

See also: AIR-SUPPORTED STRUCTURES; CABLE NETS;
COMPOSITE MATERIALS; DESIGN LIFE; DURABILITY; ETFE;
HAPPOLD, SIR TED AND BURO HAPPOLD; HOPKINS; MICHAEL;
MAINTENANCE; MINERAL FIBRES; OTTO, FREI;
PLASTICS – TYPES; ROGERS, RICHARD; ROOFS; WEATHERING.

What is a textile membrane roof?

The structural textile membranes used in building applications are typically 1 mm thick consisting of a cloth woven from polyester or glass yarns and encapsulated in a continuous polymeric coating of PVC and PTFE respectively. The cloth provides the structural strength and the coating provides weather protection to the yarns. The degree of stretch of textile materials under load is considerably greater than that of steel cables. Since membrane materials are so thin and therefore highly flexible; for all but short spans, they need to be organised into curved surface shapes so as to be prestressable. Warped or 'anti-clastic' shapes have two principal curvatures mutually opposed to one another making the surface, as a whole, prestressable. The opposing curvatures provide separate load-paths for snow and wind loads. Flat membranes can only be used in circumstances where prestress and surface inclination are sufficiently high enough to avoid the progressive collection of water and snow. Supporting structures vary in concept and details, with most using slender, elegant steel or aluminium pylons, 'push up' umbrella connectors or reinforcing cables.

Historical note

The development of this technology originates in part from the economic/social/technical changes in the 19th century. For instance the mechanised spinning of yarn and the weaving of cloth enabled large-scale production of canvas. This, coupled with the growth of railways, led to the large mobile circus tent providing entertainment to enlarging populations from 1860 onwards. The world fair held in Nizhniy-Novgorod in Russia in 1896, provided engineer V.G. Suchov with the opportunity to build several wide-span exhibition halls with thin anti-clastic surfaces using networks of thin steel straps. Post 1950 world fairs, such as Expo '70 in Osaka, continued to be the proving ground for the development of textile membrane roofs. By 1970 the Du Pont company had developed a PTFE resin coating containing microscopic glass beads which could be applied to woven glass cloth (Teflon™). The significance of this was that it was a material with high resistance to combustion, UV light and soiling from atmospheric dirt and pollutants. It was therefore suited to providing safer and more permanent enclosure to buildings (with 10–15% transmission of daylight as an added feature). In much the same period engineering methods for designing these structures were enabling a switch from physical models to numerical ones with significant advantages in dimensional accuracy and cost.

Built examples

The world's largest membrane roof is the Hajj Pilgrim Terminal built in 1980 at Jeddah Airport in Saudi Arabia, which covers 420,000 m². It is on a suitably grand scale consisting of 45 × 45 m conical PTFE/glass membrane units suspended from tall pylons. Many large textile roofs have been constructed in North America, for instance over the terminal building at Denver Airport. In Europe the first significant architectural incorporation of a tensioned membrane roof into a permanent building was the Schlumberger Cambridge Research Centre at Cambridge, UK. Completed in 1985 it stimulated a wider use in Europe of tensioned membranes within permanent building enclosures (the architect was Michael Hopkins & Partners). Hybrid structures using flatter panels of membrane tensioned over arch frameworks are to be seen in Japan, for instance the Akita Sky Dome (1982) and the Izumo Dome (1982). The ultimate example and largest application to date, of the use of flat membrane is the Millennium Dome (1999) in London, designed by Richard Rogers Partnership and Buro Happold. A radial network of cables support largely flat but inclined, membrane panels up to 17 m wide.

Further reading

Robbin, T. (1996) *Engineering a new architecture*, Yale University Press, USA.

Scheuermann, R. & Boxer, K. (1996) *Tensile architecture in the urban context*, Butterworth-Heinemann, Oxford, UK.

Vandenburg, M. (1996) *Soft canopies*, Academy Editions, John Wiley & Sons, UK.

OA

Thermal bridging

A term usually associated with building elements, which cross the boundary between two temperature zones, thereby causing a 'bridge'. It affects both energy efficiency and durability.

See also: CONDENSATION; DESIGN LIFE; DURABILITY; DYNAMIC THERMAL SIMULATION; ENERGY EFFICIENCY; FAÇADES AND FAÇADE ENGINEERING; FIRE PROTECTION; FLOORS; INSULATION; PERFORMANCE; SPECIFICATION; THERMAL COMFORT; ROOFS; WALLS.

What is thermal bridging?

This term describes a very common problem in building design, which can be resolved on paper before construction, but remains a thorny issue for many existing buildings in the UK, particularly those constructed on the basis of pre-1973 Building Regulations (before energy efficiency standards began in earnest). If a building element or material effectively crosses two zones of different temperatures then it forms a 'bridge'. The temperature difference causes condensation, which in turn can cause deterioration of the building fabric if it goes undetected. Designers should note that these 'bridges' may also contravene parts of the Building Regulations relating to fire safety.

Mechanisms of bridging

Thermal bridging actually occurs at many places within a building, but in most cases the temperature difference is slight, and not a cause for concern. However, where a major element crosses between interior and exterior (or between two different internal temperature zones), serious problems may occur because the temperature differential is much greater, and so is the potential for condensation. There are three types of thermal bridge:

Discrete bridges – where the size of the bridged area in relation to the rest of the structure is small, e.g. beams and walls;

Multi-webbed bridges – these occur in components such as slotted blocks and perforated blocks. The bridges cover a large area of the structure, so the disruption to normal heat flow characteristics is considerable;

Finned element bridges – which are formed at the junction of walls and floors and non-planar elements where the heat flow paths are complex.

Small elements such as lintels, windows and curtain walling assemblies usually incorporate insulation as a matter of course, but their surface area relative to the whole building is negligible in terms of thermal losses. However, the architectural intention to extend a roof beam or wall from interior to exterior is perhaps the worst case scenario. These large elements would form a major path for heat loss by crossing through the external envelope. Unless the design can comply with Building Regulations as a whole by using the 'combined' method to calculate U values (see below), then the element must be insulated and re-faced with cladding or an alternative material at its external end. This goes against the principle of expressing materials in an 'honest' way and so remains an 'aesthetics versus performance' moot point for many designers.

Standards and compliance

The effects of bridging elements must be taken into account when calculating U values; the 'combined method' is the most appropriate. In this case, the inverse of half the sum of both the upper and lower level thermal resistance figures for the envelope becomes its U value. This must then be multiplied by factors relating to the methods, accuracy and fixings for insulation.

Thermal bridging in domestic construction is covered by the UK Building Regulations. These recommend the avoidance of significant gaps in the insulation layers within the various elements of the fabric, at the joints between the elements and at the edges of those elements (i.e. window and door openings), in addition to reducing unwanted leakage through extraneous air paths. Increases in insulation thickness and 'deemed to satisfy' robust details will form a part of the Regulations in coming years. Where non-domestic and larger buildings are concerned the methods of compliance will include the provision of infra-red thermographic inspections prior to client hand-over, to show that the insulation is reasonably continuous.

Further reading

Building Research Establishment (2001) *Assessing the effects of thermal bridging at junctions and around openings*, BRE, Watford, UK.
Chartered Institute of Building Services Engineers, *CIBSE Guide (Section A3: Thermal Properties of Building Structures)*, CIBSE, London, UK.

WH

Human thermal comfort in offices is determined by architecture, internal environmental conditions and people's perceptions. Modern, open plan spaces such as this one (Toyota GB, Epsom) with comfortable and well-lit interiors make a real difference. Photograph by Trevor Jones, courtesy of The Concrete Society.

Thermal comfort

An individual's perception of their state of satisfaction with environmental conditions, notably temperature.

See also: AIR-CONDITIONING; AIRTIGHTNESS AND IAQ; ECOLOGICAL DESIGN; ENVIRONMENTAL DESIGN; HVAC; INSULATION; INTELLIGENT FAÇADES AND MATERIALS; NIGHT VENTILATION; PERFORMANCE; SERVICES; STACK EFFECT; VENTILATION.

What is (human) thermal comfort?

The term 'comfort' can be defined in a number of ways, but in this case it is used in the context of a person's satisfaction with the ambient environmental conditions such as temperature and humidity. Thermal comfort is a subjective measure, based on an individual's response to their climatic surroundings. There are six primary factors that affect thermal comfort, each having a unique effect.

- Activity;
- Air motion;
- Air temperature;
- Clothing;
- Humidity;
- Surface temperature.

Human comfort mechanisms

To have a built-in response to temperature is actually a very practical measure to maintain life. Human inner organs are very sensitive to temperature change; for instance, the brain and important glands depend on temperature being maintained within very narrow limits (a fraction of a degree). The extremities of the body can tolerate a much wider range – skin temperature can vary by $5-10\,°C$ with very little discomfort. The basic functions of life involve a human–environment interaction in terms of heat exchange: in the course of absorbing and digesting food the body produces gains of heat (its metabolism) but loses heat to its surroundings, by various mechanisms, to achieve a balance.

Based on air temperature and percentage humidity to be the basic components of this thermal balance, 1960s scientist Victor Olgyay postulated that a temperature range from $20-27\,°C$ and a humidity range of 20–80% RH (relative humidity) was indicative of a 'comfortable' setting for a Caucasian male, resting in the shade. This 'comfort zone' can be extended provided either radiant heating from the sun (in cooler conditions) or cooling from faster air movement (in warmer conditions) are available. Nevertheless, there are practical limits, particularly at higher temperatures (if the air is above $33\,°C$, i.e. skin temperature, people tend to perceive this as a warm air stream, rather than a cooling breeze). However, thermal comfort is not simply a matter of temperature; age, gender and clothing preferences – 'normal' environmental conditions and expectations of comfort will have a significant effect. Current R&D is based on the notion of an 'adaptive algorithm', which takes account of these and other factors ultimately for the design of building services. This is a complex field, but it is addressed in codes for environmental design and IT programs, which make design easier.

Thermal comfort in buildings

Architecture can be defined as 'shelter plus'. Buildings need to maintain an acceptable total climate in terms of temperature, sound and air quality. The problems with indoor air quality that led to 'sick building syndrome' are related to design for thermal comfort. Perceptions of thermal comfort and measurable air quality values both improve with the availability of natural/controllable heating and ventilation to adapt internal air conditions and exhaust any pollutants. Sometimes this is difficult to achieve because of deep plans or traffic pollution, so the building fabric may need to act as a 'climatic filter'. Hence the increasing use of twin-skin façades, fabric energy storage and stack effect ventilation. Developments in materials that can 'breathe' will contribute to these aspects of architectural technology in the coming years. The performance of a building in terms of thermal comfort can be surveyed as part of Post Occupancy Evaluation (POE). Nevertheless, the infinite variety of human preferences will continue to make this subject difficult to grasp for the new designer.

Further reading

Nicol, J.F., Humphreys, M.A. & Sykes, O.D. (1995) *Standards for thermal comfort: indoor air temperature standards for the 21st century*, E & FN Spon, London, UK.

Olgyay, V. (1992) *Design with climate: a bioclimatic approach to architectural regionalism*, Van Nostrand Reinhold, New York, USA.

WH/JG

Thermal mass

See: FABRIC ENERGY STORAGE; THERMOLABYRINTHS; TROMBE WALL

Thermolabyrinths

A specific application of fabric energy storage principles to pre-cool or pre-heat incoming supply air for ventilation systems.

See also: DYNAMIC THERMAL SIMULATION; ENERGY EFFICIENCY; ENVIRONMENTAL DESIGN; FABRIC ENERGY STORAGE; HEAT RECOVERY; HVAC; SERVICES; TROMBE WALLS.

Introduction

Density, specific heat capacity and conductivity determine the fabric energy storage potential of a building material. Concrete and brick have some of the highest capacities and are able to reduce heat build-up in a space and delay the peak indoor temperature – the 'thermal flywheel' effect. Although underground ice houses etc had been excavated for many years previously, the first documented evidence of the exploitation of heavyweight materials in combination with underground construction to passively manipulate air supply temperatures comes from the mid-1800s when an 'earth refrigerator' and a 'sub-earth ventilation system' were used. These devices can be described as 'thermolabyrinths', i.e. plenum spaces through which airflow is passively cooled.

Three case examples of contemporary applications for the thermolabyrinth idea are described below. The designers did not actually become aware of one another's work until 1989.

Royal Academy of Music, London, UK (1972)

In designing a ventilating system to suit the phased construction of a new theatre, internal music carrels, and rehearsal halls for the Academy (located on the busy Euston Road), building services engineer Bill Holdsworth had to devise a way to bring reasonably uncontaminated supply air into the building. An existing 70 m long basement corridor, with a glazed tiled surface finish and heavyweight walls, was used to provide a labyrinth plenum chamber away from the traffic. During summer tests (outside temperatures rose to 30 °C) the plenum air temperatures were much cooler, around 22 °C. A series of summer and winter temperature recordings were made over eight months, which justified the design decision. The thermolabyrinth resulted in substantial energy savings over the ten-year construction programme.

Elly-Heus-Knapp School, Heilbronn, Germany (1970)

Eugen Mayer, chief engineer of Heilbronn, observed that the summer, daytime air in the Elly-Heus-Knapp School entered at one end of a 60 metre underground service corridor at 31.5 °C and had cooled down to 22 °C by the time it reached the other end. Mayer devised a way to incorporate this into the general ventilation system allowing classrooms on the south and west façades of the building to be cooled to the standard of 26 °C, without any mechanical means.

Stadtheatre, Heilbronn, Germany (1982)

Based on research monitoring of the Elly-Heus-Knapp School, a government grant was given to Herr Mayer to install a thermolabyrinth system for a 700 seat theatre and 150 seat music, exhibition complex and underground garage. Within the foundations, a concrete labyrinth (6 m wide × 1.35 m high) with a surface area of 1250 m^2 was constructed. To increase the heat exchange area, profiled 'dragon's teeth' on the floor of the labyrinth added a further 450 m^2. Some 25 separate air-handling systems were connected to the outside air and the labyrinth air, together with control valves and motorised gates to interact with the air flows (based on 72 measuring plates built into the concrete passages). A detailed evaluation by the Association of German Engineers proved that on a summer's day with a maximum of 32 °C, some 90% of required cooling was provided by the thermolabyrinth.

Further reading

Holdsworth, B. & Sealey, A. (1992) *Healthy buildings: a design primer for a living environment*, Longman, Harlow, UK.

Markus, T.A. & Morris, E.N. (1980) *Buildings, climate & energy*, Pitman, UK.

WH

Thermoplastics
See: PLASTICS – TYPES; PLASTICS – FABRICATION

Thermosetting plastics
See: PLASTICS – TYPES; PLASTICS – FABRICATION

Timber

Even though architects and designers now have a wide range of materials from which to choose, timber is a very popular building material that has its own special characteristics, as well as being ecologically sound.

See also: AALTO, ALVAR; DESIGN LIFE; DURABILITY; ECOLOGICAL DESIGN; 'ECO-POINTS'; FIT-OUT; FLOORS; 'HONESTY'; ROOFS; SURFACE FINISHES; TIMBER; TIMBER – LAMINATED TIMBER; TIMBER – MANUFACTURED BOARDS; TIMBER – PRODUCTION AND FINISHES; TIMBER – STRUCTURES.

Introduction

Forests cover 30% of the Earth's land-mass – so timber is a plentiful (renewable) resource for many countries. This use can be sustained, provided the timber comes from well-managed forests. The UK imports 80% of its timber from other areas, in particular Scandinavia and North America. Although there is very keen use of timber by ecological designers, there remain many question marks such as the need for 'green' certification of imported tropical hardwoods and an improved method for tracing the origins of timber supplies. To date the Forest Stewardship Council has only certified about 1% of the global timber supply network, so specification of local UK or European timbers may prove to be the easier, and 'greener' option. This and the following four entries provide an overview of timber use in buildings, within the context of ecological concerns.

The tree is a living plant and has contributed to human development over many centuries. The timber gained from it is produced naturally (unlike many other construction materials). The range of different timber species gives a wide choice. Each species has its own characteristics and properties, and will differ in appearance, giving variations in colour, pattern, texture and finish. As well as solid timber, manufactured boards have been developed to make different structures possible and which will contribute to overcoming some of the problems with timber movement.

Timber is also used in the form of veneers, thus enabling the use of rare timbers that are not available in solid form and show a wide range of decorative features. In order to gain the best results from using timber it is necessary to know some basic facts about the material, how trees grow, how the tree is converted into usable forms and how these characteristics can be used to obtain the best results.

The structure of a tree

The tree is a very efficient structure, its trunk is the main conduit for transferring water and minerals. The leaves take in carbon dioxide, give off oxygen and absorb light, which, through the process of photosynthesis, produces nutrients. The roots absorb water and other minerals.

The trunk's structure consists of tubular cellulose cells bonded together with lignin. In hardwoods these cells run longitudinally along the trunk and branches. In softwoods these cells are shorter, food passes from cell to cell. Longitudinal resin channels may be present.

Concentric rings indicate annual growth determining a tree's age. The tree grows each year by the growth of cells in the cambium layer, which lies between the bark and the wood. These rings are described as either 'ring porous' or 'diffuse porous'. The ring porous wood shows a difference in cellular structure between wood laid down in the different growing periods of the tree, open cells when the tree is growing (such as spring or summer) and tighter grouped cells where growth slows in autumn and winter. Diffuse porous timber is found in trees where there are no marked seasonal changes and cells are much more regular in size.

A section through the tree shows the heartwood at the centre, which is mature wood that forms the structure of the tree as well as providing some food transference. Around the heartwood is the sapwood, which is where most of the transference and storage of nutrients takes place. Sapwood from most timbers is seldom used since it is not particularly resistant to fungal and insect attack. At the centre is the pith or the medulla, formed from the original sapling.

Timber use

Ecological concerns mean that forests must be maintained to ensure a continuous supply of quality trees. Therefore in the developed world the science of responsible forestry has been much improved and pressure is also being placed on developing countries in an effort to support managed forests. It has thus become difficult to use some of the endangered species of timber (e.g. tropical hardwoods); many countries are seeking to help sustain their economies by not exporting logs, but by carrying out conversion nearer the source. In a well-run forest, mature timber is extracted with care and new planting takes place to ensure continued supply.

Timber properties

Timber comes from a living tree, so its characteristics and properties will be very different both between and within individual species, or even in an individual tree. Timbers have different characteristics both structurally and visually. Some will be easy to work, others less so; some will be strong, some weaker. Specific timbers need to be chosen to suit particular applications.

Common terms used to describe timbers include:

Grain – in timber where growth has been even and the cell structure follows the main axis of the tree, the wood will be straight grained and generally easy to work. However, in some trees growth will not be so even and this may result in grain which is not straight (i.e. interlocked grain, wavy grain and curvy grain). These irregular grained woods will often be difficult to work, but can have very attractive patterns. Grain can also refer to the nature of working the wood. Timber is sawn or planed with the grain (i.e. in the direction of the wood fibres), but for timbers with irregular grain, where the grain is random, planing will be difficult.

Figure – this can be caused by grain direction but also by marked early and late wood, density of the growth rings, conversion of the trunk, and various 'imperfections' such as curl, burrs etc.

Texture – fine textured woods have closely spaced cells while coarse textured woods have large open spaced cells.

Further reading

Desch, H.E. & Dinwoodie, J.M. (1996) *Timber: structure, properties, conversion and use* (7th edition), MacMillan, Basingstoke, UK.

Gutdeutsch, G. (1996) *Building in wood, construction and details*, Birkhäuser, Basle, Switzerland.

Patterson, D. (1988) *Commercial timbers of the world*, Gower, Aldershot, UK.

Stungo, N. (1998) *The new wood architecture*, Colman and King, UK.

Zwerger, K. (1997) *Wood and wood joints: building traditions of Europe and Japan*, Birkhäuser, Basle, Switzerland.

CS

Timber – hardwoods and softwoods

The basic classification system for timber, this entry presents the common species used in architecture and construction.

See also: AALTO, ALVAR; ANDO, TADAO; CALATRAVA, SANTIAGO; DESIGN LIFE; DURABILITY; ECOLOGICAL DESIGN; 'ECO-POINTS'; FIT-OUT; FLOORS; 'HONESTY'; KAHN, LOUIS; PIANO, RENZO; ROOFS; SURFACE FINISHES; TIMBER; TIMBER – LAMINATED TIMBER; TIMBER – MANUFACTURED BOARDS; TIMBER – PRODUCTION AND FINISHES; TIMBER – STRUCTURES.

Definitions

Timber can be classified as being either softwood, or a hardwood. These terms do *not* in fact refer to the hardness or softness of specific timber species, since they are a botanical classification rather than a physical description. '**Softwood**' refers to trees that grow in colder regions, which have needles instead of leaves and are usually evergreen. '**Hardwood**' generally refers to trees which have broad leaves and are found in temperate and tropical climates and which can be either or deciduous or evergreen. Even though most hardwoods are actually hard and most softwoods soft, one of the softest timbers (balsa) is a hardwood and some softwoods can be very hard. About 80% of timber used in construction comes from softwoods. This entry gives brief descriptions of both hardwoods and softwoods.

Hardwoods

Hardwoods grow in most parts of the world, with many countries having indigenous species available, even though fashion has in the past led to the importation of particular timbers for specific uses (e.g. mahogany and teak). Common hardwoods include afrormosia, ash, beech, birch, cherry, elm, mahogany, maple, oak, sycamore, teak and walnut. Amongst hardwoods there are species with particular properties of strength, colour, grain etc. (such as bubinga, ebony, lignum vitae, padauk, rosewood, satinwood), which can be used, but because of ecological reasons may not be easy, or desirable, to obtain. Indeed, ecologically conscious groups are pressing for more stringent controls on the use of rare tropical hardwoods in construction, demanding that both designers and constructors become more responsible and accountable in their specification and use of timber.

Common species of hardwoods

Afrormosia (*Pericopsis elata*) – Generally grown in West Africa, it is a durable wood; its grain may either be straight or interlocked. In use it darkens to a yellow brown similar to that of teak and even though it has a finer texture and is not as oily, it is often used as a teak substitute. It works and finishes fairly well. In some countries it is used for construction and joinery, but often used for furniture that will be used both inside and outdoors.

Ash – European (*Fraxinus excelsior*) – Tough and straight grained, the colour is white to pale brown but sometimes the tree develops a dark stained heartwood and is known as 'olive ash'. It works well and is used where a light colour is required and where structures utilise steamed, bent components.

Beech – European (*Fagus sylvatica*) – Even textured and straight grained, it is whitish brown when sawn which turns more yellow on exposure. Some beech, depending upon its seasoning can turn a reddish brown colour. Fairly good to work and is used in interior surfaces and fittings.

Birch (*Betula alleghaniensis*) – Straight grained and even textured with a light yellow sapwood and reddish brown heartwood with distinct growth rings. It works and finishes well and is used in furniture and joinery. Constructional veneers derived from this are used in the best quality plywoods and manufactured boards.

Cherry (*Prunus avium*) – Straight grained and fairly hard, it has a fine texture and the heartwood is reddish brown. It works well and is used in quality joinery and interior surfaces and fittings.

Elm – European (English – *Ulmus procera*; Dutch – *Ulmus hollandica*) – Not unlike its American counterpart, its distinct but irregular growth rings can give it an attractive figure (pattern). It was widely used in buildings and interiors, but since the occurrence of Dutch elm disease reasonably sized logs are unavailable. What is left will be very precious timber and will only be available in the future if a way can be found to counteract the disease.

Iroko (*Chlorophora excelsa*) – Very durable, the grain can be straight or interlocked and it is very hard and resinous. It, like afrormosia, is also used as a teak substitute and thus can be used for exterior joinery and furniture. Difficult to work, but as it matures it closely resembles teak. Good fire resistance properties.

Mahogany (*Swietenia macrophylla*) – Medium texture with a range of grain patterns, the heartwood is reddish brown, which deepens on exposure. Once used widely in panelling and furniture, its availability is in serious question and other woods are often used instead and stained to the required colour. It works and finishes well but these days will be found mostly as veneer.

Maple (*Acer saccharum/rubrum*) – Straight grained with a fine texture. Hard maple is light reddish brown while soft maple is light creamy brown in colour. The hard maple is difficult to work but has lately been popular in interior fittings and furniture. It is also used for musical instruments, for turning and for butcher's blocks and flooring. Soft maple has similar uses but since it does not wear as well is not used where hardwearing properties are needed.

Oak – European (*Quercus robur/petraea*) – Straight grained but coarse textured, with distinct growth rings and showing an interesting pattern when quarter sawn. It works and finishes well and was one of the most favoured timbers in Europe when naturally grown timbers were all that was available. Since the Middle Ages it has been used extensively in building construction and very widely in boat building. A growing use of green timber and traditional structures in buildings has been evident recently.

Sycamore – European (*Acer pseudoplatanus*) – Fine textured and normally straight grained. White to slightly yellowish in colour. If examples have wavy grain when they are quarter sawn, a 'fiddleback' pattern is present. Good to work, this wood is very often used in interior fittings and furniture. (NB: fiddleback sycamore is used for violin backs).

Teak (*Tectona grandis*) – Coarse uneven texture, straight or wavy grain, this wood has a very oily feel. It is one of the best timbers for resistance to weathering and is often used in outdoor situations, and earlier in boat building. It originates from Asia, Africa and the Caribbean and can be difficult to find as solid wood and may only be available as veneer.

Walnut – European (*Junglans regia*) – Slightly coarse texture, straight or wavy grain. Grey-brown with dark streaks, the colour and pattern will vary depending on the timber's origin. Not often used in building structures, but a major timber for interior and furniture use. Good to work and can be excellent when finished.

Less widely used species

Amongst hardwoods there are species which have particular properties of strength, colour, grain etc. but because of ecological reasons may not be so easy to obtain and many will only be available as veneers; a few such species are listed below.

Bubinga (*Guilbourtia demeusei*) – Very decorative, it can have varying grain patterns, but its feature is its red-brown colour and its purple veins. When it was easily available it was commonly used in furniture and woodware.

Ebony (*Diospyros ebenum*) – Very hard, dense and heavy with an even texture and grain patterns. Difficult to work and finishes well and often used for small items of turning, musical instruments or inlay work.

Lignum vitae (*Guaiacum officinale*) – Very hard and heavy: it has a fine texture and interlocked grain and is naturally oily. Because of its hard wearing properties and its availability in smaller sizes, it was used for turnery and items such as bearings and pulleys.

Padauk (*Pterocarpus soyauxii*) – Hard and heavy, this wood has varying grain patterns and coarse texture. Most interestingly, when sawn, sawdust and faces are very bright red, but with exposure to light this changes to dark reddish-brown. It works fairly well and although it has gained in popularity, supply problems may make it difficult to obtain.

Rosewood (*Dalbergia nigra/latifolia*) – Rosewood has been a favourite with furniture makers and the two different growing areas produce quite different timber. Brazilian is hard and heavy with a medium texture and straight grain. It is highly figured with brown, violet-brown and black colours, but can be difficult to use in the solid. The Indian variety was often much darker and less highly figured.

Purchasing hardwoods

Hardwoods are cut from the tree into planks and the stated thickness of the board is the sawn size. The final thickness obtained from these boards will need to allow for planing a face side and face edge flat and square, and planing (and possibly sawing) to width and thickness.

Therefore, for example, sawn planks purchased at 25 mm will finish between 21–23 mm, depending on how much needs to be removed in order to make a component, flat, straight and square. In order to arrive at a specific dimension of 25 mm, a thicker board would have to be purchased, thus giving a large amount of waste.

Softwoods

Softwoods tend to be grown in cool climates, generally have an open grain, are easy to work and are used extensively for building and joinery work. Softwoods include cedar, fir, larch and several varieties of pine, spruce and yew.

Common species of softwoods

Cedar (*Thuja plicata*) – Often called western red cedar, it is often used in external applications for shingles (which are wooden roof tiles) and cladding on buildings. The reddish-brown colour changes on external exposure to an attractive silver/grey. It is a good timber to work and used internally with a finish, matures to a deep red/brown colour. The run off is acidic and can be detrimental to other materials e.g. metals.

Fir – Douglas (*Pseudotsuga taxifolia*) – This has a straight and pronounced grain, and although often used as a building timber since it is tough and water resistant, it can work well when used internally and for furniture. It is reasonably good to use, will accept a good finish and will darken to an attractive colour.

Fir – Silver (*Abies alba*) – Pale cream with a straight grain and fine texture with little resin. Often used in joinery and house construction, but occasionally for furniture. It is a good wood to work and looks good when a suitable finish is applied.

Larch (*Larix decidua*) – A straight grained wood of uniform texture that is tougher than many softwoods. The heartwood is a pale to rich red. It has been used for quality joinery and sometimes in boat building. Because of its toughness it might be slightly more difficult to work.

Pine – Parana (*Araucaria angustifolia*) – Straight grain with an even texture, its growth rings are not very conspicuous. The heartwood is a light brown colour sometimes with red streaks. Again used in joinery and also in furniture. It is easy to work and looks good.

Pine – White (*Pinus monticola*) – Pale yellow to reddish brown, it is straight grained and has an even texture. Again commonly used in joinery and construction but also for boat building and frequently furniture. It is easy to work and is attractive when finished.

Pine – Yellow (*Pinus strobus*) – Quite soft but has a straight grain and a fine even texture. Pale yellow to brown, often showing resin marks. A wide range of uses including joinery, pattern and model making, some musical instruments and also for furniture.

Redwood – European (*Pinus sylvestris*) – Often called Scots pine, Russian pine or Scandinavian redwood. Has a light yellow to reddish brown colour and can have a fair amount of resin present. It has a distinct figure and matures to a beautiful colour over time. Commonly used in construction work, it can look very good when used for furniture.

Spruce – Sitka (*Picea sitchensis*) – Straight grained with an even texture, non-resinous and creamy white in colour. It works very well and is strong so is often used for boat building, musical instruments and gliders as well as construction and joinery.

Yew (*Taxus baccata*) – Though botanically a softwood, it is tough, hard and was the timber used for the traditional English longbow. The heartwood is orange red while the sapwood is light and the wood is made very decorative by the growth patterns. It is a difficult wood to work, requiring great care in final finishing, but this is repaid by a glorious colour as it matures. It is therefore often used for individual furniture pieces.

Purchasing softwoods

There is a similar situation when buying sawn softwoods as with hardwoods, but sometimes softwoods can be purchased 'planed all round', (PAR), i.e. on all four sides. However the size given would be expressed in the original sawn size. For example 50 × 25 mm will finish less, approximately 46 × 23 mm, but the actual finished size will not be to an exact measurement. It will be to the nearest size that the timber yard can plane, in order to achieve a reasonable finish on all faces. Therefore purchases made at different times may differ from one another.

Built examples

Interesting buildings using timber include:

- Wohlen High School in Switzerland by Santiago Calatrava used timber arched box trusses for the roof of the assembly halls in 1998;
- Parish Church at Dormagen, Germany by Walter von Lom gives a spectacular interior with its use of large timber trusses, completed in 1989;
- Showroom and warehouse at Hergatz, Germany by Baumschlager & Eberle used timber structural arches and cladding in 1995;
- The Japanese Pavilion at Expo '92 in Seville, Spain by Tadao Ando used timber to dramatic effect;
- Weekend house using timber frames in Osaka by Hiroshi Nakao, 1991;
- Skyrose Chapel in Whittier, California by Jones and Jennings, 1997;
- Western red cedar cladding on otherwise concrete façades of the Salk Institute in La Jolla, California by Louis Kahn (1959–65).

Further reading

Desch, H.E. & Dinwoodie, J.M. (1996) *Timber: structure, properties, conversion and use* (7th edition), MacMillan, Basingstoke, UK.

Gutdeutsch, G. (1996) *Building in wood: construction and details*, Birkhäuser, Basle, Switzerland.

Patterson, D. (1988) *Commercial timbers of the world*, Gower, Aldershot, UK.
Stungo, N. (1998) *The new wood architecture*, Colman and King, UK.

CS

Timber – laminated timber

Timber growth results generally in a linear material, but with the developments in adhesive technology it can be laminated into curved or shaped forms easily.

See also: AALTO, ALVAR; CALATRAVA, SANTIAGO; DESIGN LIFE; DURABILITY; FIT-OUT; FLOORS; PIANO, RENZO; ROOFS; SURFACE FINISHES; TIMBER; TIMBER – MANUFACTURED BOARDS; TIMBER – PRODUCTION AND FINISHES; TIMBER – STRUCTURES.

Introduction

The principle of lamination is similar to the manufacture of plywood and is concerned with the glueing together of thin timber strips or sheets. In lamination, however, the strips of constructional veneer are laid with the grain of each lying in the same direction, adhesive is applied to these strips that are placed into a mould, pressure and heat are applied and the resulting form is trimmed for use. Preforming uses sheets of veneer in the same way as plywood, but in this instance the mould is shaped so that a single curvature is produced. There were several experiments during the 19th century by Thonet and others, but it was not until adhesive technology developed from natural to synthetic resins that the technique became successful.

The principle of timber lamination has been utilised in building with the manufacture of 'glulam' beams. Using the above method of construction, long curved shapes are possible and large distances can be spanned. The following examples indicate the potential of the system:

- The Jean Marie Tjibaou Cultural Centre by Renzo Piano Building Workshop situated in Nouméa, New Caledonia, uses a variety of different height vertical glulam columns in egg-shaped clusters in the most inventive use of the material to date. Each cluster surrounds part of the cultural and visitors' centre on this remote island in the Pacific.
- The Olympic Hall at Hamar, Norway, by Niels Torp, is one of the largest timber structures to be built. It uses large laminated arched trusses and the result is like a huge inverted ship from outside, but a superbly impressive interior space. It was built in 1992 for the 1994 winter Olympics.
- The 'Carisport' stadium at Cesena, Italy, by Vittorio Legnani, uses laminated timber to make two main arches and two boundary arches that give an effective, but unusual roof construction. It was completed in 1983.
- The 'College Pierre Semard', a secondary school at Bobigny, near Paris, France by Iwona Buczkowska uses a series of parabolic arches and curved beams made from laminated timber to give a very interesting arrangement of spaces. Parts of the roof are covered with cedar shingles (wood tiles) and the buildings were completed in 1994.
- Jourda and Perraudin's School of Architecture in Lyon, France features glulam columns and beams connected with cast metal connectors that are reminiscent of Victorian cast ironwork.

- Although lamella roof construction began in 1908, it is still being developed: short pieces of low grade timber can be interlocked as laminated vereer lunber (LVL) as demonstrated recently in the Homslow East Station, London. (Acanthus Lawrence & Wrightson Architects with Buro Happold). An ecologically sound option.

Historical note

In previous times when it was necessary to make curved components, it was necessary to either cut them from solid timber or to build up by gluing together shaped pieces. When the British built their oak 'men of war' ships for the Navy, the young trees were pulled into the required shapes and left to grow to that shape, in order to give strength to certain ships' timbers. This was a long-term decision and process. For furniture, wet wood was often formed; the chair makers (bodgers) in the English Chiltern woodlands used to make the bent backs from green ash or beech; they even used the suppleness of a small tree to drive their pole lathes. These 'Windsor' chairs were very ecological (before the word was even used), since components were cut, split and turned to size and shape before leaving the forest. All waste would remain where the wood was worked and rot and therefore contribute to the growing cycle.

Later it was found that if timber were steamed, bent on a mould and allowed to dry thoroughly, the shape would be permanent. There are many examples of bentwood furniture, but the most successful firm to use the technique for large production runs was the firm Thonet. The chair that came to be called the 'cafe chair' was produced in such numbers that it is almost beyond belief. Before the end of the 19th century over 4 million such chairs were shipped from Europe to America in the form of components that would be assembled far away from their point of manufacture. It took more than 50 years again before 'knock-down' (flat pack) furniture was seen regularly e.g. Ikea and MFI.

Complex curved forms

In general, board materials cannot be used for double curved forms. They have been used widely as building components to produce single curved shapes (for instance, bent and formed plywood) but until recently the production of large double curvature forms has not been possible. On the smaller product scale it has been possible to form these shapes; Arne Jacobsen designed the 'Ant' chair in the 1950s – its timber preformed shells, while shaped in one plane, also had a slight curve in the other. This, however, was only achieved by using very expensive matched steel moulds in large presses (similar to those used when forming sheet metal) and the veneer sheets used had to be tailored to enable the curves to be formed. This technique is viable when many thousands of shells are made and the expensive tooling spread over those numbers, but proves uneconomic for shorter runs or larger sizes.

Further reading

Desch, H.E. & Dinwoodie, J.M. (1996) *Timber: structure, properties, conversion and use* (7th edition), MacMillan, Basingstoke, UK.

Gutdeutsch, G. (1996) *Building in wood, construction and details*, Birkhäuser, Basle, Switzerland.

Müller, C. (2000) *Holzleimbau: laminated timber construction*, Birkhäuser, Basle, Switzerland.

Patterson, D. (1988) *Commercial timbers of the world*, Gower, Aldershot, UK.

Stungo, N. (1998) *The new wood architecture*, Colman and King, UK.

CS

Timber – manufactured boards

To overcome the inherent variability in natural timber, an industry has grown up around the use of adhesives and wood particles to make consistent board materials.

See also: AIRTIGHTNESS AND IAQ; ECOLOGICAL DESIGN; 'ECO-POINTS'; FIT-OUT; FLOORS; ROOFS; SURFACE FINISHES; TIMBER; TIMBER – LAMINATED TIMBER; TIMBER – PRODUCTION AND FINISHES; TIMBER – STRUCTURES.

Introduction

Even though the 'awkward' characteristics of natural timber are a major part of its attraction, in mass manufacture these characteristics cause problems. Therefore the timber industry has developed ways of using timber to make board materials, which are much more consistent and dimensionally stable than natural wood. To a large extent these developments have been made more practicable by the development of chemical adhesives that are not affected by heat or moisture. However the outcome is that designers have become wary of the contribution of adhesives and other chemical used in board production in relation to the outgassing that can occur in service, which may be detrimental to indoor air quality. Ecologically friendly options are now available as an alternative.

Boards can be produced to a standard thickness, which will be much more precise than sawn timbers for example. The thickness can be expressed either in metric sizes (2, 3, 4, 6 and 9 mm) or Imperial sizes (i.e. in inches). The sheet size is generally made to a standard 2400 × 1200 mm, but larger sheets are available to special order, and some of the lesser thicknesses may be sold at a different size (e.g. aeroply or 2 mm, may be found in 1500 mm sheets).

There are four main generic types of manufactured boards, which are discussed in turn.

Plywood – Boards are constructed from thin sheets of wood called constructional veneers, plys or laminates, which are bonded together with each layer at right angles to the preceding one. Usually, there is an uneven number of layers, so that the outside grain directions on the faces of the finished boards are the same.

- **Three-ply** – as its name implies, this is made from just three laminates, two face veneers, and a core, which is sometimes the same thickness. When the centre layer is thicker it is often called 'stout heart'.
- **Multi-ply** – this will be found in a variety of thicknesses, always using an odd number of laminates, but finishing in the standard board thicknesses from 6 mm–25 mm.

Interior grade plywoods are normally bonded with a urea-formaldehyde adhesive. These are suitable for interior work, but other types should be chosen for high humidity and moisture conditions. *Exterior grade plywood* (termed WBP i.e. weather and boil proof) uses phenolic adhesives, which are highly resistant to weather, wet and dry heat, insects and fungi. *Marine plywood* has laminates, which are selected so they are fault-free. For very special applications resorcinol adhesive can be used. The more specialised the adhesive used, the more expensive the board material becomes. There has been some unease about the toxicity of the adhesives used in some types, but this problem is found mainly in the manufacturing and working processes. Dust from particle and fibreboards can cause problems when being worked, although very low toxic emissions have been detected from finished products.

'Stressed skin' in the form of plywood can be used to good effect for example as seen in the work of Tim Ronalds Architects and at the recently completed Mount Stuart visitor centre on the Isle of Bute, Scotland. For the latter, architects Munckenbeck + Marshall used a plywood stressed skin panel made from 6 mm thick plywood ribs intersecting every 400 mm in both directions. This grid shell is connected to its covering of plywood sheets up to 18 mm thick by screwing and gluing. The result is a two-way spanning roof element that cantilevers up to 4.5 m in places. Steel plates are used as reinforcement where the roof meets supporting columns.

Blockboards – The most superior blockboard is called *Laminboard*. The core is constructed from strips of solid wood that are quite narrow (about 5 mm wide), usually edge glued and with two laminates on either side of the core, commonly with the outside ply's grain in line with the direction of the core strips. This is probably the most stable manufactured board available. *Blockboard* uses wider core strips (approximately 20 mm) not necessarily glued, sandwiched between outside laminate faces in one or two layers each side. A problem with this board is that the strips can show through the outside veneers, particularly if there is only one on each face. *Battenboard* is a cheaper blockboard, in which the interior strips are much wider, from 30–40 mm. Obviously show-through is much more likely. In addition to these boards, solid boards made from timber strips, jointed end to end and glued together to make a wide board have been used in the furniture industry and are becoming available in many DIY outlets. If one can visually accept the pattern of the board strips, they are stable and are a useful alternative to other boards and solid timber.

Particle boards (or chipboard) – These are made from small chips of timber, bonded together under pressure with suitable adhesive. They are generally stable but can be affected by moisture if a waterproof adhesive has not been used. Some boards are made from similar sized particles, but some have outside layers of high-density particles sandwiching a coarser core. Some boards are available with faces of wood veneer or plastic laminates. *Orientated-strand board (OSB)* and flake/wafer board ('Sterling' board) are both made from shavings or strands of wood. These are very commonly used in building work, and being the cheapest structural board material may be used for formwork, although consideration should be given to surface finish.

Fibreboards – These are made from wood reduced to its basic fibres and for some time the best known material was hardboard, which normally has one smooth and one textured face. However, manufacturers found problems with chipboard and other particle boards in that lippings, either solid or veneer had to be applied to the edges.

Medium density fibreboard (MDF) has two smooth faces, is bonded with synthetic resin adhesives and has a uniform structure throughout, which enables the edges to be machined, stained and polished without using lippings. MDF has become very popular in the interior fitting and DIY markets. However only the high-performance particleboards will be suitable in moist or variable temperature environments. Health and safety concerns mean that MDF should be worked only if appropriate protective equipment is used, e.g. face masks.

Built examples

Manufactured boards are used in buildings for floors, roofs, panelling and many interior fittings. It is most important however to ensure that the correct type and quality of board is used for specific applications. When using timber for the main structure, birch faced plywood makes an attractive and harmonious addition. Some interesting examples:

- A summerhouse at Fagloro, near Stockholm, Sweden by Per Friberg constructed in 1993, is an example of how the use of timber complements a natural site.
- At a different scale, the Centre for Understanding the Environment at the Horniman Museum in Dulwich, London shows how solid timber and board materials work very well in a public building. This was completed in 1997.

Further reading

Desch, H.E. & Dinwoodie, J.M. (1996) *Timber: structure, properties, conversion and use* (7th edition), MacMillan, Basingstoke, UK.

Gutdeutsch, G. (1996) *Building in wood, construction and details*, Birkhäuser, Basle, Switzerland.

Patterson, D. (1988) *Commercial timbers of the world*, Gower, Aldershot, UK.

Stungo, N. (1998) *The new wood architecture*, Calman and King, UK.

CS

Timber – production and finishes

The main trunk of the tree needs to be 'converted' into useable lengths and sizes, and even though some use has recently been made of green timber for specific applications, it is generally necessary to season (remove moisture) the wood before it is used.

See also: AIRTIGHTNESS AND IAQ; DESIGN LIFE; DURABILITY; ECOLOGICAL DESIGN; 'ECO-POINTS'; 'HONESTY'; OVERSIZING; PLASTICS FOR ADHESIVES AND FINISHES; SURFACE FINISHES; TIMBER; TIMBER – LAMINATED TIMBER; TIMBER – MANUFACTURED BOARDS; TIMBER – STRUCTURES.

Introduction

After extraction from the forest, logs have to be 'converted' to useful sizes. Usually only the trunks or very major limbs are used. Branches contain reaction wood, which has helped to support the tree, and therefore the timber has a high degree of movement that prevents economic use, being used for chipping for certain manufactured boards. The logs are sent to conversion units and milled into planks on large bandsaw or circular saw machines. Even though some timbers are naturally resistant, some forms of protection against fungal and insect attack may be required, which is normally carried out at the same time as other finishing methods.

Timber is a natural, organic material and so we must expect that it will have natural defects (e.g. knots and splits). In decorative work, these are often regarded as features to be made use of, but this may not be the case for structural use.

'Conversion' methods

Timber cut from different parts of the tree moves in a variety of ways. The annual rings always try to straighten out and this makes logs cut from the top planks more liable to distortion than those cut from the radial planks obtained from the centre boards. Some timber is converted 'through and through' which means the log is sawn into planks in a series of slices and therefore the boards will have different properties at the edge than those from the centre. Therefore with some expensive timbers, and where the minimum of wood movement is required, the log can be quarter sawn in order to produce as many quarter-sawn boards as possible. True quarter sawing would mean boards being tapered and since this is not economic, various ways of sawing that result in less waste are used.

Seasoning methods

All newly-cut wood contains a high percentage of water, which must be removed by drying or seasoning. The water is present either as free water or moisture that is present in the cell walls. The first stage of seasoning is to remove the free water and then, as seasoning continues and moisture is lost from the cell walls, movement and shrinkage will begin. If the seasoning takes place too quickly, stresses are created within the wood, so the process needs to be controlled carefully.

Air-drying – this is the traditional way of seasoning wood. The boards are stacked separated by spacer battens placed underneath each other. The stack is built clear of the ground and protected from rain and direct sunlight so the natural airflow gradually dries the wood. An approximate guide is that it takes one year to dry every 25 mm of plank thickness for hardwood and slightly less for softwoods. This method can only dry the timber to the ambient humidity, generally about 15%. For interior use, this needs to be reduced further in a kiln or within a controlled environment similar to that in which the timber will be used.

Kiln drying – the kiln is basically a large oven in which the temperature and humidity can be controlled carefully and will reduce the moisture content to about 8% or even less. The boards are fed into the kiln on trolleys, a controlled mixture of hot air and steam is introduced and the humidity gradually reduced to a specific moisture content. Kiln dried wood needs to be kept stored in a controlled environment since, if it is dried below the outside air RH level and then placed outside, moisture will be taken up once again.

Green timber

There has recently been more interest in the use of indigenous UK hardwoods in the construction of buildings using traditional methods, and this has lead to the use of green timber (in this sense, green means non-seasoned timber). Frames using substantial sections of timber (often oak) are made in traditional ways both structurally and jointwise. The timber will still dry out and surface cracks will often appear, but this will not reduce its strength and aesthetically it will be enhanced by the use of a material that has seasoned naturally in its environment. The use of non-processed timber can give rise to many interesting results:

- Steam bent timber was used for a Forestry Centre at Marche-en-Famenne, Belgium by Samyn et Associes to construct a toroidal dome;
- Bamboo canes were used at Fukoda, Japan by Shoei Yoh + Architects firstly to construct a form by lifting a lattice to form a folded structure and then to use this as a support for a steel mesh / concrete shell, for a community centre and school;
- Forest thinnings were used to construct Westminster Lodge student accommodation at Hooke Park, Dorset by Edward Cullinan.

An application that perhaps shows best what can be achieved is the Olivier Theatre at Bedales School, Petersfield, Hampshire by the Oak Design Group, Fielden Clegg and Roderick James, completed in 1996.

The use of green timber for cladding and sidings has become particularly popular as a means of providing an attractive and long-lasting finish in addition to achieving good environmental credentials. However, many architects remain unaware of the full range of timbers that are appropriate for this purpose. The woods that can be used untreated externally include western red cedar, European larch and Douglas Fir in addition to European oak and Iroko and other lesser-known examples. For example:

- Green oak at the Earth Centre in Doncaster by architects Feilden Clegg Bradley: horizontal oak slats are used on the façades of the restaurant;
- Feilden Clegg Bradley used Brazilian red louro as an alternative to cedar in their recent Century Court housing project in Cheltenham;
- Green oak cladding at the Sainsbury's eco-store in Greenwich, London. Chetwood Associates used American oak;
- David Chipperfield Architect's Henley River and Rowing Museum used extensive amounts of untreated oak cladding (1996);
- Nick Grimshaw's Eden project in Cornwall used cedar shingles on its visitor centre;
- Ted Cullinan used unfinished larch for the Greenwich millennium village school, in London.

Use of solid timber

Unlike metals and manufactured board, solid timber is not a material that is equally strong in all directions and its movement characteristics differ according to the grain direction. Timber is strongest in the direction of the grain (which follows the length of the trunk), but across the grain is much weaker. That is why timber construction optimises these properties by utilising frame construction. Timber will move with changes in humidity and this must always be allowed for. As an example, if we consider a board made from solid wood its greatest strength and minimal movement will be in the direction of grain. Across the grain, however, it will be weak and can break fairly easily and in this direction will have the most movement, this is partially the reason for the development of manufactured boards. When using timber as a linear timber (as beams or rails) these characteristics will not be a problem. Depending on the size of the section of a timber beam, timber can resist fire fairly well, sometimes better than steel. Even though small sections will burn readily, large sections will char on the outside. This charred layer is termed sacrificial, since its charring protects the structural integrity of the core of the beam beneath.

Veneers

Veneers are thin sheets of wood, which are used for either structural or decorative purposes.

For structural use they are called constructional veneers, cut to thicknesses of 1–3 mm and can be used in plywood in addition to laminated components. These veneers are produced by rotary-cutting where the trunk of the tree, after removal of the bark, and having been softened by steaming, is set on a machine similar to a huge lathe. As the machine revolves, a continuous sheet is cut from the log. The cutting knife reduces in radius to give an even thickness sheet. Many timbers are becoming difficult to obtain in the solid and often have such interesting surface finish characteristics that it is much more likely that in order to conserve and extend their use they will be made into veneers. This is particularly so with timbers that exhibit highly decorative grain patterns such as 'curl' mahogany. In early times, veneers were produced by sawing, the resulting veneers being fairly thick (say 3 mm) and the waste element coming from the sawdust was very high.

Preservation and finishes

Timber can be susceptible to both rot and infestation in wet environments. Even though some hardwoods are very resistant, most timbers, especially the majority of softwoods, need some measure of protection. Chemists have formulated preservatives that will enable timbers to resist both fungi and insects, and this can be applied in various ways. For in-situ timber it can be applied by brush or spray but in new work it is preferable to have the timber pressure impregnated. The timber to be treated is placed in stock on a trolley and fed into a large chamber. Air is removed from the chamber and also from much of the pores or cells of the wood. The preservative is then injected into the chamber so that the fluid will be drawn on to, and into, the timber. One of the most common systems is called 'tanalizing'. Even though protection is afforded it is still wise to ensure that wet conditions do not arise.

Timber may need to be finished, especially when it will be seen, and there are a variety of finishes available. It is now common in industry to use water-based finishes, but in the countries of Scandinavia, where much use is made of the wood aesthetic in buildings, it is common to find traditional materials and methods being used. Extensive use is made of oil-based treatments in which several coats of linseed, Danish, teak or tung oil are applied. This builds up a finish that is taken into the wood giving both protection and a beautiful natural surface, which can have a final finish of wax. The advantage is that repair and refurbishment is easy, just using abrasive paper and re-oil. For some cladding applications, the timber is left untreated. If this is the case, then designers must be clear that natural weathering (e.g. to a pale grey colour) will usually take place, but the timber may become stained in districts with heavy road traffic.

Although many internal finishes are paints that cover and hide the material to which they are applied, when using timber as a feature it is better to apply a finish in such a way as to enhance its natural beauty and characteristics. For this a clear finish is preferable, this can be either natural or synthetic. Synthetic finishes are often plastics-based, and even though they can be very hard wearing for some applications, in fact they encapsulate the wood in a plastic skin. Some designers have raised concerns about the long term outgassing from VOC based chemicals used in timber preservation; eco-friendly options are now more widely available.

Common timber defects

Some defects can arise from felling, some from careless kilning.

- **Shakes**: these are splits that can be caused by poor felling or stresses incurred during shrinkage;
- **Honeycombing**: this occurs in board if the outside stabilises before the inside is dry, leading to checking;
- **End splits**: these are caused by rapid drying of the ends of the planks and can often be prevented by sealing the ends during air-drying;
- **Bowing, warping, twisting, winding or springing**: these can be caused by poor stacking of the boards or from stresses that have built up during poor seasoning;
- **Insect or fungal attack**: these defects are often found in old buildings and furniture where there is inadequate ventilation and heating, damp conditions

allowing these pests and fungus to attack the timber; any sapwood left on the timber will suffer the worst.

It is unlikely that modern timber will suffer from these faults since much greater care is taken in extraction, conversion and seasoning, even though it may sometimes occur if proper care has not taken at source. Remember however that if damp conditions become present there is always a risk of infection.

Further reading

Desch, H.E. & Dinwoodie, J.M. (1996) *Timber: structure, properties, conversion and use* (7th edition), MacMillan, Basingstoke, UK.

Gutdeutsch, G. (1996) *Building in wood, construction and details*, Birkhäuser, Basle, Switzerland.

Hislop, P. (2001) *External timber cladding*, TRADA, High Wycombe, UK.

Patterson, D. (1988) *Commercial timbers of the world*, Gower, Aldershot, UK.

CS/JG

Timber – structures

Contemporary methods of using timber to provide a structural frame emanating from Europe and North America.

See also: BEAMS; BRACING; BUILDABILITY; COLUMN; DESIGN LIFE; DURABILITY; FLOORS; FRAMES; MODULES AND MODULAR CONSTRUCTION; OVERSIZING; ROOFS; TIMBER; TIMBER – LAMINATED TIMBER; TIMBER – MANUFACTURED BOARDS; TIMBER – PRODUCTION AND FINISHES.

Introduction

In its natural state timber offers several benefits for small-scale construction. It can usually be sourced locally, is lightweight and easy to handle, can be cut, carved and joined easily and in many countries has been part of the vernacular tradition of construction for hundreds of years. Both softwoods and hardwoods are used in a variety of ways from the more traditional approaches of using large-scale timber elements (e.g. cruck frames with individual timbers being many metres long) to modern methods using small element timbers for enhanced flexibility of use (e.g. 25 mm × 75 mm). This entry will focus mainly on the use of small-scale timber elements in contemporary methods for creating fairly simple structures.

Softwoods (e.g. pine) provide the bulk of timber used in construction in Europe, about 80% in fact. Cultivation of softwoods is swift and there is a good level of usage from each tree. These woods provide an accessible and economic material for construction. They are also very easy to work and handle. There is a range of structural configurations in which such timbers can be used. The terms below describe the ways in which timber elements can be configured to provide a structure.

Stud or stick – here, wall elements are built up piece-by-piece with the emphasis on vertical timbers (studs) as the main loadbearing components. This is a lengthy process with timbers at close centres, using many workers, but it is highly flexible and economic on materials, as the timber section sizes are minimal. In the USA this is termed 'stick' or 'stick-built' construction, and in general is used only up to 2–3 storeys.

Post and beam – in more expressive architectural projects using timber, it may be appropriate to revert to traditional methods of construction using large-scale timber elements and jointing techniques. This 'post and beam' style of building is particularly useful for projects where the timbers will be seen (exposed) to the occupants. The post elements are at wider centres than 'stick' construction with generally large cross sections. However the size (and weight) of the elements means handling is more difficult and connections need careful detailing. This approach would typically be used for work with green timber.

Platform – here, an entire storey of a structure is completed first. The floor of the upper storey is completed before work begins on the wall elements of the upper storey. Hence, the term platform, where a safe working platform is established before work progresses above. This technique originates from Europe. As well as studwork, it is also possible to erect a platform frame by using panelised wall and floor elements made off site and then erected. Timber frame buildings up to five storeys high are constructed in this way.

Panelised timber – as described above, large panels of timber are manufactured in a factory and then brought to site semi-finished. The 'engineered timber' panels are usually storey height and can incorporate openings etc.; they are built in a stick fashion usually with plywood sheathing on each side. The advantages are increased speed of construction (a house can be built in 1–3 days), increased accuracy and greater lateral stability (thus avoiding additional timbers for bracing etc).

Balloon – here, in a North American style of timber construction, the internal walls and floor elements of a building are completed first. These are followed by erection of a single element for the façade, which spans over two storeys (max.). Hence it is somewhat independent of the internal frame elements. This approach enables the two elements to process simultaneously this making construction faster.

Volumetric – here, whole rooms or modules are manufactured off site. These are structures in their own right and are simply 'stacked' together on site. The advantage of off-site manufacture is that internal fit-out works are completed in the factory, so when the module arrives, it is virtually complete. Services can also be installed. This technique is suitable for housing and other types of residential accommodation such as hotels. Modules can be used up to five storeys high.

Glued laminated timber is becoming increasingly popular for large-scale structural applications because of its attractive appearance and capacity to cover wide distances. Curved structures are more easily achieved with laminated timber as it is a fully engineered design solution, produced totally off site (see *Timber – laminated timber*). Timber grid shells, complex curves and other structural developments are currently receiving significant R&D efforts.

Further information is available from the Timber Research and Development Association.

Further reading

Brunskill, R.W. (1994) *Timber building in Britain* (2nd edition), Gollancz, London, UK.

Desch, H.E. & Dinwoodie, J.M. (1996) *Timber: structure, properties, conversion and use* (7th edition), MacMillan, Basingstoke, UK.

Gutdeutsch, G. (1996) *Building in wood, construction and details*, Birkhäuser, Basle, Switzerland.

Stungo, N. (1998) *The new wood architecture*, Colman and King, UK.

JG

Detail of column from the New Parliamentary building by Michael Hopkins & Partners. The precision in these components has been matched by good site practice, resulting in an exceptionally high standard of construction accuracy. Photograph by Trevor Jones, courtesy of The Concrete Society.

Tolerance

A 'permissible deviation' specified for the manufacture of building products or the setting out of building elements on site.

See also: AUTOMATED MANUFACTURE AND CONSTRUCTION; BEAM; BRICKS AND BLOCKS; CLADDING; COLUMNS; CONCRETE; CONNECTIONS; FLOORS; FRAME; GRIDS FOR STRUCTURE AND LAYOUT; MODULES AND MODULAR CONSTRUCTION; OFF-SITE MANUFACTURE; ON-SITE PRODUCTION; PLASTICS; SPECIFICATION; STRUCTURAL STEEL; TIMBER – STRUCTURES.

Introduction

Tolerances apply to both building products and setting out activities on site. Tolerances (i.e. maximum permissible deviations) can be set for dimensions, weight or other characteristics. It is usual for tolerances to be written in the form of 125+/−5 mm, where the 125 mm refers to the nominal dimension and the 5 mm refers to the maximum variation in that dimension. This means that anything between 120 mm and 130 mm is acceptable. In construction parlance, tolerance can also be expressed as 'to be built to the nearest (insert measurement e.g. 5 mm)' although this is more usually applied to setting out tolerances.

The accuracy with which a product is made, or building constructed, is a measure of the 'quality of tolerance' required and will be dependent on the production process employed. For example, whereas it is acceptable for buildings to be constructed to a (coarse) tolerance of +/−50 mm overall, in precision engineering (as applied to cladding and glazing) one would expect to see (fine) tolerances of +/−2 mm overall.

So, on a typical building site, one might not expect tolerances to be particularly critical, but where there is extensive use of products manufactured off-site to a high degree of accuracy, then both setting out and product tolerances become increasingly important to the construction manager. It is important that designers appreciate that tight tolerances on paper (e.g. allowing a variation of just 2–3 millimetres along the length of an 8 m long steel truss) are not likely to be achieved in reality (+/−30 mm is much more likely). Both manufacturing processes and setting out processes on site will affect tolerances – these are discussed in turn.

Product tolerance

The accuracy with which building products such as bricks, blocks, steel beams, columns or cladding panels are manufactured is determined by the characteristics of the manufacturing process itself. Common European standards exist for many building products, which specify the limits within which that product is deemed 'fit for purpose'. This setting of limits is product tolerance – establishing allowable variations in dimensions and other criteria such as weight and moisture content from the 'norm'. In product specification terms, the norm is the 'nominal' size or weight in appropriate units, and then the tolerance is stated as a finite amount or percentage variation. For example, a common house brick might have a nominal size of 215 mm × 102.5 mm × 65 mm. Dimensional tolerances for brickwork are such that the acceptable variations are about +/−3 mm in length and about +/−1.8 mm in height and thickness (see BS3921). Most common building products have their own standard (a British Standard or similar), which may contain an individual method of measurement for these tolerances. Dimensions, weight and angles etc can all be part of such standards.

In some instances, the method of connection between components can affect the selection of a tolerance value (i.e. joint tolerance). For example, cladding, erection or joint/sealant installation may require an 'interference fit' to function correctly, and this will require closer fitting than is perhaps expected.

Process (setting out) tolerance

The variations that can occur on site are separate from product tolerances, but are related. Setting out on site is the marking out of positions and alignments for elements of structure, cladding or windows for example. This may be addressed incrementally (point by point) or cumulatively (along a whole façade).

Although each building product may have its own dimensional tolerances the setting out process may need to address this and on-site variations. For example, for an in-situ concrete frame awaiting delivery of precast concrete cladding, it would be typical to use fixings that allowed some variation both in the placement and dimensions of the panels. There are various ways of 'taking up' tolerances on site such as the mortar joints in brickwork or bolts that fix into plates with slotted holes (slots allow for variations in setting out and component size).

The table below shows some 'rule of thumb' values for tolerances of some typical construction materials.

Size	Rule of thumb dimensional tolerances
Concrete floor slabs (150–1000 mm thick)	+/−6–20 mm
Concrete elements (600 mm–15 m)	+/−8–20 mm
Steel beam	+/−10 mm on plan
Precast concrete units	+/−3–5 mm over 1 m or better
Normal floor screeds	+/−3 mm over 3 m
'Superflat' floor screeds	+/−1 mm over 3 m

Note: Tolerances do not refer to relative structural movements during the life of the building/product. This must be dealt with separately through movement and/or expansion joints.

Further reading

British Standards Institute (1998) BS5606: 1990 (1998) *Guide to accuracy in building*, BSI, London, UK.

European Standards on tolerances tend to focus on precision engineering and measurement, e.g. BS EN 22768. Specific BS or EN standards for individual construction materials include appropriate tolerances and methods of measurement.

JG

Toughened glass
See: GLASS – LAMINATED AND COATED GLASS

Transom
See: WINDOWS AND CURTAIN WALLING

Transparent insulating materials
See: PHASE CHANGE MATERIALS

Trombe wall

A means of passive solar heating that uses thermal storage wall systems.

See also: BRICKS AND BLOCKS; CONCRETE; DYNAMIC THERMAL SIMULATION; ENERGY EFFICIENCY; ENVIRONMENTAL DESIGN; FABRIC ENERGY STORAGE; HEAT RECOVERY; HVAC; SERVICES; THERMOLABYRINTHS.

Introduction

The trombe wall is named after French architectural researcher Felix Trombe, who developed the idea in his experimental house in Odeillo, France, built with Jacques Michel in 1956. The term is used to describe a thermal storage wall constructed typically with concrete, solid masonry or water-filled containers (a recent development from the USA). Surfaces are usually dark on the glazing side to absorb solar heat and also to conduct heat more slowly through the wall. The thicker the masonry, the smaller the heat swings in the living space and consequently the longer the delay in conducting the heat through the wall. The technology is used typically for small buildings such as houses. Trombe walls as an element in climatic architectural design can be used in unison with other systems to suit the particular needs of the dwelling, its geographical position and its operational needs.

How does it work?

The thermal mass benefit of heavyweight building materials is a key part of the trombe wall concept. In this passive solar design device, a thick wall element is placed between a glazed façade and the living space. During the day, the wall absorbs the heat; at night it acts as a thermal buffer between the living space and the cold radiation of the glass while re-radiating stored heat to the occupied space. The performance of trombe walls can be enhanced by the use of vent openings at the top and bottom of the wall to allow the warmed air to rise by natural convection. However, this circulation route allows cool night air to enter the glazed space, creating an unwanted chilling effect. This can be overcome by the use of a lightweight film damper, top hinged, over the room side of the top vent. The best solution is to combine areas of unvented trombe walls for night operation (e.g. bedrooms etc), with direct gain through windows, together with glazed doors for daytime operation (i.e. living, dining and study rooms).

Case study

One of the best examples of a trombe wall can be found in a house designed by architect Douglas Kelburgh located in Princeton, New Jersey, USA. The house was of frame construction, with all the rooms facing south. Over a period of some eight years, Kelburgh modified the house to increase thermal performance and comfort, undertaking the following tasks:

- (1976) A second glazing layer was added to the sunspace. Installed vent wall check valves to prevent thermosiphoning. Added movable insulation to first floor windows. Added water drums to provide additional thermal storage.
- (1977) Thermal curtains were installed between the sunspace and living areas.
- (1978) Roof vents added to improve ventilation cooling of first floor bedrooms.
- (1980) Installed domestic hot water solar collector in sunspace.
- (1982) Internal storm windows were added.

Alternative options

- **Water wall systems** – due to its high specific heat, water is a very efficient heat storage medium. Trombe water wall systems collect and store heat in similar ways with one exception: water walls transfer heat through the walls as a result of the convective circulation of water in the wall. This allows the water to be mixed continually; resulting in virtually no time lag in transferring absorbed heat into the room.
- **Generative systems** – the trombe wall concept applied together with passive solar designs, which allow flexible and adaptive designs to be generated in 'sunspace' dwellings.

Further reading

Brown, G.Z. (1985) *Sun, wind, and light: architectural design strategies*, John Wiley & Sons, New York, USA.

Hastings, S.R. (1999) *Solar sir systems: built examples*, James & James, London, UK.

Hastings, S.R. & Mørck, O. (2000) *Solar air systems: a design handbook*, James & James, London, UK.

Moore, F. (1993) *Environmental control systems: heating, cooling and lighting*, McGraw-Hill International Edition, USA.

Steven Winter Associates & Crosbie, M.J. (ed.) (1998) *The passive solar design and construction handbook*, John Wiley & Sons, New York, USA.

WH

Trunking

See: RISERS AND TRUNKING

Truss

See: ROOFS; STRUCTURAL STEEL; TIMBER – STRUCTURES

Twin-skin façade

See: FAÇADES AND FAÇADE ENGINEERING

U value
See: INSULATION

UB – universal beam
See: STRUCTURAL STEEL

UC – universal column
See: STRUCTURAL STEEL

Umbrella connector
See: TEXTILE MEMBRANE ROOFS

UPVC
See: PLASTICS – TYPES

Vacuum forming

See: PLASTICS – FABRICATION

Vacuum drainage

See: WATER MANAGEMENT AND DRAINAGE

Value engineering (VE)

Value engineering (VE) is a structured process in which stakeholders in a project clarify what they want to achieve within available resources. It is part of the 'toolkit' of techniques that constitute value management (VM) and is generally used on larger projects in the construction industry.

See also: AUTOMATED MANUFACTURE AND CONSTRUCTION; BUILDABILITY; DESIGN LIFE; DURABILITY; ECOLOGICAL DESIGN; ENVIRONMENTAL DESIGN; 'LEAN' CONSTRUCTION; LIFE-CYCLE COSTING; PROCUREMENT; RISK MANAGEMENT; SPECIFICATION; SUSTAINABILITY.

Introduction

Value engineering (VE)* was applied originally in the manufacturing industry in North America during the 1940s, and has now spread to Europe, Japan and elsewhere as well as into other industries. Value engineering is a key part of value management, which encompasses a variety of approaches to problem solving, improving communications and developing strategies to meet objectives. Value management can cover the various processes that are used during a project from briefing to completion, and post-occupancy. It can therefore play a key role in the procurement of a building, during design, construction and even during post-occupancy. At their best, value techniques can help to achieve better quality and more sustainable buildings.

About value

Many people believe 'value' to be equal to function/cost or function/life-cycle cost, but it is actually a larger, more complex idea that cannot always be defined by any

* With due acknowledgement to the work of Dr Roy Woodhead (Oxford Brookes University).

one criterion. A cost-oriented view does not account for the better 'value' (in terms of criteria other than capital cost) that can be brought to a building project. Such benefits can be substantial and very persuasive to clients. For example, an increase in construction costs may be perfectly acceptable for a hotel in order that the hotel can open several weeks early and thereby enable the client to gain extra revenue from those weeks' bookings. Under 'normal' competitive procedures, such nuances may not be obvious or even assessable by the project team.

For buildings, it is most useful to employ value management techniques throughout the project, but the most effective period is at the early stages of feasibility and conceptual design, where there is the greatest potential for agreeing objectives and open-minded discussion of client requirements. Although it is thought that implementing VM techniques can add an additional 1% (approx.) on project expenditure, cost savings can be in the order of 5–25%, or even more.

Undertaking VE

Value engineering often involves a team-based, facilitated group approach (usually in a workshop), which entails a creativity procedure to generate innovative ways of achieving value. Cost reduction is not the main goal. This is often not the perception of value engineering. All too often VE is used in a simplistic manner to drive down costs, but this does not reflect the full potential of such techniques. Using VE as a means to compare alternative scenarios in terms of very basic design criteria will not illustrate fully how it can 'stretch' technical, business and strategic goals. A structured VE approach enables explicit decision making, whole team involvement and an early balancing of objectives, thus increasing overall value to the project (and the client). This is addressed by being clear about:

- Strategic goals;
- How good decisions will be recognised;
- What expertise is required to arrive at a business case that will meet those aspirations.

This 'framing' is usually carried out before a VE workshop commences. A VE workshop is typically a five-day process, which takes the project participants from their defined starting point (base case) through a series of stages:

- Function analysis;
- Creativity;
- Evaluation of ideas;
- Construction of scenarios;
- Selection of the least, moderate and high-risk scenarios.

At the end of the workshop, the client (or individual with financial control) can either stay with the base case or select one of the new scenarios to develop. Thus, VE is a decision-making process that bridges strategic and operational management. Several major UK contractors have used a model for construction projects, called the value management framework (loosely structured around the RIBA Plan of Work stages).

Endnote

The main advantage of using a VE process (for building projects) is the clear identification of an appropriate balance between cost, time and quality objectives in a team-based approach that features explicit decision making linked to project objectives. This cannot be overestimated as a vital way of ensuring success throughout design, construction and occupancy of a building. It may even lead to longer term working relationships. Although value engineering and value management techniques are used currently in the main on larger construction projects (because the potential gains are so massive); there is significant scope to extend their use to even the smallest of projects. The key to success is to employ an experienced value facilitator who is able to manage the process and help the project team to exceed its own expectations.

Further reading

Best, R. & de Valence, G. (1999) *Building in value: pre-design issues*, Butterworth-Heinemann, Oxford, UK.

Gray, C. (1996) *Value for money*, Thomas Telford, London, UK.

Institution of Civil Engineers (1996) *Creating value in engineering*, Thomas Telford, London, UK.

Kelly, J., Male, S., & Graham, D. (2001) *Value management of construction projects*, Blackwell Science, Oxford, UK.

Male, S, Kelly, J. et al. (1998) *The value management benchmark: a good practice framework for clients and practitioners*, Thomas Telford, London, UK.

Woodhead, R. & Downs, C. (2001) *Value management – improving capabilities*, Thomas Telford, London, UK.

Zimmerman, L.W. & Hart, G.D. (1982) *Value engineering: a practical approach for owners, designers and contractors*, Van Nostrand Reinhold, New York, USA.

JG

Van der Rohe, Mies

Mies van der Rohe, Ludwig (1886–1969), normally referred to as 'Mies', was the foremost proponent of a rigorous and technical architecture that came to be known as the International Style.

See also: CANTILEVERS; GLASS; GRIDS FOR STRUCTURE AND LAYOUT; GROPIUS, WALTER; HIGH TECH; LE CORBUSIER; STRUCTURAL STEEL; WINDOWS AND CURTAIN WALLING.

Perhaps the most influential architect of the 20th century, Mies van der Rohe has often shouldered the responsibility of those who came in his wake spreading non-descript glass boxes across the cities of the world. Yet he remains a hugely influential figure and his rigorous, rational architecture continues to inspire architects.

Mies was born in Aachen and started off in his father's stonemasonry workshop in that city. He moved on to become a draftsman in a stucco decorating business and later moved to Berlin where he worked in the offices of Bruno Paul and Peter Behrens, where his colleagues included Walter Gropius and Le Corbusier. In Berlin he was influenced profoundly by the neo-classical architecture of Karl Friedrich Schinkel, in particular the Altes Museum (1823–30), the proportions and plan of which would continue to influence his buildings throughout his career. The evolution of his private practice was interrupted by four years military service in 1914–18. His designs for office blocks (1921–2) featured sheer glass curtain walls and cantilevered concrete floors. Moving from a crystalline expressionism to an organic envelope shape, Mies, the trainee mason, was among the first to realise the potential freedom to be gained by the abandonment of traditional masonry structure. These visionary designs still appear remarkable today.

Mies' low-rise buildings however were redolent of the De Stijl movement and of its apologist, Theo van Doesburg who he met in 1920. Walls are treated as sculptural planes, which glide past one another and intersect while always retaining their own integrity. The abandonment of the traditional dark corner and the adoption of the 'free plan' (a misnomer as it was often governed by a remarkably rigid grid) can be attributed largely to Mies. In the Barcelona Pavilion (1928–29, rebuilt 1992) and the Tugendhat House, Brno, Czech Republic (1930) Mies built two houses which effectively introduced the world to minimalist architecture. Slender columns, broad cantilevers and planes of glass and marble were juggled with exquisite taste to form unsurpassed spaces which flowed from inside to out with the minimum of disruption. In 1930 Mies took over as director of the Bauhaus, replacing Walter Gropius. He moved with the school during its most turbulent years from Dessau to Berlin and, despite his efforts, failed to save it from closure by the Nazis regime. Mies emigrated in 1938 to the USA where he became Professor of Architecture at the Armour Institute of Technology in Chicago. His first major work in the US was a new campus for this Institute (1939). Planned like a factory, this was extreme functionalism characterised by clear-span buildings, the clean expression of structural elements and exquisite, machine-like, detailing.

The Farnsworth House, Plano, Illinois (1946–1950) became the prototype glass box, which architects are still so drawn to, and completed the severe reduction of architectonic elements which Mies savoured. His realisation of his dreams of the early 1920s and the development of the curtain-walled skyscraper dominated the next phase of Mies's career. The Promontory Apartments (1947) and Lakeshore Drive Buildings (1951) built using concrete and steel frames respectively, were radically minimal additions to Chicago's skyline. In subsequent buildings including New York's Seagram Building (1956–59) and Chicago's Federal Center (1959–64) Mies perfected the stripped-down urban box, which would be emulated by commercial architects throughout the world, with wildly varying results. In the National Gallery in Berlin (1963–68), one of the century's greatest public buildings, Mies returned to the city where he learnt his trade and paid a final, magnificent homage to his hero, Schinkel.

Mies is admired widely for his clear expression of the role of elements within his buildings. Although he has often been criticised for his love of luxurious materials (which he used in claddings) and his proclivity to stick 'I' beams on the outside of buildings to express the structure within (where steel beams were concealed necessarily behind concrete in adherence to fire regulations). Other critics have branded his world as cold and inhuman, but Mies dismissed criticism of his work being soulless saying 'I don't want to be interesting, I want to be good'.

Despite such criticism Mies's oeuvre remains hugely influential and, at its best, remains the finest and most sophisticated demonstration of the reductivist philosophy of the Modern movement encapsulated in his most famous aphorism 'Less is more'.

Further reading

Blaser, W. (ed.) (1992) *Ludwig Mies van der Rohe*, Thames & Hudson, London, UK.
Blaser, W. (ed.) (1992) *Ludwig Mies van der Rohe*, Gustavo Gili, Barcelona, Spain.
Cohen, J-L. (1996) *Mies van der* Rohe, E & FN Spon, London, UK.
Drexler, A. (1960) *Ludwig Mies van der Rohe*, Mayflower London, UK.
Riley, T. & Bergdoll, B. (2001) *Mies in Berlin*, MoMA, New York, USA.
Vandenberg, M. (1999) *20th century museums by Ludwig Mies van der Rohe, Louis Kahn and Richard Rogers*, Phaidon Press, London, UK.

EH

Ventilation

The supply of outdoor air to provide fresh air and dilute airborne contaminants.

See also: AIRTIGHTNESS AND IAQ; DYNAMIC THERMAL SIMULATION; ECOLOGICAL DESIGN; ENERGY EFFICIENCY; ENVIRONMENTAL DESIGN; FAÇADES AND FAÇADE ENGINEERING; HEAT RECOVERY; HVAC; INTELLIGENT FAÇADES AND MATERIALS; LE CORBUSIER; LOUVRES AND BRISE-SOLEIL; NEUTRA, RICHARD; NIGHT VENTILATION; SERVICES; SICK BUILDING SYNDROME; STACK EFFECT; WIND TOWERS; WINDOWS AND CURTAIN WALLING.

Introduction

Indoor air quality (IAQ) is dependent on the regular supply of fresh air from outside the building; this is called **ventilation**. It is important not only to provide fresh air for human respiration, but also to reduce the concentrations of airborne contaminants that can build up in an enclosed space. The latter point is discussed more fully in *Sick building syndrome* and *Airtightness and IAQ*. Ventilation is part of heating ventilating and air conditioning (HVAC) design and is part of the building services engineer's role. The importance of good ventilation and healthy buildings can be seen in architectural writings from the 1950s: US architect Richard Neutra was keen to develop the idea of 'better homes for people to live in'.

Various elements of a building can be used as part of the ventilation strategy, including windows, cladding, atria, louvres, façades, 'wind towers' or even staircases. Raised floor systems, suspended ceiling zones, other plenum spaces and floor slabs may also be utilised.

The rate at which 'air exchange' takes place is called the **ventilation rate** (or air change rate) and is expressed in the amount of outside air in litres required per second per person. For example, open plan spaces such as offices, retail buildings and theatres may require only 8 litre/sec/person, whereas restaurants, conference rooms and cellular offices may require up to 25 litres/sec/person (some building types will have very particular standards in this area).

The design rate selected will also take into account whether people are allowed to smoke in the space. Research has shown that a combination of smoking, body odours, small volume of space and a high concentration of people would require much higher air change rates than recommended normally. Over the past 15 years, however, the increasing R&D on sick building syndrome (SBS) and IAQ has shown that there are many more factors to be taken into account.

Designing ventilation for good IAQ

Ventilation, whether it be natural ventilation or mechanically-assisted systems, has historically been designed simply on the basis of air change rates for particular building types, with the only exceptional circumstances being laboratories and process industries. Concerns over SBS and IAQ have changed this approach, but we have yet to see these issues recognised fully in UK Building Regulations.

The buoyancy effect of air (i.e. stack effect) is a particularly effective means of utilising natural ventilation, but can be combined with 'booster' fans to ensure air change rates are always achieved. Cross ventilation can be used in combination with the stack effect (provided the building is only about 15 metres wide in total or to an atrium space). This describes an airflow across the depth of a building, driven naturally, as a response to opening windows or louvres on opposite façades (the air movement is induced by a pressure difference caused by solar gain and/or wind).

Night ventilation (purging) is a useful option to ensure any fabric energy storage is recharged overnight (reducing temperature build up during the day) and any airborne pollutants that have built up are flushed out of the space. Ecological design precepts require that wherever possible designers do not specify building materials that outgas toxic chemical compounds and provide proper night ventilation as a back-up just in case. In some instances a 'mixed mode' operation may be appropriate (combination of natural and mechanical means). In any case, the indications are that night ventilation is more important that daytime ventilation in reducing the impacts of these pollutants.

For designers concerned about such risks, new measurement techniques developed in Denmark can be used (the OLF and the DECIPOL); the latter being a correlation between the mix of pollutants and the dilution caused by ventilation. With 60% of householders in the USA alone stating their wish to occupy 'healthier' homes there is very clearly a need to revise our attitudes and approaches towards ventilation and HVAC design.

Further reading

Allard, F. (ed.) with Santamouris, M. (1998) *Natural ventilation in buildings: a design handbook*, James & James, London, UK.
CIBSE (2000) *Mixed mode ventilation: CIBSE Applications Manual 13*, CIBSE, London, UK.
Curwell, S., March, C., & Venables, R. (1990) *Buildings and health: the Rosehaugh guide*, RIBA Publications, London, UK.
Hansen, D.L. (1999) *Indoor air quality issues*, Taylor & Francis, New York, USA.
Moore, F. (1993) *Environmental control systems: heating, cooling and lighting* (International Edition), McGraw-Hill, New York, USA.
Santamouris, M. & Asimakapolous, D. (eds.) (1996) *Passive cooling of buildings*, James & James, London, UK.

WH/JG

Volumetric construction

See: MODULES AND MODULAR CONSTRUCTION; OFF-SITE MANUFACTURE; PODS; BUILDING SYSTEMS

Von Gerkan & Marg

Meinhard von Gerkan (b. 1935) and Volkwin Marg (b. 1936) and their practice 'GMP' have become known for their adventurous glazed roofs.

See also: ATRIUM; GLASS – STRUCTURAL GLAZING; HIGH TECH; RITCHIE, IAN; ROOFS; STRUCTURAL STEEL; VAN DER ROHE, MIES.

GMP first gained international attention with their design for Berlin's Tegel airport in 1975. The system of competition, which prevailed in Germany for big public buildings, allowed this young practice to compete on equal terms with large, established offices and they consistently fared exceptionally well in competition. The practice has grown to major international status and continues to produce buildings, which are well wrought and interesting. The lack of a single 'house style' ensures that new influences and site-specific solutions keep their work fresh. Their buildings could be described as a blend of High Tech and industrial architecture with a dash of the geometric rigour of Mies van der Rohe.

Their appreciation of building technology is evident from their delight in the expression of structure and, in particular, of the complex roofscapes and internal spaces created by steel trusses, which occur so frequently in their work. Confronted with a brief to provide large single spaces, GMP's response is to concentrate on the roof structure to create interest. The Neue Messe in Leipzig (1992) is a vast exhibition hall composed of a series of vast high-tech arching trusses so that the building consists only of its roof. Compared to the intricate detailing of the roof structure the interior is light and clear, entirely free of columns. The new hall at Messe Hannover (1994) has the trusses on the inside, a deep space-frame composition, which gives expression to a complex roof but similarly leaves a huge, structure-free and highly flexible interior.

GMP's most impressive recent work was at the Hannover Expo 2000 where their intelligent designs dominated the site. Halls 8 and 9 are characterised by a roof which appears to be draped over the structure and is supported on huge tubular sections, which touch the ground via twin converging braces and are then anchored to the ground externally. The excellent Christ Pavilion (1997) is a stripped ecclesiastical space in the tradition of Mies van der Rohe. Their other works include an ingenious folding bridge in Kiel-Horn (1994) in which a three part structure folds flat in a harmonica action; the Dresdner Bank in Berlin's Pariser Platz (1995), which centres around a vast drum-shaped atrium; and fine structures at Hamburg Airport and Berlin-Spandau railway station.

Further reading

Von Gerkan, Marg und Partner (1983) *Architektur 1978–1983 Von Gerkan Marg und Partner*, Deutche Verlags-Anstalt, Stuttgart, Germany.

Von Gerkan, Marg und Partner (1995) *Von Gerkan Marg und Partner* (3 volumes), Birkhäuser, Switzerland.

EH

Walls

Loadbearing elements placed in a building to support floors or roofs and also used on the exterior to provide protection from the weather.

See also: ACOUSTICS; BRACING; BRICKS AND BLOCKS; BRICKS AND BLOCKS – FINISHES; CAVITY; CONCRETE; CONCRETE – STRUCTURES; CONCRETE – FINISHES; CONDENSATION; CONNECTIONS; DRY CONSTRUCTION AND WET CONSTRUCTION; DURABILITY; EARTH CONSTRUCTION; FOUNDATIONS; FRAMES; GRIDS FOR STRUCTURE AND LAYOUT; OVERCLADDING; PERMEABILITY; PLASTERBOARD; RETAINING WALLS; STONE; SURFACE FINISHES; THERMAL BRIDGING; TOLERANCE; WEATHERING; WRIGHT, FRANK LLOYD.

Curved concrete walls form the entrance to architect Ken Shuttleworth's (Foster & Partners) own home, Crescent House. The walls continue through the house defining interior spaces and being punctured to form openings. Photograph by Nigel Young.

Introduction

The wall is one of the most primal elements in architecture. In its many and various forms the wall has provided people with protection from the weather for centuries and it is still important to today's architectural language. The historical trend has been to move from a monolithic construction (i.e. solid and thick, with one basic material, no insulation or damp proofing) to a cavity construction (less material in two layers, insulation and a measure of damp proofing). The latter is seen typically in northerly, cool and wet latitudes where energy efficiency during the long heating season is generally of more importance than passive cooling during the summer months. In hot, dry climates, the thermal mass of a thicker, solid wall is more effective for cooling purposes. Nevertheless, in most cases, the basic functions of a wall, and the materials used in its construction, are broadly consistent; the two key functions are outlined below.

Structure – walls are typically loadbearing, i.e. supporting the 'dead' loads from the structure above (i.e. floors and roof, walls) and the 'live' loads on these (e.g. people, wind and snow). Walls with no loadbearing capacity are usually called partitions or screens. Walls are not as efficient as columns at transferring vertical loads, but they can be designed to have inherent shear stability and obviously have other useful properties (see *Frames*).

Protection – this includes the wall acting as a protective layer against weather, water, noise, fire and pests. The technology to provide such functions has developed significantly such that contemporary walls provide the same functions as vernacular versions, but within just half the thickness. Protection against the weather is obviously a primary function for external walls. This is achieved in much the same way as in roofs (i.e. requiring both moistureproof layers and insulating materials) and is also governed in the UK by the standards set in the Building Regulations. Protection against noise from external sources such as traffic and from internal sources such as people, television, radio etc., is also an inherent feature of walls. The level of sound resistance afforded by the wall is determined by its thickness, density of the material and number of openings/joints etc.

Materials

Brickwork and natural stone are the most common materials used to form walls. These heavyweight building materials are generally easy to manufacture, work and place by hand. Local availability of particular types of these materials mean that wall materials often form a key part of local vernacular architecture. For example, the limestone from the Cotswolds used in Oxford and natural flint stones from the South Downs used in Sussex. The ability to hone and shape these natural materials means that there is considerable variety in use across the UK. Adobe, rammed earth or cob construction can also be seen in some areas.

In contemporary architecture, concrete in the forms of in-situ or precast concrete blocks is used extensively as it is economical, widely available and simple to use. In domestic construction, lightweight concrete blocks (with insulating properties) are particularly popular as they are also loadbearing. Glass bricks/blocks offer a useful and attractive way of getting light through a loadbearing wall without using windows.

External walls in detail

External walls using loadbearing materials are limited generally to a few storeys in height due to bearing weight and lateral stability. Such walls are thus common in domestic and low-rise construction, but very uncommon above two storeys for other types of buildings such as offices or apartments (in this case a structural frame hung with external cladding or curtain walling would be more typical). Loadbearing walls also restrict both the number and placement of openings such as windows and doors. Where an opening is formed a lintel (steel, concrete or stone) should be used to span the gap, distributing the loads into the wall on both sides of the hole.

Walls on external façades can be designed to be left as finished or to be hung with tiles or any other type of cladding. Most loadbearing external walls incorporate a cavity, hence **cavity walls**. Here, the wall has two separate leaves with a cavity (usually containing insulation) – it is the most popular form of wall for domestic construction in the UK as it deals efficiently with moisture, movement, sound protection and insulation in just over 200 mm thickness. Typically a facing brick is used on the exterior leaf with concrete blocks for the internal leaf. A damp proof course or membrane (DPC/DPM) is used at the base to prevent damp rising from ground level.

Internal walls in detail

Internal walls are less constrained by the need to provide environmental protection but may offer more than simple architectural or sculptural opportunities. The internal wall may have decorative functions, but it may also offer other performance characteristics like acoustic separation, privacy, security and fire protection. For example, in healthcare buildings walls may be designed to protect against radiation from X-ray equipment and in museums walls are used to separate different temperature and humidity zones. In warehouses with high stock (inventory) values, loadbearing walls provide the fire separation and compartment walls that are required by insurers.

Built examples

Many of Frank Lloyd Wright's early Prairie-style houses (c.1900–10) used loadbearing walls throughout. Wright was particularly skilled at placing the walls on plan, articulating the brick, stone and concrete blocks used to build the walls and using the minimum number of wall planes to support the free-flowing roof planes that dominated his work.

The in-situ concrete walls associated with Japanese architect Tadao Ando have proved highly influential. Ando designs the wall to retain a pattern of bolt holes and formwork joints that have been used to cast the concrete. In this way he expresses the construction method in his architecture and leaves the viewer with a simple rhythmic texture on the muscular concrete wall as seen in the Koshino House (1979–81).

Further reading

Allen, W. (1997) *Envelope design for buildings*, Butterworth-Heinemann, Oxford, UK.

JG

Waste
See: RECYCLING

Water management and drainage

The management of water and other wet services within a building addresses rainwater, run-off, flooding, condensation, water supplies and wastewater recycling or disposal.

See also: CLADDING; CONDENSATION; CONNECTIONS; CORE (SERVICES); DESIGN LIFE; DURABILITY; ECOLOGICAL DESIGN; ENVIRONMENTAL DESIGN; FAÇADES AND FAÇADE ENGINEERING; INTEGRATION; MAINTENANCE; OVERCLADDING; PERMEABILITY; PLASTICS; RECYCLING; RISERS AND TRUNKING; ROGERS, RICHARD; ROOFS; SERVICES; SUSTAINABILITY; WALLS.

Introduction

There are a wide range of design, construction and operational aspects that are related to, or affected by 'wet' services, i.e. those carrying some form of water. The purpose of wet services may be to supply facilities with drinking water, process water, both steam and condensates, for industries, recycle 'greywater', or to implement exit strategies for wastewater. While the building services engineer would have major responsibilities for the design and installation of wet services, for complex buildings in particular, the overall approach may be discussed with other members of the design team. For this reason it is important to have an appreciation of the basic issues involved in this discipline of 'supply and removal'.

At the scale of the whole building, the water provision forms part of the building services strategy, but has come to attract less attention than ICT installations for example, perhaps because these are more costly and of greater strategic importance to many businesses. However, wet services should be considered as one of the fundamental, most basic amenities for any building, from homes to theme parks.

Obviously for building types such as car washes and ice rinks, water inherently plays an important role! Water conservation is an important aspect of sustainability and so this vital natural resource should be well managed at all levels. This environmental perspective is reflected in practice but not adopted wholesale. So there are relatively few examples of buildings with say recycling facilities for greywater (e.g. bathwater recycled for flushing WCs).

Internal to the building

Service runs of pipes, risers, various types of plant and many items of sanitaryware are the items that most people associate with wet services in a building. The fact that these are connected in discrete systems that are often computer controlled is less known and not appreciated by all except the services engineers who designed and installed them. The construction of Rogers and Piano's Pompidou Centre in the 1970s in Paris must have been a wonderful boost for services engineers everywhere, with its proudly exposed pipework.

Nonetheless in most buildings the wet services remain unseen, but they include:

- Clean water supplies for drinking;
- Process water supply to laboratories or machinery;
- Cooling water for industry;
- Treated water or steam for industry;
- Water to heating or cooling systems;
- Water to kitchens, bathrooms and WCs;
- Wastewater from any of the above;
- Foul water from any of the above.

In some (usually hot) countries water is used as a natural cooling medium and features in the vernacular architecture as fountains or water walls (similar to trombe walls). However, not all architecture has such a holistic view of water and wet services. There can be major difficulties if these are not designed properly or develop faults, perhaps the most onerous of which is cross-contamination of drinking water supplies which can cause disease, poisoning or environmental damage. On a less dramatic level, unplanned moisture (e.g. condensation) in a building can cause localised damage to materials, fittings and furniture.

External to the building

Externally, the main effort should go into a number of areas. On the roof of a building rainwater (or snow) disposal is the priority and there are many possibilities depending on roof shape, materials and local climates. For instance, small domestic roofs using slates or tiles combined with standard PVC-U downpipes are very effective at shedding moderate amounts of rain or snow. An alternative option is the use of a group of chains hanging from the gutter as seen in McCormac Jamieson Pritchard's extension to St. John's College, Oxford – an attractive architectural option in which the water trickles down through the chains to the ground. However, for buildings with a large surface area such as a warehouse alternative options are required that provide a greater overall capacity to clear the roof of water very quickly. For example, Stansted Airport Terminal building by Foster and Partners uses a siphonic (vacuum) drainage system. The small bore downpipes contain some water all the time, but the action of rain falling causes the pressure to build and the pipes actually suck the excess away.

Rainfall and precipitation, particularly wind-driven rain, is an issue for façade design. During its service life, a façade must be able to withstand a range of weather conditions and possible impact damage. For these reasons, the construction details, joints and interfaces can be very important to the overall durability of the building.

This is best addressed in design life and specifications; it may also be useful to carry out some predictions of likely weathering patterns. In some instances, overcladding (i.e. rain screen cladding) can be used as a refurbishment measure, to better protect a deteriorating building.

Rainwater run-off from a building is contained usually within guttering and downpipes and subsequently in external hard landscaping via paving laid to a fall, which feeds underground pipe runs. Although these are designed to predicted maximum flows, designers should be aware that, in areas with high precipitation or likelihood of storms, it may be necessary to provide storm drains to cope with extreme conditions. Where high levels of rainfall are common there can be significant levels of run-off from areas of hard landscaping such as roads, plazas and parking, which can pool easily and may cause unexpected flooding. There is currently a drive towards 'sustainable urban drainage systems' (SUDS) as a means by which localised flooding can be prevented. Permeable paving, greywater holding tanks and trickle systems all help to alleviate such problems (and of course greywater could also be redirected for use elsewhere). An interesting example of technology transfer is the idea of fog-catching sails to collect water in arid areas. 1 m^2 of netting can collect 1–3 litres/day. The concept comes from traditional peruvian architecture.

Further reading
Wise, A.F.E. & Swaffield, J.A. (1995) *Water, sanitary and waste services for buildings* (4th edition), Longman, Harlow, UK.

JG

Waterproofing
See: SEALANTS

Weathering

The alteration of a building's appearance as a result of exposure to atmospheric and environmental conditions is generally termed weathering. These conditions induce visual and compositional changes within and on the surface of building materials that can decrease the value of buildings, increase maintenance requirements and compromise the aesthetic qualities of buildings.

See also: CLADDING; CONCRETE; CONCRETE – FINISHES; CONNECTIONS; CORROSION; COR-TEN®; DESIGN LIFE; DURABILITY; ENVIRONMENTAL DESIGN; FAÇADES AND FAÇADE ENGINEERING; LIFE-CYCLE COSTING; MAINTENANCE; METALS; OVERCLADDING; PERFORMANCE; PERMEABILITY; SEALANTS; SPECIFICATION; SURFACE FINISHES; WINDOWS AND CURTAIN WALLING.

About weathering
Over time all buildings go through the process of weathering. Changes in the appearance of façade elements due to weathering may affect negatively the value of a building and people's perceptions. Controlling and predicting weathering requires

a clear understanding of the causes and processes involved. The main factors causing weathering are:

- Environmental factors (i.e. climate and pollution);
- Design and construction factors (i.e. architectural details and workmanship);
- Properties of materials (i.e. porosity, texture colour and solubility of materials);
- The factor of use (i.e. general wear-and-tear).

All these factors contribute to a certain extent to the weathering and alteration of building façades. Although factors such as climate and pollution cannot be controlled by the designer, it is important to know as much as possible about the environment surrounding a building so that appropriate finishes and details may be selected. The location and orientation of the building can critically influence the manner in which it will weather. Weathering is one aspect within the umbrella term 'building pathology' (see *Further reading* below).

Types of weathering

Weathering consists of the combination of complex phenomena taking place in building materials and on their surfaces, which lead to changes in the appearance of buildings. Weathering phenomena can be generally divided in three types:

- **Physical weathering**, causing cracking erosion, and soiling/staining. These can be attributed to frost action, temperature fluctuation and the actions of wind and rain;
- **Chemical weathering**, which is usually due to the chemical reaction between water and elements existing in the atmosphere such as acids, alkalis and sulphates, and building materials, causing phenomena like oxidation, corrosion and sulphate attack efflorescence;
- **Biological weathering**, which consists of growth of organisms on the surface of building materials and is caused usually by extensive exposure to wet conditions and/or light.

Weathering of different materials

Structures often incorporate a range of different materials with varying weathering characteristics and properties. Weathering influences all materials, but some seem to be influenced more than others depending on their absorption capacity, chemical composition, texture and the context in which they are used. It is also important to be aware of the manner in which materials react with each other. The quality of materials and construction methods selected largely influence the way buildings weather and deteriorate. For example, copper develops a patina naturally (surface coating) over time, which changes its colour from glossy red to matte green.

Weathering and design

Weathering tends to become noticeable on building façades when it starts detracting from the building's original design concept. These changes tend to be more accentuated on buildings with simple façades and not many design details. Special attention is needed when designing all parts of a building where there is any differentiation in materials, volumes or textures. These points, for example protrusions, recesses and windowsills, tend to be most vulnerable to changes and breakdown, as that is where water tends to collect. There are generally three approaches to weathering in design:

- Buildings designed to stay unaltered over time by using efficient construction, high quality materials and careful detailing, thus resisting environmental impact.

This approach can prove very expensive, but highly effective in the long term. Examples include Terry Farrell's building for MI5 at Vauxhall Cross in London and John Outram's Judge Institute of Management Studies in Cambridge, both using long-lasting precast concrete and reconstituted stone.

- Buildings that can be brought back to their original appearance at regular intervals by cleaning, painting and general maintenance. This approach requires a commitment from the owners to future maintenance. For example, Denys Lasdun the architect for the National Theatre on the South Bank in London, designed it on the basis that it had a five-year maintenance cycle, but this was not sustained.
- Buildings that can weather 'gracefully' without expensive maintenance. These buildings change with time but the alterations do not disturb the initial design and composition. Changes on façades enhance rather than spoil the appearance. Examples include Ralph Erskine's copper roof on the Ark at Hammersmith in London (designed to change colour as it patinates) and David Chipperfield's Rowing Museum in Henley (1996), in which untreated exposed oak timbers were left to weather naturally and blend into the surrounding landscape.

The third approach seems difficult to put into practice but it is likely to be the cheapest in terms of life-cycle costs. Buildings designed using this approach do not necessarily use very high quality materials but are designed carefully taking into consideration the environment or, in some cases, even use materials that weather intentionally to highlight the natural transformation of matter through time.

Environmental factors, design details, construction methods and the quality and types of materials used, are all critical factors which designers must deal with when considering the future of their architecture as it exists and is effected by the ever-changing nature of weathering through time.

Further reading

Harris, S.Y. (2001) *Building pathology: deterioration, diagnostics and intervention*, John Wiley & Sons, New York, USA.

Parnham, P. (1997) *Prevention of premature staining of new buildings*, E &FN Spon, London, UK.

Watt, D. (1999) *Building pathology: principles and practice*, Blackwell Science, Oxford, UK.

EB/JG

Weathering steel

See: COR-TEN® (WEATHERING STEEL)

Wet construction

See: DRY CONSTRUCTION AND WET CONSTRUCTION

Whole-life costing

See: LIFE-CYCLE COSTING

Wind towers

Use of the stack effect and passive downdraught cooling as a substitute for conventional air conditioning.

See also: ATRIUM; BUILDING MANAGEMENT SYSTEMS;
DYNAMIC THERMAL SIMULATION; ENERGY EFFICIENCY;
ENVIRONMENTAL DESIGN; FABRIC ENERGY STORAGE;
FAÇADES AND FAÇADE ENGINEERING; HVAC; PIANO, RENZO;
STACK EFFECT; VENTILATION.

Introduction

Air movement in naturally ventilated buildings is caused by pressure differences arising from the stack effect (a buoyancy force from warm air rising and being replaced by cold air at low level) and wind flows resulting in pressure gradients over the whole building envelope. Normally, both effects are in operation, but the contribution of each varies with the geometry of the space, size and position of opening areas.

Wind towers make use of these mechanisms to passively ventilate and cool a building and are sometimes called 'solar chimneys'. This type of natural ventilation provides substantial savings in energy, running and capital costs due to the reduction in mechanical plant and associated electrical equipment. Both electricity consumption and carbon dioxide emissions are reduced and there are savings from the removal of false ceilings and raised floors.

The concept is based on the architecture of 'wind catchers' found in hot, arid climates. Many Victorian buildings were naturally ventilated using wind towers, but modern sophisticated controls including carbon dioxide sensors, rain sensors and air movement control in the stacks have enabled complete flexibility of operation of systems.

Built examples

Vertical and inclined wind towers have been used to good architectural effect in many buildings including the recently completed Portcullis House, Westminster in London by Michael Hopkins & Partners, where both stack effect mechanisms and thin 'flue' façades reduce the need for mechanical cooling to the offices. Previous to this, one of the largest applications for wind towers in an institutional building was the new School of Engineering & Manufacture (the Queen's Building), at De Montfort University, in Leicester, completed in 1993. This building by Short Ford & Associates (architects) and Max Fordham Associates (building services engineers) is a good case study for wind tower design.

The Queen's Building uses a range of different combinations of stack effect and cross-ventilation to manage airflow to lecture theatres (seating $c.150$ people), seminar rooms, workshops and circulation space. Manually controlled windows are used in some spaces, whereas others have a combination of manual air intakes, opening windows and automated air exhausts via stacks. The stacks rise more than two metres above the roofline to take advantage of the wind, which makes this building a significant landmark in the local area, but its architectural qualities are rather a moot point. The tallest stacks serve the lecture theatres, which can be used to pre-cool the spaces using the high thermal mass in the concrete and masonry structure. In the event of low wind speeds, fans have been installed within the stacks for hot, still days. The results of dynamic thermal simulation for the School showed that peak internal temperatures would not rise by more than two or three degrees above peak external temperatures and this has been broadly proved correct.

Following the completion of this building, the design team continued R&D work on wind towers via an EC-funded project into Passive Downdraught Evaporative Cooling (PDEC). Evaluations have shown that PDEC, which uses wind towers and other forms of natural stack effect ventilation, is particularly appropriate for large volume spaces, such as retail, commercial, cultural, recreational, airports and stadia.

Further reading

Battle McCarthy (1999) *Wind towers*, Academy Editions, John Wiley & Sons, London, UK.

WH

Windows and curtain walling

The use of glass in discrete frames or whole façade glazing systems to provide an opening for daylight purposes or the multifunctional 'skin' of a building. Note that much of the discussion below is also applicable to doors and other openings.

See also: AIRTIGHTNESS AND IAQ; ALUMINIUM; ATRIUM; BESPOKE; CLADDING; CONDENSATION; CONNECTIONS; DESIGN LIFE; FAÇADES AND FAÇADE ENGINEERING; GLASS; GLASS – LAMINATED AND COATED; LE CORBUSIER; LIGHTING – DAYLIGHTING; OVERCLADDING; PLASTICS – TYPES; TIMBER; VAN DER ROHE, MIES; VENTILATION; WEATHERING.

Typical application for windows – discrete openings in the 'Icon House', a prefabricated single family dwelling. High levels of energy efficiency are possible with modern double and triple glazing. Photograph courtesy of Veit Dennert KG.

Introduction

There are a number of basic principles behind the design, construction and operation of simple windows, as well as the more complex options such as curtain walling, which will be discussed here. The architectural design of a window may be affected by the orientation of the building, its geographic location and latitude as well as cultural factors which will affect the aesthetic aspects of the design. In any case, window design has a basic purpose to provide daylight into the interior of a building, while protecting against the elements (if in an exterior position). Other functions may also be performed, such as:

- Access to outdoor areas;
- Emergency access/egress;
- Explosion protection;
- Fire performance;
- Security and/or privacy;
- Solar heat gain (or exclusion);
- Sound insulation;
- Thermal performance (e.g. double or triple glazing);
- Ventilation (or to address airtightness requirements);
- Views to the exterior;
- Views to another interior space.

NB: Although the discussion further on focuses on energy efficiency, other design issues such as those listed above may be equally – if not more – important in some situations.

As a means of distinguishing between the various terms used here, the following definitions are suggested.

Windows

These are found more usually in buildings with loadbearing walls as discrete openings, or as openings within a curtain walling system although this is less typical. For information, where a window is divided into parts, the vertical members are called **mullions**, and the horizontal ones are **transoms**. Windows *per se* tend to be relatively small as the loads within the wall need to be redistributed around the opening using a lintel. Small-scale windows tend to use timber or UPVC as framing materials. It is more typical for windows to be part of a natural ventilation strategy than curtain walling (which tends to be associated with mechanical ventilation, although this is not always the case). Moisture in the form of condensation may be a problem in single glazed windows.

Curtain walling

This is somewhat different from windows. Curtain walling is almost a façade system, a 'skin' or envelope that wraps, and is supported off a framed structure. It is not part of a loadbearing structure, and usually bears only a small fraction of its own weight. It is usual for a curtain wall to use aluminium (or steel) square or rectangular profiled sections to frame glass panes, some of which may be opening windows (but this would depend on the ventilation strategy for the building). Curtain walling is much slimmer in section than a loadbearing wall and hence saves space on plan. However, the construction costs will be higher. The idea derives principally from 'patent glazing', an older metal framed window option. Curtain walling is glass-intensive cladding and is at the basic end of façade engineering solutions because it does not usually incorporate any degree of 'intelligence' or adaptivity. The first curtain walling system was designed by Gropius in 1914 for the Fagus factory at Alfeld an der Leine.

Discussion – changing standards

The changes to energy efficiency standards over the last 30 years have led to a steadily increasing requirement in terms of thermal performance for windows and other glazed elements. This is particularly so in the UK house building sector where Building Regulations are now related closely to UK carbon dioxide targets and so the thermal insulation and airtightness requirements are increasing accordingly. In parallel with these changes, there has been a change in the framing materials that are used. It is now more common to see high performance plastic and metal frames, rather than the traditional timber frames (this is also related to maintenance intervals – the inorganic materials fare better in this respect). Although double-glazing is now normal practice in most northern European countries, research into super energy efficient homes has used very high efficiency windows using triple glazing, filled with argon. In some EC countries (e.g. Scandinavia) these are now specified as standard. In other more temperate areas the cost-energy benefits can be less convincing than other improvements in a house.

Design aspects

Other changes that have occurred in window design and technology include:

- Low emissivity glass (which reduces heat loss);
- Photochromic and electrochromic glass (which adjust the amount of light coming through);
- Window and façade systems with integral louvres for shading.

These developments have occurred in parallel with progress in fire protective glass and innovations in framing systems in curtain walling and façade systems, which use framing profiles that are now much slimmer and more elegant, compared to say 15 years ago. It is now common for manufacturers to provide a standard, proprietary range of windows, doors and cladding, based on a 300 mm module, but many companies will also offer a bespoke service. It is usual to see standard windows and doors in the housebuilding market, where economies of scale can come into play. At the other end of the scale, a prestigious commercial or retail client might be prepared to pay handsomely for a bespoke curtain walling solution for a one-off building. Recent research suggests that highly-efficient vacuum panel systems incorporating PV and ventilated voids may be useful with U value of 0.001 W/m^2K and SRI of 90–120 dB.

Further reading

Button, D. & Pye, B. (eds.)(1993) *Glass in building: a guide to modern architectural glass performance*, Butterworth-Heinemann, Oxford, UK.

Muneer, T., Abodahab, N., Weir, G. & Kubie, J. (2001) *Windows in buildings: thermal, acoustic, visual and solar performance*, Butterworth-Heinemann, Oxford, UK.

Ogden, R.G. (1990) *Interfaces: curtain wall connections to steel frames*, SCI Publication 101, The Steel Construction Institute, Ascot, UK

JG

Wire-free technology

See: FIT-OUT; ICT IN BUILDINGS

Workplace design

See: FIT-OUT; ICT IN BUILDINGS; GRIDS FOR STRUCTURE AND LAYOUT

Wright, Frank Lloyd

Frank Lloyd Wright (1869–1959) was simply one of the most influential architects of the 20th century. He used technological developments as a means to realise his aesthetic visions.

See also: AIR CONDITIONING; ATRIUM; BESPOKE; BRICKS AND BLOCKS; CANTILEVERS; COLUMN; CONCRETE – STRUCTURES; CORE (SERVICES); CORE (STRUCTURAL); GROPIUS, WALTER; 'HONESTY'; INTEGRATION; NEUTRA, RICHARD; SCHINDLER, RM; STONE; SURFACE FINISHES; WALLS.

The self-proclaimed greatest architect of the age, Wright's achievements remain unique. At first influenced by the Arts and Crafts Movement in Britain, Wright began as a domestic architect, initially in the offices of his mentor and hero Louis Sullivan and later on his own. His first major innovation was a series of dwellings in the suburban Chicago area known as Prairie houses (c. 1890–1908). In these he began to dispense with the traditional systems of internal walls, while allowing roofs to overshoot the walls using expansive cantilevers, creating increasingly free-flowing and interpenetrating spaces in which interiors melted into terraces and gardens and ingenious spatial planning made these suburban houses look like prairie ranches. These designs were extremely influential on the development of the modern movement in Europe.

Unity Temple, Oak Park (1905–06) saw Wright move from the traditional construction of his domestic work (essentially unplaned timber, brick and plaster) to mass concrete. The building became the first wholly concrete church, and it was a structure that revelled in its materiality – the concrete was left exposed on the elevations. Wright also built the Larkin Building in Buffalo, NY, around this time (1904, demolished 1950), a radical office block planned around a central atrium which presaged late 20th century office design with remarkable prescience. These two buildings also dispensed with the pitched roofs, which had been so prominent in his house designs. When these buildings were published in Germany in 1910 by Wasmuth (i.e. the 'Wasmuth' portfolio) they exerted an almost unimaginable effect on the European Avant Garde and were at least partly responsible for the look of the Modern and De Stijl movements.

After Midway Gardens, Chicago (1913) and the Imperial Hotel in Tokyo (1916–23), Wright returned to domestic work and explorations of the possibilities of concrete. Wright's role as a pioneer of the use of precast concrete elements is often overlooked as critics concentrate on the spatial innovation of the Prairie houses. The Hollyhock House, Los Angeles (1921) was a massive poured concrete structure with precast concrete decorative details and represented a staggering departure from his earlier, ground-hugging houses. From here Wright went on to develop what he called the 'knit- or textile-block' technique in which walls of prefabricated concrete elements are held in place using steel-ties. This technique allowed Wright to incorporate intricate geometric patterns in the walls, finally creating what he saw as an organic integration of structure and decoration in one element. The decorative forms were based on indigenous American patterns, often those of Mayan buildings. His next great house was Falling Water, Bear Run, Pennsylvania (1936–39). Certainly among the greatest houses of the 20th century, Falling Water was a deceptively simple composition of cantilevered reinforced concrete horizontals and random rubble verticals of local stone. The structure was tied back to the rock upon which it sat freeing the rooms to sit above the waterfall in a display of structural acrobatics.

In the same years he designed Falling Water, Wright gained the commission for the Johnson Wax Administrative Center, Racine, Wisconsin. In this building he developed the ideas he had formulated at the Larkin Building, creating a horizontal version of his top-lit workers' paradise. In this case, the structure was a series of slender reinforced concrete mushroom columns (which have been compared to golf tees in shape), their heads great disks with glazing in the interstices. These columns allowed Wright to lighten the brick walls and insert horizontal bands of glazing (unusually composed of welded glass tubing) and to dispense with traditional corners in favour of a sleek, streamlined shape. In 1943–45 Wright added an elegant laboratory tower to the structure. Based on the structure of a tree (rather than the steel grid) the building was constructed around a hollow reinforced concrete service and structural core, its cantilevered floors tapering to the outer walls where they became visible as continuous horizontal bands. The rounded corners echo the streamlining of the older structures.

At around the same time Wright was designing a series of 'Usonian Houses' which he intended as archetypes for semi-affordable dwelling for Middle America and in which he stripped down and simplified the tectonic language of his prairie houses for standardised production. During the 1940s his domestic and public buildings took on a different character as Wright adopted sharp angular forms although volumes continued to flow into one another. Some of the best examples of these buildings can be seen at his Taliesin settlements in Wisconsin (initially 1911 and then in another phase from 1925) and at Scottsdale, Arizona (from 1927). His major urban monument is the Guggenheim Museum overlooking Central Park in New York, the design and construction of which spanned from 1942 to 1959. One of the most recognisable of all

Modern buildings, the museum is the organic snail-shape which Wright had always wanted to build, a single, reinforced concrete ramp (which comprises the main gallery designed to be seen in descent) spiralling to a central roof light.

Further reading

Blake P. (1960) *Frank Lloyd Wright: architecture and space*, Gollancz, London, UK.

Levine, N. (1996) *The architecture of Frank Lloyd Wright*, Princeton University Press, Princeton, USA.

Patterson, T.L. (1994) *Frank Lloyd and the meaning of materials*, Van Nostrand Reinhold, New York, USA.

Scully, V. (1960) *Frank Lloyd Wright*, George Braziliere, New York, USA.

EH

X-bracing

See: BRACING

Yeang, Ken

A knowledgeable and enthusiastic proponent of ecological design, Ken Yeang is perhaps best known for his work on 'bioclimatic skyscrapers'.

See also: ECOLOGICAL DESIGN; ENVIRONMENTAL DESIGN; FAÇADES AND FAÇADE ENGINEERING; CORE (SERVICES).

Dr Kenneth Yeang,
AA Dip, APAM, FSIA, RIBA, Hon. FAIA, PhD (Cantab.)
Professor of the Graham Willis Chair, Sheffield University, UK,
Adjunct Professor of RMIT, Melbourne, the University of New South Wales, Sydney, the University of Malaya and the University of Hawaii.

Ken Yeang was born in 1948. A pupil in Malaysia and England, he graduated in architecture from the Architectural Association School, (AA) London in 1971, undertook Landscape planning studies at the University of Pennsylvania, Philadelphia, USA in 1973 and in 1975 obtained his PhD from Wolfson College, Cambridge. Yeang is an architect who practises what he preaches. He believes that most of today's architects and designers are theoretically and technically ill-equipped to respond to the new demands to design in a responsive way to meet the needs of the changing environment. Most important is that almost all architects (except landscape architects) lack a serious educational background in ecology and environmental biology.

In conjunction with architect Tengku Robert Hamzah, a prince in the Malay Royal family, who also studied at the AA School, London, the international architectural firm of T.R. Hamzah & Yeang Sdn. Bhd, was founded in 1976, with its headquarters in Kuala Lumpur, Malaysia. With affiliated offices in London, Stuttgart, Sydney, Tokyo and Beijing, the firm has received over 20 awards including the Aga Khan Award for Architecture in 1995 and the RAIA International Award in 1997 and 1999. The firm's expertise is their ecological approach for the design of large projects and buildings that include consideration given to their impacts of the site's ecology and to the building's use of energy and materials over its life-cycle. Much of the firm's early work pioneers the passive low-energy design of skyscrapers, as the 'bioclimatic skyscraper'. Key projects include the high-rise National Library Board building, Singapore, the 24-storey IBM Building, Malaysia and the 15-storey Mesiniaga Building, Malaysia.

The design criteria for all of Yeang's design work is based on his own well-published writing. He sees ecological design as being environmentally beneficial and productive and a positive contribution to the natural environment. Furthermore, he believes that it can become a positive act of repair, restoration and renewal of the natural system of the environment. Yeang sees ecology as being all about linkages, interdependence and creative adaptation as opposed to compartmentalised causality. In his book, *The Green Skyscraper: the basis for designing sustainable intensive buildings* he sets down the parameters and technologies that he uses and continues to develop as being the basis of his buildings operational systems. Building form and shape are climatically adapted. Increasing technology tends to increase energy and the balance seems to be 'mixed mode' operations. Form, shape and operational technologies are all affected by the different impacts of the global regions. Ken Yeang puts down his design pointers in the knowledge that with the increasing population of cities and the increasing loss of arable land, a new ecological and sustainable use of the skyscraper is necessary:

> *The final design should incorporate adequate fenestration to make use of free solar energy and natural daylight while optimising heat losses and avoiding glare.*
>
> *As an alternative to shading devices, the building can have cut-in transitional spaces at its façade to provide useable 'places-in-the-sky' as well as recessed shading. Such 'skycourts' and recessed terraces serve as interstitial zones between the inside and the outside. These 'parks-in-the-sky' balance the inorganic mass of the building's hardware and components with an organic mass to effect a more balanced ecosystem.*
>
> The Green Skyscraper: the basis for designing sustainable intensive buildings – Ken Yeang

Selected projects

Menara Umno, Penang, Malaysia (1998) – a 21 storey tower with total area (including car parking) 10,900 m². All office floors can be ventilated and all desks are close to openable windows for natural sunlight and ventilation. The building has wing-walls to direct wind to special balconies.

Beijing World Science and Trade Centre, China – (in design) this will comprise three apartment towers of 50, 62 and 72 storeys; four office towers of 43 storeys, a 25 storey hotel convention centre and an 11 storey serviced apartment building. Ecological/bioclimatic design features include maximum daylighting, cross-ventilation and apartments with sky-garden terraces. Other features are the modification of the internal environment by scooping wind in to the atrium space.

Elephant & Castle, South London, UK – (in design) two 35 storey and one 12 storey residential eco-towers for this major regeneration project where Yeang's 'City-in-the-sky' concept will be fully tested.

Further reading

Harrison, A., Lee, E. & Read, J. (eds.) *Intelligent buildings in south east Asia*, E & FN Spon, London, UK.

Yeang, K. (1994) *Designing with nature*, McGraw-Hill, USA.

Yeang, K. (1996) *The skyscraper: bioclimatically considered*, Academy Editions, John Wiley & Sons, London, UK.

Yeang, K. (1998) *Bioclimatic skyscrapers*, (2nd Edn), Ellipsis, London, UK.

Yeang, K. (1998) *The Green Skyscraper: the basis for designing sustainable intensive buildings*, Prestel Verlag, Munich, Germany.

Yeang, K. (2000) *Service cores in buildings*, Academy Editions, John Wiley & Sons, London, UK.

WH

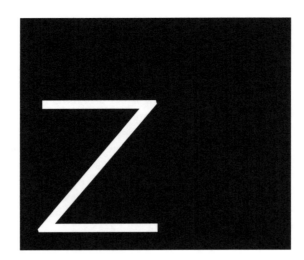

Zinc

A commonly used metal found in roofing, cladding and as a protective coating to steel (galvanising).

See also: ALUMINIUM; CEMENT; CLADDING; CONCRETE; COPPER; CORROSION; DESIGN LIFE; DURABILITY; GALVANISING; 'HONESTY'; LEAD; METALS; ROOFS; STAINLESS STEEL; STANDING SEAM ROOF; SURFACE FINISHES; TIMBER – HARDWOODS AND SOFTWOODS; WEATHERING.

What is zinc?

Zinc is a hard, silvery coloured metal that is used in roofing and cladding. It is also associated with other applications because it can be added to steel as a coating to protect against rust (in a process called galvanising). Industrial production of zinc began in the 18th century and its use in buildings began about a century later. It is manufactured from a natural ore (zinc blende) and goes through several processes, depending on what grade (quality) is required. Zinc is processed into sheet or strip using casting and rolling. It can be obtained in its pure form or as an alloy. The alloy contains small amounts of titanium and copper, which gives it better durability, increased strength and lower thermal expansion. Both types can be worked easily by hand at room temperature, which makes this metal particularly useful for complex details and junctions on roofs for example.

Uses and applications

For buildings, zinc is used most often as a roofing material, with more use being made in continental Europe (especially Germany, Switzerland and Eastern Europe) than in the UK. Zinc is versatile and easily worked, so is very useful for architecture with difficult geometries and intricate detailing. However, it can also be rolled out in lengths as a standing seam roofing sheet, covering vast areas efficiently and attractively. Zinc alloy sheets come in sheets up to six metres in length and are usually fixed to some form of timber decking. Sheets range from 0.6–1.10 mm in thickness. Zinc sheets can also be used as vertical cladding, which is a modern, commercial alternative to the diamond-shaped (parallelogram) interlocking zinc 'tiles' that appear in European traditional architecture. Several cladding systems are available such as profiled, corrugated and plug-in options. Self-supporting elements and rainwater goods are also available. Architectural ornamentation including finials, gargoyles, elaborate